Iran
a country study

Federal Research Division
Library of Congress
Edited by
Glenn E. Curtis and
Eric Hooglund

On the cover: A bas-relief of a bearded sphinx, ca. 500 B.C., from Persepolis

Fifth Edition, First Printing, 2008.

Library of Congress Cataloging-in-Publication Data

Iran: a country study/edited by Glenn E. Curtis and Eric Hooglund. – 5th ed.
  p. cm.
Includes bibliographical references and index.
ISBN 978–0–8444–1187–3
1. Iran. 2. Iran–History. I. Curtis, Glenn E. (Glenn Eldon), 1946– II. Hooglund, Eric J. (Eric James), 1944–
DS254.5.I732 2008
955–dc22

2008011784

For sale by the Superintendent of Documents, U.S. Government Printing Office
Internet: bookstore.gpo.gov Phone: toll free (866) 512–1800; DC area (202) 512–1800
Fax: (202) 512–2250 Mail: Stop SSOP, Washington, DC 20402–00001

ISBN 978–0–8444–1187–3

Foreword

This volume is one in a continuing series of books prepared by the Federal Research Divison of the Library of Congress under the Country Studies/Area Handbook Program, formerly sponsored by the Department of the Army and revived in FY 2004 with congressionally mandated funding under the sponsorship of the Joint Chiefs of Staff, Strategic Plans and Policy Directorate (J–5).

Most books in the series deal with a particular foreign country, describing and analyzing its political, economic, social, and national security systems and institutions, and examining the interrelationshps of those systems and the ways they are shaped by historical and cultural factors. Each study is written by a multidisciplinary team of social scientists. The authors seek to provide a basic understanding of the observed society, striving for a dynamic rather than a static portrayal. Particular attention is devoted to the people who make up the society, their origins, dominant beliefs and values, their common interests and the issues on which they are divided, the nature and extent of their involvement with national institutions, and their attitudes toward each other and toward their social system and political order.

The books represent the analysis of the authors and should not be construed as an expression of an official U.S. government position, policy, or decision. The authors have sought to adhere to accepted standards of scholarly objectivity. Corrections, additions, and suggestions for changes from readers will be welcomed for use in future editions.

Chief
Federal Research Division
Library of Congress
Washington, DC 20540–4840
E-mail: frds@loc.gov

Acknowledgments

The editors wish to acknowledge the contributions of the authors of the 1989 edition of *Iran: A Country Study*, edited by Helen Chapin Metz, on which this revised edition is based.

The editors are grateful to individuals in various government agencies and private institutions who contributed their time, research materials, and expertise to the production of this book. In particular, the editors would like to acknowledge the generosity of the individuals and public and private agencies that allowed their photographs to be used in this study.

The editors also wish to thank members of the Federal Research Division staff who contributed directly to the preparation of the manuscript. These individuals include Sandra W. Meditz, who reviewed all graphic and textual materials and managed editing and book production; and Janie L. Gilchrist, who did the word processing. Outside contributors include Vincent Ercolano, who edited chapters, and Christopher S. Robinson, who prepared the book's graphics as well as the final digital manuscript for the printer. Special thanks are owed to Theresa E. Kamp, who designed the cover artwork and the illustrations on the title page of each chapter.

Contents

List of Figures

Preface

Like its predecessor, this study is an attempt to treat in a concise and objective manner the dominant social, political, economic, and military aspects of contemporary Iran. Sources of information included scholarly journals and monographs, official reports of governments and international organizations, foreign and domestic newspapers, and numerous periodicals and Internet sources. Chapter bibliographies appear at the end of the book; at the end of each chapter is a brief comment on some of the more valuable sources suggested as further reading. The Glossary provides supplementary explanations of words and terms used frequently or having particular importance. Measurements are given in the metric system; a conversion table is provided to assist those readers who are unfamiliar with metric measurements (see table 1, Appendix).

The use of foreign words and terms has been confined to those essential to understanding the text, with a brief definition upon first usage and additional treatment in the Glossary. The transliteration of Persian words and phrases posed a particular problem. The expertise of Dr. Eric Hooglund was most helpful in identifying the most acceptable forms. For words that are of direct Arabic origin—such as Muhammad (the Prophet) and Muslim—the authors followed a modified version of the system for Arabic adopted by the U.S. Board on Geographic Names and the Permanent Committee on Geographic Names for British Official Use, known as the BGN/PCGN system. (The modification is a significant one, entailing the deletion of all diacritical marks and hyphens.) The BGN/PCGN system also was used to transliterate Persian words, again without the diacritics. However, place-names that are widely known by another spelling have been rendered in that form when the use of the BGN/PCGN system might have caused confusion. For example, the reader will find Basra for the city rather than Al Basrah. Similarly, where variants exist, the names of well-known individuals have been rendered in the form thought to be most familiar to readers—for example, Khamenei rather than Khamenehi for Iran's Leader.

Readers not familiar with the Iranian calendar should be aware, when consulting Iranian sources, that the Iranian calendar differs in several significant respects from the Gregorian calendar used in the West. The Iranian calendar is a solar calendar that begins each year at the vernal equinox (usually March 21). Years in the Iranian calendar are counted beginning with 622 A.D., the year of Muhammad's flight from Mecca to Medina. The current Iranian calendar year, which began in March 2008, is 1387.

Research for this revised volume began in late 2004, and updates of drafts written primarily in 2005 continued throughout 2006 and into 2007. Although a comprehensive update of the entire volume could not be undertaken, updated information has been incorporated where available. The book's overall information cutoff date is October 2007.

Table A. Chronology of Important Events

EARLY HISTORY

ca. 3400 B.C.	Elamite kingdom emerges in southwestern Iran and Mesopotamia.
ca. 2000 B.C.	Nomadic peoples—Scythians, Medes, and Persians move from Central Asia to Iranian plateau.

SIXTH CENTURY B.C.

ca. 553–550 B.C.	Cyrus II (also known as Cyrus the Great or Cyrus the Elder) overthrows Medean king; becomes ruler of Persia and Media; founds Achaemenian Empire.
539 B.C.	Cyrus captures Babylon, releases Jews from captivity.
525 B.C.	Cyrus's son Cambyses II conquers Egypt.
522 B.C.	Darius I becomes king; restablishes and extends empire, carries out administrative reorganization.

FIFTH CENTURY B.C.

490 B.C.	Darius invades Greek mainland; defeated at the Battle of Marathon.

FOURTH CENTURY B.C.

334 B.C.	Alexander the Great begins Persian campaign; completes conquest of Persia and Mesopotamia, 330 B.C.
323 B.C.	Death of Alexander; division of empire among generals; Seleucids emerge as principal heirs in Iran.

THIRD CENTURY B.C.

247 B.C.	Parthians overthrow Seleucids; establish own dynasty.

THIRD CENTURY A.D.

A.D. 224	Ardeshir overthrows last Parthian ruler; establishes Sassanian dynasty with capital at Ctesiphon.
A.D. 260	Shahpur I wages campaign against Romans, takes emperor Valerian captive.

SEVENTH CENTURY

637	Muslim armies capture Ctesiphon, Sassanian Empire begins to crumble.
641–42	Sassanian army defeated at Nahavand; Iran comes under Muslim rule.
661	After assassination of Ali, son-in-law of Muhammad, Umayyads establish new dynasty with capital at Damascas.

EIGHTH CENTURY

750	Abbasids, from base in Khorasan, overthrow Umayyads, establish capital at Baghdad.

NINTH–TENTH CENTURIES

	Emergence of virtually independent local dynasties in northeastern and eastern Iran; court patronage leads to flowering of Persian language, poetry, and literature.

Table A. Chronology of Important Events (Continued)

ELEVENTH CENTURY

1055	Seljuk chief Tughril Beg consolidates rule over Iran; receives title "King of the East" from caliph in Baghdad.

THIRTEENTH CENTURY

ca. 1219	Beginning of Mongol invasion under Genghis (Chinggis) Khan.
1258	Mongols sack Baghdad and consolidate rule over Iran.
1295	Ghazan Khan, a convert to Islam, becomes Mongol ruler, aided by his famous Iranian vizier, Rashid ad Din; period of reform, stabilization.

FOURTEENTH CENTURY

ca. 1335	End of centralized Mongol rule.
1381	Timur, also called Tamerlane (Timur the Lame), makes himself master of Iran.

FIFTEENTH CENTURY

1405	Death of Timur; rapid disintegration of his empire; long period of fragmented rule in Iran.

SIXTEENTH CENTURY

1501	Safavis seize power in Tabriz; Ismail Safavi proclaimed shah.
1587	Shah Abbas succeeds to the throne; his reign (1587–1629) marks apogee of Safavi power, cultural flowering.

EIGHTEENTH CENTURY

1722	Afghan tribesmen enter Esfahan; Safavi Empire collapses.
1729	Tahmasp Quli, chief of Afshar tribe, expels Afghans, rules in name of Safavis.
1736	Tahmasp Quli assumes throne in own name as Nader Shah.
ca. 1738–39	Nader Shah, in series of military campaigns, extends Iran's borders into Georgia, Armenia, and Afghanistan; sacks Delhi.
1747	Assassination of Nader Shah; his empire fragments.
1750	Karim Khan Zand consolidates power in southern Iran with his capital at Shiraz; adopts title of *vakil al ruaya*, or deputy of the subjects.
1779	Death of Karim Khan; tribal struggle for succession ensues.
1795	Agha Mohammad Qajar, having made himself master of Iran, is crowned king, inaugurating Qajar dynasty; establishes capital at Tehran.
1797	Death of Agha Mohammad; succession of Fath Ali Shah.

NINETEENTH CENTURY

1812	First Russo-Persian War ends in Treaty of Gulistan. Iran cedes territory to Russia in Caucasus.
1828	Second Russo-Persian War ends in Treaty of Turkmanchay. Iran cedes additional territory in Caucasus, pays indemnity, extends capitulatory rights to Russian (and later to other European) subjects.
1834	Death of Fath Ali Shah; succession of Mohammad Shah.
1848	Death of Mohammad Shah; succession of Naser ad Din Shah.

Table A. Chronology of Important Events (Continued)

1851	Founding of Dar ol Fonun, first school based on European model.
	Amir Kabir, Naser ad Din Shah's powerful prime minister, dismissed, executed on shah's orders.
ca. 1853	Beginning of Russian expansion in Central Asia into territories claimed by Iran.
1857	British land troops in south; force Iran to end second siege of Herat in Afghanistan (first siege had ended under British pressure in 1837). Treaty of Paris signed with Britain; Iran gives up all claims to Herat.
1871	Appointment of Mirza Hosain Khan Moshir od Dowleh as prime minister, marking start of era of reform, including cabinet-style government, advisory council to the shah, and foreign concessions.
1872	Shah grants railroad concession to British national, Baron Julius de Reuter; later cancels concession after protests by high officials, clergy.
1888	Shah opens Karun River in Khuzestan Province to international commercial traffic; Imperial Bank of Persia established under concession to Reuter.
1891–92	Shah grants tobacco monopoly to a British national. Nationwide protests force him to cancel it.
1896	Naser ad Din Shah assassinated by follower of Jamal ad Din al Afghani; succeeded by Muzaffar ad Din Shah.
TWENTIETH CENTURY	
1900, 1902	Shah contracts first and second Russian loans.
1901	British speculator William D'Arcy receives a concession to explore and develop southern Iran's oil resources.
1905–6	Antigovernment protests culminate in demand for a constitution.
1906	Muzaffar ad Din Shah issues a decree promising a constitution.
	Majlis (parliament) ratifies constitution, shah signs it, changing government to a constitutional monarchy.
1907	Supplementary Laws to constitution enacted.
	Anglo-Russian Agreement signed, dividing Iran into spheres of influence.
1908	Mohammad Ali Shah bombards parliament, suspends constitution.
	Oil is discovered in Iran.
1909	Overthrow of Mohammad Ali Shah, restoration of the constitution; Ahmad Shah begins reign.
	Anglo-Persian Oil Company (APOC) is formed.
1911	American Morgan Shuster arrives as financial adviser.
	Russian ultimatum and invasion, dismissal of Shuster, closure of parliament.
1914	Britain gains control of APOC.
1914–19	Iran declares neutrality in World War I but becomes battleground for Russian, British, and Turkish forces.
1919	Anglo-Persian Agreement signed, establishing a virtual British protectorate in Iran.
1921	Anglo-Persian Agreement rejected by the Majlis.

Table A. Chronology of Important Events (Continued)

1921–25	Army commander Reza Khan brings tribes under control.
1923	Ahmad Shah names Reza Khan prime minister, leaves Iran, never to return.
1924	Campaign to establish a republic abandoned after clerical objections.
1925	Qajars deposed by act of Majlis.
	Reza Khan named shah by Majlis, establishes Pahlavi dynasty.
1927–32	New civil code enacted.
1932	Uniform European dress code imposed.
	Shah cancels agreement under which the Anglo-Persian Oil Company (APOC) produced and exported Iran's oil.
1933	A new 60-year Anglo-Persian oil agreement is signed.
1935	APOC is renamed the Anglo-Iranian Oil Company (AIOC).
	Tehran University inaugurated.
1936	Abolition of the wearing of the veil.
	Troops fire on protesters inside the shrine of Imam Reza in Mashhad, eroding the shah's popular support.
August 1941	Anglo-Russian invasion of Iran after shah, who had declared Iran neutral in World War II, refuses to expel German nationals.
September 1941	Abdication of Reza Shah; Mohammad Reza Shah becomes ruler.
December 1945	Azarbaijan Democratic Party declares autonomous republic.
	Kurdish Republic of Mahabad declared in Kurdistan.
December 1946	Iranian army moves into Azarbaijan; autonomy movement, Kurdish Republic of Mahabad collapse.
March 1951	Majlis nationalizes oil industry.
April 1951	Mohammad Mossadeq becomes prime minister.
August 1953	Mossadeq overthrown in a coup engineered by the U.S. Central Intelligence Agency and Britain's MI–5, supported by Iranian royalists.
1954	A new agreement divides profits equally between the National Iranian Oil Company (NIOC) and the multinational consortium that replaced the Anglo-Iranian Oil Company (AIOC).
October 1955	Iran is a charter member of the U.S.-supported Baghdad Pact (renamed the Central Treaty Organization—CENTO—after Iraq's withdrawal in 1958).
January 1962	Government approves law mandating breakup of large landholdings.
January 1963	Shah's "White Revolution" approved in a national referendum.
June 1963	Riots in Tehran and other major cities support Ayatollah Sayyid Ruhollah Musavi Khomeini.
November 1964	Khomeini sent into exile.
1971	Celebrations held to mark 2,500 years of Iranian monarchy.
1974	Organization of the Petroleum Exporting Countries (OPEC) quadruples oil prices; Iran's oil revenues rise dramatically.
1975	Algiers Agreement establishes the "thalweg" as the border between Iran and Iraq in the Shatt al Arab, giving Iran equal navigation rights in the waterway.
1978	Riots rock major Iranian cities.
January 1979	Shah leaves Iran.

Table A. Chronology of Important Events (Continued)

February 1979	Khomeini returns from exile, names provisional government and Revolutionary Council; collapse of Pahlavi monarchy.
March–April 1979	National referendum approves establishment of Islamic Republic, which is declared on April 1.
May 1979	Khomeini authorizes establishment of the Islamic Revolutionary Guard Corps.
June–July 1979	Private-sector banks, insurance companies, industrial enterprises, and large businesses are nationalized or expropriated.
November 1979	Iranian "students of the Imam's Line" occupy the U.S. embassy compound in Tehran and take American diplomats hostage. United States and Iran break diplomatic relations.
December 1979	Second national referendum approves new constitution, vesting supreme authority in the *faqih*, or Islamic religious law expert.
January 1980	Abolhasan Bani Sadr elected first president of the Islamic Republic.
April 1980	United States tries but fails to rescue embassy hostages.
September 1980	Iraq invades Iran, launching Iran–Iraq war.
January 1981	U.S. Embassy hostages released.
June 1981	Bani Sadr impeached. Bloody struggle between regime and opposition forces ensues.
October 1981	Sayyid Ali Khamenei elected president.
August 1985	Khamenei elected to a second term as president.
1985–86	"Iran–Contra Affair," covert selling of U.S. arms to Iran for money given to anticommunist "contra" groups in Nicaragua, causes major scandal in United States.
August 1988	Iran–Iraq war ends with cease-fire, after about 1 million casualties and major shifts in regional politics; reform factions gain seats in parliamentary elections.
February 1989	Khomeini appoints Expediency Council composed of 12 ex-officio members and his own representative, with wide powers to resolve differences between the Majlis and Guardians Council.
	Khomeini issues a fatwa against Salman Rushdie for his novel *The Satanic Verses*, deemed insulting to the Prophet.
June 1989	Khomeini dies. Hojjatoleslam Ali Khamenei succeeds him as Leader of the Revolution.
July 1989	Ali Akbar Hashemi Rafsanjani elected president.
1990	Large-scale protests against economic conditions begin, continue through early 1990s.
1992	Iran asserts sovereignty over southern half of Persian Gulf island of Abu Musa, in violation of a 1971 Memorandum of Understanding, thus beginning a territorial dispute with the United Arab Emirates.
June 1993	Rafsanjani reelected president, with declining support.
1995	Russia agrees to assume construction of nuclear reactors at Bushehr.
1996	Iran–Libya Sanctions Act (ILSA) passed by the U.S. Congress places economic sanctions on Iran.
May 1997	Election of Mohammad Khatami as president, at the head of a reform movement; in ensuing years, struggle heightens in courts and parliament between reformist and conservative factions.
1998	Iran announces first test-firing of Shahab-3 ballistic missile.
February 1999	First local elections since the Revolution are held.

Table A. Chronology of Important Events (Continued)

February 2000	Guardians Council disqualifies large numbers of reformist candidates for parliamentary elections, but reformists make significant gains.

TWENTY-FIRST CENTURY

March 2001	Russia agrees to complete nuclear reactor construction at Bushehr.
June 2001	Khatami wins second term as president, but conservatives retain control of Guardians Council.
September 2001	Iranian officials express deep sympathy with the United States following the terrorist attacks of September 11.
2002	Iran continues to support Northern Alliance forces in Afghanistan in successful anti-Taliban campaign.
	Repression of press and dissident activities increases in Iran; student demonstrators are arrested.
January 2002	Israel intercepts the freighter *Karine A* in the Mediterranean Sea. The ship was carrying Iranian weapons believed to be bound for the Palestinian Authority. U.S. President George W. Bush links Iran with Iraq and North Korea in an "axis of evil."
February 2003	Conservatives make large gains in local elections.
	International Atomic Energy Administration (IAEA) begins examination of Iran's nuclear program.
March 2003	United States deposes Saddam Hussein in Iraq; Iran opposes ensuing occupation but remains neutral.
May 2003	Guardians Council vetoes key reform legislation of Khatami.
July 2003	Death of a Canadian journalist in an Iranian jail causes international outcry.
October 2003	Human rights lawyer Shirin Ebadi wins the Nobel Peace Prize.
December 2003	Earthquake destroys the Iranian city of Bam.
February and May 2004	After many reformist candidates are disqualified, conservatives gain a parliamentary majority in elections.
September 2004	Three new provinces, North Khorasan, South Khorasan, and Razavi Khorasan, are created from the province of Khorasan.
March 2005	United States offers economic incentives for Iran to suspend uranium enrichment.
June 2005	In a runoff election, Mahmoud Ahmadinejad is elected president with a populist platform.
October 2005	Iran reconfirms its right to develop peaceful nuclear technology.
April 2006	IAEA officially reports Iran's failure to suspend uranium enrichment, as mandated by the United Nations (UN) Security Council.
June 2006	United States offers to join talks on Iran's nuclear program; international powers offer new incentives for Iran to suspend uranium enrichment.
December 2006	UN Security Council imposes limited sanctions on Iran.
March 2007	UN Security Council widens scope of the December 2006 sanctions against Iran.
May 2007	U.S. and Iranian negotiators meet, for first time in 27 years, to discuss stability in Iraq.
August 2007	Iran and the IAEA reach agreement on a timetable according to which Iran will allow IAEA inspectors to resume inspecting declared nuclear sites.

Table A. Chronology of Important Events (Continued)

October 2007	Iran's chief nuclear negotiator (Ali Larijani) resigns and is replaced by a close associate of President Ahmadinejad.
	United States unilaterally imposes tougher new economic sanctions on Iran, focusing on the Revolutionary Guards, Ministry of Defense, and a number of Iranian individuals, banks, and companies.
November 2007	An official U.S. government intelligence report concludes that Iran likely ceased work on its nuclear weapons program in 2003, although uranium enrichment continued.
March 2008	Ahmadinejad is the first Iranian president since the Revolution to visit Iraq.
	UN Security Council tightens existing economic sanctions against Iran.

Country Profile

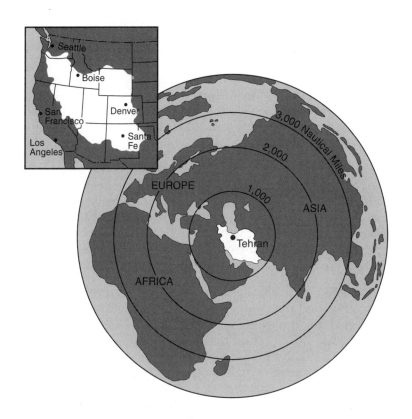

Country

Formal Name: Islamic Republic of Iran.

Short Form: Iran.

Term for Citizen(s): Iranian(s).

Capital: Tehran.

Other Major Cities (in order of population): Mashhad, Esfahan, Tabriz, Karaj, Shiraz, Qom, and Ahvaz.

Independence: In the modern era, Iran has always existed as an independent country.

Historical Background

The first Iranian state was the Achaemenian Empire, which was established by Cyrus the Great in about 550 B.C. Alexander the Great conquered the empire in 330 B.C. The Arabs conquered Iran in A.D. 642, bringing with them Islam, which eventually became the predominant religion. In the centuries that followed, Iran was ruled by a succession of Arab, Iranian, Turkic, and Mongol dynasties. In 1501 the Iranian Safavis created a strong centralized empire under Ismael I and established Shia Islam as the official religion.

In 1795 the Qajar family established a dynasty that would rule Iran until 1925. In the nineteenth century, Iran lost much of its territory to Russia. The Constitutional Revolution of 1905–7 led to the formation of Iran's first parliament. When the Qajar dynasty was overthrown in 1925, Reza Khan established the Pahlavi dynasty, which ruled until 1979 under Reza Shah Pahlavi, as Reza Khan was renamed, and his son, Mohammed Reza Shah Pahlavi.

In the 1960s, the authoritarian rule of the shah provoked political discontent, and the cleric Ayatollah Ruhollah Musavi Khomeini developed an antigovernment movement. The movement grew into a nationwide revolution in 1978, toppling the shah. In 1979 Khomeini took the position of Leader in the newly established Islamic Republic of Iran. That year the occupation of the U.S. embassy in Tehran and the taking hostage of 53 U.S. diplomats led to a decisive break in U.S.-Iranian relations. Between 1980 and 1988, Iran fought an indecisive, costly war with Iraq.

The death of Khomeini in 1989 began a period of struggle among political factions in Iran. The presidencies of moderates Ali Akbar Hashemi Rafsanjani (1989–97) and Mohammad Khatami (1997–2005) encountered strong resistance from radical elements. Conservatives regained control of the parliament in the 2004 elections, and the election in 2005 of Mahmoud Ahmadinejad as president strengthened the conservative hold on government. In the early 2000s, Iran's international relations were eroded by ostensible support of terrorist groups in the Middle East, controversy over Iran's nuclear program, and Ahmadinejad's confrontational rhetoric.

Geography

Size and Location: Iran, which occupies nearly 1.65 million square kilometers, is located in the Middle East, between Turkey and Iraq on the west and Afghanistan and Pakistan on the east.

Topography: Iran has rugged mountain chains surrounding several basins collectively known as the Central Plateau, which has an average elevation of about 900 meters. East of the Central Plateau are two large desert regions. Lowland areas are located along the Caspian coast, in Khuzestan Province at the head of the Persian Gulf, and at several dispersed locations along the Persian Gulf and Gulf of Oman coasts. Iran has no major rivers. The only navigable river is the Karun.

Climate: Iran's climate is mostly arid and semi-arid, with a humid rain-forest zone along the Caspian coast.

Natural Resources: Iran has enormous reserves of oil and natural gas. Oil reserves are estimated at more than 130 billion barrels (third in the world behind Saudi Arabia and Iraq; about 11 percent of world proven reserves) and natural gas reserves at more than 32 trillion cubic meters (second in the world behind Russia). Mineral resources currently exploited include bauxite, chromium, coal, copper, gold, iron ore, limestone, red oxide, salt, strontium, sulfur, turquoise, and uranium. About 11 percent of Iran's land surface is classified as arable. The most productive agricultural land, bordering the Caspian Sea, makes up about 5.5 percent of the country's total land.

Environmental Factors: Especially in urban areas, vehicle emissions, refinery operations, and industrial effluents contribute to poor air quality. Tehran is rated as one of the world's most polluted cities. Much of Iran's territory suffers from desertification and/or deforestation. Industrial and urban wastewater runoff has contaminated rivers and coastal waters and threatened drinking water supplies. Iran has not developed a policy of sustainable development because short-term economic goals have taken precedence.

Society

Population: Iran's population is about 70 million according to preliminary data from the decennial census conducted in late

2006; of that number, approximately one-third is rural and two-thirds urban. Urbanization has been steady. Population density averages 42 people per square kilometer, but with significant regional variations. The annual population growth rate was about 1 percent in 2006. According to a 2007 estimate, 23.2 percent of Iran's population was 14 years of age or younger, and 5.4 percent was 65 or older; the population was about 51 percent male. In 2007 life expectancy was 69.1 years for men, 72.1 years for women. The birthrate was 16.6 per 1,000 and the death rate, 5.6 per 1,000. Between 1979 and 2007, the fertility rate decreased from about 7.0 to 1.7 children born per woman.

Ethnic Groups and Languages: The main ethnic groups in Iran are Persians (65 percent), Azerbaijani Turks (16 percent), Kurds (7 percent), Lurs (6 percent), Arabs (2 percent), Baluchis (2 percent), Turkmens (1 percent), Turkish tribal groups such as the Qashqai (1 percent), and non-Persian, non-Turkic groups such as Armenians, Assyrians, and Georgians (less than 1 percent). Persian, the official language, is spoken as a mother tongue by at least 65 percent of the population and as a second language by a large proportion of the remaining 35 percent. Other languages in use are Azeri Turkish and Turkic dialects, Kurdish, Luri, Arabic, and Baluchi.

Religion: The constitution declares Shia Islam to be the official religion of Iran. At least 90 percent of Iranians are Shia Muslims, and about 8 percent are Sunni Muslims. Other religions present in Iran are Christianity (more than 300,000 followers), the Baha'i faith (at least 250,000), Zoroastrianism (about 32,000), and Judaism (about 30,000). The constitution recognizes Christianity, Zoroastrianism, and Judaism, but not the Baha'i faith, as legitimate minority religions.

Education and Literacy: In 2003 the literacy rate of the population was 79.4 percent (85.6 percent for males and 73 percent for females). Under the constitution, primary education (between ages six and 10) is compulsory, and primary enrollment was nearly 98 percent in 2004. Secondary school attendance is not compulsory. Hence, enrollment rates are lower—about 90 percent for middle school and 70 percent for high school in 2004. Primary, secondary, and higher education is free, although private schools and universities charge tuition. The majority of Iran's 113,000 pre-collegiate public schools are single-sex beyond kindergarten. Universities are coeducational. By 2004, Iran had more than 200 public and more than 30 private institutions of higher education, enrolling a total of nearly 1.6 million students.

Health: The overall quality of public health care improved dramatically after the 1978–79 Revolution because public health has been a top government priority. Most Iranians receive subsidized prescription drugs and vaccinations. An extensive network of public clinics offers basic care, and the Ministry of Health operates general and specialty hospitals. In large cities, well-to-do persons use private clinics and hospitals that charge high fees. In the early 2000s, estimates of the number of physicians varied from 8.5 to 11 per 10,000 population. There were about seven nurses and 11 hospital beds per 10,000 population. Some 650 hospitals were in operation. In the early 2000s, the main natural causes of death were cardiovascular disease and cancer. Opium and other drug addictions constitute a growing health problem.

Welfare: Iran's Ministry of Social Affairs supervises public programs for pensions, disability benefits, and income for minor children of deceased workers. Welfare programs for the needy are managed by more than 30 public agencies and semi-state organizations, as well as by several private nongovernmental organizations. In 2003 the government began to consolidate its welfare organizations in an effort to eliminate redundancy and inefficiency. The largest welfare organization is the Bonyad-e Mostazafin (Foundation of the Disinherited), a semi-public foundation that operates a variety of charitable activities.

Economy

Overview: Iran's economy is dominated by the oil industry, which is part of the state sector. In the early 2000s, more than 80 percent of export earnings came from oil and gas. The state also owns and administers several large industries. The private sector includes automobile, textile, metal manufacturing, and food-processing factories as well as thousands of small-scale enterprises such as workshops and farms. Smuggling and other illegal economic activities occupy an increasingly large part of the overall economy. Traditional import-export merchants, collectively known as the bazaar, occupy an influential place in economic policy making. Government economic planning is done in five-year development plans, the fourth of which began in March 2005. Although economic diversification has been a goal in the early 2000s, little progress has been made in that direction.

Gross Domestic Product (GDP): In 2006 Iran's GDP was estimated at US$194.8 billion, an increase of about 6 percent over the 2005 figure, yielding about US$2,978 per capita. Services contributed 47.1 percent, industry 41.7 percent, and agriculture 11.2 percent of GDP.

Inflation: The government's anti-inflationary policies have reduced inflation from the average rate of 23 percent in the 1977–98 period. The official rate for 2006 was 15.8 percent.

Agriculture: Iran's diversity of terrain and climate enable cultivation of a variety of crops, most notably wheat, barley, rice, pistachio nuts, cotton, sugar beets, and sugarcane. Because of droughts, the area under cultivation has decreased since 2000, and Iran depends on imports for some of its grains and other food items. About one-third of agricultural income comes from livestock, chiefly chickens, sheep, beef cattle, and dairy cows.

Mining and Minerals: In 2006 Iran produced more than 15 different nonradioactive metals and 27 nonmetal minerals. The mined products yielding the greatest value were iron ore, decorative stones, gravel and sand, coal, copper ore, and limestone. The fastest growing nonpetroleum extraction industry is copper. Iran has an estimated 4 percent of the world total of copper.

Industry and Manufacturing: Iran's most important industries are those associated with the extraction and processing of oil and gas. The petrochemicals industry has grown rapidly in the early 2000s; the Fourth Economic Development Plan (2005–10) calls for a major expansion of annual petrochemical output, from 9 million tons in 2001 to 27 million tons in 2015. The steel industry, centered in Ahvaz, Esfahan, and Mobarakeh, also has grown rapidly since 1990. Automobile manufacture has benefited from licensing agreements with European and Asian manufacturers. Processing of agricultural products and production of textiles also are important industries. The construction industry has grown rapidly since 2000 because of government investment in infrastructure projects and increased demand for private housing.

Energy: Oil output averaged 4 million barrels per day in 2006, but infrastructure is aging. Natural gas output in 2006 was 105 billion cubic meters. A large share of Iran's natural gas reserves are believed to remain untapped, and massive government investments are planned in that sector. In 2004 Iran's electric power plants had a total installed capacity of more than 39,000 megawatts. Of that amount, in 2006 about 50 percent was based on natural gas, 18 percent on oil, and 6 percent on hydroelectric power. New gas-fired and hydroelectric plants are planned to meet Iran's fast-growing power demand. The first nuclear power plant at Bushehr may come on line in 2008 after a series of delays.

Services: In the financial sector, the Central Bank of Iran, also known as Bank Markazi, oversees all state and private banks. Wealthy Iranians use foreign banks, especially for savings accounts. The Fourth Five-Year Economic Development Plan (2005–10) calls for the introduction of foreign banks, but such a move has met with substantial resistance. The trading of shares on the Tehran Stock Exchange was limited in the post-Revolution years, but activity has increased sharply since 2002. Beginning in the 1990s, Iran's tourism industry has revived after being decimated during the Iran–Iraq War.

Labor: In mid-2007 an estimated 14 percent of Iran's labor force was unemployed; the unemployment rate was much higher among younger workers, and underemployment was common. Skilled labor has been in short supply. In 2004 some 47.7 percent of the labor force was employed in services, 30.6 percent in industry, and 21.7 percent in agriculture. In 2005 the minimum wage was about US$120 per month.

Foreign Economic Relations: The Iran Sanctions Act, in existence since 1996 and until 2006 known as the Iran–Libya Sanctions Act, is a full U.S. trade embargo against Iran. Other countries, including members of the European Union (EU), have continued trade with Iran, but Western countries have blocked the export to Iran of dual-use items. In the early 2000s, China emerged as an important trade partner in both imports and exports. Japan retained the position that it assumed in the mid-1990s as Iran's best export customer. In order of volume, the main purchasers of Iran's exports in 2006 were Japan, China, Italy, Turkey, and South Korea. In order of volume, the main source countries for Iran's imports in 2006 were Germany, China, the United Arab Emirates, South Korea, and France. The main commodities imported are basic manufactures, chemicals, food (chiefly rice and wheat), and machinery and transport equipment. The main commodities exported are petroleum, carpets, chemical products, fruit and nuts, iron and steel, natural gas, and copper.

Trade Balance: In 2006 Iran's estimated income from exports was US$63 billion, 85 percent of which came from petroleum and natural gas. The estimated payment for imports in 2006 was US$45 billion, yielding a trade surplus of US$18 billion.

Balance of Payments: In 2006 Iran's current account balance, determined mainly by its merchandise trade surplus and its smaller services trade deficit, was US$13.3 billion. Its foreign exchange reserves, determined primarily by oil prices, were estimated at US$58.5 billion.

External Debt: Since 2001 Iran's foreign debt has risen as international borrowing has increased. In mid-2006 the estimate was US$18.6 billion, compared with US$10.2 billion in 2003.

Foreign Investment: Foreign investment has been hindered by unfavorable or complex operating requirements in Iran and by international sanctions, although in the early 2000s the Iranian government liberalized investment regulations. Foreign investors have concentrated their activity in a few sectors of the economy: the oil and gas industries, vehicle manufacture, copper mining, petrochemicals, foods, and pharmaceuticals. The most active investors have been British, French, Japanese, South Korean, Swedish, and Swiss companies.

Currency and Exchange Rate: The value of the rial, Iran's unit of currency, declined substantially between 2002 and 2007. In 2002 a multiple exchange rate was replaced by a single floating rate. In late February 2008, the exchange rate was about 9,400 rials to the U.S. dollar. The tuman, which is worth 10 rials, is the preferred unit of currency in commerce.

Fiscal Year: In accordance with the Iranian calendar, the fiscal year begins March 21.

Transportation and Telecommunications

Roads: In 2003 Iran had a total of 100,000 kilometers of paved roads and nearly 80,000 kilometers of graded, unpaved roads. The three national auto routes are the A–1 across northern Iran, the A–2 across southern Iran, and the Tehran–Qom–Esfahan–Shiraz highway, which traverses central Iran from north to south.

Railroads: The rail system, which originally was constructed in the 1920s and 1930s, has been undergoing constant expansion since 1989. In 2006 Iran had a total of 8,367 kilometers of rail line. Only 13 of Iran's 30 provinces had railroad service in the early 2000s. The five main lines of the national system radiate from Tehran. Tehran also has a combined underground and surface rail commuter system.

Ports: In 2004 about 53 million tons of cargo were unloaded and 30 million tons loaded at Iran's 14 ports. More than one-third of total traffic came through Bandar-e Abbas on the Strait of Hormuz. The main oil terminal is on Khark Island in the northeastern Persian Gulf. Since 1992, Caspian ports have handled more trade as commerce with the Central Asian countries has increased. Modernization projects are underway in Bandar-e Anzali on the Caspian Sea and Chabahar on the Gulf of Oman.

Inland Waterways: In 2006 Iran had 850 kilometers of inland waterways. The most important is the 193-kilometer-long Shatt al Arab (Arvanrud in Persian), which is formed in Iraq by the confluence of the Tigris and Euphrates rivers and then forms the Iran–Iraq border until it flows into the Persian Gulf. The ports of Abadan and Khorramshahr are located along the Shatt al Arab.

Civil Aviation and Airports: In 2006 Iran had 321 airports, 129 of which had paved runways. Of those, 41 had runways 3,000 meters or longer. International airports are located at Tehran, Tabriz, Mashhad, Bandar-e Abbas, Bushehr, Esfahan, and Shiraz, and on the islands of Kish in the Persian Gulf and Qeshm in the Strait of Hormuz. Some 15 heliports also were in operation. In 2006 the national airline, Iran Air, served 25 cities in Iran with connections to the Persian Gulf and European and Asian cities.

Pipelines: In 2006 Iran had 17,099 kilometers of natural gas pipelines, 8,521 kilometers of oil pipelines, 7,808 kilometers of pipelines for refined products, 570 kilometers of pipelines for liquid petroleum gas, and 397 kilometers of pipelines for gas condensate. In 2007 a new 160-kilometer line to Armenia began operations. However, a 2,600-kilometer line to Pakistan, which potentially also could supply India, remained under negotiation.

Telecommunications: Most phases of telecommunications services are controlled by the state. Between 1995 and 2006, the number of telephone land lines increased from 86 to 330 per 1,000 population. A large-scale modernization program has aimed at improving and expanding urban service and reaching rural areas. In 2006 an estimated 13.7 million subscribers had mobile telephone service. In 2005 an estimated 7.5 million Iranians had access to the Internet. However, the state filters Internet content intensively.

Government and Politics

Political System: The Islamic Revolution of 1978–79 established the Islamic Republic of Iran as a republic with nominal separation of powers among the executive, judicial, and legislative branches. The senior figure in the system is the *faqih,* an expert in religious law, who is referred to in the constitution as the Leader of the Revolution (Leader). Leaders are elected by a majority vote of the Assembly of Experts, a body of senior clergymen who are elected in national elections. The legal system is based on sharia (Islamic law).

Executive Branch: The Leader, who exercises many de facto executive functions, is elected by a majority vote of the Assembly of Experts, an 86-member body of senior clergymen who are elected by popular vote to eight-year terms. The Leader chooses the commanders of the military services and the head of the judiciary, sets general state policy, declares war and peace, and commands the armed forces. The executive branch is headed by the president, who in practice is the second-highest government official. He is elected in national elections every four years and is limited to two consecutive terms. The current president, Mahmoud Ahmadinejad, was elected in 2005. The president selects several vice presidents and the 21 cabinet ministers.

The relationship between the president and the Leader, not well defined by the constitution, has varied with the personalities in power. In the early 2000s, the reluctance of Ahmadinejad's moderate predecessor, Muhammad Khatami, to engage in confrontational politics enabled conservatives to strengthen the office of the Leader. In his early presidency, Ahmadinejad took a bolder position vis-à-vis the Leader.

Legislative Branch: The legislative branch consists of a parliament, or Majlis, and the Guardians Council. The 290 Majlis deputies are elected directly to four-year terms. The speaker presides over parliament, assisted by two deputies and 22 permanent committees. The Majlis may both propose and pass legislation, and the executive branch cannot dissolve it. All bills passed by the Majlis must be reviewed by the 12-member Guardians Council, which is appointed by the Leader and the Majlis. If the Guardians Council finds a bill unconstitutional or un-Islamic, the bill is sent back to the Majlis for revision. The Expediency Council resolves disputes between the Majlis and the Guardians Council. In practice, the Expediency Council has divided its decisions between the two bodies.

Judicial Branch: The highest judicial authority is the Supreme Court. The head of the judiciary, who is appointed to a five-year term by the Leader, appoints members of the Supreme Court. The court nominally has 33 regional branches, to which its chief assigns cases, but all but two are located in Tehran. The Supreme Court oversees enforcement of the laws by lower courts, sets judicial precedent, and acts as a court of appeal. Public courts try conventional civil and criminal cases at province and local levels. Revolutionary courts try cases involving political offenses and national security. The Clerical Court, overseen directly by the Leader, deals with crimes committed by members of the clergy, including misinterpretation of religious precepts. Iran also has special courts for members of the security forces and government officials. The judges of all courts must be experts in Islamic law.

Administrative Divisions: Iran is divided into 30 provinces, which are subdivided into counties (321 in 2007), districts, and villages.

Provincial and Local Government: Each province is administered by a governor general appointed by the central government. The governor general, in consultation with the Ministry of Interior, then appoints the governor of each county in the province and, in consultation with the latter, the chief of each district. At the local level, directly elected city and village councils have exerted substantial authority since the first local elections in 1999. Conservative candidates swept most of the local council elections held in 2003, but moderates won the majority of local council seats in the 2007 elections.

Judicial and Legal System: Although the constitution provides for an independent judiciary, in practice the judicial branch is influenced strongly by political and religious institutions. Defendants have the right to public trial, choice of a lawyer, and appeal. Judicial authority is concentrated in the judge, who also acts as prosecutor and investigator with no legal counsel. In the early 2000s, reformers tried unsuccessfully to gain Majlis approval for the introduction of jury trials. The Islamic revolutionary courts have authority to hold suspects on unspecified charges without the benefit of counsel.

Electoral System: Suffrage is universal at age 16. Direct elections every four years choose the Majlis, the president, and local councils. The Ministry of Interior and a committee of the Guardians Council vet candidates for direct election to national offices. Local boards supervise elections at the lowest governmental levels. The selection process favors candidates demonstrating strong loyalties to the Revolution and Islamic law. In recent elections, the Guardians Council has used its vetting capacity to disqualify a high percentage of reformist candidates.

Politics and Political Parties: Political parties were legalized in 1998. However, official political activity is permitted only to groups that accept the principle of political rule known as *velayat-e faqih*, literally, the guardianship of the *faqih* (religious jurist). Allegiances, still based on special interests and patronage, remain fluid. In 1998, 18 parties joined in a broad coalition called the Second of Khordad coalition. All were reformist parties that supported the political and economic proposals of President Mohammad Khatami; in the early 2000s, internal differences over specific economic policies hampered the coalition's effectiveness, however. During that period, the conservatives were more united, despite the existence of several major conservative parties. The Islamic Iran Builders Council (known as Abadgaran) emerged as a powerful conservative coalition beginning in 2003, leading the conservatives to victory in the 2004 parliamentary elections and the 2005 presidential election.

Mass Media: The constitution guarantees freedom of the press, provided that published material complies with Islamic principles. Freedom of speech is not guaranteed. In 1997 and 1998, publishing restrictions were relaxed, but since that time reformist publications have encountered various legal and illegal obstacles. The newspapers with the largest circulation are published in Tehran and include the conservative *Jomhuri-e Islami* (Islamic Republic), *Kayhan* (World), and *Resalat* (Prophetic Mission). The state news service is the Islamic Republic News Agency, which publishes the English-language *Iran Daily.* Several foreign news agencies maintain offices in Tehran. Radio and television broadcasting is controlled by the state.

Foreign Relations: The election of Mohammad Khatami as president in 1997 led to improved relations with Iran's neighbors and with most of the West, excluding Israel and the United States. The Khatami government stressed commercial and geopolitical relations with Western Europe and Japan. However, in the early 2000s, the regime failed to normalize bilateral relations with the United States. The Bush administration's inclusion of Iran as part of an "axis of evil" in 2002 brought relations to a new low in the post-1989 period. Beginning in 2004, relations deteriorated further because U.S. officials believe that Iran intends to develop a nuclear weapons program and actively supports insurgent activity in various parts of the Middle East. The nuclear issue also caused relations with Europe to decline in this period.

Since the overthrow of Iraqi President Saddam Hussein in 2003, Iran has established cooperative relations with the Shia-dominated government of Iraq. In the early 2000s, relations with other regional Arab countries have varied. Iran has had relatively good relations with China, India, and Russia, particularly in the area of military cooperation. Relations with neighbors Pakistan and Turkey have been correct but not close.

National Security

Armed Forces Overview: In 2007 the armed forces, under a unified command with the Leader as commander in chief, included about 420,000 active personnel in the regular forces and 125,000 in the auxiliary Islamic Revolutionary Guard Corps. Iran has eschewed military alliances, although it has reached military supply agreements with a number of countries. Modernization of the navy, seen as vital for protecting interests in the Persian Gulf, is a high priority. Technology purchased from North Korea and China, and refined by the domestic defense industry, supports a growing missile force that is considered the most important element of air defense policy. In 2001 Iran signed a 10-year military-technical agreement with Russia that included assistance in aircraft maintenance and design estimated to be worth US$4 billion.

Defense Budget: Iran's defense budget for 2006 was estimated at US$6.6 billion, which was a significant increase over the 2005 level of US$5.6 billion. The 2004 budget was US$3.3 billiion.

Major Military Units: In 2007 the army had about 350,000 active personnel assigned to four armored divisions, six infantry divisions, two commando divisions, one airborne brigade, one special forces brigade, and six artillery groups. The navy had about 18,000 active personnel in 2006, of whom 2,600 were in naval aviation and 2,600 in marine units. The navy operates bases at Bandar-e Abbas, Bushehr, Khark Island, Bandar-e Anzali, Bandar-e Khomeini, Bandar-e Mah Shahr, and Chabahar. The air force had about 52,000 active personnel in 2006, including 15,000 assigned to air defense units. Air force combat forces were organized in nine ground-attack fighter squadrons, five fighter squadrons, and one reconnaissance squadron.

Major Military Equipment: In 2006 the army had 1,613 main battle tanks, 610 armored infantry fighting vehicles, 640 armored personnel carriers, 2,010 pieces of towed artillery, 310 pieces of self-propelled artillery, 876 multiple rocket launchers, 5,000 mortars, 75 antitank guided weapons, 1,700 antiaircraft guns, and 50 attack helicopters. The navy had 3 submarines, 3 frigates, 140 patrol and coastal combatants, 5 mine warfare vessels, and 13 amphibious vessels. The air force ground-attack fighter units had F–4D, F–4E, F–5E, Su–24MK, Su–25K, and Mirage F–1E aircraft; the fighter units had F–14, F–7M, and MiG–29A aircraft. The air force also had 34 helicopters.

Military Service: Males are legally eligible for conscription between ages 18 and 50, for an active service term of 18 months. Individuals may volunteer for active duty at age 16.

Paramilitary Forces: The volunteer paramilitary force, the Popular Mobilization Army, or Basij, includes an estimated 300,000 personnel (40,000 active), mainly youths, with an estimated capability to expand to 1 million if needed. The Basij are under the authority of the Islamic Revolutionary Guard Corps.

Police: About 40,000 police serve under the Ministry of Interior, including border patrol personnel. The Police–110 unit specializes in rapid-response activities in urban areas and dispersing gatherings deemed dangerous to public order.

Internal Threat: Despite strong government countermeasures, Iran is a main transit country for narcotics from neighboring Afghanistan and Pakistan and destined for Europe, Central Asia, and the Gulf region. Considerable quantities of these narcotics are sold illegally in Iran and are the main source of a serious and growing addiction problem. In the early 2000s, other types of smuggling increased rapidly, especially in Iran's impoverished border provinces. Corruption in the border police is a major factor in this trade.

Human Rights: International human rights organizations have cited major abuses in Iran's judicial system, including arbitrary arrest, lack of due process, denial of access to attorneys, restrictions on family visits, prolonged periods in solitary confinement, and inhumane punishments in unofficial detention centers. Prison conditions are poor, particularly regarding food and medical care. The government controls all television and radio broadcast facilities. Domestic and foreign publications and films are censored. The state also filters Internet content. Members of religions not specifically protected by the constitution (Christianity, Islam, Judaism, and Zoroastrianism), such as members of the Baha'i faith, do not have full rights to assemble and may be subject to discrimination and even persecution. Marriage law discriminates against women in divorce, child custody, and inheritance from deceased spouses. Although women have equal access to education, social and legal conditions limit their professional activities.

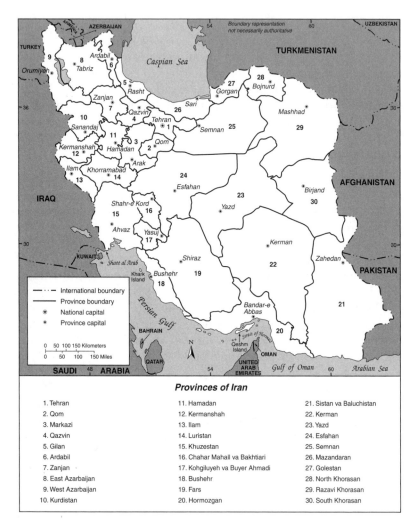

Figure 1. Administrative Divisions

Provinces of Iran

1. Tehran	11. Hamadan	21. Sistan va Baluchistan
2. Qom	12. Kermanshah	22. Kerman
3. Markazi	13. Ilam	23. Yazd
4. Qazvin	14. Luristan	24. Esfahan
5. Gilan	15. Khuzestan	25. Semnan
6. Ardabil	16. Chahar Mahall va Bakhtiari	26. Mazandaran
7. Zanjan	17. Kohgiluyeh va Buyer Ahmadi	27. Golestan
8. East Azarbaijan	18. Bushehr	28. North Khorasan
9. West Azarbaijan	19. Fars	29. Razavi Khorasan
10. Kurdistan	20. Hormozgan	30. South Khorasan

Introduction

CONTEMPORARY IRAN is a country whose people retain memories of legendary heroes and rulers, some of whom lived more than two millennia ago. Its national language, Persian, is equally ancient as a written tongue. Some customs, such as the annual New Year's celebrations that are observed on the spring equinox, also have their roots deep in history. The religion of at least 98 percent of Iranians is Islam, which initially was brought into Iran by Arabs in the mid-seventh century. Thus, history, Persian literature, cultural traditions, and Islam have been longtime and persistent influences on Iran. Although the Islamic Revolution of 1978–79 led to the creation of the Islamic Republic, an event that marked a break with the long political tradition of rule by monarchs (shahs) and institutionalized a dominant political role for the Shia (see Glossary) clergy, Iran's development otherwise has demonstrated numerous continuities with its pre-1979 past.

Iranians generally consider their ancient history as a period of national greatness, while they view their more recent history, especially the 150 years preceding the 1978–79 Revolution, as a time of national humiliation and foreign intervention. Ancient Iranians, also known as Persians, organized three powerful empires—the Achaemenian (550–330 B.C.), Parthian (247 B.C.–A.D. 224), and Sassanian (A.D 224–642). At their heights, those empires extended east into modern Afghanistan and Central Asia and west as far as Anatolia and the Mediterranean Sea. Following the overthrow of the Sassanian dynasty by Arab armies, Iran did not exist as an independent polity for 850 years. Nevertheless, between the eighth and twelfth centuries Iranian Muslim scholars contributed to the development of classical Sunni Islam, and by the eleventh century modern Persian had acquired equal status with Arabic as a language of culture throughout most of the Islamic world.

After Shah Ismail Safavi reestablished it as an independent country in 1501, Iran was a major power for the next two centuries. Ismail also established Shia Islam as the official religion, thus setting Iran apart from the predominantly Sunni Islamic world. By 1722, when the Safavi dynasty was overthrown, the majority of Iranians had become Shias, and the Shia denomination of Islam has been identified closely with Iran since that time. Under the Safavis, the state and the Shia clergy maintained close relations, but under later dynasties, particularly the Qajars (1795–1925) and Pahlavis (1925–79), the clergy tended to view their role as protecting the people from the power of the state. In fact, the clergy played a significant role in several major antigovernment movements, including the Tobacco Rebellion of 1891, the Constitutional Revolution of 1905–7, and the Islamic Revolution of 1978–79.

The fall of the Safavi dynasty precipitated a civil war that continued intermittently until the Qajars established control over the entire country in the late 1700s. However, by the beginning of the Qajar dynasty Iran's status had so declined that its territorial integrity and even national sovereignty were threatened by the European empires of Britain and Russia. After losing two disastrous wars to Russia in the early nineteenth century, Iran's leaders sought to achieve military parity with the Europeans by adopting Western military tactics and technology. Thus began a national reform or Westernization project that would preoccupy Iran's rulers for some 90 years. The Qajars desired a strong state that could deter foreign threats and quell domestic unrest, but they also feared the destabilizing effects of exposing their subjects to new ideas that challenged their absolute rule. Because of this ambivalence toward change, the overall reform effort was dilatory. By the end of the nineteenth century, unrest was increasing among secular intellectuals, merchants, and the Shia clergy, who saw no improvement in Iran's resistance to foreign economic and political penetration.

Discontent culminated in the Constitutional Revolution of 1905–7, which featured the organization of long economic strikes in major cities—a tactic that would be repeated 70 years later during the Islamic Revolution. The Constitutional Revolution forced the shah to grant a representative assembly (the Majlis—see Glossary), a free press, and a constitution. But Iran's first experience with constitutional government exposed serious political differences between secular and clerical intellectuals that have persisted to the present. Secular political leaders wanted to apply European economic, political, and social principles in Iran, including strict separation of religion and government. Religious leaders feared that the secularists' reforms would undermine the role of religion in Iranian society. These differing perspectives paralyzed the Majlis and created conditions for British and Russian political interference.

In 1921 the army officer Reza Khan provided military support for a coup d'état that led to far-reaching economic, political, and social changes. After the Majlis deposed the Qajar dynasty in 1925, Reza Khan became shah, taking the dynastic name Pahlavi. He then implemented a wholesale modernization program intended to return Iran to its historical stature. Reza Shah's economic policies transformed urban Iran, but his intolerance of political dissent alienated intellectuals, who had hoped for democratic government, and Shia clerics, who perceived his secular policies as an attack on religion.

Reza Shah was forced to abdicate in 1941 after Britain and the Soviet Union, discontented with Iran's neutral position in World War II, invaded the country. He was succeeded by his son, who ascended the throne as Mohammad Reza Shah Pahlavi. Reza Shah's removal led to a restoration of constitutional government, the re-emergence of a relatively free press, and the resumption of the religious-secular debates over the desirability of Westernization. In 1944 a mid-ranking cleric, Ruhollah Musavi Khomeini, authored a book denouncing the anticlerical policies of Reza Shah's regime and advocating a role for high-ranking clergy in selecting the ruler and advising the government on legislation. Later, in the 1970s, Khomeini would elaborate on these ideas and put forth his concept of *velayat-e faqih* (see Glossary).

Meanwhile, Mohammad Reza Shah's undemocratic rule met increasing resistance from secular politicians, who agreed with his goals of modernization. Mohammad Mossadeq, the leading advocate of democracy in the Majlis, formed a National Front to promote national development and democratic politics. The National Front viewed the country's large, British-owned oil industry as a threat to Iran's independent development. With strong public support, the Majlis enacted an oil nationalization bill in 1951, and Mossadeq was named prime minister. But in 1953 British and U.S. intelligence agencies supported a military coup d'état that overthrew the Mossadeq government.

After the 1953 coup, Mohammad Reza Shah ruled as a virtual dictator with an acquiescent Majlis. He implemented development programs that expanded industrialization and education, stimulated urbanization, and led to the creation of a Westernized, technocratic elite. He also firmly aligned Iran with the United States and its European allies in the Cold War. However, secular and religious opponents were unified by the shah's undemocratic rule and his alliance with countries identified with the ouster of the popular Mossadeq. In 1962–64 Khomeini achieved national prominence by his vocal opposition to the shah's domestic and foreign policies, which led to his forcible exile to Turkey and later Iraq. From exile Khomeini formed a clandestine network of opposition to the shah's regime, which gradually expanded throughout the country in the late 1960s and during the 1970s.

Other secular and religious opposition groups formed in the same period, despite repression by the shah's secret police organization, SAVAK (in full, Sazman-e Ettelaat va Amniyat-e Keshvar; Organization for Intelligence and National Security). Two groups, the Marxist Fedayan (Fedayan-e Khalq, or People's Warriors) and the Islamist Mojahedin (Mojahedin-e Khalq, or People's Fighters), initiated guerrilla warfare against the government in 1971, with the aim of overthrowing the shah's regime. Between 1976 and 1978, an increasing tide of intellectual, middle class, and religious opposition gradually coalesced into a nationwide revolutionary movement. In 1978 the charismatic exile Khomeini led this movement through strikes and mass demonstrations to ultimate victory: the overthrow of the Pahlavi dynasty in February 1979 and the establishment of an Islamic republic.

The national unity that brought an end to monarchy in Iran began to disintegrate in the initial postrevolutionary period. Secular leaders did not want the clergy to exercise a political role in the government, but they were marginalized quickly because Khomeini had widespread support. A constitution drafted with heavy influence from Khomeini's followers enshrined his concept of *velayat-e faqih* as the basis of Iran's new Islamic government. Nevertheless, among religious leaders and their lay allies differing perspectives on the nature of Islamic government led to the formation of distinct political factions. Since the early 1990s, the two most important factions have been referred to as the reformists and the conservatives. In the early postrevolutionary years, the reformist groups advocated using the country's substantial oil revenues to improve social justice and benefit low-income people, while the conservatives distrusted policies for the redistribution of wealth, contending that an Islamic government's obligation was to protect private property.

Increasingly in the postrevolutionary period, the divisive force of differences on domestic policy was limited by the perceived need to remain united against foreign threats. Although the Revolution had demonstrated that a peaceful national movement based on Islamic values could overthrow a powerful dictator backed by a foreign superpower, the revolutionary leaders believed that the United States aimed to repeat the successful reinstatement of the shah that had occurred in 1953. This mindset led to the incident that has had the strongest, most enduring influence on U.S-Iranian "non-relations": the taking hostage of U.S. embassy personnel by young Iranian radicals in November 1979.

Khomeini promoted Iran's experience as a model for movements in other countries seeking freedom from U.S. political influence (the Persian Gulf states, for example) and the Soviet Union (Afghanistan, for example). Iraq's invasion of Iran in September 1980, at a time when Iran still was embroiled with the United States in the hostage crisis, led to a traumatic eight-year war that ignited tremendous patriotic fervor. The general isolation that Iran experienced during that war reinforced the impression that many foreign countries opposed the Islamic Republic.

The end of the war prompted the political elite to focus attention on reconstructing the country and normalizing Iran's external relations with other countries. However, Khomeini died barely a year later. His successor as Leader of the Revolution, Sayyid Ali Khamenei, did not possess the latter's charisma or scholarly reputation, and many reformers believed he was against them in their factional struggle with the conservatives. This suspicion fostered controversy over the degree of the Leader's authority and political freedom in the Islamic Republic. Although the constitution stipulates that the institutions and structure of government are under the supervision and protection of the Leader, neither it nor the first Leader, Khomeini, articulated specific functions of the office. Hence, conservatives and reformists have interpreted the Leader's powers differently. The reformists hold that all officials, including the Leader, are accountable to the people for their decisions and policies. In this conception, the Leader is a neutral arbiter who encourages political groups to work out compromises for the overall national good; if a Leader takes a partisan position, he loses legitimacy and therefore can be removed.

The conservatives, by contrast, have seen the Leader as an adviser to the political leadership whenever executive or legislative decisions come into conflict with Islamic values. Many conservatives hold that the Leader has absolute authority in protecting the public from the undesirable exercise of freedom of speech, such as insults to religious values and religious personalities, and by extension to government officials and agencies. Since the late 1990s, conservatives have used this conception of the Leader's responsibilities to justify closing reformist newspapers that criticized the rulings of the Leader or other senior clergy. As their attitude toward the press has demonstrated, conservatives believe in the necessity of setting definite limits on the exercise of popular sovereignty. They distrust the masses, who, they suspect, would not behave in accordance with Islamic values if they were to have unfettered freedom. Conservatives insist that their version of Islamic democracy is superior to a Western-style democracy. They believe that in the latter every kind of religious and moral ideal is under attack in the name of freedom, undermining the moral values that bind societies together.

Conservatives generally have seen a free press, demonstrations, political meetings, and unions as potentially disruptive of the social order. Centrist president Ali Akbar Hashemi Rafsanjani (1989–97) oversaw a partial lifting of media and organizational restrictions, and the administration of his successor, Mohammad Khatami (1997–2005), accelerated this process. After the conservatives had succeeded in blocking many, but not all, of the reforms proposed by the Khatami administration, the extent of personal and political freedom was marginally greater in 2007 than it had been 10 years earlier.

In 2005 Khatami was succeeded as president by a conservative, Mahmoud Ahmadinejad, who defeated former president Rafsanjani in an election that extended to a second round when no candidate reached the minimum of 50 percent in the initial balloting. Although Ahmadinejad is a conservative in terms of political philosophy, i.e., a firm supporter of the notion of an authoritative *faqih*/Leader, his ideas on social justice issues, such as increasing subsidies for poor families, implementing programs to end poverty, increasing government regulation of the economy, and opposing "dependence" on foreign capital and investment, were not favored by the conservatives, especially those politicians with ties to the bazaar (see Glossary). Consequently, the conservative-dominated parliament succeeded in blocking most of Ahmadinejad's economic proposals during his first two years in office. The political dispute over economic policies was not conducive to private investment in the types of activities that promote job creation.

In fact, between the late 1990s and 2007, private investment remained at a low level, and in each year of that period the number of new job-seekers exceeded the number of available jobs. One result was an increasing unemployment rate among youth aged 16 to 25. In 2007 that rate was estimated at between 20 and 25 percent, compared with the official overall unemployment rate of 14 percent.

In the early part of his term, Ahmadinejad did not show particular concern for the social issues that preoccupy the fundamentalist conservatives, and he did not endorse campaigns to restrict or roll back the social freedoms that had become common by the second Khatami administration. On foreign policy issues, however, Ahmadinejad proved very unlike the moderate Khatami or the pragmatic Rafsanjani. His critics in Iran described him as a "super-patriot sensitive to the tiniest insult to national pride." His handling of the nuclear energy dispute since 2005 has demonstrated a focus on Iran's national right to develop nuclear fuel technology, especially the enrichment of uranium, and an inability or unwillingness to comprehend the concerns of the International Atomic Energy Agency (IAEA) that such activity could lead to the production of weapons-grade uranium fuel. The consequent impasse over Iran's position prompted the IAEA in 2006 to refer Iran to the United Nations (UN) Security Council, where the United States advocated international sanctions against Iran to force compliance with UN and IAEA demands to stop the enrichment of uranium. Because not all permanent members of the Security Council supported the imposition of sanctions, a compromise was reached in June 2006 to send Iran a letter offering negotiations in return for its suspension of nuclear enrichment. The reply of the Ahmadinejad administration was delayed for several months, leaving the international community divided over the appropriate way to deal with Iran. Ahmadinejad took the position that Iran was prepared to negotiate over its nuclear program, but that it would not accept any pre-conditions (i.e., the suspension of uranium enrichment) for such talks. Within the country, Ahmadinejad's tough stance on the nuclear program garnered him widespread popular support, even among those Iranians who disliked his domestic economic and/or political policies.

In 2007 the standoff over the nuclear issue continued. In defiance of international warnings, Iran expanded its uranium enrichment capacity and refused to provide key documentation on its nuclear industry requested by the IAEA. The UN Security Council voted to impose relatively mild sanctions on Iran as part of its strategy to pressure the country into complying with IAEA inspections. The sanctions were a compromise between the tough measures favored by Britain, France, and the United States on the one hand and the lack of enthusiasm for any sanctions on the part of China and Russia on the other hand. Officials in the former countries periodically issued harsh statements about the dangers of a suspected secret nuclear program in Iran while simultaneously stressing the need to find a diplomatic settlement of the impasse. These tactics seemed to have achieved some results, when in August 2007 the Ahmadinejad government and the IAEA reached agreement on a timetable by which Iran would provide the nuclear agency responses to several outstanding questions pertaining to its nuclear program and also allow IAEA inspectors to resume inspecting declared nuclear sites. However, in October 2007, the resignation of Ali Larijani, Iran's chief international negotiator on the nuclear issue, indicated a possible hardening of Iran's stance.

In November 2007, a National Intelligence Estimate by the U.S. government concluded that Iran likely had ceased production of equipment for nuclear weapons in 2003, although enrichment of uranium continued. Although controversial, that document softened international condemnation of Iran's nuclear program at the end of 2007. In Iran that change diverted attention from the international threat to the increasingly worrisome economic situation, and Khamenei expressed dissatisfaction with the economic policies of President Ahmadinejad. At the end of 2007, experts also observed other signs of Khamenei's diminishing support for Ahmadinejad, who with the Leader's tacit approval had exceeded the official ceremonial prerogatives of the presidency during his first two years in office.

Meanwhile, in May 2007, U.S. and Iranian ambassadors to Iraq met in Baghdad to discuss the security situation. This meeting marked the first time in 27 years that diplomats from the two countries had met openly to discuss an issue of mutual concern. Their talks, which included two subsequent sessions during the summer, came amid increased tension caused by Iran's jailing of four individuals with joint Iranian and U.S. citizenship and a spate of accusations by U.S. diplomatic and military officials that Iran was supplying arms to Shia insurgents in Iraq.

During 2006 and 2007, Iran's economy continued to grow at a moderate rate (a gross domestic product (GDP) increase of about 6 percent in 2006) as state policy continued to strive unsuccessfully for a diversity that would wean the economy from its excessive reliance on the petroleum industry. Because the labor force grew faster than the economy, the unemployment rate increased from the 12 percent official figure for 2006 to an unofficial rate of about 14 percent by mid-2007. The government also tried to limit the high consumer demand for gasoline during 2007. Up to 40 percent of domestic gas consumption had to be imported as a result of the inadequate capacity of the country's refineries. To reduce gasoline imports, gas rationing for cars went into effect at the beginning of the summer. This policy was greatly unpopular and prompted demonstrations and even riots in several cities, although the population seemed to have adjusted to the rationing by the end of the summer. In the fall of 2007, the government reduced gasoline subsidies in another effort to reduce demand. However, continuing shortages of consumer goods, related to Ahmadinejad's import and industrial policies, resulted in price rises. The official inflation rate rose to 19 percent at the end of 2007. The rising inflation was attributed, at least in part, to the UN-imposed economic sanctions, because, prodded by their governments, international banks based in European Union member countries began resticting or halting financial transactions with Iranian banks. Consequently, Iranian businesses, which for years had relied on low-interest, short-term credit from these banks to finance imports, were forced to turn to Asian banks, which charged significantly higher rates of interest. These credit costs were passed on to the consumer in the form of higher prices for all imported goods.

Meanwhile, in July 2006, Khamenei declared a renewed campaign to privatize portions of Iran's economy, following several years in which official privatization goals were not met. Khamenei's intent was to improve performance in many industries that had been rendered unproductive by high state subsidies and to prepare Iran for possible membership in the World Trade Organization. The privatization program for 2007 included smaller banks, some electric power stations, some major mining and metallurgical companies, most airlines, and some telecommunications companies. In a step to improve the lot of Iran's poor, beginning in 2006 shares in many state companies were offered to people below the poverty line (a segment of the population estimated at 12 million in 2007) and to rural residents. The privatization program also relied on substantial purchases of shares by the Iranian expatriate community; access to shares by foreign firms was strictly limited, however.

Despite increases in oil revenues estimated at 15 percent in 2006, extensive government subsidy programs continued to cause shortfalls in the national budget. To help cover the deficit foreseen for fiscal year (see Glossary) 2007, the government removed US$12 billion from the Oil Stabilization Fund, which was set aside to minimize the effect of fluctuations in oil prices. In 2006 and 2007, Iran sought to expand economic relationships on several fronts. For example, it signed a new bilateral trade agreement with Persian Gulf neighbor Oman and sought major new investments in its petroleum industry from China and Japan, both of which have relied heavily on Iran for oil. Thus, in 2007 important aspects of both the domestic and international sectors of Iran's economy were in a state of uncertainty and transition.

February 19, 2008   Eric Hooglund

Chapter 1. Historical Setting

Members of the Achaemenian royal bodyguard, from a bas-relief at Persepolis

THE ISLAMIC REVOLUTION OF 1978–79 brought a sudden end to the rule of the Pahlavi dynasty, which for 50 years had been identified with the attempt to modernize and westernize Iran. The Revolution replaced the monarchy with an Islamic republic, vesting ultimate power in the hands of a clerical leader and the clerical class as a whole. It brought new elites to power, altered the pattern of Iran's foreign relations, and led to a substantial transfer of wealth from private ownership to state control. There were continuities across the watershed of the Revolution, however; bureaucratic structure and behavior, attitudes toward authority and individual rights, and the arbitrary use of power remained much the same. Nonetheless, combined with sweeping purges and executions, violent power struggles within the revolutionary coalition, and the Iran–Iraq War (1980–88), the Revolution amounted to a great upheaval in Iranian political and social life. The Revolution also was rooted in the idea of government based on the will of the people, and the reform movement ushered in by the election of Mohammad Khatami to the presidency in 1997 reflected the aspiration of many Iranians to greater freedom and the rule of law. But by 2000, the reform movement had suffered severe setbacks, and it was unclear whether the democratic or the autocratic legacy of the Islamic Revolution would prevail.

The Revolution ended a pattern of monarchical rule that had been an almost uninterrupted feature of Iranian government for nearly 500 years. The tradition of monarchy itself was even older. In the sixth century B.C., Iran's first empire, the Achaemenian Empire, was already established. It had an absolute monarch, centralized rule, a highly developed system of administration, aspirations to world rule, and a culture that was uniquely Iranian even as it borrowed, absorbed, and transformed elements from other cultures and civilizations. Although Alexander the Great brought the Achaemenian Empire to an end in 330 B.C., under the Sassanian dynasty (A.D. 224–642) Iran once again became the center of an empire and a great civilization.

The impact of the Islamic conquest in the seventh century was profound. It introduced a new religion and new social and legal systems. The Iranian heartland became part of a world empire whose center was not in Iran. Nevertheless, historians have found striking continuities in Iranian social structure, administration, and culture. Iranians contributed significantly to all aspects of Islamic civilization; in many ways, they helped shape the new order. By the ninth century, there was a revival of the Persian (Farsi) language and of a literature that was uniquely Iranian but also was enriched by Arabic and Islamic influences.

The breakup of the Islamic empire led, in Iran as in other parts of the Islamic world, to the establishment of local dynasties. Iran, like the rest of the Middle East, was affected by the rise to power of the Seljuk Turks and then by the destruction wrought first by the Mongols and then by Timur, also called Tamerlane (Timur the Lame).

With the rise of the Safavi dynasty (1501–1722), Iran was reconstituted as a territorial state within borders not very different from those prevailing today. Shia (see Glossary) Islam became the state religion, and monarchy once again the central institution. Persian became unquestionably the language of administration and high culture. Although historians no longer assert that under the Safavis Iran emerged as a nation-state in the modern sense of the term, nevertheless by the seventeenth century the sense of Iranian identity and of Iran as a state within roughly demarcated borders was more pronounced.

The Qajar dynasty (1795–1925) attempted to revive the Safavi Empire, in many ways patterning their administration after that of the Safavis. But the Qajars lacked the claims to religious legitimacy available to the Safavis. Also, they failed to establish strong central control and faced an external threat from technically, militarily, and economically superior European powers, primarily Russia and Britain. Foreign interference in Iran, Qajar misrule, and new ideas on government in 1905 led to protests and eventually to the Constitutional Revolution (1905–7), which, at least on paper, limited royal absolutism, created a constitutional monarchy, and recognized the people as a source of legitimacy. Various factors, however, resulted in the failure of the constitutional experiment: royalist counterrevolution, internal divisions, clerical opposition, the traditional attitudes of much of Iranian society, foreign interference, and the fact that, despite popular enthusiasm, the meaning of constitutionalism was understood only by a small elite—and then only imperfectly.

The rise of Reza Shah Pahlavi, who as Reza Khan seized power in 1921 and established a new dynasty in 1925, reflected the failure of the constitutional experiment. His early actions also resulted from the aspirations of educated Iranians to create a state that was strong, centralized, free of foreign interference, economically developed, and possessed of those characteristics thought to distinguish the more advanced states of Europe from the countries of the East.

Modernization continued under the second Pahlavi monarch, Mohammad Reza Shah Pahlavi. In the 1960s and 1970s, he further expanded industry, widened access to employment and other economic opportunities, increased the availability of education, built up the central government and the military, limited foreign influence, and gave Iran an influential role in regional affairs.

However, major unresolved tensions were revealed in Iranian society by rioting during the 1951–53 oil nationalization crisis and in 1963 during the Muslim month of Moharram, in response to the announcement of certain government reforms. These responses stemmed from inequities in the distribution of wealth; the concentration of power in the hands of the crown and the bureaucratic, military, and entrepreneurial elites; demands for political participation by a growing middle class and members of upwardly mobile lower classes; a belief that Westernization posed a threat to Iran's national and Islamic identity; and a growing polarization between the religious classes and the state. Although by the mid-1970s Iranians as a whole were enjoying considerably higher standards of living and greater employment and educational opportunities, these social tensions remained unresolved. They were exacerbated by growing royal autocracy, economic dislocations caused by the huge infusion of new oil wealth, corruption, and a perception that the shah, in the rush to modernize, was heedless of Iranian national and religious traditions.

Discontent was expressed in public protests, then riots and demonstrations, which began in 1977 and spread rapidly in the following year. These upheavals, along with the emergence of a charismatic leader in the person of Ayatollah Sayyid Ruhollah Musavi Khomeini and the paralysis of the monarchy in response to the rising protest movement, cleared the way for the Islamic Revolution. During the decades that followed, that revolution fundamentally changed governance within Iran as well as Iran's relations with the rest of the world.

Ancient Iran

Pre-Achaemenian Iran

Iran's history as a nation of people speaking an Indo-European language did not begin until the middle of the second millennium B.C. Before then, Iran was occupied by peoples with a variety of cultures. There are numerous artifacts attesting to settled agriculture, permanent sun-dried-brick dwellings, and pottery making as early as the sixth millennium B.C. The most advanced area technologically was Susiana (present-day Khuzestan Province; see fig. 1). By the fourth millennium B.C., the inhabitants of Susiana, the Elamites, were using semipictographic writing, probably learned from the highly advanced civilization of Sumer in Mesopotamia (the ancient name for much of the area now known as Iraq) to the west.

Sumerian influence in art, literature, and religion became particularly strong when the Elamite lands were occupied by, or at least came under the domination of, two Mesopotamian cultures, those of Akkad and Ur, during the middle of the third millennium. By 2000 B.C., the Elamites had become sufficiently unified to destroy the city of Ur. Elamite civilization developed rapidly from that point, and by the fourteenth century B.C. its art was at its most impressive.

Immigration of the Medes and the Persians

Small groups of nomadic, horse-riding peoples speaking Indo-European languages began moving into the Iranian cultural area from Central Asia near the end of the second millennium B.C. Population pressures, overgrazing in their home area, and hostile neighbors may have prompted these migrations. Some of the groups settled in eastern Iran, but others, those who were to leave significant historical records, pushed farther west toward the Zagros Mountains.

Three major groups are identifiable—the Scythians, the Medes (the Amadai or Mada), and the Persians (also known as the Parsua or Parsa). The Scythians established themselves in the northern Zagros Mountains and clung to a seminomadic existence in which raiding was the chief form of economic enterprise. The Medes settled over a huge area, reaching as far as modern Tabriz in the north and Esfahan in the south. They had their capital at Ecbatana (present-day Hamadan) and annually paid tribute to the Assyrians. The Persians were established in three areas: to the south of Lake Urmia (called Lake Rezaiyeh under the Pahlavis), on the northern border of the kingdom of the Elamites; and in the environs of modern Shiraz, which would be their eventual settling place and to which they would give the name Parsa (roughly coterminous with present-day Fars Province).

During the seventh century B.C., the Persians were led by Hakamanish (Achaemenes, in Greek), ancestor of the Achaemenian dynasty. A descendant, Cyrus II (also known as Cyrus the Great or Cyrus the Elder), led the combined forces of the Medes and the Persians to establish the most extensive empire known in the ancient world.

The Achaemenian Empire, 550–330 B.C.

By 546 B.C., Cyrus had defeated Croesus, the Lydian king of fabled wealth, and had secured control of the Aegean coast of Asia Minor, Armenia, and the Greek colonies along the Levant (see fig. 2). Moving east, he took Parthia (land of the Arsacids, not to be confused with Parsa, which was to the southwest), Chorasmia (Khwarezm), and Bactria. He besieged and captured Babylon in 539 B.C. and released the Jews who had been held captive there, thus earning his immortalization in the Book of Isaiah. When Cyrus died in 529 B.C., his kingdom extended as far east as the Hindu Kush in present-day Afghanistan.

Cyrus's successors were less successful. His unstable son, Cambyses II, conquered Egypt in 525 B.C. but later committed suicide during a revolt led by a priest, Gaumata, who held the throne until 522 B.C., when he was overthrown by a member of a lateral branch of the Achaemenian family, Darius I (also known as Darayarahush and Darius the Great). Darius attacked the Greek mainland, which had supported rebellious Greek colonies under his aegis, but his defeat at the Battle of Marathon in 490 B.C. forced him to retract the limits of the empire to Asia Minor.

The Achaemenians thereafter consolidated areas firmly under their control. It was Cyrus and Darius who, by sound and farsighted administrative planning, brilliant military maneuvering, and a humanistic worldview, established the greatness of the Achaemenians, raising them in less than 30 years from an obscure tribe to a world power.

The quality of the Achaemenians as rulers began to disintegrate, however, after the death of Darius in 486 B.C. His son and successor, Xerxes, chiefly occupied himself with suppress-

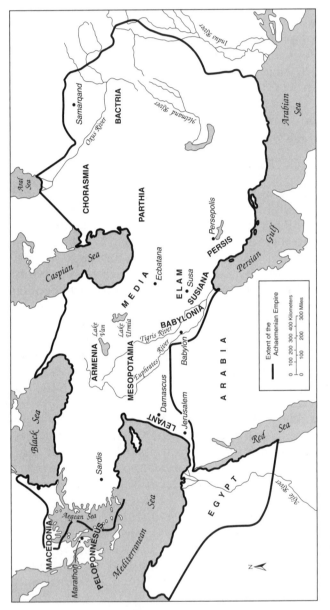

Source: Based on information from *Hammond World Atlas*, Maplewood, New Jersey, 1971; and Herbert H. Vreeland, ed., *Iran*, New Haven, 1957.

Figure 2. Persian Empire, ca. 500 B.C.

ing revolts in Egypt and Babylonia. He also attempted to conquer the Greek Peloponnesus, but, encouraged by a victory at Thermopylae, he overextended his forces and suffered overwhelming defeats at Salamis and Plataea. By the time his successor, Artaxerxes I, died in 424 B.C., the imperial court was beset by factionalism among the lateral family branches, a condition that persisted until the death in 330 B.C. of the last of the Achaemenians, Darius III, at the hands of his own subjects.

The Achaemenians were enlightened despots who allowed a certain amount of regional autonomy in the form of the satrapy system. A satrapy was an administrative unit, usually organized on a geographical basis. A satrap (governor) administered the region, a general supervised military recruitment and ensured order, and a state secretary kept official records. The general and the state secretary reported directly to the central government. The 20 satrapies were linked by a 2,500-kilometer highway, the most impressive stretch being the royal road from Susa to Sardis built by command of Darius I. Relays of mounted couriers could reach the most remote areas in 15 days. As if to remind the satrapies of their limited independence, royal inspectors, the "eyes and ears of the king," would tour the empire and report on local conditions. Inclinations toward restiveness were further discouraged by the existence of the king's personal bodyguard of 10,000 men, called the Immortals. The most common language in the empire was Aramaic. Old Persian was the "official language" but was used only for inscriptions and royal proclamations.

Darius I revolutionized the economy by placing it on a system of silver and gold coinage. Trade was extensive, and under the Achaemenians an efficient infrastructure facilitated the exchange of commodities among the far reaches of the empire. As a result of this commercial activity, Persian words for typical items of trade became prevalent throughout the Middle East and eventually entered the English language; examples include *asparagus, bazaar, lemon, melon, orange, peach, sash, shawl, spinach, tiara,* and *turquoise.* Trade was one of the empire's main sources of revenue, along with agriculture and tribute. Other accomplishments of Darius's reign included codification of the *data,* a universal legal system upon which much of later Iranian law would be based, and construction of a new capital at Persepolis, where vassal states would offer their yearly tribute at the festival celebrating the spring equinox. In its art and architecture, Persepolis reflected Darius's

9

perception of himself as the leader of conglomerates of people to whom he had given a new, single identity. The Achaemenian art and architecture found there is at once distinctive and highly eclectic. The Achaemenians took the art forms and the cultural and religious traditions of many of the ancient Middle Eastern peoples and combined them into a single form. This Achaemenian artistic style is evident in the iconography of Persepolis, which celebrates the king and the office of the monarch.

Alexander the Great, the Seleucids, and the Parthians

Envisioning a new world empire based on a fusion of Greek and Iranian culture and ideals, Alexander the Great of Macedon accelerated the disintegration of the Achaemenian Empire. He was first accepted as leader by the fractious Greeks in 336 B.C., and by 334 B.C. had advanced to Asia Minor, an Iranian satrapy. In quick succession, he took Egypt, Babylonia, and then, over the course of two years, the heart of the Achaemenian Empire—Susa, Ecbatana, and Persepolis—the last of which he burned. Alexander married Roxana (Roshanak), the daughter of the most powerful of the Bactrian chiefs, and in 324 B.C. commanded his officers and 10,000 of his soldiers to marry Iranian women. The mass wedding, held at Susa, manifested Alexander's desire to consummate the union of the Greek and Iranian peoples. But this hope was dashed in 323 B.C., when Alexander was stricken with fever and died in Babylon, leaving no heir. His empire was divided among four of his generals. One, Seleucus, who became ruler of Babylon in 312 B.C., gradually reconquered most of Iran. The rulers descended from him are known as the Seleucids. Under Seleucus's son, Antiochus I, many Greeks entered Iran, and Hellenistic motifs in art, architecture, and urban planning became prevalent.

Although the Seleucids faced challenges from the Ptolemaic kings of Egypt and from the growing power of Rome, the main threat came from the province of Fars. Arsaces (of the seminomadic Parni tribe), revolted against the Seleucid governor in 247 B.C. and established a dynasty, the Arsacids, or Parthians, who would rule for nearly five centuries. During the second century, the Parthians were able to extend their rule to Bactria, Babylonia, Susiana, and Media, and, under Mithradates II (123–87 B.C.), Parthian conquests stretched from India to Armenia. After the victories of Mithradates II, the Parthians began to claim descent from both the Greeks and the Achae-menians. They spoke a language similar to that of the Achae-menians, used the Middle Persian Pahlavi script that had developed from the Aramaic alphabet, and established an administrative system based on Achaemenian precedents.

Early in the third century A.D., Ardeshir, son of the priest Papak, who claimed descent from a legendary hero Sasan, became the Parthian governor in the Achaemenian home province of Fars. In A.D. 224 he overthrew the last Parthian king and established the Sassanian dynasty, which was to last 400 years.

The Sassanians, A.D. 224–642

The Sassanians established an empire roughly within the frontiers achieved by the Achaemenians, with its capital at Cte-siphon (see fig. 3). The Sassanians sought to resuscitate Iranian traditions and to obliterate Greek cultural influence. Their rule was characterized by centralization, ambitious urban plan-ning, agricultural development, and technological improve-ments. Sassanian rulers adopted the title *shahanshah* (king of kings), as sovereigns over numerous petty rulers, known as *shahrdars*. Historians believe that society was divided into four classes: priests, warriors, secretaries, and commoners. The royal princes, petty rulers, great landlords, and priests together con-stituted a privileged stratum, and the social system appears to have been fairly rigid. Sassanian rule and the system of social stratification were reinforced by Zoroastrianism, which had arisen in Persia between 1500 B.C. and 1000 B.C. and became the state religion under the Sassanians. The Zoroastrian priest-hood became immensely powerful. The head of the priestly class, the *mobadan mobad,* along with the military commander, the *eran spahbod,* and the head of the bureaucracy, were among the great men of the state. The Roman Empire had replaced Greece as Iran's principal western enemy, and hostilities between the two empires were frequent. Shahpur I (A.D. 241–72), son and successor of Ardeshir, waged successful campaigns against the Romans and in A.D. 260 even took the emperor Valerian prisoner.

Chosroes I (531–79), also known as Anushirvan the Just, is the most celebrated of the Sassanian rulers. He reformed the tax system and reorganized the army and the bureaucracy, tying the army more closely to the central government than to local lords. His reign witnessed the rise of the *dihqans* (literally,

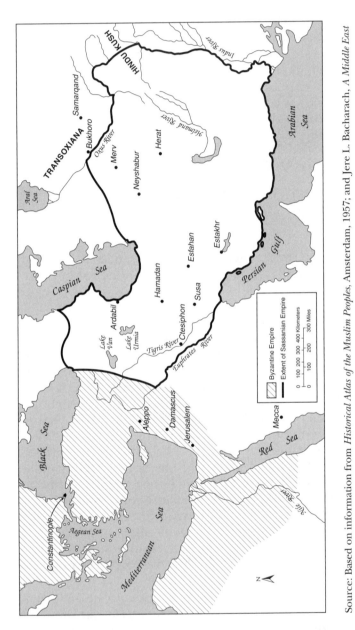

Source: Based on information from *Historical Atlas of the Muslim Peoples*, Amsterdam, 1957; and Jere L. Bacharach, *A Middle East Studies Handbook*, Seattle, 1984.

Figure 3. Sassanian Empire, Sixth Century A.D.

village lords), the petty landholding nobility who were the backbone of later Sassanian provincial administration and the tax collection system. Chosroes was a great builder, embellishing his capital, founding new towns, and constructing new buildings. Under his auspices, too, many books were brought from India and translated into Pahlavi. Some of these later found their way into the literature of the Islamic world. The reign of Chosroes II (591–628) was characterized by the wasteful splendor and lavishness of the court.

Toward the end of Chosroes II's reign, his power declined. In fighting with the Byzantine Empire (the successor to the eastern half of the Roman Empire), he enjoyed initial successes, captured Damascus, and seized the Holy Cross (upon which Christ presumably was crucified) in Jerusalem. But counterattacks by the Byzantine emperor Heraclius brought enemy forces deep into Sassanian territory. Years of warfare exhausted both the Byzantines and the Iranians. The later Sassanians were further weakened by economic decline, heavy taxation, religious unrest, rigid social stratification, the increasing power of the provincial landholders, and a rapid turnover of rulers. These factors would facilitate the Arab invasion in the seventh century.

Islamic Conquest

The bedouin Arabs who toppled the Sassanian Empire were propelled not only by a desire for conquest but also by a new religion, Islam. The Prophet Muhammad, a member of the Hashimite clan of the powerful tribe of Quraysh, proclaimed his prophetic mission in Arabia in 612 and eventually won over the city of his birth, Mecca, to the new faith. Within one year of Muhammad's death in 632, Arabia itself was secure enough to allow his secular successor, Abu Bakr, the first caliph, to begin a campaign against the Byzantine and Sassanian empires.

Abu Bakr defeated the Byzantine army at Damascus in 635 and then began his conquest of Iran. In 637 the Arab forces occupied the Sassanian capital of Ctesiphon (which they renamed Madain), and in 641–42 they defeated the Sassanian army at Nahavand. After that, Iran lay open to the invaders. The Islamic conquest was aided by the material and social bankruptcy of the Sassanians; the native populations had little to lose by cooperating with the conquering power. Moreover, the Muslims offered relative religious tolerance and fair treatment to populations that accepted Islamic rule without resistance. It was not until around 650, however, that resistance in Iran was quelled. Conversion to Islam, which offered certain advantages, was fairly rapid among the urban population but occurred more slowly among the peasantry and the *dihqans*. The majority of Iranians did not become Muslim until the ninth century.

Although the conquerors, especially the Umayyads (the Muslim rulers whose dynasty succeeded Muhammad and ruled from 661 to 750), tended to stress the primacy of Arabs among Muslims, the Iranians were gradually integrated into the new community. The Muslim conquerors adopted the Sassanian coinage system and many Sassanian administrative practices, including the office of vizier, or minister, and the *divan*, a bureau or register for controlling state revenue and expenditure that became a characteristic of administration throughout Muslim lands. Later caliphs adopted Iranian court ceremonial practices and the trappings of Sassanian monarchy. Men of Iranian origin served as administrators after the conquest, and Iranians contributed significantly to all branches of Islamic learning, including philology, literature, history, geography, jurisprudence, philosophy, medicine, and the sciences.

The Arabs were in control, however. As the new state religion, Islam imposed its own system of beliefs, laws, and social mores. In regions that submitted peacefully to Muslim rule, landowners kept their land. But crown land, land abandoned by fleeing owners, and land taken by conquest passed into the hands of the new state. This included the rich lands of the Sawad, an alluvial plain in central and southern Iraq. Arabic became the official language of the court in 696, although Persian continued to be widely used as the spoken language. The *shuubiyya* literary controversy of the ninth through the eleventh centuries, in which Arabs and Iranians each lauded their own and denigrated the other's cultural traits, suggests the survival of a certain sense of distinct Iranian identity. In the ninth century, the emergence of more purely Iranian ruling dynasties witnessed the revival of the Persian language, enriched by Arabic loanwords and using the Arabic script, and of Persian literature.

Another legacy of the Arab conquest was Shia Islam, which, although it has come to be identified closely with Iran, was not initially an Iranian religious movement. Rather, it originated with the Arab Muslims. In the great schism of Islam, one group among the community of believers maintained that leadership of the community following the death of Muhammad rightfully belonged to his son-in-law, Ali, and to Ali's descendants. This group came to be known as the Shiat Ali, the partisans of Ali, or the Shias. Another group, supporters of Muawiya for the caliphate, challenged Ali's election to that position in 656. After Ali was assassinated while praying in a mosque at Kufa in 661, Muawiya was declared caliph by the majority of the Islamic community. He became the first caliph of the Umayyad dynasty, which had its capital at Damascus.

Ali's youngest son Hussein refused to pay the homage commanded by Muawiya's son and successor Yazid I and fled to Mecca, where he was asked to lead the Shias in a revolt. At Karbala, now in Iraq, Hussein's band of 200 male and female followers, unwilling to surrender, were cut down by about 4,000 Umayyad troops in 680. The Umayyad leader received Hussein's head, and the date of Hussein's death, on the tenth of Moharram, continues to be observed as a day of mourning by all Shias (see Shia Islam in Iran, ch. 2).

The largest concentration of Shias in the first century of Islam was in southern Iraq. It was not until the sixteenth century, under the Safavis, that a majority of Iranians became Shias. Shia Islam became then, as it is now, the state religion.

The Abbasids, who overthrew the Umayyads in 750, while sympathetic to the Iranian Shias, were clearly an Arab dynasty. They revolted in the name of descendants of Muhammad's uncle, Abbas, and the House of Hashim. Hashim was an ancestor of both the Shia and the Abbas, or Sunni (see Glossary), lines, and the Abbasid movement enjoyed the support of both Sunni and Shia Muslims. The Abbasid army consisted primarily of people from Khorasan and was led by an Iranian general, Abu Muslim. It contained both Iranian and Arab elements, and the Abbasids enjoyed both Iranian and Arab support.

The Abbasids, although interested in retaining Shia support, did not encourage the more extreme Shia aspirations. The Abbasids established their capital at Baghdad. Al Mamun, who seized power from his brother Amin and proclaimed himself caliph in 811, had an Iranian mother and thus a base of support in Khorasan. The Abbasid dynasty continued the centralizing policies of its predecessors. Under its rule, the Islamic world experienced a cultural efflorescence and the expansion of trade and economic prosperity. These were developments in which Iran shared.

Subsequent ruling dynasties drew their rulers from the descendents of nomadic, Turkic-speaking warriors who had been moving out of Central Asia for more than a millennium. The Abbasid caliphs had begun using these people as slave warriors as early as the ninth century. Shortly thereafter the real power of the Abbasid caliphs began to wane; eventually they became religious figureheads under the control of the erstwhile slave warriors. As the power of the Abbasid caliphs diminished, a series of independent and indigenous dynasties rose in various parts of Iran, some with considerable influence and power. Among the most important of these overlapping dynasties were the Tahirids in Khorasan (820–72), the Saffarids in Sistan (867–903), and the Samanids (875–1005), originally at Bukhoro, a city in what is now Uzbekistan. The Samanids eventually ruled an area from central Iran to India. In 962 a Turkish slave governor of the Samanids, Alptigin, conquered Ghazna (in present-day Afghanistan) and established a dynasty, the Ghaznavids, that lasted to 1186.

Several Samanid cities had been lost to another Turkish group, the Seljuks, a clan of the Oghuz (or Ghuzz) Turks, who lived north of the Oxus River (now called the Amu Darya). Their leader, Tughril Beg, turned his warriors against the Ghaznavids in Khorasan. He moved south and then west, conquering but not wasting the cities in his path. In 1055 the caliph in Baghdad gave Tughril Beg robes, gifts, and the title "King of the East." Under Tughril Beg's successor, Malik Shah (1072–92), Iran enjoyed a cultural and scientific renaissance, largely attributed to his brilliant Iranian vizier, Nizam al Mulk. The Seljuks established the observatory where Umar (Omar) Khayyam did much of his research toward development of a new calendar, and they built religious schools in all the major towns. They brought Abu Hamid Ghazali, one of the greatest Islamic theologians, and other eminent scholars to the Seljuk capital at Baghdad and encouraged and supported their work.

A serious internal threat to the Seljuks, however, came from the Ismailis, a secret sect with headquarters at Alumut, between Rasht and Tehran. They controlled the immediate area for more than 150 years and sporadically sent out adherents to strengthen their rule by murdering important officials. The word *assassins*, which was applied to these murderers, developed from a European corruption of the name applied to them in Syria, *hashishiyya*, because folklore had it that they smoked hashish before their missions.

Invasions of the Mongols and Tamerlane

After the death of Malik Shah in 1092, rule of Iran once again reverted to petty dynasties. During this time, Genghis (Chinggis) Khan brought together a number of Mongol tribes and led them on a devastating sweep through China. Then, in 1219, he turned his 700,000 forces west and quickly devastated the cities of Bukhoro, Samarqand, Balkh, Merv, and Neyshabur. Before his death in 1227, he had reached western Azarbaijan, pillaging and burning cities along the way.

The Mongol invasion was disastrous to the Iranians. Destruction of the *qanat* irrigation systems destroyed the pattern of relatively continuous settlement, producing numerous isolated oasis cities in a land where they had previously been rare. Many people, particularly males, were killed; between 1220 and 1258, the population of Iran dropped drastically.

The Mongol rulers who followed Genghis Khan did little to improve Iran's situation. Genghis's grandson, Hulagu Khan, turned to foreign conquest, seizing Baghdad in 1258 and killing the last Abbasid caliph. He was stopped at Ain Jalut in Palestine by the Mamluks, Egypt's ruling military caste. Afterward, Hulagu Khan returned to Iran and spent the rest of his life in Azarbaijan. A later Mongol ruler, Ghazan Khan (1295–1304), and his famous Iranian vizier, Rashid ad Din, brought Iran a brief, partial economic revival. The Mongols reduced taxes for artisans, encouraged agriculture, rebuilt and extended irrigation works, and improved the safety of the trade routes. As a result, commerce increased dramatically. Items from India, China, and Iran passed easily across the Asian steppes, and these contacts culturally enriched Iran. For example, Iranians developed a new style of painting based on a unique fusion of solid, two-dimensional Mesopotamian painting with the feathery brush strokes and other motifs characteristic of China. But after Ghazan's nephew Abu Said died in 1335, Iran again lapsed into petty dynasties—the Salghurid, Muzaffarid, Inju, and Jalayirid—under Mongol commanders, old Seljuk retainers, and regional chiefs.

Tamerlane, variously described as of Mongol or Turkic origin, was the next ruler to achieve emperor status. He conquered Transoxiana proper and by 1381 established himself as sovereign. He did not have the huge forces of earlier Mongol leaders, so his conquests were slower and less savage than those of Genghis Khan or Hulagu Khan. Nevertheless, Shiraz and Esfahan were virtually leveled. Tamerlane's regime was characterized by its inclusion of Iranians in administrative roles and its promotion of architecture and poetry. His empire disintegrated rapidly after his death in 1405, however, and Mongol tribes, Uzbeks, and Turkmens ruled an area roughly coterminus with present-day Iran until the rise of the Safavi dynasty, the first native Iranian dynasty in almost 1,000 years.

The Safavis, 1501–1722

The Safavis, who came to power in 1501, were leaders of a militant Sufi order of Islamic mystics. The Safavis traced their ancestry to Sheikh Safi ad Din (died ca. 1334), the founder of the Sufis, who claimed descent from Shia Islam's Seventh Imam, Musa al Kazim. From their home base in Ardabil, the Safavis recruited followers among the Turkmen tribesmen of Anatolia and forged them into an effective fighting force and an instrument for territorial expansion. In the mid-fifteenth century, the Safavis adopted Shia Islam, and their movement became highly millenarian in character. In 1501, under their leader Ismail, the Safavis seized power in Tabriz, which became their capital. Ismail was proclaimed shah of Iran. The rise of the Safavis marks the reemergence in Iran of a powerful central authority within geographical boundaries attained by former Iranian empires. The Safavis declared Shia Islam the state religion and used proselytizing and force to convert the large majority of Muslims in Iran to the Shia sect. Under the early Safavis, Iran was a theocracy. Ismail's followers venerated him as the *murshid-kamil*, the perfect guide, who combined in his person both temporal and spiritual authority. In the new state, he was represented in both these functions by the *vakil*, an official who acted as a kind of alter ego. The *sadr* headed the powerful religious organization; the vizier, the bureaucracy; and the *amir alumara*, the fighting forces. These forces, the *qizilbash*, came primarily from the seven Turkic-speaking tribes that had supported the Safavi bid for power.

The Safavis faced the problem of integrating their Turkic-speaking followers with the native Iranians, their fighting traditions with the Iranian bureaucracy, and their messianic ideology with the exigencies of administering a territorial state. The institutions of the early Safavi state and subsequent efforts at state reorganization reflect attempts, not always successful, to strike a balance among these various elements. The Safavis also faced external challenges from the Uzbeks to the northeast and the Ottoman Empire to the west. The Uzbeks were an unstable

Part of the Porch of Xerxes at Persepolis
Courtesy LaVerle Berry

element who raided into Khorasan, particularly when the central government was weak, and blocked the Safavi advance northward into Transoxiana. Based in present-day Turkey, the Ottomans, who were Sunnis, were rivals for the religious allegiance of Muslims in eastern Anatolia and Iraq and pressed territorial claims in both these areas and in the Caucasus.

The Safavi Empire received a blow that was to prove fatal in 1524, when the Ottoman sultan Selim I defeated Safavi forces at Chaldiran and occupied the Safavi capital, Tabriz. Although he was forced to withdraw because of the harsh winter and the Safavis' scorched-earth policy, and although Safavi rulers continued to assert claims to spiritual leadership, the defeat shattered belief in the shah as a semidivine figure and weakened his hold on the *qizilbash* chiefs. In 1533 the Ottoman sultan Süleyman occupied Baghdad and then extended Ottoman rule to southern Iraq. Except for a brief period (1624–38) when Safavi rule was restored, Iraq remained firmly in Ottoman hands. The Ottomans also continued to challenge the Safavis for control of Azarbaijan and the Caucasus until the Treaty of Qasr-e Shirin in 1639 established frontiers in both Iraq and in the Caucasus that remain virtually unchanged.

The Safavi state reached its apogee during the reign of Shah Abbas (1587–1629). The shah gained breathing space to confront and defeat the Uzbeks by signing a largely disadvantageous treaty with the Ottomans. He then fought successful campaigns against the Ottomans, reestablishing Iranian control over Iraq, Georgia, and parts of the Caucasus. He counterbalanced the power of the *qizilbash* by creating a body of troops composed of Georgian and Armenian slaves who were loyal to the person of the shah. He extended state and crown lands and the provinces directly administered by the state, at the expense of the *qizilbash* chiefs. He relocated tribes to weaken their power, strengthened the bureaucracy, and further centralized the administration.

Shah Abbas made a show of personal piety and supported religious institutions by building mosques and religious seminaries and by making generous endowments for religious purposes. However, his reign witnessed the gradual separation of religious institutions from the state and an increasing movement toward a more independent religious hierarchy.

In addition to reorganizing the Iranian polity supporting religious institutions, Shah Abbas promoted commerce and the arts. The Portuguese had previously occupied Bahrain and the island of Hormoz off the Persian Gulf coast in their bid to dominate trade in the Indian Ocean and the Persian Gulf, but in 1602 Shah Abbas expelled them from Bahrain, and in 1623 he enlisted the British (who sought a share of Iran's lucrative silk trade) to expel the Portuguese from Hormoz. He significantly enhanced government revenues by establishing a state monopoly over the silk trade and encouraged internal and external trade by safeguarding the roads and welcoming British, Dutch, and other traders to Iran. With the encouragement of the shah, Iranian craftsmen excelled in producing fine silks, brocades, and other cloths, as well as carpets, porcelain, and metalware. When Shah Abbas built a new capital at Esfahan, he adorned it with fine mosques, palaces, schools, bridges, and a bazaar (see Glossary). He patronized the arts, and the calligraphy, miniatures, painting, and architecture of his period are particularly noteworthy.

The Safavi Empire declined after the death of Shah Abbas in 1629 as a result of weak rulers, interference by the women of the harem in politics, the reemergence of *qizilbash* rivalries, maladministration of state lands, excessive taxation, reduced trade, and the weakening of Safavi military organization. (Both the *qizilbash* tribal military organization and the standing army composed of slave soldiers were deteriorating.) The last two Safavi rulers, Shah Sulayman (1669–94) and Shah Sultan Hussein (1694–1722), were voluptuaries. Once again the eastern frontiers began to be breached, and in 1722 a small body of Afghan tribesmen won a series of easy victories before entering and taking the capital itself, ending Safavi rule.

Afghan supremacy was brief. Tahmasp Quli, a chief of the Afshar tribe, soon expelled the Afghans in the name of a surviving member of the Safavi family. Then, in 1736, he assumed power in his own name as Nader Shah. He went on to drive the Ottomans from Georgia and Armenia and the Russians from the Iranian coast of the Caspian Sea and restored Iranian sovereignty over Afghanistan. He also took his army on several campaigns into India, sacking Delhi in 1739 and bringing back fabulous treasures. Although Nader Shah achieved political unity, his military campaigns and extortionate taxation proved a terrible drain on a country already ravaged and depopulated by war and disorder, and in 1747 he was murdered by chiefs of his own Afshar tribe.

A period of anarchy marked by a struggle for supremacy among Afshar, Qajar, Afghan, and Zand tribal chieftains followed Nader Shah's death. Finally, Karim Khan Zand (1750–79) was able to defeat his rivals and unify the country, except for Khorasan, under a loose form of central control. He refused to assume the title of shah, however, preferring to rule as *vakil al ruaya,* or deputy of the subjects. He is remembered for his mild and beneficent regime.

The Qajars, 1795–1925

At Karim Khan Zand's death, another struggle for power among the Zands, Qajars, and other tribal groups again disrupted economic life and plunged the country into disorder. This time Agha Mohammad Qajar defeated the last Zand ruler outside Kerman in 1794, thus beginning the Qajar dynasty, which would last until 1925. Under Fath Ali Shah (1797–1834), Mohammad Shah (1834–48), and Naser ad Din Shah (1848–96), a degree of order, stability, and unity returned to the country. The Qajars revived the concept of the shah as the shadow of God on earth and exercised absolute power over the servants of the state. They appointed royal princes to provincial governorships and, in the course of the nineteenth century, increased their power in relation to that of the tribal chiefs, who provided contingents for the shah's army. Under the Qajars, the merchants and the ulama, or religious leaders, remained important members of the community. A large bureaucracy assisted the chief officers of the state, and, in the second half of the nineteenth century, new ministries and offices were created. The Qajars were unsuccessful, however, in their attempt to replace an Iranian military based on tribal levies with a European-style standing army characterized by regular training, organization, and uniforms.

Early in the nineteenth century, the Qajars began to face pressure from two great world powers, Russia and Britain. Britain's interest in Iran arose from the need to protect trade routes to India, while Russia's came from a desire to expand into Iranian territory from the north. In two disastrous wars with Russia, which ended with the Treaty of Gulistan (1812) and the Treaty of Turkmanchay (1828), Iran lost all its territories in the Caucasus north of the Aras River. Then, in the second half of the century, Russia forced the Qajars to give up all claims to territories in Central Asia. Meanwhile, Britain twice landed troops in Iran to prevent the Qajars from reasserting a claim to the city of Herat, lost after the fall of the Safavis. Under the Treaty of Paris in 1857, Iran surrendered to Britain

The tomb, in Hamadan, of Ibn Sina (known as Avicenna to the West),
a famous Persian mathematician who died in A.D. 1037
Courtesy LaVerle Berry

all claims to Herat and other territories in the present-day state of Afghanistan.

Britain and Russia also came to dominate Iran's trade and interfered in Iran's internal affairs. The two great powers enjoyed overwhelming military and technological superiority and could take advantage of Iran's internal problems. Iranian central authority was weak; revenues were generally inadequate to maintain the court, bureaucracy, and army; the ruling class was divided and corrupt; and the people suffered exploitation by their rulers and governors.

When Naser ad Din acceded to the throne in 1848, his prime minister, Mirza Taqi Khan Amir Kabir, attempted to strengthen the administration by reforming the tax system, asserting central control over the bureaucracy and the provincial governors, encouraging trade and industry, and reducing the influence of the Islamic clergy and foreign powers. He established a new school, the Dar ol Fonun, to educate members of the elite in the new sciences and in foreign languages. The power he concentrated in his hands, however, aroused jealousy within the bureaucracy and fear in the king. In 1851 Kabir was dismissed and then executed, a fate shared by earlier powerful prime ministers.

In 1858 officials such as Malkam Khan began to suggest in essays that the weakness of the government and its inability to prevent foreign interference lay in failure to learn the arts of government, industry, science, and administration from the advanced states of Europe. In 1871, with the encouragement of his new prime minister, Mirza Hosain Khan Moshir od Dowleh, the shah established a European-style cabinet with administrative responsibilities and a consultative council of senior princes and officials. In 1872 he granted a concession for railroad construction and other economic projects to a Briton, Baron Julius de Reuter, and visited Russia and Britain. Opposition from bureaucratic factions hostile to the prime minister and from clerical leaders who feared foreign influence, however, forced the shah to dismiss his prime minister and to cancel the concession. Nevertheless, internal demand for reform was slowly growing. Moreover, Britain, to which the shah turned for protection against Russian encroachment, continued to urge him to undertake reforms and open the country to foreign trade and enterprise as a means of strengthening the country. In 1888, heeding this advice, the shah opened the Karun River in Khuzestan Province to foreign shipping and gave Reuter permission to open Iran's first bank, the Imperial Bank of Persia. In 1890 the shah gave another British company a monopoly over the country's tobacco trade. The tobacco concession was obtained through bribes to leading officials and aroused considerable opposition among the clerical classes, the merchants, and the people. When a leading cleric, Mirza Hasan Shirazi, issued a fatwa (religious ruling) forbidding the use of tobacco, the ban was universally observed, and the shah was once again forced to cancel the concession, at considerable cost to an already depleted treasury.

The last years of Naser ad Din's reign as shah were characterized by growing royal and bureaucratic corruption, oppression of the rural population, and indifference on the shah's part. The tax machinery broke down, and disorder became endemic in the provinces. New ideas and demands for reform were also becoming more widespread. In 1896, reputedly encouraged by Jamal ad Din al Afghani (called Asadabadi because he came from the town of Asadabad), a well-known Islamic preacher and political activist, a young Iranian assassinated the shah.

The Constitutional Revolution

Naser ad Din Shah's son and successor, Muzaffar ad Din Shah (1896–1907), was a weak ruler. Royal extravagance and the absence of revenues exacerbated financial problems. The shah quickly spent two large loans from Russia (1900 and 1902), partly on trips to Europe. Public anger fed on the shah's propensity for granting concessions to Europeans in return for generous payments to him and his officials. People began to demand a curb on royal authority and the establishment of the rule of law as their concern over foreign, and especially Russian, influence grew.

The shah's failure to respond to protests by the religious establishment, the merchants, and other classes led the merchants and clerical leaders in January 1906 to take sanctuary from probable arrest in mosques in Tehran and outside the capital. When the shah reneged on a promise to permit the establishment of a "house of justice," or consultative assembly, 10,000 people, led by the merchants, took sanctuary in June in the compound of the British legation in Tehran. In August the shah was forced to issue a decree promising a constitution. In October an elected assembly convened and drew up a constitution that provided for strict limitations on royal power; an elected parliament, or Majlis (see Glossary), with wide powers to represent the people; and a government with a cabinet subject to confirmation by the Majlis. The shah signed the constitution on December 30, 1906. He died five days later. The Supplementary Fundamental Laws approved in 1907 provided, within limits, for freedom of the press, speech, and association, and for security of life and property. According to scholar Ann K. S. Lambton, what became known as the Constitutional Revolution marked the end of the medieval period in Iran. The hopes for constitutional rule were not realized, however.

Muzaffar ad Din's successor, Mohammad Ali Shah, was determined to crush the constitution. After several disputes with the members of the Majlis, in June 1908 he used his Russian-officered Persian Cossacks Brigade to bomb the Majlis building, arrest many of the deputies, and close down the assembly. Resistance to the shah, however, coalesced in Tabriz, Esfahan, Rasht, and elsewhere. In July 1909, constitutional forces marched from Rasht and Esfahan to Tehran, deposed the shah, and reestablished the constitution. The ex-shah went into exile in Russia.

Although the constitutionalists had triumphed, they faced serious difficulties. The upheavals of the Constitutional Revolution and civil war had undermined stability and trade. In addition, the ex-shah, with Russian support, attempted to regain his throne, landing troops on the Caspian shore in July 1910. Most serious of all, the hope that the Constitutional Revolution would inaugurate a new era of independence from the great powers ended when, under the Anglo-Russian Agreement of 1907, Britain and Russia agreed to divide Iran into spheres of influence. The Russians were to enjoy the exclusive right to pursue their interests in the northern sphere, the British in the south and east; both powers would be free to compete for economic and political advantage in a neutral sphere in the center. Matters came to a head when Morgan Shuster, an administrator from the United States hired as treasurer general by the Iranian government to reform its finances, sought to collect taxes from powerful officials who were Russian protégés and to send members of the treasury gendarmerie, a tax department police force, into the Russian zone. When in December 1911 the Majlis unanimously refused a Russian ultimatum demanding Shuster's dismissal, Russian troops, already in the country, moved to occupy the capital. To prevent this, on December 20 chiefs of Bakhtiari tribes and their troops surrounded the Majlis building, forced acceptance of the Russian ultimatum, and shut down the assembly, once again suspending the constitution. There followed a period of government by Bakhtiari chiefs and other powerful notables.

World War I

Iran hoped to avoid entanglement in World War I by declaring its neutrality but ended up as a battleground for Russian, Turkish, and British troops. When German agents tried to arouse the southern tribes against the British, Britain created an armed force, the South Persia Rifles, to protect its interests. Then a group of Iranian notables led by Nezam os Saltaneh Mafi, hoping to escape Anglo-Russian dominance and sympathetic to the German war effort, left Tehran, first for Qom and then for Kermanshah, where they established a provisional government. The provisional government lasted for the duration of the war but failed to capture much support.

At the end of the war, because of Russia's preoccupation with its own revolution, Britain was the dominant influence in Tehran. The foreign secretary, Lord Curzon, proposed an agreement under which Britain would provide Iran with a loan and with advisers to the army and virtually every government department. The Iranian prime minister, Vosuq od Dowleh, and two members of his cabinet who had received a large financial inducement from the British, supported the agreement. The Anglo-Persian Agreement of 1919 was widely viewed as establishing a British protectorate over Iran. However, it aroused considerable opposition, and the Majlis refused to approve it. The agreement was already dead when, in February 1921, Persian Cossacks Brigade officer Reza Khan, in collaboration with prominent journalist Sayyid Zia ad Din Tabatabai, marched into Tehran and seized power, inaugurating a new phase in Iran's modern history.

The Era of Reza Shah, 1921–41

Tabatabai became prime minister, and Reza Khan became commander of the armed forces in the new government. Reza Khan, however, quickly emerged as the dominant figure. Within three months, Tabatabai was forced out of the government and into exile. Reza Khan became minister of war. In 1923 Ahmad Shah, who had succeeded his father as shah in 1909, agreed to appoint Reza Khan prime minister and to leave for Europe. The shah was never to return. Reza Khan seriously considered establishing a republic, as his contemporary Kemal Atatürk had done in Turkey, but abandoned the idea in the face of clerical opposition. In October 1925, a Majlis dominated by Reza Khan's men deposed the Qajar dynasty; in December the Majlis conferred the crown on Reza Khan and his heirs. The military officer who had become master of Iran was crowned as Reza Shah Pahlavi in April 1926.

Even before he became shah, Reza Khan had taken steps to create a strong central government and to extend government control over the country. Now, as Reza Shah, with the assistance of a group of army officers and younger bureaucrats, many trained in Europe, he launched a broad program of change designed to bring Iran into the modern world. To strengthen central authority, he built up Iran's heterogeneous military forces into a disciplined army of 40,000, and in 1926 he persuaded the Majlis to approve universal military conscription. Reza Shah used the army not only to bolster his own power but also to pacify the country and to bring the tribes under control. In 1924 he broke the power of Sheikh Khazal, who was a British protégé and practically autonomous in Khuzestan Province. In addition, Reza Shah forcibly settled many of the tribes.

To extend government control and promote Westernization, the shah overhauled the administrative machinery and vastly expanded the bureaucracy. He created an extensive system of secular primary and secondary schools and, in 1935, established the country's first European-style university in Tehran. These schools and institutions of higher education became training grounds for the new bureaucracy and, along with economic expansion, helped create a new middle class. The shah also expanded the road network, successfully completed a trans-Iranian railroad, and established a string of state-owned factories to produce such basic consumer goods as textiles, matches, canned goods, sugar, and cigarettes.

Many of the shah's measures were consciously designed to break the power of the religious hierarchy. His educational reforms ended the clerics' near-monopoly on education. To limit further the power of the clerics, he undertook a codification of the laws that created a body of secular law, applied and interpreted by a secular judiciary outside the control of the religious establishment. He excluded the clerics from judgeships, created a system of secular courts, and transferred the important and lucrative task of notarizing documents from the clerics to state-licensed notaries. The state even encroached on the administration of *vaqfs* (religious endowments) and on the licensing of graduates of religious seminaries.

Among other components, the new secular law included a civil code, the work of Justice Minister Ali Akbar Davar, enacted between 1927 and 1932; the General Accounting Act (1934–35), a milestone in financial administration; a new tax law; and a civil service code.

Determined to unify what he saw as Iran's heterogeneous peoples, end foreign influence, and emancipate women, Reza Shah imposed European dress on the population. He opened the schools to women and brought them into the workforce. In 1936 he forcibly abolished the wearing of the veil.

Reza Shah initially enjoyed wide support for restoring order, unifying the country, and reinforcing national independence, and for his economic and educational reforms. In accomplishing all this, however, he took away effective power from the Majlis, muzzled the press, and arrested opponents of the government. His police chiefs were notorious for their harshness. Several religious leaders were jailed or sent into exile. In 1936,

*The tomb of Persian poet
Umar (Omar) Khayyam,
1048–1131, Neyshabur
Courtesy Nader Davoodi*

in one of the worst confrontations between the government and religious authorities, troops violated the sanctity of the shrine of Imam Reza in Mashhad, where worshipers had gathered to protest Reza Shah's reforms. Dozens of worshipers were killed and many injured. In addition, the shah arranged for powerful tribal chiefs to be put to death; bureaucrats who became too powerful suffered a similar fate. Reza Shah jailed and then quietly executed Abdul Hosain Teimurtash, his minister of court and close confidant; Davar, the justice minister, committed suicide.

As time went on, the shah grew increasingly avaricious and amassed great tracts of land. Moreover, his tax policies weighed heavily on the peasants and the lower classes. The great landowners' control over land and the peasantry increased, and the condition of the peasants worsened during his reign. As a result, by the mid-1930s there was considerable dissatisfaction in the country.

Meanwhile, Reza Shah initiated changes in foreign affairs as well. In 1928 he abolished the capitulations under which Europeans in Iran had, since the nineteenth century, enjoyed the privilege of being subject to their own consular courts rather than to the Iranian judiciary. Suspicious of both Britain and the Soviet Union, the shah circumscribed contacts with foreign

embassies. Relations with the Soviet Union had already deteriorated because of that country's commercial policies, which in
the 1920s and 1930s adversely affected Iran. In 1932 the shah
offended Britain by canceling the agreement under which the
Anglo-Persian Oil Company (formed in 1909) produced and
exported Iran's oil. Although a new and improved agreement
eventually was signed in 1933, it did not satisfy Iran's demands
and left bad feeling on both sides. To counterbalance British
and Soviet influence, Reza Shah encouraged German commercial enterprise in Iran. On the eve of World War II, Germany
was Iran's largest trading partner.

World War II and the Azarbaijan Crisis

At the outbreak of World War II, Iran declared its neutrality,
but the country was soon invaded by both Britain and the
Soviet Union. Britain had been annoyed when Iran refused
Allied demands that it expel all German nationals from the
country. When German forces invaded the Soviet Union in
1941, the Allies urgently needed to transport war matériel
across Iran to the Soviet Union, an operation that would have
violated Iranian neutrality. As a result, Britain and the Soviet
Union simultaneously invaded Iran on August 26, 1941, the
Soviets from the northwest and the British across the Iraqi frontier from the west and at the head of the Persian Gulf in the
south. Resistance quickly collapsed. Reza Shah knew the Allies
would not permit him to remain in power, so he abdicated on
September 16 in favor of his son, who ascended the throne as
Mohammad Reza Shah Pahlavi. Reza Shah and several members of his family were taken by the British first to Mauritius
and then to Johannesburg, South Africa, where Reza Shah died
in July 1944.

The occupation of Iran proved of vital importance to the
Allied cause and brought Iran closer to the Western powers.
Britain, the Soviet Union, and the United States together managed to move more than 5 million tons of munitions and other
war matériel across Iran to the Soviet Union. In addition, in
January 1942 Iran signed a tripartite treaty of alliance with Britain and the Soviet Union under which it agreed to extend nonmilitary assistance to the war effort. The two Allied powers, in
turn, agreed to respect Iran's independence and territorial
integrity and to withdraw their troops from Iran within six
months of the end of hostilities. In September 1943, Iran
declared war on Germany, thus qualifying for membership in

the United Nations (UN). In November at the Tehran Conference, President Franklin D. Roosevelt, Prime Minister Winston
Churchill, and Prime Minister Josef Stalin reaffirmed a commitment to Iran's independence and territorial integrity and a
willingness to extend economic assistance to Iran.

The effects of the war were very disruptive for Iran, however.
Food and other essential items were scarce. Severe inflation
imposed great hardship on the lower and middle classes, while
fortunes were made by individuals dealing in scarce items. The
presence of foreign troops accelerated social change and also
fed xenophobic and nationalist sentiments. An influx of rural
migrants into the cities added to political unrest. The Majlis,
dominated by the propertied interests, did little to ameliorate
these conditions. With the political controls of the Reza Shah
period removed, meanwhile, party and press activity revived.
The communist Tudeh Party was especially active in organizing
industrial workers. Like many other political parties of the left
and center, it called for economic and social reform.

Eventually, collusion between the Tudeh and the Soviet
Union brought further disintegration to Iran. In September
1944, while American companies were negotiating for oil concessions in Iran, the Soviets requested an oil concession in the
five northern provinces. In December, however, the Majlis
passed a law forbidding the government to discuss oil concessions before the end of the war. This led to fierce Soviet propaganda attacks on the government and agitation by the Tudeh
in favor of a Soviet oil concession. In December 1945, the
Azarbaijan Democratic Party, which had close links with the
Tudeh and was led by Jafar Pishevari, announced the establishment of an autonomous republic. In a similar move, activists in
neighboring Kurdistan established the Kurdish Republic of
Mahabad. The Soviets supported the autonomy of both autonomous republics, but Soviet troops remained in Khorasan, Gorgan, Mazandaran, and Gilan. Other Soviet troops prevented
government forces from entering Azarbaijan and Kurdistan.
Soviet pressure on Iran continued as British and American
troops evacuated in keeping with treaty commitments while
Soviet troops remained in the country. Prime Minister Ahmad
Qavam had to persuade Stalin to withdraw his forces by agreeing to submit a Soviet oil concession to the Majlis and to negotiate a peaceful settlement to the Azarbaijan crisis with the
Pishevari government.

In April 1946, the government signed an oil agreement with the Soviet Union; in May, partly as a result of U.S., British, and UN pressure, Soviet troops withdrew from Iranian territory. Qavam took three Tudeh members into his cabinet. Qavam was able to reclaim his concessions to the Soviet Union, however, when an anticommunist tribal revolt in the south provided an opportunity to dismiss the Tudeh cabinet officers. In December, ostensibly in preparation for new Majlis elections, Qavam sent the Iranian army into Azarbaijan. Without Soviet backing, the Pishevari government collapsed, and Pishevari himself fled to the Soviet Union. A similar fate befell the Kurdish Republic of Mahabad. In the new Majlis, a strong bloc of deputies, organized as the National Front and led by Mohammad Mossadeq, helped defeat the Soviet oil concession agreement by 102 votes to two. The Majlis also passed a bill forbidding any further foreign oil concessions and requiring the government to exploit oil resources directly.

Soviet influence diminished further in 1947, when Iran and the United States signed an agreement providing for military aid and for a U.S. military advisory mission to help train the Iranian army. In February 1949, the Tudeh was blamed for an abortive attempt on the shah's life, and its leaders fled abroad or were arrested. The party was banned.

Mossadeq and Oil Nationalization

Beginning in 1948, sentiment for nationalization of Iran's oil industry grew. That year the Majlis approved the first economic development plan (1948–55; see Glossary), which called for comprehensive agricultural and industrial development. The Plan Organization was established to administer the program, which was to be financed in large part with oil revenues. Politically conscious Iranians were aware, however, that the British government derived more revenue from taxing the concessionaire, the Anglo-Iranian Oil Company (AIOC—formerly the Anglo-Persian Oil Company), than the Iranian government derived from royalties. The oil issue figured prominently in elections for the Majlis in 1949, and nationalists in the new Majlis were determined to renegotiate the AIOC agreement. In November 1950, the Majlis committee concerned with oil matters, headed by Mossadeq, rejected a draft agreement in which the AIOC had offered the government slightly improved terms. These terms did not include the 50–50 profit-sharing provision that was part of other new Persian Gulf oil concessions.

Subsequent negotiations with the AIOC were unsuccessful, partly because General Ali Razmara, who became prime minister in June 1950, failed to convince the oil company of the strength of nationalist feeling in the country and in the Majlis. By the time the AIOC finally offered 50–50 profit sharing in February 1951, sentiment for nationalization of the oil industry had become widespread. Razmara advised against nationalization on technical grounds and was assassinated in March 1951 by a member of the militant Islamic Warriors (Fedayan-e Islami). On March 15, the Majlis voted to nationalize the oil industry. In April the shah yielded to Majlis pressure and demonstrations in the streets by naming Mossadeq prime minister.

Oil production came to a virtual standstill as British technicians left the country, and Britain imposed a worldwide embargo on the purchase of Iranian oil. In September 1951, Britain froze Iran's sterling assets and banned the export of goods to Iran. It also challenged the legality of the oil nationalization, taking its case against Iran to the International Court of Justice at The Hague. The court found in Iran's favor, but the dispute between Iran and the AIOC remained unsettled. Under U.S. pressure, the AIOC improved its offer to Iran. The excitement generated by the nationalization issue, anti-British feeling, agitation by radical elements, and the conviction among Mossadeq's advisers that Iran's maximum demands would, in the end, be met, however, led the government to reject all offers. The economy began to suffer from the loss of foreign exchange and oil revenues.

Mossadeq's growing popularity and power led to political chaos and eventual U.S. intervention. Mossadeq had come to office on the strength of support from the National Front and other parties in the Majlis and as a result of his great popularity. His popular appeal, growing power, and intransigence on the oil issue were creating friction between the prime minister and the shah. In the summer of 1952, the shah refused the prime minister's demand for the power to appoint the minister of war (and, by implication, to control the armed forces). Mossadeq resigned, three days of pro-Mossadeq rioting followed, and the shah was forced to reappoint Mossadeq to head the government.

As domestic conditions deteriorated, Mossadeq's populist style grew more autocratic. In August 1952, the Majlis acceded to his demand for full powers in all affairs of government for a six-month period. These special powers subsequently were extended for a further six-month term. Mossadeq also obtained approval for a law to reduce, from six years to two, the term of the Senate (established in 1950 as the upper house of the Majlis), thus bringing about the dissolution of that body. Mossadeq's support in the lower house of the legislature was dwindling, however, so on August 3, 1953, he conducted a plebiscite for the dissolution of the Majlis, claimed a massive vote in favor of the proposal, and dissolved the legislative body.

The administration of President Harry S. Truman initially had been sympathetic to Iran's nationalist aspirations. However, in 1953, with the onset of the administration of President Dwight D. Eisenhower, the United States came to accept the view of the British government that no reasonable compromise with Mossadeq was possible and that, by working with the Tudeh, the Iranian prime minister was making probable a communist-inspired takeover. Mossadeq's intransigence and his inclination to accept Tudeh support, the Cold War atmosphere, and the fear of Soviet influence in Iran also shaped U.S. thinking. In June 1953, the Eisenhower administration approved a British proposal for a joint Anglo-American operation, code-named Operation Ajax, to overthrow Mossadeq. Kermit Roosevelt of the U.S. Central Intelligence Agency (CIA) traveled secretly to Iran to coordinate plans with the shah and the Iranian military, which was led by General Fazlollah Zahedi.

In accord with the plan, on August 13 the shah appointed Zahedi prime minister to replace Mossadeq. Mossadeq refused to step down and arrested the shah's emissary. This triggered the second stage of Operation Ajax, which called for a military coup. The plan initially seemed to fail, so the shah fled the country and Zahedi went into hiding. After four days of rioting, however, the tide turned. On August 19, pro-shah army units and street crowds defeated Mossadeq's forces. The shah returned to the country. Mossadeq was sentenced to three years' imprisonment for trying to overthrow the monarchy, but he was subsequently allowed to remain under house arrest in his village outside Tehran, where he died in 1967. His minister of foreign affairs, Hussein Fatemi, was executed. Hundreds of National Front leaders, Tudeh Party officers, and political activists were arrested; several army officers who were Tudeh members also were sentenced to death.

The Post-Mossadeq Era and the Shah's White Revolution

To help the Zahedi government through a difficult period, the United States arranged for US$45 million in immediate economic assistance. The Iranian government restored diplomatic relations with Britain in December 1953, and a new oil agreement was concluded the following year. The shah, fearing both Soviet influence and internal opposition, sought to bolster his regime by edging closer to Britain and the United States. In October 1955, Iran joined the Baghdad Pact, which brought together the "northern tier" countries of Iraq, Turkey, and Pakistan in an alliance that included Britain, with the United States serving as a supporter but not a full member. (The pact was renamed the Central Treaty Organization—CENTO—after Iraq's withdrawal in 1958.) In March 1959, Iran signed a bilateral defense agreement with the United States. In the Cold War atmosphere, relations with the Soviet Union were correct but not cordial. The shah visited the Soviet Union in 1956, but Soviet propaganda attacks and Iran's alliance with the West continued. Internally, a period of political repression followed the overthrow of Mossadeq, as the shah concentrated power in his own hands. He banned or suppressed the Tudeh, the National Front, and other parties; muzzled the press; and strengthened the secret police agency, SAVAK (Sazman-e Ettelaat va Amniyat-e Keshvar). Elections to the restored Majlis in 1954 and 1956 were closely controlled. The shah appointed Hussein Ala to replace Zahedi as prime minister in April 1955 and thereafter named a succession of prime ministers who were willing to do his bidding.

Attempts at economic development and political reform were inadequate. Rising oil revenues allowed the government to launch the second economic development plan (1955–62) in 1956. Several large-scale industrial and agricultural projects were initiated, but economic recovery from the disruptions of the oil nationalization period was slow. The infusion of oil money led to rapid inflation and spreading discontent, but strict controls provided no outlets for political unrest. When martial law, which had been instituted in August 1953 after the coup, ended in 1957, the shah ordered two of his senior officials to form a majority party and a loyal opposition as the basis for a two-party system. These became known as the Melliyun and the Mardom parties. These officially sanctioned parties did not satisfy demands for wider political representation, however. During Majlis elections in 1960, charges of widespread fraud could not be suppressed, and the shah was forced to cancel balloting. Jafar Sharif Emami, a staunch loyalist, became prime minister. After renewed and more strictly controlled elections, the Majlis convened in February 1961. But with economic conditions and political unrest both worsening, the Sharif Emami government fell in May 1961.

Yielding both to domestic demands for change and to pressure for reform from U.S. President John F. Kennedy's administration, the shah named Ali Amini, a wealthy landlord and senior civil servant, as prime minister. Amini received a mandate from the shah to dissolve parliament and rule for six months by cabinet decree. Known as an advocate of reform, Amini loosened controls on the press, permitted the National Front and other political parties to resume activity, and ordered the arrest of a number of former senior officials on charges of corruption. Under Amini, the cabinet approved the third economic development plan (1962–68) and undertook a program to reorganize the civil service. In January 1962, in the single most important measure of the 14-month Amini government, the cabinet approved a law on land distribution.

The Amini government, however, was beset by numerous problems. Belt-tightening measures ordered by the prime minister were necessary, but in the short term they intensified recession and unemployment. This recession caused discontent in the bazaar and business communities. In addition, the prime minister acted in an independent manner, and the shah and senior military and civilian officials close to the court resented this challenge to royal authority. Moreover, although they were enjoying limited freedom of activity for the first time in many years, the National Front and other opposition groups pressed the prime minister for elections and withheld cooperation. When Amini was unable to close a large budget deficit, the shah refused to cut the military budget, and the United States, which had previously supported the prime minister, refused further aid. As a result, Amini resigned in July 1962.

Amini was replaced by Asadollah Alam, a confidant of Mohammad Reza Shah. Building on the credit earned in the countryside and in urban areas by the land distribution program, the shah submitted six measures to a national referendum in January 1963. In addition to land reform, these measures included profit sharing for industrial workers in private-sector enterprises, nationalization of forests and pasture-land, the sale of government factories to finance land reform, amendment of the electoral law to give more representation on supervisory councils to workers and farmers, and establishment of the Literacy Corps, an institution that would enable young men to satisfy their military obligation by working as village reading teachers. The shah described the package as his White Revolution (see Glossary), and when the referendum votes were counted, the government announced a 99 percent majority in favor of the program. In addition to these other reforms, the shah announced in February that he was extending the right to vote to women.

The reforms earned the government considerable support among certain sectors of the population, but they did not deal immediately with sources of unrest. Economic conditions were still difficult for the poorer classes. Many clerical leaders opposed land reform and the extension of suffrage to women. These leaders were also concerned about the extension of government and royal authority that the reforms implied. In June 1963, Ayatollah Sayyid Ruhollah Musavi Khomeini, a religious leader in Qom, was arrested after a fiery speech in which he directly attacked the shah. The arrest sparked three days of the most violent unrest the country had witnessed since the overthrow of Mossadeq a decade earlier. The shah severely suppressed the riots, and, for the moment, the government appeared to have triumphed over its opponents.

State and Society, 1964–74

Elections to the twenty-first Majlis in September 1963 led to the formation of a new political party, Iran Novin (New Iran), committed to a program of economic and administrative reform and renewal. The Alam government had opened talks with National Front leaders earlier in the year, but no accommodation had been reached, and the talks had broken down over such issues as freedom of activity for the front. As a result, the front was not represented in the elections, which were limited to the officially sanctioned parties, and the only candidates on the slate were those presented by the Union of National Forces, an organization of senior civil servants and officials and workers' and farmers' representatives put together with government support. After the elections, the largest bloc in the new Majlis, with 40 seats, was a group called the Progressive Center. An exclusive club of senior civil servants, the center had been established by Hasan Ali Mansur in 1961 to study and make policy recommendations on major economic and social issues. In June 1963, the shah had designated the center as his personal research bureau. When the new Majlis convened in October, 100 more deputies joined the center, giving Mansur a majority. In December Mansur converted the Progressive Center into a political party, Iran Novin. In March 1964, Alam resigned, and the shah appointed Mansur prime minister at the head of a government led by Iran Novin.

The events leading to the establishment of Iran Novin and the appointment of Mansur as prime minister represented a renewed attempt by the shah and his advisers to create a political organization that would be loyal to the crown, attract the support of the educated classes and the technocratic elite, and strengthen the administration and the economy. Iran Novin drew its membership almost exclusively from a younger generation of senior civil servants, Western-educated technocrats, and business leaders. Initially, membership was limited to 500 hand-picked persons and was allowed to grow very slowly. In time it came to include leading members of the provincial elite and its bureaucratic, professional, and business classes. Even in the late 1960s and early 1970s, when trade unions and professional organizations affiliated themselves with the party, full membership was reserved for a limited group.

In carrying out economic and administrative reforms, Mansur created four new ministries and transferred the authority for drawing up the budget from the Ministry of Finance to the newly created Budget Bureau. The bureau was attached to the Plan Organization and was responsible directly to the prime minister. In subsequent years, it introduced greater rationality in planning and budgeting. Mansur appointed younger technocrats to senior civil service posts, a policy continued by his successor. He also created the Health Corps, modeled after the Literacy Corps, to provide primary health care to rural areas.

In the Majlis, the government enjoyed a comfortable majority, and the nominal opposition, the Mardom Party, generally voted with the government party. An exception, however, was the general response to a bill establishing a status of forces agreement to grant diplomatic immunity to U.S. military personnel serving in Iran and to their staffs and families. In effect, the agreement would allow these Americans to be tried by U.S. rather than Iranian courts for crimes committed on Iranian soil. For Iranians this provision recalled the humiliating capitulatory concessions extracted from Iran by the imperial powers in the nineteenth century. Feeling against the bill was sufficiently strong that 65 deputies absented themselves from the legislature, and 61 opposed the bill when it was put to a vote in October 1964.

The status of forces legislation also aroused strong feeling outside the Majlis. Khomeini, who had been released from house arrest in April 1964, denounced the measure in a public sermon before a huge congregation in Qom. Tapes of the sermon and a leaflet based on it were circulated widely and attracted considerable attention. Khomeini was arrested again in November within days of the sermon and sent into exile in Turkey. In October 1965, he was permitted to take up residence in the city of An Najaf, Iraq—the site of numerous Shia shrines—where he was to remain for the next 13 years.

Although economic conditions were soon to improve dramatically, the country had not yet fully recovered from the recession of 1959–63, which had been particularly hard on the poorer classes. Mansur attempted to close a budget deficit of an estimated US$300 million (at then-prevalent rates of exchange) by imposing heavy new taxes on gasoline and kerosene and on exit permits for Iranians leaving the country. Because kerosene was the primary heating fuel for the working classes, the new taxes proved highly unpopular. Taxicab drivers in Tehran went on strike, and Mansur was forced to rescind the fuel taxes in January 1965, six weeks after they had been imposed. An infusion of US$200 million in new revenues (US$185 million from a cash bonus for five offshore oil concessions granted to U.S. and West European firms and US$15 million from a supplementary oil agreement concluded with the Consortium, a group of foreign oil companies) helped the government through its immediate financial difficulties.

With this assistance, Mohammad Reza Shah Pahlavi was able to maintain political stability despite the assassination of his prime minister and an attempt on his own life. On January 21, 1965, Mansur was murdered by members of a radical Islamic group. Evidence made available after the Islamic Revolution revealed that the group had affiliations with clerics close to Khomeini. A military tribunal issued death sentences to six of those charged and sentenced the others to long prison terms. In April there was also an attempt on the shah's life, organized by a group of Iranian graduates of British universities. To replace Mansur as prime minister, the shah appointed Amir

Abbas Hoveyda, a former diplomat and an executive of the National Iranian Oil Company (NIOC). Hoveyda had helped Mansur found the Progressive Center and Iran Novin and had served as his minister of finance.

Hoveyda's appointment marked the beginning of nearly a decade of impressive economic growth and relative political stability. During this period, the shah also used Iran's enhanced economic and military strength to secure a more influential role for the country in the Persian Gulf region, and he improved relations with Iran's immediate neighbors and the Soviet Union and its allies. Hoveyda remained in office for the next 12 years, the longest term of any of Iran's modern prime ministers. During this period, Iran Novin dominated the government and the Majlis. It won large majorities in the 1967 and 1971 elections, both of which were carefully controlled by the authorities. Only the Mardom Party and, later, the Pan-Iranist Party, an extreme nationalist group, were allowed to compete with Iran Novin. Neither opposition party was able to secure more than a handful of Majlis seats, and neither engaged in serious criticism of government programs.

In 1969 and again in 1972, the shah appeared ready to permit the Mardom Party, under new leadership, to function as a genuine opposition, that is, to criticize the government openly and to contest elections more energetically, but these developments did not occur. Iran Novin's domination of the administrative machinery was made further evident during municipal council elections held in 136 towns throughout the country in 1968. Iran Novin won control of a large majority of the councils and of every seat in 115 of them. Only 10 percent of eligible voters cast ballots in Tehran, however, a demonstration of public indifference that was not confined to the capital.

Under Hoveyda the government improved its administrative machinery and launched what was dubbed "the education revolution." It adopted a new civil service code and a new tax law and appointed better-qualified personnel to key posts. Hoveyda also created several additional ministries in 1967, including the Ministry of Science and Higher Education, which was intended to help meet the need for an expanded and more specialized workforce. In mid-1968, the government began a program that, although it did not resolve problems of overcrowding and uneven quality, substantially increased the number of institutions of higher education, brought students from provincial and lower middle-class backgrounds into the new community colleges, and created a number of institutions of high academic standing, such as Tehran's Arya Mehr Technical University (see Education, ch. 2).

In 1960 the queen, Farah Diba Pahlavi, had given birth to a male heir, Reza. In 1967, because the crown prince was still very young, steps were taken to regularize the procedure for the succession. Under the constitution, if the shah were to die before the crown prince came of age, the Majlis would meet to appoint a regent. There might be a delay in the appointment of a regent, especially if the Majlis was not in session. A constituent assembly, convened in September 1967, amended the constitution, providing for the queen to become regent automatically unless the shah in his lifetime designated another individual.

In October 1967, believing his achievements finally justified such a step, the shah celebrated his long-postponed coronation. Like his father, he placed the crown on his own head. To mark the occasion, the Majlis conferred on the shah the title of Arya Mehr, or "Light of the Aryans." This glorification of the monarchy and the monarch, however, was not universally popular with Iranians. In 1971 celebrations were held to mark what was presented as 2,500 years of uninterrupted monarchy (there were actually gaps in the chronological record) and the twenty-fifth centennial of the founding of the Iranian empire by Cyrus the Great. The ceremonies were designed primarily to celebrate the institution of the monarchy and to affirm the position of the shah as the country's absolute and unchallenged ruler. The lavish ceremonies (which many compared to a Hollywood-style extravaganza), the virtual exclusion of Iranians from the celebrations at which the honored guests were foreign heads of state, and the excessive adulation of the person of the shah in official propaganda generated much adverse domestic comment. A declaration by Khomeini condemning the celebrations and the regime received wide circulation. In 1975, when the Majlis, at government instigation, voted to alter the Iranian calendar so that year one of the calendar coincided with the first year of the reign of Cyrus rather than with the beginning of the Islamic era, many Iranians viewed the move as a gratuitous insult to religious sensibilities.

Iran, meantime, experienced a period of unprecedented and sustained economic growth. It also was a period of relatively little serious political unrest, attributable in large part to the land distribution program launched in 1962, along with steadily expanding job opportunities, improved living standards, and moderate inflation between 1964 and 1973.

In foreign policy, the shah used the relaxation in East-West tensions to improve relations with the Soviet Union. In an exchange of notes in 1962, he gave Moscow assurances he would not allow Iran to become a base for aggression against the Soviet Union or permit foreign missile bases to be established on Iranian soil. In 1965 Iran and the Soviet Union signed a series of agreements under which the Soviets provided credits and technical assistance to build Iran's first steel mill in exchange for shipments of Iranian natural gas. This led to construction of an almost 2,000-kilometer trans-Iranian pipeline from the southern natural gas fields to the Iranian-Soviet frontier. The shah also bought small quantities of arms from the Soviet Union and expanded trade with East European states. Although Soviet officials did not welcome the increasingly close military and security cooperation between Iran and the United States, especially after 1971, Moscow did not allow this to disrupt its own rapprochement with Tehran.

In 1964 the shah joined the heads of state of Turkey and Pakistan to create an organization, Regional Cooperation for Development (RCD), for economic, social, and cultural cooperation among the three countries "outside the framework of the Central Treaty Organization." The establishment of the RCD was seen as a sign of the diminishing importance of CENTO and, like the rapprochement with the Soviet Union, of the shah's increasing independence in foreign policy. The three RCD member states undertook a number of joint economic and cultural projects, though none on a large scale.

The shah also began to play a larger role in Persian Gulf affairs. He supported the royalists in the Yemen Civil War (1962–70) and, beginning in 1971, assisted the sultan of Oman in putting down a rebellion in Dhofar. He also reached an understanding with Britain on the fate of Bahrain and three smaller islands in the Persian Gulf that Britain had controlled since the nineteenth century but that Iran continued to claim. Britain's decision to withdraw from the Gulf by 1971 and to help organize the Trucial States into a federation of independent states (eventually known as the United Arab Emirates— UAE) necessitated resolution of that situation. In 1970 the shah agreed to give up Iran's long-standing claim to Bahrain and to abide by the desire of the majority of its inhabitants that it become an independent state. The shah, however, continued

The shah and his family, with eldest son, Reza Cyrus Pahlavi,
standing in rear (Photo taken in the mid-1970s)

to press his claim to three islands, Abu Musa (controlled by the sheikh of Sharjah) and the Greater and Lesser Tunbs (controlled by the sheikh of Ras al Khaymah). He secured control of Abu Musa by agreeing to pay the sheikh of Sharjah an annual subsidy, and he seized the two Tunbs by military force, immediately following Britain's withdrawal.

This incident offended Iraq, however, which broke diplomatic relations with Iran as a result. Relations with Iraq remained strained until 1975, when Iran and Iraq signed the Algiers Agreement, under which Iraq acceded to Iran's long-standing demand for equal navigation rights in the Shatt al Arab (see Glossary), and the shah agreed to end support for the Kurdish rebellion in northern Iraq.

Tehran maintained generally good relations with the other Persian Gulf states. Iran signed agreements with Saudi Arabia and other Gulf states delimiting frontiers along the continental shelf in the Gulf, began cooperation and information sharing on security matters with Saudi Arabia, and encouraged closer cooperation among the newly independent Gulf sheikhdoms through the Gulf Cooperation Council.

To enhance Iran's role in the Persian Gulf, the shah expanded and provided additional equipment for the Iranian army, air force, and navy, using oil revenues to pay for the upgrades. His desire that Iran play the primary role in guaranteeing Gulf security in the aftermath of the British withdrawal coincided with President Richard M. Nixon's hopes for the region. In the Nixon Doctrine, enunciated in 1969, the U.S. president had expressed his preference that U.S. allies shoulder greater responsibility for regional security. During his 1972 visit to Iran, Nixon took the unprecedented step of allowing the shah to purchase any conventional weapon in the U.S. arsenal in quantities the shah believed necessary for Iran's defense. U.S.-Iranian military cooperation deepened when the shah allowed the United States to establish two listening posts in Iran to monitor Soviet ballistic missile launches and other military activity.

Renewed Opposition

In the years that followed the riots of June 1963, there was little overt political opposition. The political parties that had been prominent from 1950 to 1963 were weakened by arrests, exile, and internal splits. Political repression continued, and it proved more difficult to articulate a coherent policy of opposition in a period of economic prosperity, foreign policy successes, and such reform measures as land distribution. Nonetheless, opposition parties were gradually reorganized, new groups committed to more violent forms of struggle were formed, and more radical Islamic ideologies were developed to revive and fuel the opposition movements. Both the Tudeh and the National Front underwent numerous splits and reorganizations. The Tudeh leadership remained abroad, and the party did not play a prominent role in Iran until after the Islamic Revolution. Of the National Front parties that managed to survive the post-1963 clampdown, the most prominent was the Nehzat-e Azadi-ye Iran, or the Iran Freedom Movement (IFM), led by Mehdi Bazargan. Bazargan worked to establish links between his movement and the moderate clerical opposition. Like others who looked to Islam as a vehicle for political mobilization, Bazargan was active in preaching the political pertinence of Islam to a younger generation of Iranians. Among the best-known thinkers associated with the IFM was Ali Shariati, who argued for an Islam committed to political struggle, social justice, and the cause of the deprived classes.

Khomeini, in exile in Iraq, continued to issue antigovernment statements, to attack the shah personally, and to organize supporters. In a series of lectures delivered to his students in An Najaf in 1969 and 1970 and later published in book form under the title of *Velayat-e Faqih* (Rule of the Islamic Jurist), he argued that monarchy was a form of government abhorrent to Islam, that true Muslims must strive for the establishment of an Islamic state, and that the leadership of the state belonged by right to the *faqih* (see Glossary), or Islamic jurist. A network of clerics worked for Khomeini in Iran, having returned from periods of imprisonment and exile to continue their activities. Increasing internal difficulties in the early 1970s gradually won Khomeini a growing number of followers.

In the meantime, some younger Iranians, disillusioned with what they perceived to be the ineffectiveness of legal opposition to the regime and attracted by the example of guerrilla movements in Cuba, Vietnam, and China, formed a number of underground groups committed to armed struggle against the regime. Most of these groups were uncovered and broken up by the security authorities, but two survived: the Fedayan (Fedayan-e Khalq, or People's Warriors) and the Mojahedin (Mojahedin-e Khalq, or People's Fighters). The Fedayan were Marxist in orientation, whereas the Mojahedin sought to find in Islam the inspiration for an ideology of political struggle and economic radicalism. Nevertheless, both movements used similar tactics in attempting to overthrow the regime: attacks on police stations; bombing of U.S., British, and Israeli commercial or diplomatic offices; and assassination of Iranian security officers and U.S. military personnel stationed in Iran. In February 1971, the Fedayan launched the first major guerrilla action against the state: an armed attack on a post of the Imperial Iranian Gendarmerie (the internal security and border guard) at Siahkal in the Caspian forests of northern Iran. Several similar actions followed. A total of 341 members of these guerrilla movements died between 1971 and 1979 in armed confrontations with security forces, by execution or suicide, or while in the hands of their jailers. Many more served long terms in prison.

The Coming of the Revolution

By late 1976, it was evident that the Iranian economy was in trouble. The shah's attempt to use Iran's vastly expanded oil revenues after 1973 for an unrealistically ambitious expansion of industry and infrastructure and a massive military buildup greatly strained Iran's human and institutional resources and caused severe economic and social dislocation. Widespread official corruption, rapidly increasing inflation, and a growing income gap between the wealthier and the poorer social strata fed public dissatisfaction.

In response, the government attempted to provide the working and middle classes with some immediate and tangible benefits of the country's new oil wealth. The government nationalized private secondary schools and community colleges, made secondary education free for all Iranians, started a free meal program in schools, and extended financial support to university students. It also reduced income taxes, inaugurated an ambitious health insurance plan, and accelerated implementation of a program introduced in 1972 under which industrialists were required to sell 49 percent of the shares of their companies to their employees. The programs were badly implemented, however, and did not adequately compensate for the deteriorating economic position of civil servants and the urban working class. To deal with inflation and soaring housing costs, the government adopted policies that appeared threatening to the propertied classes and to the people of the bazaars, businesspeople, and industrialists (see Urban Society, ch. 2).

For example, in an effort to bring down rents, municipalities were empowered to take over empty houses and apartments and to rent and administer them in place of the owners. In an effort to bring down prices in 1975 and 1976, the government declared a war on profiteers, arrested and fined thousands of shopkeepers and petty merchants, and sent two prominent industrialists into exile.

Moreover, by 1978 there were 60,000 foreigners in Iran—45,000 of them Americans—engaged in business or in military training and advisory missions. This foreign presence tended to intensify the perception that the shah's modernization program was threatening the society's Islamic and Iranian values and identity. Increasing political repression and the establishment of a one-party state in 1975 further alienated the educated classes.

Beginning in early 1977, the shah took a number of steps to counter both domestic and foreign criticism of Iran's human rights record. Amnesty International and other human rights organizations were drawing attention to mistreatment of political prisoners and violation of the rights of the accused in Iranian courts. U.S. president Jimmy Carter, who took office in January 1977, also was making an issue of human rights violations in countries associated with the United States. The shah released political prisoners and announced new regulations to protect the legal rights of civilians brought before military courts. In July the shah replaced Hoveyda, his prime minister of 12 years, with Jamshid Amuzegar, who had served for more than a decade in various cabinet posts. However, Amuzegar also became unpopular, as he attempted to slow the overheated economy with measures that, however necessary, triggered a downturn in employment and private-sector profits.

Leaders of the moderate opposition, professional groups, and the intelligentsia took advantage of the political opening allowed by the shah to organize and speak out. They addressed open letters to prominent officials demanding adherence to the constitution and restoration of basic freedoms. Lawyers, judges, university professors, and writers formed professional associations to press these demands. The National Front, the IFM, and other political groups resumed activity.

The protest movement took a new turn in January 1978, when a government-inspired article in *Ettelaat,* one of the country's leading newspapers, cast doubt on Khomeini's piety and suggested that he was a British agent. Senior clerics denounced the article. Seminary students took to the streets in Qom and clashed with police, and a number of demonstrators were killed. On February 18, mosque services and demonstrations were held in several cities to honor those killed in the Qom demonstrations. In Tabriz these demonstrations turned violent, and it was two days before order could be restored. By the summer, riots and antigovernment demonstrations had swept dozens of towns and cities.

The cycle of protests that began in Qom and Tabriz in 1978 differed in nature, composition, and intent from the protests of the preceding year. The 1977 protests were primarily the work of middle-class intellectuals, lawyers, and secular politicians. They took the form of letters, resolutions, and declarations and were aimed at the restoration of constitutional rule. The protests that rocked Iranian cities in the first half of 1978, by contrast, were led by religious elements and were centered on mosques and religious events. They drew on traditional groups in the bazaar and the urban working class for support. The protesters used a form of calculated violence to achieve their ends, attacking and destroying carefully selected targets that represented objectionable features of the regime: nightclubs and cinemas, as symbols of moral corruption and the influence of Western culture; banks, as symbols of economic exploitation; offices of Rastakhiz (the party created by the shah in 1975 to run the one-party state) and police stations, as symbols of political repression. The protests, moreover, aimed at fundamental change: In slogans and leaflets, the protesters demanded the shah's removal, depicting Khomeini as their leader and an Islamic state as their ideal. From his exile in Iraq, Khomeini continued to urge further demonstrations, rejected compromise with the regime, and demanded the overthrow of the shah.

The government's position deteriorated further in August 1978, when more than 400 people died in a fire at the Rex Cinema in Abadan. The fire was started by religiously inclined students, but the opposition carefully cultivated a widespread conviction that it was the work of SAVAK agents. Following the Rex Cinema fire, the shah removed Amuzegar and named Jafar Sharif Emami prime minister. Sharif Emami, a former prime minister and a trusted royalist, had for many years served as president of the Senate. He eased press controls and permitted more open debate in the Majlis. He released a number of imprisoned clerics, revoked the imperial calendar, closed gambling casinos, and obtained from the shah the dismissal from court and public office of members of the Baha'i faith, a religion to which the clerics strongly objected (see Non-Muslim Minorities, ch. 2). These measures, however, did not quell public protests. On September 4, more than 100,000 took part in the public prayers to mark the end of Ramazan (Ramadan), the Muslim fasting month. Growing antigovernment demonstrations continued for the next two days, taking on an increasingly radical tone. After the government declared martial law in Tehran and 11 other cities, troops fired into a crowd of demonstrators in Tehran's Jaleh Square. A large number of protesters, certainly many more than the official figure of 87, were killed. The day of the Jaleh Square shooting came to be known as "Black Friday." The shootings further radicalized the opposition movement and made compromise with the regime, even by the moderates, less likely.

Khomeini, expelled from Iraq, went to France in October and established his headquarters at Neauphle-le-Château, outside Paris. His arrival in France gave Khomeini and his movement exposure in the world press and media. It made possible easy telephone communication with lieutenants in Iran, thus permitting better coordination of the opposition movement. It also allowed Iranian political and religious leaders to visit him for direct consultations. One such visitor, National Front leader Karim Sanjabi, met with Khomeini in early November 1978 and issued a three-point statement that for the first time committed the National Front to the Khomeini demand for the deposition of the shah and the establishment of a "democratic and Islamic" government.

In September, workers in the public sector, including the oil industry, had begun striking on a large scale. Their demands for improved salaries and benefits quickly escalated into demands for changes in the political system. The unavailability of fuel oil and freight transport and shortages of raw materials resulting from a customs strike, meanwhile, led to a shutdown of most private-sector industries in November.

On November 5, after violent demonstrations in Tehran, the shah replaced Prime Minister Sharif Emami with General Gholam Reza Azhari, commander of the Imperial Guard. Addressing the nation for the first time in many months, the shah declared that he had heard the people's "revolutionary message," promised to correct past mistakes, and urged a period of quiet to permit promised reforms. Presumably to placate public opinion, the shah allowed the arrest of 132 former leaders and government officials, including former Prime Minister Hoveyda, an ex-chief of SAVAK, and several former cabinet ministers. He also ordered the release of more than 1,000 political prisoners, including a Khomeini associate, Ayatollah Hosain Ali Montazeri.

The appointment of Azhari as prime minister brought about a short-lived abatement of the strike fever, and oil production improved. Khomeini dismissed the shah's promises as worthless, however, and called for continued protests. The strikes resumed, virtually shutting down the government, and clashes between demonstrators and troops became a daily occurrence. On December 9 and 10, 1978, several hundred thousand persons participated in antiregime marches in Tehran and the provinces.

During December the shah finally began exploratory talks with members of the moderate opposition. Discussions with the National Front's Karim Sanjabi proved unfruitful; Sanjabi was bound by his agreement with Khomeini. At the end of December, another National Front leader, Shapour Bakhtiar, agreed to form a government on condition that the shah leave the country. Bakhtiar secured a vote of confidence from the two houses of the Majlis on January 3, 1979, and presented his cabinet to the shah three days later. The shah left the country on January 16. As his aircraft took off, celebrations broke out across the country.

The Bakhtiar Government

Once installed as prime minister, Bakhtiar took several measures designed to appeal to elements in the opposition movement. He lifted restrictions on the press; the newspapers, on strike since November, resumed publication. He freed all remaining political prisoners and promised the dissolution of SAVAK, the lifting of martial law, and free elections. He announced Iran's withdrawal from CENTO, canceled arms orders worth US$7 billion from the United States, and announced that Iran would no longer sell oil to South Africa or Israel. Although Bakhtiar won the qualified support of leading moderate clerics such as Ayatollah Kazem Shariatmadari, he did not win the support of Khomeini and the main opposition elements, who were now committed to ending the monarchy and establishing a new political order. The National Front expelled Bakhtiar, and Khomeini declared his government illegal. Some normalcy returned to the bazaar, and oil production improved slightly in the wake of Bakhtiar's appointment. But strikes in both the public and private sectors and large-scale demonstrations against the government continued. When, on January 29, 1979, Khomeini called for a street "referendum" on the monarchy and the Bakhtiar government, there was a massive turnout.

Khomeini returned to Iran from Paris on February 1, received a rapturous welcome from millions of Iranians, and announced that he would "smash in the mouth of the Bakhtiar government." Khomeini established his headquarters in a girls' secondary school in Tehran, and the *komiteh-ye imam,* or the imam's committee (imam—see Glossary), coordinated opposition activity. On February 5, Khomeini named Mehdi Bazargan prime minister of a provisional government, reinforcing the conditions of dual authority that had characterized the closing days of the Pahlavi monarchy. In many large urban centers, local *komitehs* (revolutionary committees) had assumed responsibility for municipal functions, including neighborhood security and the distribution of such basic necessities as fuel oil. Government ministries and such services as the customs and mail service remained largely paralyzed. Bakhtiar's cabinet ministers proved unable to assert their authority or, in many instances, even to enter their offices. The loyalty of the armed forces was being seriously eroded by months of confrontation with protesters, and desertions were increasing. Clandestine contacts under way between Khomeini's representatives and a number of military commanders were being encouraged by U.S. ambassador William Sullivan, who had no confidence in the Bakhtiar government and believed that only an accommodation between the armed forces and the Khomeini camp could assure stability in Iran.

On February 8, uniformed airmen appeared at Khomeini's home and publicly pledged their allegiance to him. On February 9, air force technicians at the Doshan Tappeh Air Base outside Tehran mutinied. The next day, the air base arsenal was opened, and weapons were distributed to crowds outside. Over the next 24 hours, revolutionaries seized police barracks, prisons, and public buildings. On February 11, a group of 22 senior military commanders met and announced that the armed forces would observe neutrality in the confrontation between the government and the people. The army's withdrawal from the streets was tantamount to a withdrawal of support for the Bakhtiar government and acted as a trigger for a general uprising. By late afternoon on February 11, Bakhtiar was in hiding, and key points throughout the capital were in rebel hands. The Pahlavi monarchy had collapsed.

The Revolution

Bazargan and the Provisional Government

Mehdi Bazargan became the first prime minister of the revolutionary regime in February 1979. Bazargan, however, headed a government that controlled neither the country nor even its own bureaucratic apparatus. Central authority had broken down. Hundreds of semi-independent revolutionary committees, not answerable to central authority, were performing a variety of functions, both lawful and unlawful, in major cities and towns across the country. The committees policed neighborhoods in urban areas, guarded prisons and government buildings, made unauthorized arrests, served as execution squads of the revolutionary tribunals, intervened in labor-management disputes, and seized property. Factory workers, civil servants, white-collar employees, and students often were in control, demanding a say in running their organizations and choosing their chiefs. Governors, military commanders, and other officials appointed by the prime minister frequently were rejected by the lower ranks or local inhabitants. A range of political groups, from the far left to the far right, from secular to ultra-Islamic, were vying for political power and demanding immediate action from the prime minister. Clerics led by Ayatollah Mohammad Beheshti established the Islamic Republican Party (IRP), which emerged as the organ of the clerics around Khomeini and the major political organization in the country. Not to be outdone, followers of the more moderate senior cleric Shariatmadari established the Islamic People's Republican Party (IPRP), with a base in Azarbaijan Province, Shariatmadari's home province.

Multiple centers of authority emerged within the government. As the Leader, Khomeini did not consider himself to be bound by the government. He alone made policy pronouncements, named personal representatives to key government organizations, established new institutions, and announced decisions without consulting his prime minister. The prime minister had to share power with the Revolutionary Council, which Khomeini had established in January 1979. The cabinet was to serve as the executive authority, but the Revolutionary Council exercised supreme decision-making and legislative authority.

Differences quickly emerged between the cabinet and the Revolutionary Council over appointments, the role of the revolutionary courts and other revolutionary organizations, foreign policy, and the general direction of the Revolution. Bazargan and his cabinet colleagues were eager for a return to normalcy and rapid reassertion of central authority. Clerics of the Revolutionary Council, more responsive to the Islamic and popular temper of the mass of their followers, generally favored more radical economic and social measures. They mobilized the street crowds and the revolutionary organizations to achieve their ends. In July 1979, clerical members of the Revolutionary Council joined the government, and cabinet officers were given seats on the council, but this failed to ease tensions.

The revolutionaries quickly turned their attention to bringing to trial and punishing members of the former regime whom they considered responsible for political repression, corruption, damaging economic policies, and the foreign exploitation of Iran. A revolutionary court set to work almost immediately in Tehran. Revolutionary courts were established in provincial centers shortly thereafter. The Tehran court issued its first death sentences for four of the shah's generals on February 16, 1979; the four were executed by firing squad on the roof of the building housing Khomeini's headquarters. More executions, of military and police officers, SAVAK agents, cabinet ministers, Majlis deputies, and officials of the shah's regime, followed on an almost daily basis.

The activities of the revolutionary courts became a focus of intense controversy. Left-wing political groups and populist clerics pressed hard for "revolutionary justice" for miscreants of the former regime. But lawyers and human rights groups protested the arbitrary nature of the revolutionary courts, the vagueness of charges, and the absence of defense lawyers. Bazargan, too, was critical of the courts' activities. At the prime minister's insistence, the revolutionary courts suspended their activities on March 14, 1979; but new regulations issued on April 5 formalized the revolutionary courts and authorized them to try a variety of broadly defined crimes, such as "sowing corruption on earth," "crimes against the people," and "crimes against the Revolution." The courts resumed their work on April 6. The following day, despite international pleas for clemency, Hoveyda, who had served as the shah's prime minister for 12 years, was put to death. Executions of other former regime officials resumed. Beginning in August 1979, the courts tried and passed death sentences on members of ethnic minorities involved in antigovernment movements. Some 550 persons had been executed by the time Bazargan resigned in November 1979, having failed to bring the revolutionary committees under his control. Despite abuses committed by the revolutionary committees, members of the Revolutionary Council wanted to control the committees rather than eliminate them. In February 1979, the council appointed a senior cleric as head of the Tehran revolutionary committee and charged him with supervising the committees countrywide. The revolutionary committees endured, serving as one of the coercive arms of the revolutionary government.

In May 1979, Khomeini authorized the establishment of the Islamic Revolutionary Guard Corps or Revolutionary Guards (Pasdaran; in full, Pasdaran-e Enghelab-e Islami). The Revolutionary Guards organization was conceived by the men around Khomeini as a military force loyal to the Revolution and to the clerical leaders, a counterbalance to the regular army, and a weapon against the guerrilla organizations of the left, which also were arming. The force expanded rapidly.

Two other important organizations were established in the regime's formative period. In March 1979, Khomeini established the Foundation of the Disinherited (Bonyad-e Mostazafin; see Welfare, ch. 2). The organization was to take charge of the assets of the shah's philanthropic Pahlavi Foundation and to use the proceeds from their liquidation to assist low-income groups. The new foundation eventually became one of the largest conglomerates in the country, controlling hundreds of expropriated and nationalized factories, trading firms, farms, and apartment and office buildings, as well as two large newspaper chains. Crusade for Reconstruction (Jihad-e Sazandegi or Jihad), established in June, recruited young people to build clinics, local roads, schools, and similar facilities in villages and rural areas. This organization also grew rapidly, assuming functions in rural areas that had previously been handled by the Planning and Budget Organization (which had replaced the Plan Organization in 1973) and the Ministry of Agriculture.

In March 1979, three different disputes broke out in different parts of Iran, concerning, respectively, the Turkmens, the Kurds, and the Arabic-speaking population of Khuzestan Province (see Languages and Peoples, ch. 2). The disputes in the Turkmen region of Gorgan Province were over land rather than claims for Turkmen cultural identity or autonomy. In Khuzestan, the center of Iran's oil industry, members of the Arabic-speaking population demanded a larger share of oil revenues for the region, more jobs for local inhabitants, the use of Arabic as a semiofficial language, and a larger degree of local autonomy. Both these disturbances were put down by the use of troops and the arrest of leaders and activists.

The Kurdish uprising proved more persistent and deeply rooted. The Kurdish leaders were disappointed that the Revolution had not brought them local autonomy. Scattered fighting began in March 1979 between government and Kurdish forces; attempts at negotiation proved abortive. The Kurdistan Democratic Party, led by Abdol Rahman Qasemlu, and a more radical group led by Sheikh Ezz ad Din Husseini, demanded the enlargement of the Kurdistan region to include all Kurdish-speaking areas in Iran and considerable financial, administrative, linguistic, and law enforcement autonomy, with the central government limited to national defense, foreign affairs, and central banking functions. With the rejection of these demands, serious fighting broke out in August 1979. Khomeini used the army against other Iranians for the first time since the Revolution. No settlement was reached with the Kurds during Bazargan's tenure as prime minister.

With the Bazargan government powerless, control over security passed into the hands of clerics in the Revolutionary Council and the IRP, who ran the revolutionary courts and had influence with the Revolutionary Guards, the revolutionary committees, and the club-wielding *hezbollahis* (see Glossary), or "followers of the party of God." The clerics deployed these forces to curb rival political organizations. In June 1979, the Revolutionary Council promulgated a restrictive press law. More than 40 opposition newspapers were closed down in August. The Revolutionary Council proscribed the National Democratic Front, a newly organized left-of-center political movement, and issued a warrant for the arrest of its leader. *Hezbollahis* closed the Tehran headquarters of the Fedayan and the Mojahedin organizations. On September 8, the two largest newspaper enterprises in the country, *Kayhan* and *Ettelaat*, were expropriated, with control transferred to the Foundation for the Disinherited.

In June and July 1979, the Revolutionary Council also passed a number of major economic measures, whose effect was to transfer considerable private-sector assets to the state. It nationalized banks, insurance companies, major industries, and certain categories of urban land; expropriated the wealth of leading business and industrial families; and appointed state managers to run many private-sector industries and other private companies.

The New Constitution

Khomeini had charged the provisional government with the task of drawing up a draft constitution. A step in this direction was taken on March 30 and 31, 1979, when a national referendum was held to determine the country's political system. The only form of government on the ballot was an Islamic republic, and voting was not by secret ballot. The government reported more than 98 percent in favor; Khomeini proclaimed the establishment of the Islamic Republic of Iran on April 1, 1979.

The provisional government unveiled a draft constitution on June 18. Aside from substituting a president for the monarch, the draft did not differ substantially from the 1906 constitution and accorded no special role to the clerics in the new state. A 73-member Assembly of Experts, dominated by clerics and IRP supporters, convened on August 18 to consider the draft constitution. The majority rewrote the constitution to establish the basis for the clerical domination of the state and to vest ultimate authority in Khomeini as the *faqih*, the Islamic jurisprudent to be known as the Leader of the Revolution and as the heir to the mantle of the Prophet. Last-minute attempts by centrist and liberal groups, by Shariatmadari's followers, and by Bazargan and some cabinet members to stave off this eventuality failed. The Assembly of Experts completed its work on November 15. The constitution was approved in a national referendum on December 2 and 3, once again, according to government figures, by more than 98 percent of the voters. Shariatmadari's followers in Tabriz organized protest demonstrations and seized control of the radio station. A potentially serious challenge to the dominant clerical hierarchy floundered, however, when Shariatmadari wavered in his support for the protesters, and the pro-Khomeini forces organized massive counterdemonstrations in the city. Fearing reprisals, the IPRP announced its own dissolution in December.

Few foreign initiatives were possible in the early months of the Revolution. The Bazargan government attempted to maintain correct relations with the Persian Gulf states, despite harsh denunciations of the Gulf rulers by senior clerics and revolutionary leaders. Anti-American feeling was widespread and was fanned by Khomeini himself, populist preachers, and the left-wing parties. Bazargan, however, continued to seek military spare parts from Washington and asked for intelligence information on Soviet and Iraqi activities in Iran. Then, on October 22, 1979, the shah, who was seriously ill, was admitted to the United States for medical treatment. The revolutionaries feared that the shah would use this visit to the United States to secure U.S. support for an attempt to overthrow the Islamic Republic. On November 1, Bazargan met with President Carter's national security adviser, Zbigniew K. Brzezinski, in Algiers, where the two men were attending Independence Day celebrations. That same day, hundreds of thousands marched in Tehran to demand the shah's extradition, while the press denounced Bazargan for meeting with a key U.S. official. On November 4, young men who later designated themselves "students of the Imam's line" occupied the U.S. embassy compound and took U.S. diplomats hostage. Bazargan resigned two days later; no prime minister was named to replace him.

The Revolutionary Council took over the prime minister's functions, pending presidential and Majlis elections. The elections for a new president were held in January 1980. Abolhasan Bani Sadr, an independent associated with Khomeini who had written widely on the relationship of Islam to politics and economics, received 75 percent of the vote.

The Bani Sadr Presidency

Bani Sadr's program as president was to reestablish central authority, phase out the Revolutionary Guards and the revolutionary courts and committees and have other government organizations absorb their functions, reduce the influence of the clerical hierarchy, and launch a program for economic reform and development. Against the wishes of the IRP, Khomeini allowed Bani Sadr to be sworn in as president in January 1980, before the convening of the Majlis. Khomeini further bolstered Bani Sadr's position by appointing him chairman of the Revolutionary Council and delegating to the president his own powers as commander in chief of the armed forces. On the eve of the Iranian New Year on March 20,

Khomeini issued a message to the nation designating the coming year as "the year of order and security" and outlining a program reflecting Bani Sadr's own priorities.

However, like Bazargan before him, Bani Sadr found that he was competing for primacy with the clerics and activists of the IRP. Bani Sadr failed to secure the dissolution of the Revolutionary Guards and the revolutionary courts and committees. He also failed to establish control over the judiciary or the radio and television networks. Khomeini appointed IRP members Ayatollah Mohammad Beheshti as chief justice and Ayatollah Abdol Karim Musavi Ardabili as prosecutor general. Bani Sadr's appointees to head the state broadcasting services and the Revolutionary Guards were forced to resign within weeks of their appointments.

Parliamentary elections were held in two stages, in March and May 1980, amid charges of fraud. The official results gave the IRP and its supporters 130 of 241 seats decided; elections were not completed in all 270 constituencies. Candidates associated with Bani Sadr and with Bazargan's IFM each won a handful of seats; other left-of-center secular parties fared no better. The Majlis began its deliberations in June. Ali Akbar Hashemi Rafsanjani, a cleric and founding member of the IRP, was elected Majlis speaker. After a two-month deadlock between the president and the Majlis over the selection of a prime minister, Bani Sadr was forced to accept the IRP candidate, Mohammad Ali Rajai; after a long standoff, Bani Sadr was forced to accept IRP candidates for many key cabinet positions as well.

The president's inability to control the revolutionary courts and the persistence of revolutionary temper were both demonstrated in May 1980, when executions, which had become rare in the previous few months, began again on a large scale. Some 900 executions were carried out, most of them between May and September. Meanwhile, a remark by Khomeini in June 1980 that "royalists" were still to be found in government offices led to a new wave of purges. Some 4,000 civil servants and between 2,000 and 4,000 military officers lost their jobs before the purges ended. Around 8,000 military officers had been dismissed or retired in previous purges.

The Kurdish problem proved intractable. Renewed negotiations failed when Kurdish leaders refused to compromise on their demand for autonomy, and fighting resumed. Bani Sadr's various attempts to resolve the American hostage crisis also

Demonstrators outside the U.S. Embassy in Tehran in late 1979
Copyright Lehtikuva/PHOTRI

Voters cast their ballots
in the presidential election, January 1980.
Copyright Lehtikuva/PHOTRI

proved abortive. The "students of the Imam's line" were using the hostage issue and documents found in the embassy to radicalize the public temper, challenge the authority of the president, and undermine the reputations of moderate politicians and public figures. The crisis had shattered relations with the United States and was badly straining ties with West European countries. The shah, meantime, had made his home in Panama, but, fearing extradition, he abruptly left for Egypt in March 1980, where he died four months later.

In April 1980, the United States attempted unsuccessfully to rescue the hostages by landing aircraft and troops near Tabas in eastern Iran. Radical factions in the IRP and left-wing groups charged that Iranian officers opposed to the Revolution had secretly helped the U.S. aircraft to escape radar detection. Bani Sadr prevented another purge of the military but was forced to reshuffle the top military command. In June the chief judge of the Army Military Revolutionary Tribunal announced the discovery of an antigovernment plot centered on the military base in Piranshahr in Kurdistan Province. Twenty-seven junior and warrant officers were arrested. In July the authorities announced that they had uncovered a plot centered on the Shahrokhi Air Base in Hamadan Province. Ten of the alleged plotters were killed when members of the Revolutionary Guards broke into their headquarters. Approximately 300 officers, including two generals, were arrested. The government charged the accused with plotting to overthrow the state and seize power in the name of exiled former prime minister Bakhtiar. As many as 140 officers were shot on orders of the military tribunal; wider purges of the armed forces followed.

In September 1980, perhaps believing that the hostage crisis could serve no further diplomatic or political end, the Rajai government opened secret talks with U.S. representatives in West Germany. The talks continued for the next four months, with the Algerians acting as intermediaries. The hostages were released on January 20, 1981, concurrently with Ronald W. Reagan's inauguration as president of the United States. In return, the United States released more than US$11 billion in Iranian funds that had been frozen by presidential order. Iran also agreed to repay US$5.1 billion in syndicated and nonsyndicated loans owed to U.S. and foreign banks and to place another US$1 billion in an escrow account, pending the settlement of claims filed against Iran by U.S. firms and citizens. These claims, and Iranian claims against U.S. firms, were adjudicated by a special tribunal of the International Court of Justice at The Hague, established under the terms of what came to be known as the Algiers Agreement.

One incentive for Iran to settle the hostage crisis was the onset of full-scale hostilities with Iraq in September 1980. The conflict stemmed from Iraqi anxieties that the fever of the Iranian Revolution would infect Iraq's Shia Muslims, who constituted a majority of Iraq's population, The Iraqi president, Saddam Hussein, also desired to undo the 1975 Algiers Agreement (not to be confused with the agreement resulting from the 1980–81 United States–Iran negotiations) in order to bring about the overthrow of the Khomeini regime and to establish a more friendly government in Iran. On September 17, he abrogated the Algiers Agreement. Five days later, Iraqi troops and aircraft began a massive invasion of Iran (see fig. 4).

The war did nothing to moderate the friction between Bani Sadr and the Rajai government, with its clerical and IRP backers. Bani Sadr championed the cause of the army; his IRP rivals championed the cause of the Revolutionary Guards. Bani Sadr accused the Rajai government of hampering the war effort; the prime minister and his backers accused the president of planning to use the army to seize power. The prime minister also fought the president over control of foreign and domestic economic policy. In late 1980, Bani Sadr attempted to persuade Khomeini to dismiss the Rajai government and dissolve the Majlis, the Supreme Judicial Council, and the Guardians Council and to give him, as president, wide powers to run the country during the war emergency. Khomeini refused.

Supporters of Bani Sadr and others critical of the activities of the IRP and the revolutionary courts and committees organized rallies in November and December in Mashhad, Esfahan, Tehran, and Gilan. In December, merchants of the Tehran bazaar associated with the National Front called for the resignation of the Rajai government. In February 1981, Bazargan denounced the government at a mass rally. A group of 133 writers, journalists, and academics issued a letter protesting the suppression of basic freedoms. Senior clerics questioned the legitimacy of the revolutionary courts, widespread property confiscations, and the power exercised by Khomeini as *faqih*. The IRP retaliated by using its *hezbollahi* gangs to break up Bani Sadr rallies in various cities and to harass opposition organizations; the offices of Bani Sadr's newspaper, *Enqelab-e Islami*, and

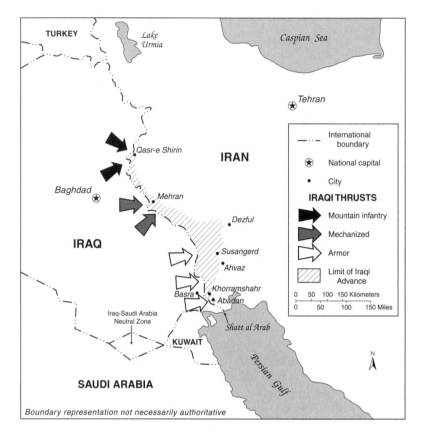

Figure 4. Initial Iraqi Attack on Iran, September–November 1980

the IFM newspaper, *Mizan*, were smashed and the newspapers closed down; prominent Bani Sadr supporters were arrested.

Khomeini's various attempts to mediate the differences between Bani Sadr and the Rajai government and the IRP failed. In May 1981, the Majlis passed measures to permit the prime minister to appoint caretakers to ministries still lacking a minister, to deprive the president of his veto power, and to allow the prime minister rather than the president to appoint the governor of the Central Bank of Iran. Within days the governor was replaced by a Rajai appointee.

By the end of May, Bani Sadr appeared to be losing Khomeini's support as well. On June 10, Khomeini removed Bani Sadr from his post as the acting commander in chief of the military. On June 12, a motion for the impeachment of the president was presented by 120 deputies. Soon afterward, fearing for his life, Bani Sadr went into hiding. When the Mojahedin called for "revolutionary resistance in all its forms," the government responded harshly. Twenty-three protesters were executed on June 20 and 21, as the Majlis debated the motion for impeachment. On June 21, with 30 deputies absenting themselves or abstaining, the Majlis decided for impeachment by a vote of 177 to one. The revolutionary movement had brought together a coalition of clerics, middle-class liberals, and secular radicals against the shah. The impeachment of Bani Sadr represented the triumph of the clerical party over the other members of this coalition.

Terror and Repression

Following the fall of Bani Sadr, opposition elements attempted to reorganize so as to overthrow the government by force. The regime responded with a policy of repression and terror. Bani Sadr remained in hiding for several weeks, formed an alliance with Mojahedin leader Masoud Rajavi, and in July 1981 escaped with Rajavi from Iran to France. In Paris Bani Sadr and Rajavi announced the establishment of the National Council of Resistance (NCR) and committed themselves to work for the overthrow of the Khomeini regime. The Kurdistan Democratic Party, the National Democratic Front, and a number of other small groups and individuals subsequently announced their association with the NCR.

Meanwhile, violent opposition to the government continued. On June 28, 1981, a powerful bomb exploded at the headquarters of the IRP while a meeting of party leaders was in progress. Seventy-three persons were killed, including the chief justice and party secretary general Mohammad Beheshti, four cabinet ministers, 27 Majlis deputies, and several other government officials. Elections for a new president were held on July 24, and Rajai, the prime minister, was elected to the post. On August 5, the Majlis approved Rajai's choice of Mohammad Javad Bahonar as prime minister.

Rajai and Bahonar, along with the chief of the Tehran police, lost their lives when a bomb went off during a meeting at the office of the prime minister on August 30. The Majlis named another cleric, Mohammad Reza Mahdavi Kani, as interim prime minister. In a new round of elections on October 2, Sayyid Ali Khamenei was elected president. On October 28, the Majlis elected Mir Hosain Musavi, a protégé of the late

Mohammad Beheshti, as prime minister. The Mojahedin claimed responsibility for a spate of other assassinations. Among those killed in the space of a few months were the Friday prayer leaders in the cities of Tabriz, Kerman, Shiraz, Yazd, and Bakhtaran; a provincial governor; the warden of the notorious Evin Prison in Tehran; the chief ideologue of the IRP; and several revolutionary court judges and Majlis deputies.

In September 1981, expecting to spark a general uprising, the Mojahedin sent their young followers into the streets to demonstrate against the government and deployed their very limited military units for armed attacks against the Revolutionary Guards. Smaller left-wing opposition groups, including the Fedayan, attempted similar guerrilla activities. In July 1981, members of the Union of Communists tried to seize control of the Caspian town of Amol. At least 70 guerrillas and Revolutionary Guards members were killed before the uprising was put down. The government responded to the armed challenge of the guerrilla groups with widespread arrests, jailings, and executions. Fifty executions a day became routine; there were days when more than 100 persons were executed. Amnesty International documented 2,946 executions in the 12 months following Bani Sadr's impeachment; this probably was a conservative figure. The pace of executions slackened considerably at the end of 1982, partly as a result of a deliberate government decision but primarily because, by then, the back of the armed resistance movement had largely been broken.

By the end of 1983, key leaders of the Fedayan, Peykar (a Marxist-oriented splinter group of the Mojahedin), the Union of Communists, and the Mojahedin in Iran had been killed; thousands of the rank and file had been executed or were in prison; and the organizational structure of these movements was gravely weakened. Only the Mojahedin managed to survive by moving its headquarters to Paris.

During this period, the government was also able to crush its other active and potential political opponents and armed groups. In June 1982, the authorities captured Khosrow Qashqai, who had returned to Iran after the Revolution and had led his Qashqai tribesmen in a local uprising (see Turkic-Speaking Groups, ch. 2). He was tried and publicly hanged in October. The government reasserted control over major towns in Kurdistan in 1982, and Kurdish armed resistance in the countryside came to an end in the following year.

In the fall of 1982, former Khomeini aide and foreign minister Sadeq Qotbzadeh and some 70 military officers were tried and executed for allegedly plotting to kill Khomeini and overthrow the state. The government implicated the respected religious leader Shariatmadari in the alleged plot. In an unprecedented move, members of the Association of the Seminary Teachers of Qom voted to strip Shariatmadari of his title of *marja-e taqlid* (a jurist who particularly merits emulation), and he was placed under virtual house arrest.

Moves to crush opposition gave freer rein to the Revolutionary Guards and the revolutionary committees. Members of these organizations entered homes, made arrests, conducted searches, and confiscated goods at will. The government organized "Mobile Units of God's Vengeance" to patrol the streets and to impose Islamic dress and Islamic codes of behavior. Instructions issued by Khomeini in December 1981 and in August 1982 admonishing the revolutionary organizations to exercise proper care in entering homes and making arrests were ignored. "Manpower renewal" and "placement" committees in government ministries and offices resumed large-scale purges in 1982.

By the end of 1982, the country was experiencing a reaction against the widespread executions and the arbitrary actions of the revolutionary organizations and purge committees. Also, the government realized that domestic insecurity was exacerbating economic difficulties. Accordingly, in December 1982 Khomeini issued an eight-point decree prohibiting the revolutionary organizations from entering homes, making arrests, conducting searches, and confiscating property without legal authorization. He also banned unauthorized tapping of telephones, interference with citizens in the privacy of their homes, and unauthorized dismissals from the civil service. He urged the courts to respect the life, property, and honor of citizens. Although the decree did not end repression, it led to a marked decrease in executions, tempered the worst abuses of the Revolutionary Guards and the revolutionary committees, and brought a measure of security to individuals not engaged in opposition activity.

However, the December decree implied no increased tolerance of the political opposition. For instance, the Tudeh initially had secured a measure of freedom by declaring loyalty to Khomeini and supporting the clerics against liberal and left-wing opposition groups. But the government began a crackdown on the Tudeh in 1981, branding its members agents of a foreign power. In February 1983, the government arrested Tudeh leader Nureddin Kianuri, other members of the party central committee, and more than 1,000 party members. The party was proscribed, and Kianuri was produced on television to confess to spying for the Soviet Union and to "espionage, deceit, and treason."

Consolidation of the Revolution

As the government eliminated the political opposition and successfully prosecuted the war with Iraq, it also took further steps to consolidate and institutionalize its authority. It reorganized the Revolutionary Guards, the Crusade for Reconstruction, and the state security organization as full ministries (respectively, in 1982, 1983, and 1984); placed the revolutionary committees under the Ministry of Interior; and nominally incorporated the revolutionary courts into the regular court system. These measures met with only limited success in reducing the considerable autonomy and budgetary independence of the revolutionary organizations.

In 1985 the Assembly of Experts (not to be confused with the constituent assembly that went by the same name), a body charged under the constitution with electing Khomeini's successor, agreed to designate its choice, Ayatollah Hosain Ali Montazeri, merely as Khomeini's "deputy." This action placed Montazeri in line for the succession without actually naming him as the heir apparent.

Elections to the second Majlis were held in the spring of 1984 and were contested only by candidates of the IRP and other groups and individuals in the ruling hierarchy. The second Majlis, more radical in temper than the first, convened in May 1984. With some prodding from Khomeini, it gave Mir Hosain Musavi a renewed vote of confidence as prime minister. In 1985 Khamenei, who was virtually unchallenged, was elected to another four-year term as president.

Opposition to the ruling hierarchy was barely tolerated. Bazargan, as leader of the IFM, continued to protest the suppression of basic freedoms. He addressed a letter on these issues to Khomeini in August 1984; he also spoke out against the war with Iraq and urged a negotiated settlement. In retaliation, in February 1985 the *hezbollahis* smashed the offices of the party, and the party newspaper was once again shut down. Bazargan was denounced from pulpits and was barred from running for president in the 1985 election.

There were, however, increasing signs of factionalism within the ruling group itself over questions of social justice, economic policy, the succession, and, to a lesser degree, foreign policy and the war with Iraq. The economic policy debate arose partly from disagreements over redistribution of wealth and partly from differences over the roles of the state and the private sector in the economy. Divisions also arose between the Majlis and the Guardians Council, a group composed of senior Islamic jurists and other experts in Islamic law that was empowered by the constitution to veto, or demand the revision of, any legislation it considered in violation of the constitution or of the precepts of Islam. In this dispute, the Guardians Council emerged as the collective champion of private-property rights. In the years 1982–85, the Guardians Council vetoed a law that would have nationalized foreign trade; the Law for the Expropriation of the Property of Fugitives, which would have allowed the state to seize the property of any Iranian living abroad who failed to return to Iran; a law for state takeover and distribution to farmers of large agricultural landholdings; and a measure for state control over the domestic distribution of goods. The Guardians Council forced the Majlis to substantially revise a law for the state takeover of urban land, giving landowners more protection; and in 1984 and 1985, it blocked attempts by the Majlis to revive measures for nationalization of foreign trade and for major land distribution. However, in 1984 the council approved a law, based on Article 49 of the constitution, that made all wealth obtained in a manner violating Islamic principles subject to confiscation. In 1986, after demanding revisions, it also approved a limited land-distribution law, under which less than 750,000 hectares of land, seized in the turmoil immediately following the Revolution and belonging to between 5,000 and 5,600 landowners, was distributed to approximately 120,000 cultivators.

The deadlock between the Majlis and the Guardians Council led to two significant developments. In an important letter addressed to President Khamenei in January 1988 in connection with another dispute on economic issues between the Majlis and the Guardians Council, Khomeini articulated an unusually broad—even unlimited—definition of the powers of the Islamic state. Such a state, he said, derives its authority from the vice regency entrusted by God to the Prophet and rules by divine sanction. In the interests of the community, Islam, and the country, he said, an Islamic government can revoke contracts it makes with the people, prohibit commercial transactions considered lawful under Islamic law, and even suspend the exercise of the five pillars of the faith required of every Muslim. In February 1989, Khomeini appointed an Expediency Council (in full, Council for the Discernment of Expediency) composed of 12 ex-officio members and his own representative, with wide powers to resolve differences between the Majlis and the Guardians Council.

Khomeini's Last Years

In a series of offensives in the spring and summer of 1982, Iran had almost entirely expelled Iraqi forces from Iranian territory. Some in the senior leadership advocated crossing the border into Iraq and pursuing the war until the overthrow of Saddam Hussein; others argued for ending military action at Iran's borders. The advocates of going into Iraq won out, prolonging the war for another five years. Iranian forces secured slices of Iraqi territory in offensives in 1983, came close to cutting the strategic Basra–Baghdad Highway in 1985, and captured the Fao Peninsula along the strategic Shatt al Arab in February 1986. In January 1987, in Operation Karbala V, its largest, best-prepared offensive in five years, Iran seriously threatened the port city of Basra. But a decisive victory eluded the Iranians. Saddam Hussein retaliated by using aircraft and missiles acquired from the Soviet Union and France to renew the "tanker war," bomb oil facilities at Khark (Kharg) Island, and launch missile and bomb attacks against Iranian cities. He also used poison gas against Iranian forces.

Iran's January 1987 offensive was made possible by arms acquired not only from China and the Democratic People's Republic of Korea (North Korea) but also from the United States. In what came to be known as the Iran–Contra Affair, during 1985–86 the Reagan Administration sold to Iran more than 2,000 antitank missiles and parts for antiaircraft missile systems to fund anticommunist "contra" forces in Nicaragua. The arms-for-hostages deal led to contacts between senior Iranian and U.S. officials. Three U.S. hostages being held in Lebanon were released. But the clandestine agreement, leaked to a Lebanese weekly in November 1986, proved highly controversial in Iran and the United States and could not be sustained once it became public. In addition, fearing the disruptive effects on Arab allies of an Iranian victory over Iraq, the Reagan Administration changed tack and began to assist Saddam Hussein with intelligence, financial assistance, some arms, and diplomatic support. In July 1987, the United States also agreed to reflag and provide escorts for Kuwaiti tankers in the Persian Gulf. Iran had begun to target these tankers in retaliation for Kuwaiti assistance to Iraq's war effort. The arrival of a large fleet of U.S. battleships and aircraft carriers, and Saddam Hussein's ability to rearm even while Iran was virtually shut out of the international arms market, helped tip the balance of the war against Iran. Between April and July 1988, with clandestine U.S. assistance, Iraqi forces expelled Iranian forces from Iraqi territory and went on to retake large swaths of Iranian territory. On July 18, 1988, Iran finally accepted UN Resolution 598, which called for a cease-fire in place. Khomeini described the decision as "more lethal to me than poison."

The war with Iraq had led the government to seek to repair its relations with the international community. As early as October 1984, Khomeini had endorsed such an initiative. The government subsequently took steps to improve ties with Turkey and Pakistan, Britain and other West European states, and also with the Soviet Union. Relations had been strained by the Soviet supply of arms to Iraq and the Soviet military presence in Afghanistan. But hard-liners in Iran repeatedly undermined these efforts. For example, relations with France were again disrupted when an Iranian embassy employee in Paris was implicated in bombings in the French capital; relations with Britain were damaged when a British diplomat in Tehran was abducted and badly beaten after an Iranian consular official was charged with shoplifting in Manchester. In February 1989, Khomeini wrecked months of careful fence-mending by Rafsanjani in Europe by issuing a death sentence against the British novelist Salman Rushdie, whose novel *The Satanic Verses* he deemed insulting to the Prophet.

In March 1989, Khomeini created another crisis by dismissing Ayatollah Montazeri as his successor designate, describing him as unsuitable for the role of Leader. The two men had been very close, but Montazeri had become publicly critical of restrictions on the press, the treatment of political prisoners, and prison conditions, which he described as "far worse than under the Shah." He accused Khomeini of stifling debate and losing touch with public opinion. Montazeri also refused Khomeini's demand that he disassociate himself from a relative, Mehdi Hashemi, who used his armed retainers to interfere in domestic and foreign affairs.

The dismissal of Montazeri and the necessity of making arrangements for the post-Khomeini period led to the convening of a constitutional assembly in May 1989 to consider amendments to the constitution. Khomeini named 20 leading officials and clerics to the council and invited the Majlis to name five others. The assembly made a number of major revisions to the 1979 constitution, aimed at the centralization of authority, enhancement of the powers of the Leader, and solidification of clerical control of the institutions of the state. The constitutional convention completed its work in mid-July. The amendments to the constitution were approved in a national referendum on July 28, when Rafsanjani also was elected president.

Khomeini died on June 3, 1989, before the assembly could complete its work, and he was buried two days later. The Assembly of Experts quickly convened and named Khamenei his successor.

The Post-Khomeini Era

The Rafsanjani Presidency

The end of the Iran–Iraq War in 1988, Khomeini's death in 1989, and the election of Ali Akbar Hashemi Rafsanjani to the presidency that same year permitted a turn toward more pragmatic policies. The end of the war allowed the government to redirect its resources and energies to the long-neglected economy. The death of Khomeini gave his lieutenants greater room to chart their own course. The amended constitution vested expanded powers in the president. As president, Rafsanjani emphasized the need to eschew sloganeering and to focus on postwar reconstruction, job creation, and economic rationalization. He eased social (though not political) controls at home. He also set about repairing Iran's international relations. Progress was made in each of these areas; but by Rafsanjani's second term, due to opposition inside the ruling group and institutional obstruction, each of these programs was in serious trouble.

The U.S.-led 1990–91 Gulf War to expel Iraq from Kuwait yielded Iran immediate benefits. Saddam Hussein was forced to evacuate Iranian territory that Iraq had occupied since the 1988 cease-fire. The Gulf War greatly weakened a better-armed and menacing enemy. Iranian policy during and after the war reflected a new, more moderate strain in foreign policy. Rafsanjani skillfully kept Iran out of the war, in effect (if not in rhetoric) aligning Iran with the aims of the U.S.-led alliance. At the end of the war, Iran showed restraint in the limited aid it extended to fellow Shias when Saddam Hussein brutally crushed an uprising in southern Iraq.

Rafsanjani used the cover of the war to resume diplomatic relations with Morocco, Egypt, and Saudi Arabia. After the war, he used Iranian influence with Hizballah to secure the release of the remaining American hostages in Lebanon. Iran assiduously courted better relations with Turkey, Saudi Arabia, Kuwait, and the other Arab states of the Persian Gulf. It muted its criticism of the military basing agreement that Kuwait signed with the United States and the support that Arab states of the Persian Gulf gave to the Oslo peace process (which Iran strongly opposed). Iran did not attempt to stir up Islamic sentiments in the newly independent states of Central Asia and the Caucasus. Iran's relations with Turkey remained correct despite increased cooperation between the Turkish and Israeli militaries.

As a counterweight to the United States, with which relations remained strained, Iran deliberately set out to cultivate other major powers, including Russia, China, Japan, Germany, and France. This policy proved advantageous. Iran secured sources of arms, industrial goods, credits, and occasional diplomatic support, despite considerable U.S. pressure for comprehensive trade sanctions.

But Iran did not abandon its support for radical causes abroad or for policies that tended to exacerbate relations with the countries it was courting. Both pragmatic and ideological considerations characterized foreign policy. Iran adopted an uncompromisingly hostile stand toward the Oslo peace process and the 1993 Palestinian-Israeli agreement, labeling Israel an illegitimate state that should cease to exist. Along with Syria, Iran was a principal sponsor of Hizballah in Lebanon and supported Hizballah's military arm with money, arms, and training. Hizballah used these resources to shell Israeli settlements along the Israeli-Lebanese border and to attack Israel's military surrogates in southern Lebanon. Hizballah was also implicated in two bombings in Buenos Aires, of the Israeli embassy in 1992 and of a Jewish cultural center in 1995, in which a total of more than 100 persons were killed. Palestinian Islamic Jihad, another

Iran-supported group, was implicated in bombings in Tel Aviv in 1995 and Jerusalem in 1996 that took many Israeli lives. In the early 1990s, Iran moved with alacrity to support the new "Islamic" government in Sudan, although that move damaged Iran's fragile relations with Egypt.

These linkages in Iran's foreign policy, Iran's attempt to secure medium-range and long-range missile capabilities, and suspicions that Iran was seeking nuclear weapons exacerbated the already problematic United States–Iran relationship. The United States maintained extensive sanctions against Iran and pressured its allies to limit economic cooperation with the Islamic Republic. U.S. pressure played a large role in the German decision at the end of the Iran–Iraq War not to resume work on an Iranian nuclear power plant at Bushehr and in limiting World Bank loans to Iran, investment by international firms in Iran's oil and gas industry, and the transfer to Iran of dual-use nuclear technology.

For its part, Iran chafed at the sanctions, the large U.S. military presence in the Persian Gulf, and the "terrorist" label applied by the United States. Although Iran's military had been ravaged by eight years of war with Iraq and insecurity was endemic along the Iran–Iraq border, Iran continued to be denied Western weapons, even as Saudi Arabia, Kuwait, and other Persian Gulf states were heavily rearming. In 1995, however, Iran offered an American company, Conoco, a major contract to develop the offshore Pars gas field. This overture probably represented an attempt by Iran to uncouple U.S.-Iranian economic relations from the other issues between the two countries. The strategy did not work. President William J. Clinton responded by banning American companies from doing business in Iran. In 1996 the United States Congress passed the Iran–Libya Sanctions Act (ILSA), which imposed sanctions on foreign companies investing more than US$40 million (later reduced to US$20 million) in Iran's oil and gas sector. However, objections by the European Union (EU) prevented strict enforcement of ILSA-mandated sanctions.

The radical element in Iran's foreign policy served several purposes. Khamenei believed that uncompromising hostility to Israel and the United States enhanced his standing with important constituencies at home and with Islamic constituencies abroad. Opposition to Israel, for example, identified Iran with the Palestinian masses and the Palestinian diaspora and distinguished the Islamic Republic from the supposedly pliant Arab states that had acquiesced in a United States–sponsored pro-Israeli peace plan. Support for Hizballah or Palestinian Islamic Jihad, not very costly in financial terms, enhanced Iran's weight and role in the region. By playing the role of spoiler in the Arab-Israeli peace process, Iran sought leverage against the United States and Israel. Such policies also satisfied the aspirations of the radical faction within the ruling group. Khomeini's fatwa sanctioning the killing of Salman Rushdie, for example, was a serious obstacle to improved relations with the EU countries. However, Rafsanjani's attempts to explain away the decree were repeatedly undermined by hard-line elements at home.

Before his death in 1989, Khomeini already had given his approval for a five-year economic development plan (see Glossary) that pointed to a more market-oriented economic program. The plan provided for a larger share in the economy for the domestic and foreign private sectors and allowed the government to borrow up to US$27 billion abroad for development projects—both controversial measures. Together with the technocrats he appointed to head key economic organizations such as the central bank, the Planning and Budget Organization, and the Ministry of Finance, President Rafsanjani began to move Iran away from a state-controlled war economy. In 1991 the government reduced the multiple exchange rates for the rial (for value of the rial—see Glossary) from seven to three and in 1993 declared full convertibility. Controls on imports, foreign currency, and prices were eased; state subsidies for essential goods were reduced; and prices for utilities and fuel were raised.

New regulations permitted foreign investors equity participation of up to 49 percent in joint ventures. Free-trade zones were established on the islands of Qeshm and Kish in the Persian Gulf. Several hundred government factories were slated for privatization. The government promised to reduce its own role in the economy—as much as 97 percent of all investments were being made by the public sector—although the five-year plan foresaw ambitious government investments in petrochemicals, gas, steel, and other industries. Real gross domestic product (GDP—see Glossary) grew by more than 10 percent per year in the early 1990s.

However, the liberalization program soon ran into difficulties. Privatization stalled in the face of resistance from the Foundation of the Disinherited, the parastatal organization that controlled hundreds of nationalized and expropriated enterprises, and because of fear that privatization would lead to economic dislocation. Inefficient, overstaffed state enterprises could not be sold off until they were made profitable. Government efforts to persuade expatriate Iranian businessmen to return and invest in Iran were unsuccessful. The easing of import and currency restrictions led to a doubling of imports, which depleted foreign-exchange reserves and saddled the country with short-and medium-term foreign debts of nearly US$30 billion.

Severe retrenchment followed. Unable to meet its repayment obligations, the government had to reschedule about US$12 billion of debt, primarily with Germany, other European states, and Japan. At the same time, the open-market value of the rial dropped nearly 60 percent. Credit to the private sector was restricted. Imports were cut sharply, forcing many factories to operate at 50 percent of capacity because of scarcities of spare parts and raw materials. Continued deficit spending contributed to severe inflation. The start of the second five-year development plan was postponed for a year. The government re-imposed multiple exchange rates and import-export controls and threatened measures to control consumer prices.

In 1992 economic hardship led to severe riots in the cities of Mashad, Arak, and Shiraz and to angry protests over inadequate municipal services and higher bus fares in two working-class districts near Tehran in 1995. The government responded by strengthening the paramilitary forces and the secret police apparatus, while the Majlis approved a new security law that provided for lengthy prison sentences for even the most ordinary political activities deemed threatening to the stability of the state.

Despite economic crises and heightened political repression, the early years of the Rafsanjani presidency witnessed an easing of some social and cultural controls. Restrictions on women's dress and public intermixing between young men and women were relaxed. Rafsanjani's first minister of culture, Mohammad Khatami, pursued less restrictive policies toward the arts, theater, and book publishing. A number of intellectual and literary journals, such as *Kiyan, Goftegu, Gardun, Iran-e Farda,* and *Kelk,* were allowed to publish. These journals carried on a lively discussion on issues of civil society, the relationship between religion and state, and the role of clerics in government. *Kiyan* published the essays of the thinker and philosopher Abdol Karim Soroush, who implicitly challenged the clerical monopoly on political power by arguing for an Islam that is pluralistic, tolerant, open to reinterpretation, and compatible with democracy. The newspaper *Salaam*, published by a clerical insider, was allowed to criticize the government from a leftist perspective.

The extent of this opening was limited, however, and did not extend to the political sphere. Factionalism among elite groups created some space for political competition within the ruling clerical establishment, but opposition political groups and newspapers were suppressed. Even the centrist IFM, which proclaimed loyalty to the Islamic Republic, was barely tolerated. Elections continued to be closely controlled. The judiciary remained an instrument of state policy. The role of the security agencies was pervasive and menacing.

The majority of the ruling clerics were grouped around two organizations, the Combatant Clerics Association and the Militant Clerics Association. The Combatant Clerics represented the right wing and the Militant Clerics the left wing of the clerical establishment. The conservatives used a kind of electoral gerrymandering to exclude the left wing from the Assembly of Experts in elections held in 1990 and from the Majlis in elections held in 1992. (The Militant Clerics reemerged to play a role in the 1997 presidential election, however.)

Although he assisted or acquiesced in these efforts to neutralize the radicals on the left, Rafsanjani proved unable or unwilling to stand up to conservatives on the right or to the security agencies, which grew increasingly assertive during his second presidential term (1993–97). The conservative majority in the Majlis forced the resignation of Rafsanjani's minister of culture and the head of national broadcasting on grounds of excessively liberal policies. In his role as Leader, Khamenei spearheaded a campaign against the Western "cultural onslaught," encouraging a crackdown on the press and the arts. The morals police reemerged in force to harass women and the young. Several newspapers were shut down. With clerical encouragement, attacks occurred in 1995–96 against the offices of the publisher of a novel considered hostile to Islam, cinemas, and a bookstore. Women cyclists in a Tehran park were beaten. Officially sanctioned, club-wielding thugs broke up public gatherings of which the government did not approve. In November 1994, the prominent writer Ali Akbar Saidi Sirjani died while in police custody. In 1996 Ahmad Mir

Alai, a writer and translator, was found dead on a street in his hometown, Esfahan. The essayist and translator Ghaffar Hosseini was found dead in his apartment in November 1996. The writer Farhad Sarkuhi was arrested repeatedly and badly tortured in 1996. Many observers suspected the complicity of the intelligence agencies in these acts of violence against intellectuals. Rafsanjani did nothing to investigate them, nor did he forthrightly condemn them.

Iran was also implicated in the assassination of Iranian dissidents abroad. Iranian opposition figures were killed in Paris, Berlin, Vienna, Istanbul, Geneva, and elsewhere. Among them were former prime minister Bakhtiar (in Paris); the leader of the Kurdistan Democratic Party, Abdol Rahman Qasemlu (in Vienna); and Qasemlu's successor, Sadeq Sharifkandi (in Berlin). German authorities eventually charged Iran's minister of intelligence (state security) and implicated Iran's highest officials in Sharifkandi's murder.

By the end of Rafsanjani's second term, the Majlis and—with rare exceptions—the press were quiescent. Political life, defined in terms of genuine competition and debate over ideas and policies, was virtually nonexistent, even within the ruling group. Rafsanjani's close association with Khamenei, his insider status, and the extensive business interests of his family meant that he would not risk an open split with the conservative faction. In his second term, Rafsanjani's centrist policies were in retreat, and the conservatives once again were in the ascendant.

Khatami and the Reform Movement

In 1996–97 two events sparked the second major attempt in the post-Khomeini decade to set the Revolution on a different course. First, on the eve of the 1996 Majlis elections, a small group of ministers and high-ranking officials closely associated with Rafsanjani broke away from the Combatant Clerics (with Rafsanjani's blessing) to form a new association, the Executives of Construction. They contested the elections on a separate slate, stressing their commitment to efficient management and to the industrial and entrepreneurial sector rather than to the bazaar, and won nearly 30 percent of the 270 Majlis seats. Thus, the elections unexpectedly led to a significant split within the dominant conservative clerical camp; indicated substantial public support for centrist, pragmatic politics; and made possible a debate on policy alternatives within the ruling establishment.

The second event was the surprise election of Mohammad Khatami to the presidency in 1997. Khatami, Rafsanjani's one-time minister of culture, was running against the Majlis speaker, Ali Akbar Nateq Nuri, who was the candidate of the Combatant Clerics. Nuri had been endorsed by the principal clerical organizations and personalities, by commanders of the Revolutionary Guards, and, implicitly, by Khamenei. Nuri was widely expected to win. But Khamenei and the ruling clerics desired a large turnout. Khamenei prevailed upon the left-leaning Militant Clerics, who had withdrawn in a huff from active politics after their exclusion from the 1992 Majlis elections, to contest the election.

The Militant Clerics named Khatami as their candidate, and he galvanized voters by running on a platform that emphasized the rule of law, expanded freedoms for Iranians, the need for a society-wide dialogue on problems of national concern, the idea of civil society, and dialogue rather than confrontation with the West. Khatami was further assisted by effective organization. The mayor of Tehran, Hussein Karbaschi, a Rafsanjani protégé, contributed the support of his widely read newspaper *Hamshsahri* and the considerable resources of the Tehran municipality. The Executives of Construction, who endorsed Khatami, proved effective organizers. The press, taking advantage of a small political opening, provided a forum for debate and discussion among competing political groups. Nearly 80 percent of eligible voters cast ballots; Khatami secured nearly 70 percent of the vote. Khatami's election reflected the widespread desire for change and helped launch a movement for wide-ranging reform and the expansion of civil society.

*   *   *

The Cambridge History of Iran (seven volumes) provides learned and factual essays by specialists on history, literature, the sciences, and the arts for various periods of Iranian history from the earliest times to the end of the Pahlavi period. Gene Garthwaite's *The Persians* is a handy one-volume survey of Iranian history from the Achaemenians to the present.

For the history of ancient Iran and the period from the Achaemenians until the Islamic conquest, Roman Ghirshman's

Iran: From the Earliest Times to the Islamic Conquest and A. T. Olmstead's *History of the Persian Empire*, although somewhat dated, continue to be standard works. More recent books on the period are Richard Frye's *The Heritage of Persia* and its companion volume, *The Golden Age of Persia*. For the early Islamic period, few books are devoted specifically to Iran, and readers therefore must consult general works on early Islamic history. Recommended studies are Marshall G. S. Hodgson's three-volume work *The Venture of Islam* and Ira Lapidus's *A History of Islamic Societies*. Much useful information on the early as well as the later Islamic period can be culled from E. G. Browne's four-volume *A Literary History of Persia*. Ann K. S. Lambton's *Landlord and Peasant in Persia* is excellent for both administrative history and land administration up to the 1950s.

For the period of Reza Shah, *A History of Modern Iran* by Joseph M. Upton is both concise and incisive. *Iran and the Rise of Reza Shah* by Cyrus Ghani is a rich political history of the background to Reza Shah's rise and early years in power, covering the period up to 1925. Stephanie Cronin's *The Army and the Creation of the Pahlavi State in Iran, 1910–1926* examines the army Reza Shah built and its role as he rose to power. *Modern Iran* by L. P. Elwell-Sutton, although written in the 1940s, is still a useful factual study, and Amin Banani's *The Modernization of Iran, 1921–1941* offers similar coverage of that same period.

For the period of Mohammad Reza Shah's rule, *Iran: The Politics of Groups, Classes, and Modernization* by James A. Bill and *The Political Elite of Iran* by Marvin Zonis are studies of elite politics and elite structure. Fred Halliday's *Iran: Dictatorship and Development* is a critical account of the nature of the state and the shah's rule; Robert Graham's *Iran: The Illusion of Power* covers the last years of the shah's reign. A more sympathetic assessment can be found in George Lenczowski's *Iran under the Pahlavis*. Relations between the state and the religious establishment for the whole of the Pahlavi period are covered in Shahrough Akhavi's *Religion and Politics in Contemporary Iran*. Iran's foreign policy is surveyed in Ruhollah Ramazani's *Iran's Foreign Policy, 1941–1973*. The U.S.-Iranian relationship in the period 1941–80 is the focus of James Bill's *The Eagle and the Lion: The Tragedy of American-Iranian Relations* and of Barry Rubin's *Paved with Good Intentions: The American Experience and Iran*.

Books that examine the roots and causes of the Islamic Revolution of 1978–79 include Jahangir Amuzegar, *The Dynamics of the Iranian Revolution*; Misagh Parsa, *Social Origins of the Iranian*

Revolution; and Hossein Bashiriyeh, *The State and Revolution in Iran, 1962–1982*. The U.S.-Iranian relationship in the period preceding and immediately following the Islamic Revolution is covered in Gary Sick's *All Fall Down: America's Tragic Encounter with Iran*. The foreign policy of the Islamic Republic is covered in Ramazani's *Revolutionary Iran: Challenge and Response in the Middle East*. Shaul Bakhash's *Reign of the Ayatollahs: Iran and the Islamic Revolution*, in its second edition, is a political history of the Islamic Revolution up to 1990. In *Who Rules Iran: The Structure of Power in the Islamic Republic*, Wilfried Buchta looks at the institutional and personal power structures in the Islamic Republic. Bahman Bakhtiari's *Parliamentary Politics in Revolutionary Iran* covers the period up to 1994. Daniel Brumberg's *Reinventing Khomeini: The Struggle for Reform in Iran* is a rich interpretive essay on the conflicting ideas and ideologies that have fueled the Islamic Revolution. The economy in the post-revolution period is addressed in Jahangir Amuzegar's factual and analytical *The Iranian Economy under the Islamic Republic*. The Iran–Iraq War is covered in Dilip Hiro's *The Longest War: The Iran–Iraq Military Conflict* and in Shahram Chubin and Charles Tripp, *Iran and Iraq at War*. (For further information and complete citations, see Bibliography.)

Chapter 2. The Society and Its Environment

A fifth-century B.C. drinking vessel in the shape of a winged lion, from Hamadan

THE CREATION OF THE ISLAMIC REPUBLIC of Iran in 1979 resulted in the destruction of the power and influence of the predominantly secular and Western-oriented political elite that had ruled Iran since the early part of the twentieth century. The new political elite that replaced this group was composed of Shia (see Glossary) Muslim clergymen and lay technocrats of middle-class and lower-class origins. The programs that they implemented have had cultural consequences, specifically in the promotion of religious ideals and values in public life. The general trend of social changes since 1979 has been for lower-income groups to benefit considerably from broader access to educational facilities, health services, and welfare programs. However, large discrepancies in household income between the richest and poorest strata of the population have not been eliminated. Government investments in social programs have helped to stimulate a major rural-to-urban migration, which has led to a shift in the distribution of the population, from about 65 percent rural in 1976 to 68 percent urban by 2006.

From the outset, establishing an "ideal" religious society was a professed aim of the Islamic Republic. However, pursuit of this goal was impeded by the eight-year war with Iraq (1980–88), a conflict that, at least in its initial years, threatened the existence of both the regime and the country. Even during the war years, however, the government implemented several programs to benefit the *mostazafin* (literally, the disinherited, meaning the poor; see Glossary). For example, a nationwide literacy program targeted both men and women over the age of 15. A campaign to provide the country's villages with amenities comparable to those in the cities improved the rural road system and the delivery of electricity, piped water, and natural gas supplies to rural households. The government also invested amply in schools, public libraries, cultural centers, public parks, hospitals, and health clinics in both rural and urban areas. Although there was consensus among the revolutionary elite that the government should provide infrastructure for the *mostazafin*, there was also contention over the kinds of social welfare programs for which the government should assume responsibility.

Every major cultural and social group in Iran has been affected by the changes resulting from the establishment of the

Islamic Republic. One significant impact has been the government's ongoing effort to recast society according to religiously prescribed behavioral codes. The secularized, Western-educated upper and middle classes of the prerevolutionary period resent laws that impose standards of social behavior they disdained when they had elite status. In particular, they dislike *hejab* (see Glossary), a code that regulates strictly how women may dress, and the prohibition on the production and distribution of alcoholic beverages. Both the religious middle class, generally identified with the merchants and artisans of the bazaar (see Glossary), and the lower classes tend to support these laws because they reinforce the values of their generally conservative lifestyles. In turn, the clergy and lay political leaders have targeted secular groups for their "immoral" lifestyles.

Geography

Iran is one of the world's most mountainous countries, and its topography has helped to shape the political, economic, and social history of the country. The mountains enclose several broad elevated basins, or plateaus, on which major agricultural and urban settlements are located. Until the twentieth century, when major highways and railroads were constructed through the mountains to connect the population centers, these basins tended to be relatively isolated from one another. Historically, transportation was by means of caravans that followed routes traversing gaps and passes in the mountains. The mountains also impeded easy access to the Persian Gulf and the Caspian Sea.

Located in southwestern Asia between the Caspian Sea and the Persian Gulf, Iran has an area of 1,648,000 square kilometers, about one-fifth that of the continental United States. Iran is the seventeenth largest country in the world. It shares land borders with seven countries and marine boundaries with nine countries. To the north are Armenia, the Republic of Azerbaijan, and Turkmenistan; on the west are Turkey and Iraq; on the east are Afghanistan and Pakistan. Some 1,700 kilometers long, Iran's southern border consists entirely of the northern shorelines of the Persian Gulf and Gulf of Oman. Iran shares marine boundaries in the Persian Gulf with Bahrain, Kuwait, Qatar, Saudi Arabia, and the United Arab Emirates; its sea boundary in the Gulf of Oman is with the sultanate of Oman and the United Arab Emirates. Iran also has a 740-kilometer coast along the Caspian Sea, whose waters it shares with the Republic of Azerbaijan, Kazakhstan, Russia, and Turkmenistan.

Topography

The topography of Iran consists of rugged mountains surrounding high interior basins. The main mountain chain is the Zagros Mountains, a series of parallel ridges interspersed with plains that bisect the country from northwest to southeast. Many peaks in the Zagros exceed 3,000 meters above sea level, and at least five peaks in the south-central region of the country are higher than 4,000 meters. As the Zagros chain continues into southeastern Iran, the average elevation declines dramatically, to less than 1,500 meters. A narrow but high range, the Alborz Mountains, rims the Caspian Sea littoral. Volcanic Mount Damavand (5,600 meters), located in the center of the Alborz, is the country's highest peak, and the highest mountain on the Eurasian landmass west of the Hindu Kush range (see fig. 5).

The center of Iran consists of several closed basins that collectively are referred to as the Central Plateau. The average elevation of this plateau is about 900 meters, but several of the mountains that tower over it exceed 3,000 meters. The eastern part of the plateau is covered by two deserts, the Dasht-e Kavir (Salt Desert) and the Dasht-e Lut (Desert of Emptiness). Except for some scattered oases, these deserts are uninhabited.

Iran has two notable expanses of lowlands: the Khuzestan Plain in the southwest and the Caspian Sea coastal plain in the north. The Khuzestan Plain is a flat, roughly triangular extension of the Mesopotamia Plain averaging about 160 kilometers in width. It extends about 120 kilometers inland, then meets abruptly with the first foothills of the Zagros. Much of the Khuzestan Plain is covered with marshes. The Caspian coastal plain is both longer and narrower. It extends about 640 kilometers along the Caspian shore, but its greatest width is less than 50 kilometers. South of Khuzestan, there are extensive stretches of the Persian Gulf and Gulf of Oman coasts where the Zagros Mountains meet the shore. There are fairly broad coastal lowlands to the east and west of the city of Bushehr and along the Strait of Hormuz, but annual precipitation in both regions is too low and unreliable to sustain the diverse agriculture that characterizes the Khuzestan Plain and the Caspian coastal plain.

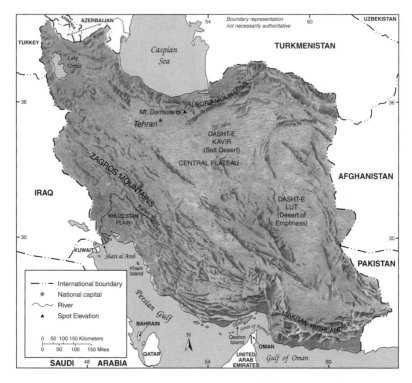

Figure 5. Physical Features

Iran has no major rivers. The only navigable river is the Karun, which shallow-draft boats can negotiate from Khorramshahr, where the Karun joins the Shatt al Arab (Arvand Rud in Persian; see Glossary), north to Ahvaz for about 180 kilometers. The Karun and several other permanent rivers and streams, such as the Dez and the Karkheh, originate in the southwestern Zagros Mountains. However, with the notable exception of the Karun and its main tributary the Dez, few of these watercourses reach the Persian Gulf. The Karkheh, for example, is a major feeder for the marshes that straddle the Iran–Iraq border. Farther north, most rivers drain into interior basins that form shallow salt lakes in the winter and spring but are dry beds in the summer months. Of the major permanent saltwater bodies, the largest is Lake Urmia (also cited as Orumiyeh or Urmiyeh) in the northwest, which is too briny to support fish or most other forms of aquatic life. Several connected salt lakes also exist along the Iran–Afghanistan border.

Climate

Iran has a variable climate. In the northwest and west, winters are cold, with heavy snowfall and subfreezing temperatures from December to February. Spring and fall are relatively mild, with rain in the early spring and late autumn. Summers are dry; days can be hot, but nights are mild to cool. In Tehran and the central part of the country, winters are less severe and summers warmer than in the west. Along the Caspian coastal plain, winters generally are mild, with rare frosts; summers are warm and humid. In the south, winters are mild and the summers very hot, with average daily temperatures in July exceeding 40° C along the Persian Gulf coast. On the Khuzestan Plain, summer heat is accompanied by high humidity.

In general, Iran's climate is arid; most of the relatively scant annual precipitation falls from October through April. In most of the country, yearly precipitation averages 250 millimeters or less. Some basins of the Central Plateau receive 100 millimeters or less. These dry conditions mean that agriculture in most areas of Iran must depend on irrigation.

Two regions enjoy relatively generous amounts of precipitation: the higher mountain valleys of the Zagros and the Caspian coastal plain. In both, precipitation averages at least 500 millimeters annually. In the western part of the Caspian coastal plain, rainfall exceeds 1,300 millimeters annually and is distributed relatively evenly throughout the year.

Environment

Iran's mountains are in an active earthquake zone, and several low-magnitude quakes that cause little destruction and few or no casualties occur annually. More powerful earthquakes, exceeding six on the open-ended Richter scale, also are frequent. A December 2003 earthquake centered under the city of Bam in the southeastern Zagros Mountains destroyed more than 12,000 homes and buildings and caused the deaths of 26,000 people. A 1990 earthquake in the western Alborz Mountains caused 40,000 deaths.

Various human activities have had adverse effects on the environment. Excessive use of fertilizers and pesticides in agriculture, for example, has contributed to soil degradation in many rural areas, while the drilling of deep wells has lowered water tables and caused some pastures to dry up. Industrialization and urbanization, ongoing since the 1960s, have caused pollution of the water even as they have introduced competing demands for this scarce resource. Although environmental nongovernmental organizations (NGOs) and some political leaders have been advocating water conservation policies since at least the early 1990s, an effective national water consumption plan has not been developed.

The Environmental Protection Organization (EPO), which is headed by a vice president and thus has de facto cabinet rank, is the main governmental body that monitors and works to control atmospheric pollution. Since the early 1990s, it has cited air pollution, especially in Tehran, as the country's major environmental problem. According to the EPO, 94 percent of all urban air pollution is attributable to auto vehicle emissions. Air pollution generally is most severe in winter because low-pressure air masses—composed of dirty air—remain suspended for several days over the high-altitude basins in which are located major cities such as Esfahan, Mashhad, Shiraz, Tabriz, and Tehran. The EPO issues health alerts whenever its professional monitors deem the measured level of toxic pollutants in the air sufficiently high to pose a hazard if inhaled by vulnerable populations, including all children under age 14. The city of Tehran annually closes all public schools several days at a time each winter in response to these EPO alerts.

The EPO also monitors water pollution from both household and industrial waste. In certain areas, the illegal dumping of toxic wastes into water sources has made the affected water unfit for consumption and even killed aquatic life. The EPO has been moderately effective in prompting municipalities and private enterprises along the densely populated Caspian coast to limit the dumping of wastes into streams that empty into the Caspian Sea, where pollution has become a threat to undersea spawning areas for many fish species and has fouled nesting sites of migratory birds and the habitat of the endangered Caspian seal. Other major environmental problems are deforestation and the overgrazing and desertification of agricultural land.

Population

According to preliminary data from the October–November 2006 decennial census, Iran's total population was 70,049,262. This figure represents a 16.6 percent increase over the total population of 60,055,488 enumerated in the previous national census conducted in October 1996 or an average of 1.66 percent per year. Iran's population growth rate has been declining steadily since 1986, when it was at a twentieth-century high of 3.2 percent per annum. Because of a very active birth-control program promoted by the Ministry of Health since 1988, the growth rate had declined to 1.1 percent in 2006. The fertility rate dropped from about 7.0 to 1.7 children born per woman between 1979 and 2007. In 2007 the birthrate was 16.6 per 1,000 population, and the death rate was 5.6 per 1,000 population. Also in 2007, an estimated 23.2 percent of the population was 14 years of age or younger, 5.4 percent was 65 and older, and 71.4 percent was 15 to 64. In 2006 those percentages were 26.1, 4.9, and 69.0, respectively (see fig. 6). Males constituted 50.9 percent of the population and females 49.1 percent in the 2006 census.

According to the 2006 census, Iran has an average population density of 42 persons per square kilometer. However, in the provinces of East Azerbaijan in the northwest, Gilan and Mazandaran along the Caspian coast, and Tehran, the population density is significantly greater. Much of eastern Iran is more sparsely populated, with some areas having fewer than 10 persons per square kilometer.

Also according to the 2006 census, 68.4 percent of the population was living in urban areas, defined as incorporated places with a minimum population of 5,000. Tehran, the capital and largest city, had a total population of 7,160,094 in 2006, while six other cities—Mashhad, Esfahan, Tabriz, Karaj, Shiraz, and Qom—had populations in excess of 1 million (see table 2, Appendix). As of 1996, an additional 48 cities each had a population of more than 100,000 (see table 3, Appendix). The most populous province is Tehran, with a population of 13,328,011 according to preliminary 2006 census data. The least populous province is Ilam, with 543,729 inhabitants in 2006.

Emigration

During and immediately following the Iranian Revolution of 1978–79, an estimated 200,000 to 300,000 Iranians voluntarily left the country to resettle abroad, primarily in the United Kingdom, France, Germany, and the United States. Most emigrants were from the wealthiest families, who collectively took with them an estimated US$30 billion. During the conflict between the government and armed opposition groups in the early 1980s, several thousand Iranians fled the country clandestinely and obtained refugee status in various European Union

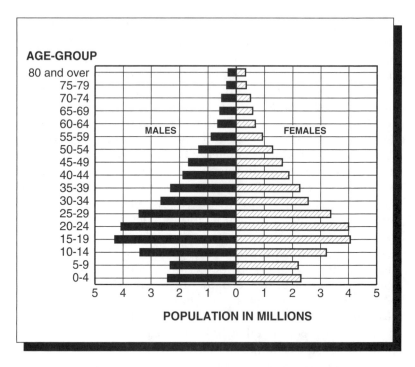

AGE-GROUP

Source: Based on information from U.S. Census Bureau, International Data Base, "IDB
Population Pyramids," www.census.gov/ipc/www/idbpyr.html.

Figure 6. Population Distribution by Age and Sex, 2006

(EU) countries, Australia, Canada, and the United States. Since the early 1990s, several hundred to several thousand Iranians, most with a college education, have emigrated annually. The largest community outside Iran lives in the United States, where 338,266 people claimed Iranian ancestry (i.e., were born in Iran or in the United States of Iran-born parents) in the 2000 census; half of this number resided in California. An estimated 300,000 more Iranians were living in Canada, the countries of the EU, and Turkey.

Refugees

During the 1980s, an estimated 2.5 million Afghans fled to Iran as refugees from the civil war between the Soviet-backed Afghan government and Afghan anti-Soviet militia groups known collectively as the mujahedin. In addition, 300,000 Iraqis, primarily Shia Muslims, were registered as refugees in Iran; two-thirds of these refugees were Iraqis who were descendants of Iranian clergy and pilgrims who had settled in Iraq but whom the government of Saddam Hussein forcibly expelled during 1979–80. In March 1991, an estimated 1.8 million Iraqis fled to Iran following the Iraqi government's suppression of uprisings among the Iraqi Shias (who were Arabs) and Kurds. The International Committee of the Red Cross and Red Crescent Societies began repatriating Afghan and Iraqi Kurdish refugees from Iran in 1992. Nonetheless, the 1996 census identified 1.4 million Afghans and 400,000 Iraqis, primarily Arab Shias, living in Iran. Since the late 1990s, many Afghans have resisted repatriation, migrating from refugee camps in eastern Iran to large cities to find work and avoid detection by the authorities. During 2003 and 2004, an estimated 250,000 Iraqi refugees returned independently to Iraq.

Languages and Peoples

Iran has a heterogeneous population speaking a variety of Indo-Iranian, Semitic, and Turkic languages (see fig. 7; table 4, Appendix). The largest language group consists of speakers of Indo-Iranian languages, who in 1996 made up more than 75 percent of the population. Speakers of Indo-Iranian languages include speakers of Persian, the official language of the country, and its various dialects; speakers of a set of related dialects, called Kirmanji, spoken by the Kurds of western Iran; speakers of Luri, the language of the Bakhtiaris and Lurs, who live in the central Zagros; and Baluchi (also seen as Balochi), the language of the semitribal people of the same name who live in southeastern Iran (see Baluchis, this ch.). Approximately 20 percent of the population speaks various dialects of Turkish. Speakers of Semitic languages include Arabs and Assyrians.

The Persian Language and People

The official language of Iran is Persian (the Persian term for which is Farsi). It is the language of government and public instruction and is the native tongue of at least 65 percent of the population. A large proportion of the other 35 percent speak Persian as a second language. Many different dialects of Persian are spoken in various parts of the Central Plateau, and people from each city usually can be identified by their speech.

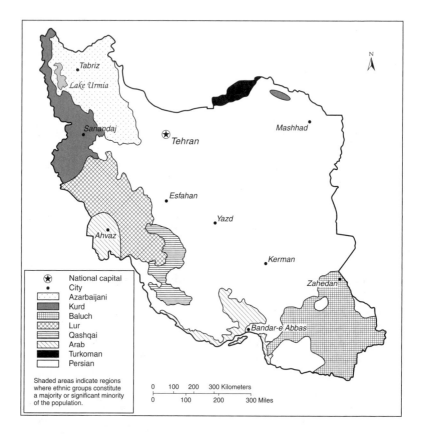

Figure 7. Major Ethnic Groups

Some dialects, such as Gilaki and Mazandarani, spoken along the Caspian coastal plain, are distinct enough to be virtually unintelligible to a Persian speaker from Tehran or Shiraz.

As part of the Indo-European family of languages, Persian is distantly related to Latin, Greek, the Slavic and Teutonic languages, and English. Persian is an ancient language that has developed through three historical stages: Old Persian, ca. 500 B.C. to ca. A.D. 250, was written in cuneiform and used exclusively for royal proclamations and announcements; Middle Persian, or Pahlavi, was in use from ca. 250 to ca. 900 and written in an ideographic script; modern Persian is written in a modified Arabic script. Modern Persian has a well-established literary tradition, especially in poetry, from as early as the thirteenth century. Persian speakers regard their language as exceptionally beautiful, and they take great pleasure in listening to the verses of medieval poets such as Ferdowsi, Hafez, Rumi, and Sadi, as well as to contemporary poetry. The language is a living link with the past, and historically it has been important in binding the nation together.

The Persians are the largest ethnic group in Iran. They predominate in the major urban areas of central and eastern Iran—in the cities of Tehran, Esfahan, Mashhad, Shiraz, Arak, Kashan, Kerman, Qom, and Yazd; in the villages of the Central Plateau; and along the Caspian coast. Persians generally take great pride in their art and music, both of which have uninterrupted historical roots almost as old as Persian literature. The vast majority of Persians are Shia Muslims (see Shia Islam in Iran, this ch.). Since at least the beginning of the nineteenth century, Persians have dominated the higher ranks of the Shia clergy and have provided important clerical revolutionary leaders such as Ayatollah Sayyid Ruhollah Musavi Khomeini and former presidents Ali Akbar Hashemi Rafsanjani and Mohammad Khatami. Fewer than 3 percent of Persians adhere to other faiths. These include a community of Sunni (see Glossary) Muslim Persians in the Lar region of Fars Province, Baha'is, Jews, and members of the pre-Islamic Zoroastrian faith (see Sunni Muslims; Non-Muslim Minorities, this ch.).

Other Indo-Iranian–Speaking Groups

Kurds

In the early 2000s, an estimated 4.3 to 4.6 million Kurds lived in Iran, accounting for about 7 percent of the total population. They are the third-largest ethnic group in the country, after the Persians and Azerbaijanis (see Turkic-speaking Groups, this ch.). The Kurds are concentrated in the Zagros Mountains along the western frontiers with Turkey and Iraq, adjacent to the Kurdish populations of both those countries. The Kurdish area of Iran includes the southern counties of West Azarbaijan Province and all of Kurdistan and Kermanshah provinces. There are also Kurdish villages in Hamadan, Ilam, and Luristan provinces and a predominantly Kurdish area in North Khorasan Province.

Historically, Iran's Kurdish population has been both rural and urban. As late as the 1930s, some 80 percent of the Kurds lived in rural settings, and at one time as many as half of rural Kurds were nomads. Since the late 1950s, however, the Kurdish population has been increasingly urbanized. According to the 1996 census, more than 50 percent of the population in the Kurdish provinces of Kermanshah and Kurdistan was urban and less than 2 percent was nomadic. Kermanshah (formerly Bakhtaran) historically has been the largest Kurdish city.

During the twentieth century, the gradual urbanization and education of Kurdish society aroused ethnic consciousness and a feeling of community with Kurds in other countries. The neighboring Iraqi Kurds' struggle for autonomy, which began in 1960, influenced the formation of two clandestine political parties, the Kurdistan Democratic Party (KDP) and the Komela. After supporting the Iranian Revolution of 1978–79, these parties, which, like the population of Kurdistan itself, were predominantly Sunni, undertook four years of ultimately unsuccessful regional guerrilla activity against the Islamic Republic in an effort to gain the autonomy that they had expected would result from the Revolution. The campaign found little support in the regions around Bakhtaran (now Kermanshah), where non-Sunni Kurds were integrated economically and politically with the rest of Iran. Since the guerrillas' suppression in 1984, the Sunni Kurd population has complained of discrimination by the central government in the distribution of development funds, the status of the Kurdish language, and access to employment and university admission.

Although Sunni Islam is the predominant religion among the Kurds, significant numbers practice Shia Islam and a heterodox version of Islam, Ahl-e Haqq (see Shia Islam in Iran, this ch.). Iran's Kurds also include small communities of Yazidis, another heterodox Islamic group, and Jews.

The Kurds' closely related dialects, known collectively in Iran as Kirmanji, are divided into northern and southern groups. All contain numerous Persian loanwords. Persians have used the proximity of Kurdish to Persian as an argument against the use of Kurdish in schools in majority-Kurdish areas. Because Persian has been the medium of instruction in schools for more than 50 years, educated Kurds tend to be bilingual.

Lurs

The Lurs are an ethnic group residing in the central and southern Zagros. They speak Luri, a language closely related to Persian and Kurdish. Like the Persians, the Lurs are predominantly Shia Muslims, although a minority adhere to Ahl-e Haqq. Luri is not a written language, but it has a rich oral culture of music and poetry. Since the 1980s, the lack of a literary tradition has contributed to a trend for Lur children, especially in urban areas, of using the Persian that they learn in school for everyday speech. A majority of the estimated 3.5 million Lurs live in Luristan Province, which in the early twentieth century was occupied by 60 distinct tribal groups. Tribal identities have weakened under the impact of steady urbanization. By 1996, more than 60 percent of the province's population lived in cities. Khorramabad and Borujerd are Luristan's main urban centers.

Historically, the Bakhtiari were the most famous and powerful of the Lur tribes. By the 1920s, their long and arduous nomadic treks had become the subject of Western travel lore and even cinema. The Bakhtiari tribal leaders, or *khans,* became involved in national politics and were considered part of the prerevolutionary elite. Detribalized Bakhtiaris, especially those who settled in urban areas, tend to become assimilated into Persian culture. Although small numbers of Bakhtiaris continue to practice nomadic livestock raising, by 2000 the overwhelming majority lived in towns and villages. The Bakhtiari Lurs have their own province, Chahar Mahall va Bakhtiari, southeast of Luristan.

Other Lurs live south of the Bakhtiari in Kohgiluyeh va Buyer Ahmadi Province and in Ilam Province. Once considered among the fiercest of Iranian tribes, the Lurs, like other nomadic tribes, were forcibly settled in the 1930s. After the Revolution, the Islamic Republic designated Ilam Province and Kohgiluyeh va Buyer Ahmadi Province especially "deprived," or underdeveloped, and targeted them for special infrastructure development projects.

Baluchis

The Baluchis, who live predominantly in Sistan va Baluchistan Province, numbered approximately 800,000 in Iran in the early 2000s. They are part of a larger group that forms the majority of the population of Balochistan Province in Pakistan and of adjacent areas in southwestern Afghanistan. In Iran the Baluchis are concentrated in the Makran Highlands, an area that stretches eastward along the Gulf of Oman to the Pakistan border and includes some of the most barren landscape in Iran. The Baluchis speak an Indo-Iranian language distantly related to Persian and more closely related to Pashtu (Pashto). Baluchi is solely an oral language in Iran. The majority of Baluchis are Sunni rather than Shia Muslims. This religious difference has been a persistent source of tension, especially in the provincial capital, Zahedan.

About 10 percent of the Baluchis are seminomadic or nomadic; the remainder are settled farmers and town dwellers. Tribal organization remains intact among rural Baluchis. The Baluchis have been one of the most difficult tribal groups for the central government to control, in large part because of poor communications between Tehran and the province of Sistan va Baluchistan. Most of the principal Baluchi tribes live along the borders with Pakistan and Afghanistan.

With the exception of the city of Zahedan, neither the monarchy nor the Islamic republic has invested significant funds in local development projects. As a result, since the 1980s a major source of income for residents has been smuggling goods, especially illegal narcotics, into Iran from Afghanistan and Pakistan. In highland areas, limited agriculture is practiced where groundwater is sufficient for irrigation. In the late 1990s, a prolonged drought severely affected the entire province, prompting thousands of Baluchis to abandon their villages and resettle in Zahedan and elsewhere in Iran.

Other Indo-Iranian Groups

Scattered throughout central, southern, and eastern Iran are small groups, some nomadic or seminomadic, speaking many different Indo-Iranian languages. Some tribes in the provinces of North Khorasan, Razavi Khorasan, and South Khorasan are related to groups in neighboring Afghanistan and Turkmenistan. Also in those three provinces are an estimated 30,000 Tajiks, settled farmers related to the Tajiks of Afghanistan and Tajikistan. Several smaller Indo-Iranian–speaking minorities exist in tribally organized settled groups: the Hazarah, Barbai, Teimuri, Jamshidi, and Afghani in the provinces of North, Razavi, and South Khorasan; the Qadikolahi and Pahlavi in Mazandaran Province; and the Agajani in the Talesh region of Gilan Province.

Turkic-Speaking Groups

Turkic speakers constitute about 20 percent of Iran's total population. They are concentrated in northwestern Iran, where they form the overwhelming majority of the population of Ardabil and East Azarbaijan provinces and a majority in West Azarbaijan and Zanjan provinces. They also constitute a significant minority in the provinces of Fars, Gilan, Hamadan, Mazandaran, North Khorasan, Qazvin, Razavi Khorasan, South Korasan, and Tehran. Except for the Azerbaijanis, most Turkic-speaking groups are tribally organized. Some Turkic-speaking tribes continue to lead a nomadic or seminomadic life. Educated Turkic speakers in the large cities also speak Persian.

The Turkic languages belong to the Ural-Altaic family, which includes many languages of Central Asia and western China, as well as Turkish, Hungarian, and Finnish. The various Turkic languages spoken in Iran tend to be mutually intelligible. Of these, only Azerbaijani is written to any extent. In Iran it is written in the Arabic script, in contrast to the practice in the Republic of Azerbaijan, where a modified Latin alphabet is used.

Azerbaijanis

The Azerbaijanis account for 90 percent of all Turkic speakers in Iran. Most Azerbaijanis are concentrated in the northwestern corner of the country, where they form the majority population in an area between the Caspian Sea and Lake Urmia and the segment of the northern border formed by the Aras River south to the latitude of Tehran. Their language, Azerbaijani (also called Azeri or Turkish), is structurally similar to the Turkish spoken in Turkey. More than 65 percent of all Azerbaijanis live in urban areas. Major Azerbaijani cities include Tabriz, Ardabil, Khoi, Maragheh, and Zanjan. In addition, about 40 percent of the population of the region of Urmia in West Azarbaijan Province is Azerbaijani, as is one-third of Tehran's population. There are sizable Azerbaijani minorities in the major cities of northwestern Iran. The lifestyles of urban Azerbaijanis do not differ from those of Persians, and there is considerable intermarriage within the upper and middle classes in cities with mixed populations. Similarly, customs among Azerbaijani villagers do not appear to differ markedly from those of Persian villagers. The majority of Azerbaijanis, like the majority of Persians, are Shia Muslims, although some Azerbaijanis are Ahl-e Haqq Muslims or non-Muslim Baha'is.

Qashqais

The Qashqais are the second-largest Turkic-speaking group in Iran. Numbering about 600,000, they are a confederation of several Turkic-speaking tribes in Fars Province in south-central

Iran. Historically, the Qashqais were pastoral nomads who moved between summer pastures in the higher elevations of the Zagros Mountains north of Shiraz and winter pastures at low elevations south of Shiraz. Most Qashqais are Shia Muslims.

The Qashqai confederation emerged in the eighteenth century, and during the nineteenth century it became one of the best-organized and most powerful tribal groups in Iran. Reza Shah Pahlavi (r. 1925–41) forcibly settled the Qashqais in the early 1930s, but, like the Bakhtiaris and other forcibly settled tribes, they returned to nomadic life upon Reza Shah's exile in 1941. However, the reduction in numbers and disorganization they had suffered after their settlement kept the Qashqais from regaining their previous strength and independence. Since the mid-1960s, Qashqais have been settling in villages and towns. According to some estimates, up to 75 percent of all Qashqais had settled by the early 2000s. Both Qashqai and non-Qashqai Turkic speakers in Fars Province recognize a common ethnic identity in relation to non-Turks. All the Turkic-speaking groups of the region speak mutually intelligible dialects that are closely related to Azerbaijani.

Other Turkic-Speaking Groups

Many small Turkic-speaking groups are scattered throughout Iran, mainly in the northern tier of provinces. The largest of these are the Turkmens, divided into several tribes, some of which are sections of larger tribes living across the border in Turkmenistan. The Turkmens live to the northeast of the Caspian Sea, in a region of Golestan Province known as the Turkmen Sahra. Largely pastoral nomads before the 1930s, the Turkmens subsequently settled in permanent villages and engaged in agriculture, especially cotton cultivation. Since the 1980s, they have been migrating to regional urban centers. In 1996, of an estimated 500,000 Turkmens in Iran, about 20 percent lived in the city of Gonbad-e Kavus, while another 20 percent lived in other towns and the ethnically mixed provincial capital, Gorgan.

In the northeastern part of Ardabil Province live some 50 tribes collectively called the Ilsavan (formerly known as the Shahsavan). The Ilsavan, whose population in Iran is estimated at 75,000 to 100,000, are largely pastoral nomads who spend summer on the high slopes of Mount Sabalan and winter in the lowland Dasht-e Moghan, adjacent to the Aras River, which forms the frontier between Iran and the Republic of Azer-

A nomadic Qashqai family moving to new grazing ground
Courtesy United Nations (S. Jackson)

baijan. The Afshars, of approximately equal numbers as the Ilsavan, are scattered throughout Iran. A seminomadic people who speak a dialect akin to Azerbaijani, the Afshars are found along the shores of Lake Urmia, around the city of Zanjan, along the borders of Kurdistan, south of the city of Kerman, and in North, Razavi, and South Khorasan provinces. These separated groups are estimated to total 100,000, but they do not recognize a common identity or have any political unity. Nevertheless, they all refer to themselves as Afshars and differentiate themselves from other groups, both Turkic and non-Turkic, that surround them. Among several other very small Turkic-speaking groups, the Qajars are the most notable. The Qajars, who live in rural areas of Mazandaran Province, are the tribe of the royal family that Reza Shah dethroned in 1925.

Semitic Groups

Arabic and Assyrian are the two Semitic languages spoken in Iran. The Arabic dialects are spoken in Khuzestan Province and along the Persian Gulf coast. They are modern variants of the older Arabic that formed the base of the classical literary language and all the colloquial languages of the Arabic-speaking world. There is no linguistic relationship between Arabic and Persian, although Persian vocabulary has many loanwords

99

from Arabic. Arabic also continues to be the language of prayer of all Muslims in Iran. Children in school learn to read the Quran in Arabic. Persian- and Turkic-speaking Iranians who have commercial interests in the Persian Gulf area often learn Arabic for business purposes.

In 1996 an estimated 1.0 to 1.3 million Arabs lived in Iran. A majority lived in Khuzestan Province, where they constituted a significant ethnic minority. Most other Arabs lived along the Persian Gulf coast between Bushehr and Bandar-e Abbas, although there also were small scattered tribal groups living in central and eastern Iran. About 50 percent of Arabs are urban dwellers, concentrated in such cities as Abadan, Ahvaz, Bandar-e Abbas, Bushehr, and Khorramshahr. The majority of urban Arab adult males are unskilled workers, especially in the oil industry. Arabs also work in commerce and services, and a small group of Arab professionals has been emerging since the 1980s. Some urban Arabs and most rural Arabs are tribally organized. The rural Arabs of Khuzestan tend to be farmers and fishermen. Many Arabs who live along the Persian Gulf coast derive family incomes from fishing or from operating dhows (small boats) involved in the lucrative trade between Iran and the Arab states of the Persian Gulf. There are some Arab pastoral tribes.

Both the urban and rural Arabs of Khuzestan are intermingled with the Persians, Turks, and Lurs who also live in the province and collectively outnumber the Arabs. The Khuzestan Arabs are Shia Muslims, and this common religion facilitates intermarriage between Arabs and other Iranians. Nevertheless, the Arabs tend to regard themselves as separate from non-Arabs and usually are so regarded by other Iranians. Both before and after the Revolution, the government of neighboring Iraq claimed that the Khuzestan Arabs suffered discrimination and asserted its readiness to assist their "liberation" from Tehran. When Iraq invaded Iran in 1980, however, an anticipated uprising of the Arab population did not occur; most local Arabs fled the area together with the non-Arab population. The Arabs in the area stretching from Bushehr to Bandar-e Abbas are predominantly Sunni Muslims who differentiate themselves by religion from the Arabs in Khuzestan as well as from most non-Arab Iranians.

The other Semitic people of Iran are the Assyrians, a Christian group that speaks modern dialects of Assyrian, an Aramaic language that evolved from Old Syriac. Language and religion provide a strong cohesive force and give the Assyrians a sense of identity with their coreligionists in Iraq, in other parts of the Middle East, and in the United States. Most Assyrians belong to the Assyrian Church of the East (sometimes referred to as the Nestorian Church); a smaller group of Roman Catholic Assyrians generally are referred to as Chaldeans (see Non-Muslim Minorities, this ch.).

The 1996 census identified about 32,000 Assyrians in Iran. More than 50 percent of Assyrians live in Tehran, which has been a magnet for this minority since the early 1950s. However, more than 15,000 Assyrians still live in and around Orumiyeh, which has been the traditional home of Assyrians in Iran for centuries. Since 1979, many Assyrians have emigrated, resettling primarily in the United States. As a result of this migration, the Assyrian population in Iran has not increased since the Revolution.

Armenians

The Armenians, a non-Muslim minority that traditionally has lived in northwestern Iran, speak an Indo-European language that is distantly related to Persian. Large numbers of Armenians have emigrated since the Revolution; in 2000 the Armenian population was estimated at 300,000, about 15 percent less than in 1979. Iran's Armenians are predominantly urban dwellers. An estimated 65 percent of them live in Tehran, which since the early 1970s has been the primary Armenian cultural center in Iran. Sizable Armenian communities also live in Esfahan, Tabriz, and Orumiyeh. Armenians in Iran tend to be relatively well educated, maintain their own schools, and support Armenian-language newspapers.

Most Armenians are Gregorian Christians, although some are Roman Catholic and Protestant as a result of European and American missionary work in Iran during the nineteenth and early twentieth centuries. Although Iranian Armenians welcomed the independence of Armenia in 1991, few of them have immigrated there; virtually all Armenian emigration from Iran has been to the United States.

Structure of Society

Iranians have a very strong sense of class structure. In the past, they referred to their society as being divided into three tiers, or *tabagheh*: the first, corresponding to the upper classes;

the second, to the middle classes; and the third, to the lower classes. Under the influence of revolutionary ideology, society is now perceived as being divided into the wealthy, a term generally having negative connotations; the middle class; and the *mostazafin*. In reality, Iranian society always has been more complex than the three-tier division implies because each of the three broad classes is subdivided into several social groups. These divisions have existed in both urban and rural areas.

Urban Society

Historically, towns in Iran have been administrative, commercial, and manufacturing centers. The traditional political elite consisted of the shah and his family as well as non-royal families, whose wealth was derived from land and/or trade and from which were recruited the official representatives of the central government. In larger cities, these families traced their power and influence back several generations. In the largest cities, the families of Shia clergy also were influential. The middle stratum included merchants and owners of artisan workshops. The lowest class of urban society included artisans, laborers, and providers of personal services such as barbers, bath attendants, shoemakers, tailors, and servants. Most artisans were organized into trade associations or guilds and worked in the covered bazaars, historically the heart of Iranian towns. Merchants also had their shops in the bazaars, which in the largest cities also contained warehouses, restaurants, baths, mosques, schools, and gardens.

The modernization policies of the Pahlavi shahs both preserved and transformed urban society. The extension of central government authority throughout the country fostered the expansion of administrative apparatuses in all major provincial centers. Parts of the traditional bazaars were demolished to create new streets lined with European-style stores. By the 1970s, modern factories had displaced numerous artisan workshops in the bazaars, and merchants were encouraged to locate retail shops along the new streets rather than in the bazaars. During the last years of the Pahlavi dynasty, the political elite described the bazaars as symbols of backwardness and advanced plans to replace them with modern shopping malls.

One consequence of the Revolution was the revitalization of the traditional bazaar, especially in larger cities. Another consequence was the intensive rural-to-urban migration of the 1980s. This population movement led to the development of sprawl-

Rooftops in Yazd, central Iran
Courtesy Nader Davoodi

ing cities with new suburban areas, or *shahraks* (literally, little towns), where European-style shopping streets and even American-style enclosed shopping malls were built rather than traditional bazaars. The growth of cities proceeded in tandem with the spread of education; the expansion of medical services, electrification, water delivery systems, communications, and highways; and the emergence of many new urban occupations in manufacturing and services. This job diversity has contributed to a greater differentiation of social groups.

The Revolution swept aside the old political elite—the shah, his family, and the official representatives of the monarchy in the capital and provincial centers. Although members of the old political elite were not physically removed, they were stripped of their power. The new elite consisted of the higher ranks of the Shia clergy and the nonclerical political leaders who had organized antigovernment demonstrations and work strikes over the course of several months. The most important administrative, military, and security positions were filled by these lay politicians who supported the rule of the clergy. Most members of the lay political elite had their origins in the pre-revolutionary middle class, especially the bazaar families, but a significant minority were of rural origin.

103

Social Class in Contemporary Iran

In the postrevolutionary era, access to political power, an important basis for measuring influence and elite status in pre-revolutionary Iran, has continued to be important for ascribing status, even though the composition of the political elite has changed. For 10 years after 1979, gaining entry to the political elite at the national or provincial level depended on having revolutionary credentials, that is, being able to provide evidence of having participated in the demonstrations and other revolutionary activities during 1978–79, and having a reputation for being a good Muslim, that is, attending public prayers and observing Islamic codes of conduct in one's private life. Revolutionary credentials became less significant for the generation that matured after the early 1990s. Education, especially a college degree, became an informal substitute for revolutionary credentials.

The Upper Class

The postrevolutionary upper class consisted of some of the same social groups as the old elite, such as large landowners, industrialists, financiers, and large-scale merchants. These groups had remained in Iran after 1979 and had retained much of their wealth. For the most part, however, such persons did not occupy positions of political influence, although they maintained various ties to politically influential people. Those with political influence comprised senior clergy, high-ranking bureaucrats, executive officers of public and private corporations and charitable foundations, and wealthy entrepreneurs; none had been part of the prerevolutionary economic and social elite. Although a reputation for piety and loyalty to the ideals of the Revolution initially was a more important attribute than family or wealth for participation in the postrevolutionary political elite, those who attained politically powerful positions received generous salaries that elevated them to the top income brackets and opened access to multiple legitimate opportunities for acquiring more wealth. The children of the new elite generally have been encouraged to get college educations, and postgraduate degrees from foreign universities have become status symbols since the mid-1990s. These social trends have gradually but informally altered the criteria for recruitment into the political elite: Possessing a university degree and having ties to a prominent religious or revolutionary family have become advantageous in the competition for politically influential positions.

The Middle Class

After the Revolution, the composition of the middle class did not change significantly, but its size doubled from about 15 percent of the population in 1979 to more than 32 percent in 2000. Several prerevolutionary social groups still were identifiable, including entrepreneurs, bazaar merchants, physicians, engineers, university teachers, managers of private and public concerns, civil servants, teachers, medium-scale landowners, junior military officers, and the middle ranks of the Shia clergy. New groups also emerged, including technicians in specialized fields such as communications, computers, electronics, and medical services; owners of small-scale factories employing fewer than 50 workers; owners of construction firms and transport companies; and professional staff of broadcast and print media. Merchants, especially those with ties to bazaar-based organizations even though their stores were physically located outside the traditional covered bazaars, gained access to political power that they had lacked before the Revolution.

The prerevolutionary cultural divide between those middle-class individuals who had a secular outlook and those who valued a role for religion in both public and private life did not disappear. Since 1979, however, the political relationship between these two contrasting views has reversed. Whereas under the monarchy the state tried to restrict religion to the private sphere, under the Islamic Republic the state consciously has promoted religion in public life. Secularly oriented Iranians have tended to resent this dominant role of the religious outlook in politics and society, especially its manifestations in numerous laws and regulations that they perceive as interfering with their personal lives. Whereas the secular-religious divide cuts across all occupational groups, in general those who promote religious values and the public observance of prayers and religious rituals tend to be more heavily concentrated in the bazaar, security forces, and managerial positions in the bureaucracies than in other lines of work and other professions.

The Working Class

An urban industrial working class separate from the traditional artisan class of the towns has been in the process of formation since the early twentieth century. The industrialization programs of the Pahlavi shahs provided the impetus for the expansion of this class. By the early 1970s, a distinct working-class identity, *kargar,* had emerged, although those who applied this term to themselves did not constitute a unified group. Rather, the working class was segmented by economic sectors: the oil industry, manufacturing, construction, and transportation; also, many members of the working class were employed as mechanics. The largest component, factory workers, numbered about 2.5 million on the eve of the Revolution, double the number in 1965, accounting for 25 percent of Iran's total labor force (see The Distribution of Employment, ch. 3).

Since 1979, the urban working class has continued to expand; by the early 2000s, it constituted more than 45 percent of the employed labor force. As was the situation before the Revolution, however, the workers within any one occupation did not share a common identity but rather were divided according to their perceived skills. For example, skilled construction workers, such as carpenters, electricians, and plumbers, earned significantly higher wages than the more numerous unskilled workers and tended to look down on them. Similar status differences were common among workers in the oil industry and manufacturing. An estimated 7 percent of all workers were Afghan refugees in the early 2000s. These workers were concentrated in unskilled jobs, especially in construction. Because most Afghan workers did not have work permits after 1992 and thus worked illegally, employers could pay them less than the daily minimum wage rates and not provide them with benefits required for Iranian workers.

Under both the monarchy and the republic, the government has strictly controlled union activity. After the Revolution, the Ministry of Labor established the Workers' House to sponsor Islamic unions in large manufacturing concerns. These unions discourage strikes through a combination of cooptation of workers through periodic raises and bonuses and cooperation with authorities to identify and discipline workers who exhibit tendencies toward independence. The Islamic unions generally have been effective in preventing major strikes by workers; a long history of factionalism among different working-class occupational groups and between skilled and unskilled workers within individual industries has contributed to this relative success. Nevertheless, since the early 1990s scattered strikes have defied union control. In some instances, the strikes have been

A provincial coffeeshop
Courtesy Nader Davoodi

resolved peacefully through negotiations, while in other cases
they have been repressed violently by security forces.

The Lower Class

The working class is part of the overall urban lower class, or
mostazafin, a social stratum that includes all families whose
household incomes place them marginally above, at, or below
the officially defined poverty line. In cities with populations
greater than 250,000, the lower class makes up an average of 40
to 50 percent of the total population; the lower-class proportion generally is less in smaller cities (50,000 to 250,000 population) and towns.

The lower class can be divided into two groups: the marginally poor, who receive regular incomes on a weekly or monthly
basis; and the very poor, whose incomes vary from month to
month and who thus experience difficulty in paying for food,
housing, and utilities. Recipients of regular incomes include
pensioners, industrial and construction workers, and people
employed in the diverse services sector, such as attendants in
barbershops, beauty salons, and public bathhouses, bakery
workers, sales clerks, domestic servants, gardeners, garbage and
trash collectors, painters and plasterers (of homes), porters,
street cleaners, peddlers, street vendors, office cleaners, and

laundry workers. These job categories, as well as others, also include at least 1 million workers who are employed only occasionally or seasonally, primarily as a result of the shortage of full-time positions in an economy that has had an official unemployment rate ranging between 10 and 15 percent of the labor force since the early 1990s. Although many government agencies and private charities provide assistance to the poor, a social stigma is associated with accepting such aid, especially among adult men, whom others judge according to their ability to support a family. Among some marginally poor people in the largest cites, especially families with female heads of household, there has been an increasing tendency since the mid-1990s to rely on begging to supplement income, A few poor neighborhoods in the largest cities, such as Khakh-e sefid in southeasten Tehran Province, have acquired negative reputations because gangs have established safe houses there for illegal activities such as prostitution, gambling, and drug trafficking.

Urban Migration

A main characteristic of the burgeoning urban lower class is its peasant origins. The rapid expansion of this class since the 1960s has been the result of migration from villages to cities. By the early 1970s, urban services no longer could keep pace with the population growth, and slum neighborhoods developed in Tehran and other large cities. Immediately after the Revolution, the government initiated two programs aimed at improving conditions in urban slums and villages. In the latter case, the programs also had the objective of stanching rural-to-urban migration. New *shahraks* replaced slum neighborhoods and offered low-income families affordable housing with electricity, piped water, and sewerage connections. Schools, libraries, cultural centers, health clinics, and sports facilities were integral parts of the new *shahraks*. These new neighborhoods could not eliminate poverty, but they improved the overall quality of life for most low-income residents in urban areas. The same also has been true for the villages, although the major improvement in the quality of rural life did not halt rural-to-urban migration, which continued at an even higher rate between 1980 and 1996 than in the prerevolutionary years.

Rural Society

At the time of the Revolution, Iran had 70,000 villages. Social organization in these villages was less stratified than in urban areas, but a hierarchy of political and social relationships and patterns of interaction could be identified. At the top of the village social structure was the largest landowner or owners. In the middle stratum were peasants who owned medium-sized farms. In the larger villages, the middle stratum also included local merchants and artisans. The lowest level, which predominated in most villages, consisted of landless villagers and peasants who owned subsistence plots. Traditionally, the *kadkhoda* (see Glossary)—not to be confused with the head of the smallest tribal unit, a clan—was responsible for administering village affairs and for representing the village in relations with governmental authorities and other outsiders.

The land reform and various rural development programs undertaken prior to the Revolution did not help most villagers. Economic conditions for most village families stagnated or deteriorated at the same time as manufacturing and construction were experiencing an economic boom in urban areas. Consequently, there was a significant increase in rural-to-urban migration. Between the 1966 and the 1976 censuses, a period when the population of the country as a whole was growing at the rate of 2.7 percent per year, most villages actually lost population, and the rural population's overall growth rate was barely 0.5 percent annually. This migration was primarily of young villagers attracted to cities by the prospect of seasonal or permanent work opportunities. By the late 1970s, this migration had depleted the labor force of many villages. This was an important factor in the relative decline in production of such basic food crops as cereals because many farming families were forced to sow their agricultural land with less labor-intensive crops.

The problems of rural stagnation and agricultural decline had surfaced in public debate by the eve of the Revolution. During the immediate turmoil surrounding the fall of the monarchy, peasants in many villages took advantage of the unsettled conditions to expropriate the property of large landowners whom they accused of being un-Islamic. These actions forced the new republican government to tackle the land problem. This issue was hotly contested between officials who saw peasant expropriations as a solution to inequitable land distribution and others who opposed such expropriations on the ground that Islamic law protects private property. In the end, no national policy was formulated; local courts adjudicated the land disputes on a case-by-case basis, and less than 10 percent of cultivated land in Iran actually was transferred from large to smaller owners.

Unlike land redistribution, rural development was widely considered a high priority among the postrevolutionary political elite. A new organization for rebuilding villages, the Crusade for Reconstruction (Jihad-e Sazandegi, or Jihad), was created in 1979. At first it consisted of high-school-educated youth, largely from villages, who initiated such village improvement projects as providing electrification and piped water, building feeder roads, constructing mosques and bathhouses, and repairing irrigation networks. The operational approach was to involve the villagers in the projects, including their planning, construction, and even partial financing, although overall direction was from Tehran via the provincial Jihad offices. As a result of these activities, more than 90 percent of villages had electricity and piped water by 2000, as well as access to rural schools, health clinics, and improved secondary roads that connected to highways. This rural infrastructure significantly improved the overall quality of life in villages. However, because the prerevolutionary pattern of landownership was not altered—about 75 percent of farmers continued to cultivate the equivalent of subsistence plots—the majority of rural households remained poor.

Nomadic Society

The long-standing decline in the number of tribally organized, pastoral nomads continued after the Revolution. According to the 1996 census, about 1.2 million persons in 180,000 households continued to practice pastoral nomadism on a year-round basis. This represented a decrease of 40 percent from the mid-1960s, when 400,000 families (about 2 million persons) engaged in pastoral nomadism. The nomadic population practices a form of seasonal migration known as transhumance: one migration in the spring to upland summer pastures and a fall migration to lowland winter pastures. Each tribe claims the use of fixed territories for its pastures and the right to use a specified migration route between these areas, which can be separated by as much as 300 kilometers. In the past, each migration could take as much as two months, but since the early 1990s an increasing reliance on pickup trucks has shortened this process to a few days.

The movements of the tribes appear to be an adaptation to the ecology of the Zagros Mountains. In summer, when the low

Residential neighborhood in the village of Masooleh, northern Iran
Dates drying in the village of Abyaneh, central Iran
Courtesy Nader Davoodi

valleys are parched, the tribes are at the verdant higher elevations. When night frosts begin to limit pasture growth in the higher valleys, the tribes migrate to low-lying pastures that remain green throughout the winter because of the seasonal rainfall. The nomadic tribes keep large herds of sheep and goats, animals that traditionally have provided the main source of red meat for Iranians. During migrations the tribes trade their live animals, wool, hair, hides, dairy products, and various knotted and woven textiles with villagers and townspeople for manufactured and agricultural goods. This economic interdependence between the nomadic and settled populations of Iran has been an important characteristic of society for several centuries.

During the Qajar dynasty (1795–1925), when the central government was especially weak, the nomadic tribes formed tribal confederations and acquired a great deal of power and influence. In many areas, these confederations were virtually autonomous, negotiating with the local and national governments for extensive land rights. Reza Shah moved against the tribes with the new national army that he created. His tribal

111

policy had two objectives: to break the authority and power of the great tribal confederation leaders, whom he perceived as a threat to his goal of centralizing power, and to gain the allegiance of urban political leaders, who had historically resented the power of the tribes. In addition to military maneuvers against the tribes, Reza Shah used economic and administrative techniques such as confiscating tribal properties and holding chiefs' sons as hostages. Eventually, many nomads were subdued and placed under army control. Some were given government-built houses and forced to lead a sedentary life. Mohammad Reza Shah Pahlavi (r. 1941–79) continued the policy of weakening the political power of the nomadic tribes, but efforts to coerce them into settling were abandoned. Several tribal leaders were exiled, and the military was given greater authority to regulate tribal migrations. Tribal pastures were nationalized during the 1960s as a means of permitting the government to control access to grazing. In addition, various educational, health, and vocational training programs were implemented to encourage the tribes to settle voluntarily.

Following the Revolution, several former tribal leaders attempted to revitalize their tribes as major political and economic forces. But many factors worked against this effort, including the hostile attitude of the central government, the decline in size of the nomadic population as a result of the settlement of large numbers of tribal people in the 1960s and 1970s, and, as a consequence of settlement, a change in attitudes toward nomadic life, especially among tribal youth raised in villages and towns. By the mid-1980s, the nomadic tribes were no longer a political force in Iranian society. The central government had demonstrated its ability to control the migration routes, and the leadership of the tribes effectively was dispersed among a new generation of nonelite tribesmen who did not share the views of the old elite.

The Family

For most Iranians, the reciprocal obligations and privileges that define relations among kinfolk—from the parent-child bond to more distant connections—are more important than those associated with any other kind of social alignment. Economic, political, and other forms of institutional activity have been affected significantly by family ties. This is true not only for the nuclear family of parents and offspring but also for the aggregate kinfolk, near and distant, who together represent the extended family.

Historically, an influential family was one whose members were distributed strategically throughout the most vital sectors of society, with each person prepared to support the others in order to ensure overall family prestige and status. Since the Revolution, this has meant that each of the elite families of Tehran and the major provincial centers includes a cadre of clergy, bureaucrats, and the Islamic Revolutionary Guard Corps or Revolutionary Guards (Pasdaran; in full, Pasdaran-e Enghelab-e Islami; see The Islamic Revolutionary Guard Corps (IRGC), ch. 5). Successful members are expected to help less successful ones get their start. Iranians view this inherent nepotism as a positive value, not as a form of corruption. Business operations continue to be family affairs; often, large government loans for business ventures are obtained simply because entrepreneurs are recognized as members of families with good Islamic and revolutionary credentials. Political activities also follow family lines. Several brothers or first cousins, for example, tend to be aligned with the same political faction. This is true even in the case of armed opposition groups, such as the Mojahedin-e Khalq (People's Fighters). A person without family ties has little status in the society at large.

The head of the household—the father and husband—traditionally expected obedience and respect from others in the family. In return, he was obligated to support them and to satisfy their spiritual, social, and material needs. In practice, family roles have been undergoing considerable change since the Revolution, and the father's role as a strict disciplinarian has been challenged by the postrevolutionary generation. The average age of first marriage has risen significantly for both men and women, which means that children—both daughters and sons—have been remaining in their parental home until they are in their 20s. Since the late 1980s, many fathers, especially in small towns and rural areas, have encouraged daughters to delay marriage in favor of obtaining a secondary school and even college education.

Religious law defines the conditions for marriage, divorce, inheritance, and guardianship. Additional laws have been passed by the parliament (Majlis—see Glossary) that reinforce and refine religious law and are designed to protect the integrity of the family. Marriage regulations are defined by Shia religious law, although non-Shias are permitted to follow their own religious practices. Before the Revolution, the legal marriage age was 21 for males and 18 for females, although most couples married at a younger age. Immediately after the Revolution, the minimum legal age of marriage for males and females was lowered to 15 and 13 years, respectively. The average age of first marriage fell immediately, and by the mid-1980s an estimated 2.4 percent of girls younger than 15 were married. However, when the generation of youth who participated in the Revolution (aged 18–25 during 1978–79) began assuming positions of political authority in the early 1990s, they initiated various reforms, including enactment of a law that raised the legal marriage age to 18 for males and 15 for females. As a result, by 2002 the average age at first marriage had risen to 22 for men and 19 for women.

The selection of a marriage partner normally is determined by customary preference, economic circumstances, and geographic considerations. Traditionally, there was a distinct preference for marriage within extended kin networks, which accounted for a a high incidence of marriages among first and second cousins. An "ideal" marriage was between the children of two brothers, although this kind of consanguineous marriage was becoming less common among the old regime elite and secular middle class by the eve of the Revolution. In the early 2000s, although a majority of marriages were still between couples with some kinship relationship, surveys found that more than 60 percent of men and more than 40 percent of women disapproved of such marriages.

Marriage arrangements continue to follow traditional patterns. When a young man is ready for marriage, he asks his parents to visit the parents of a girl whom he would like to marry. If the girl's parents are agreeable, the two families negotiate the amount of the bride-price that will be given to the bride's family at the time of marriage. The exact sum varies according to the wealth, social position, and degree of kinship of the two families. Once they have agreed to the marriage, the prospective bride and groom are considered engaged. Generally, the engagement lasts less than 12 months. The actual marriage involves a contractual ceremony and a public celebration, or wedding. One significant feature of the marriage contract is the *mahriyeh* (see Glossary), a stipulated sum that the husband must give his wife in the event of divorce.

In the early 2000s, polygyny was still practiced in Iran. It is regulated by Islamic custom, which permits a man to have as many as four wives simultaneously, provided that he treats them equally. During the 1990s, the Majlis enacted laws that required a man to provide evidence of his first wife's noncoerced agreement to his taking a second spouse and of adequate financial resources to support two households. The incidence of polygyny actually is very low because of widespread social disapproval, especially among men and women born after 1950.

Shia Islam, unlike Sunni Islam, also recognizes a form of temporary marriage called *muta*. In a *muta* marriage, the man and woman sign a contract agreeing to live together as husband and wife for a specified time, which can be as brief as several hours or as long as 99 years. The man agrees to pay a certain amount of money for the duration of the contract. Provision also is made for the support of any offspring. The number of *muta* marriages that a man may contract is not limited. Although *muta* marriages may be registered as legal contracts, there is widespread social disapproval of the practice; some women's groups openly condemn *muta* as legalized prostitution. In the early 2000s, the practice appeared to be limited to some members of the political and economic elite.

Traditionally, in Iran men could divorce their wives unilaterally according to the guidelines of Islamic law; women were permitted to leave their husbands only on narrowly defined grounds, such as insanity or impotence. Although the postrevolutionary government initially rescinded monarchy-era legislation that had liberalized access to divorce for women, by 1985 new laws permitted women to initiate divorce proceedings in certain limited circumstances. Women's right to divorce was strengthened in the 1990s, and by the end of the decade women actually were initiating more divorce petitions than men. The divorce rate in Iran is low in comparison with that in many European countries and the United States because of family and societal pressures on couples to work out their differences. By the early 2000s, the rate had risen to 0.7 divorces per 1,000 marriages.

Gender Issues

Traditional Attitudes Toward Segregation of the Sexes

With the exception of the Westernized and secularized upper and middle classes, Iranian society before the Revolution practiced public segregation of the sexes. Women generally wore the chador when in public and indoors when males not related to them were present. The majority of Iranians envisioned an ideal society as one in which women stayed at home, performing domestic tasks associated with managing a household and rearing children. Men worked in the public sphere—fields, factories, bazaars, and offices. Deviations from this ideal, especially in the case of women, tended to reflect adversely on the reputation of the family. Gender segregation also was practiced in the public education system, which maintained separate schools for boys and girls at the elementary through secondary levels.

By the late 1960s, the majority attitudes on the segregation of women clashed sharply with the views and customs of the secularized upper and middle classes, especially in Tehran. For these latter groups, mixed gatherings, both public and private, became the norm. During the Pahlavi era, the government was the main promoter of change with respect to social attitudes toward gender segregation. It banned the wearing of the chador at official functions and encouraged mixed participation in a variety of public gatherings. One result was to bring the government into conflict with non-elite social values, which were defended by the Shia clergy.

Among the ideas imported into Iran from the West was the notion that women should participate in the public sphere. The Pahlavi government encouraged women's education and their participation in the labor force. After Reza Shah banned the chador in 1936, veiling came to be perceived among the elite and secular middle-class women, who were a minority among female Iranians, as a symbol of oppression. Before the Revolution, Iranian society already was polarized between the values of the majority of women and those of a minority who embraced American and European feminist values. Some of the latter had a genuine interest in improving the status of all women. As early as 1932, such women held a meeting of the Oriental Feminine Congress in Tehran at which they called for the right of women to vote, compulsory education for both boys and girls, equal salaries for men and women, and an end to polygyny. The White Revolution reforms of 1963 included granting women the right to vote and to hold public office (see The Post-Mossadeq Era and the Shah's White Revolution, ch. 1).

Female Participation in the Workforce

On the eve of the 1979 Revolution, only about 14 percent of women aged 10 years and older participated in the paid labor force. Three patterns of work existed among women. Among the upper classes, women worked either as professionals or volunteers. Whereas secular middle-class women aspired to follow this model, traditional middle-class women worked outside the home only from dire necessity. Lower-class women frequently worked outside the home, especially in major cities, because their incomes were needed to support their households.

Women were active participants in the revolution that toppled the shah. Some activists were professional women of the secular middle class, among whom political antagonists to the regime had long been recruited. Like their male counterparts, such women had nationalist aspirations and denounced the shah's regime as a U.S. puppet. Some women also participated in guerrilla groups such as the Fedayan-e Khalq (People's Warriors) and the Mojahedin-e Khalq (People's Fighters). More significant, however, were the large numbers of lower-class women in the cities who participated in street demonstrations during the latter half of 1978 and early 1979. They responded to Khomeini's call for all Muslims to demonstrate opposition to the tyranny of the shah.

Following the Revolution, the new republican government called for the participation of women in an "Islamic society," because such a society would not be "morally corrupt" like the deposed monarchy. Observance of *hejab* would assure respect for women. *Hejab* eventually was defined as clothing that concealed the shape of a woman's figure, such as loose outer garments, and covered her hair and skin, leaving only her face and hands exposed. The requirement to observe *hejab* in public was controversial among the minority of secularized women who never had worn a chador. However, for the majority of women who always had worn the chador, *hejab* served to legitimate their presence in the public sphere, especially in work outside the home. Nevertheless, because so many professional women with jobs emigrated from Iran between 1979 and 1981 and because the postrevolutionary government compelled families to send underage girls to school rather than to work, the number of women in the paid labor force declined form 14 percent in 1976 to 9 percent in 1986; it rose gradually to 11 percent by 1996.

In the early 2000s, women made up 16 percent of the urban labor force and 14 percent of the rural labor force. The government was a major employer of women, especially the ministries of education and health. Moreover, the variety of jobs available for women expanded in the private sector, including positions for women as bus and taxi drivers. The increasing numbers of employed women prompted interest in work-related discrimination against women. Several women deputies in the Majlis, for example, sponsored legislation that required employers to give women workers the same pay and fringe benefits received by their male counterparts. The monthly magazine *Zanan* regularly published articles dealing with issues of concern to working women. The magazine's periodic sample surveys documented positive developments in urban areas, such as declining fertility, the rise in the age of first marriage for women, and steadily increasing numbers of women entering college. However, the surveys also showed that few qualified women were promoted to managerial positions in either the public or private sector. In the late 1990s, women's rights groups began launching campaigns to sensitize the public to issues such as unequal pay, the lack of paid maternity leave, inadequate job-site nurseries and childcare facilities, and limited access for women employees to training programs. All these activities contributed to a heightened public awareness about the status of working women. Government responses included the establishment of women's affairs divisions in several government ministries and in the president's office, as well as financial support for women's studies centers in the public colleges and universities.

Religion

Shia Islam in Iran

The overwhelming majority of Iranians—at least 90 percent of the total population—are Muslims who adhere to Shia Islam. In contrast, the majority of Muslims throughout the world follow Sunni Islam. Of the several Shia sects, the Twelve Imam, or Twelver *(ithna-ashari)*, is dominant in Iran; most Shias in Bahrain, Iraq, and Lebanon are also members of this sect. All the Shia sects originated among early Muslim dissenters in the first three centuries following the death of the Prophet Muhammad in A.D. 632 (see Islamic Conquest, ch. 1).

The principal belief of Twelvers, but not of other Shias, is that the spiritual and temporal leadership of the Muslim community passed from Muhammad to his cousin and son-in-law Ali and then sequentially to 11 of Ali's direct male descendants. Sunnis reject this tenet. Over the centuries, various other theological differences have developed between Twelver Shias and Sunnis.

Distinctive Beliefs

Although Shias have lived in Iran since the earliest days of Islam, it is believed that most Iranians were Sunnis before the seventeenth century. The Safavi dynasty (1501–1722) made Shia Islam the official state religion in the sixteenth century. The early Safavi shahs imported Shia clergy from historical Shia centers in Bahrain, Iraq, and Lebanon and supported an aggressive proselytization campaign on behalf of the new religion. Historians believe that by the end of the sixteenth century most people in what is now Iran had become Shias.

All Twelver Shia Muslims share with all Sunni Muslims three basic principles of Islam: there is one God who is a unitary being, not, as Christians believe, a trinitarian being; Muhammad is the last of a line of prophets beginning with Abraham and including all the Old Testament prophets, as well as Jesus, and God chose Muhammad as his final messenger to humankind; and there is a resurrection of the body and soul on the last, or judgment, day. Shias also believe in two additional principles of Islam: that divine justice will reward or punish believers based on actions undertaken through their own free will, and that the Twelve Imams were successors to Muhammad. Among Shias, the term imam (see Glossary) traditionally has been applied only to Ali and his 11 descendants. In Sunni Islam, an imam is the leader of congregational prayer.

All Shia Muslims believe that there are seven pillars of faith, which detail the acts necessary to demonstrate and reinforce faith. The first five of these pillars are shared with Sunni Muslims. They are *shahada,* or the confession of faith; *namaz,* or ritual prayer; *zakat,* or almsgiving; *sawm,* fasting and contemplation during daylight hours during the lunar month of Ramazan (Ramadan); and hajj, or pilgrimage to the holy cities of Mecca and Medina once in one's lifetime if financially feasible. The other two pillars, which are not shared with Sunnis, are jihad, or personal struggle to protect Islamic lands, beliefs, and institutions; and the requirement to do good works and to avoid all evil thoughts, words, and deeds. In addition to the seven principal tenets of faith, traditional religious practices also are intimately associated with Shia Islam. These include the observance of the month of martyrdom, Moharram, and pilgrimages to the shrines of the Twelve Imams and their various descendants. The Moharram observances commemorate the death of the Third Imam, Hussein, who was the son of Ali and Fatima and the grandson of Muhammad. Hussein was killed in battle near Karbala in present-day Iraq in A.D. 680. Hussein's death is commemorated by Shias with passion plays and is an intensely religious time.

The distinctive dogma and institution of Shia Islam is the Imamate, which includes the idea that the successor of Muhammad is not merely a political leader but also must be a spiritual leader. Thus, the imam must have the ability to interpret the inner mysteries of the Quran and sharia (Islamic law—see Glossary). Twelver Shias believe further that the Twelve Imams who succeeded the Prophet were sinless and free from error and had been chosen by God through Muhammad. The Imamate began with Ali, who also is accepted by Sunni Muslims as the fourth of the "rightly guided caliphs" to succeed the Prophet. Shias revere Ali as the First Imam, whose descendants continued the line of the imams until the Twelfth, who is believed to have ascended to a supernatural state and will return to earth on judgment day. Shias cite the close lifetime association of Muhammad with Ali as evidence for their beliefs. Shias believe that Ali was the first person to make the declaration of faith in Islam. He fought in all of Muhammad's battles except one, and the Prophet chose him to be the husband of his favorite daughter, Fatima.

The Shia doctrine of the Imamate was not elaborated fully until the tenth century. Other dogmas were developed still later. A characteristic of Shia Islam is the continual exposition and reinterpretation of doctrine. The most recent example is Ayatollah Khomeini's expounding of the doctrine of *velayat-e faqih* (see Glossary), or the political guardianship of the community of believers by scholars trained in religious law. This is an innovation rather than a traditional idea in Shia Islam. Its essential idea is that the clergy, by virtue of their superior knowledge of the laws of God, are the best qualified to rule the society of believers who are preparing themselves on earth to live eternally in heaven. The concept of *velayat-e faqih* thus provides the doctrinal basis for theocratic government, an experiment that Twelve Imam Shias had not attempted prior to the Iranian Revolution in 1978–79.

Religious Institutions and Organizations

Historically, the most important religious institution in Iran has been the mosque. In towns and cities, congregational prayers, as well as prayers and rites associated with religious observances and important phases in Muslim life, took place in mosques. Primarily an urban phenomenon, mosques did not exist in most Iranian villages. In the years preceding the Revolution, Iranian Shias generally attached diminishing significance to institutional religion, and by the 1970s there was little emphasis on mosque attendance, even for the Friday congregational prayers. During the Revolution, however, mosques in large cities played a prominent social role in organizing people for large demonstrations. Since that time, the mosques have continued to play important political and social roles, in addition to their traditional religious functions.

Another religious institution of major significance has been the *hoseiniyeh*, or Islamic center. Wealthy patrons financed construction of *hoseiniyehs* in urban areas to serve as sites for recitals and performances commemorating the martyrdom of Hussein, especially during the month of Moharram. In the 1970s, *hoseiniyehs* such as the Hoseiniyeh Irshad in Tehran became politicized as prominent clerical and lay preachers helped to lay the groundwork for the Revolution by referring to the symbolic deaths as martyrs of Hussein and the other imams in veiled but obvious criticism of Mohammad Reza Shah's regime.

Institutions providing religious education include madrassas, or seminaries, and *maktabs*, or primary schools run by the clergy. The madrassas historically were important settings for advanced training in Shia theology and jurisprudence. Each madrassa generally was associated with a noted Shia scholar who had attained the rank of ayatollah. Some older madrassas functioned like religious universities at which several scholars taught diverse religious and secular subjects. Students, or *talabehs*, lived on the grounds of the madrassas and received stipends for the duration of their studies, usually a minimum of seven years, during which they prepared for the examinations that qualify a seminary student to be a low-level preacher, or mullah (see Glossary). At the time of the Revolution, there were slightly more than 11,000 *talabehs* in Iran, approximately 60 percent of them at the madrassas in Qom. From 1979 to 1982, the number of *talabehs* in Qom more than tripled from 6,500. There were just under 25,000 *talabehs* at all levels of study

A prayer meeting at the University of Tehran
Courtesy United Nations (John Isaac)

in Qom seminaries in the early 2000s, as well as about 12,000 *talabehs* at seminaries in other Iranian cities.

Maktabs started to decline in number and importance in the first decades of the twentieth century, once the government began developing a national public school system. Nevertheless, *maktabs* continued to exist as private religious schools until the Revolution. Because the overall emphasis of public schools has remained secular subjects, since 1979 *maktabs* have continued to serve children whose parents want them to have a more religious education (see Education, this ch.).

Another major religious institution in Iran is the shrine. Pilgrimage to the shrines of imams is a specific Shia custom, undertaken because Shia pilgrims believe that the imams and their relatives have the power to intercede with God on behalf of petitioners. Of the more than 1,100 shrines in Iran, the most important are those for the Eighth Imam, Reza, in Mashhad, for Reza's sister Fatima in Qom, and for Khomeini in Tehran. Each of these is a huge complex that includes the mausoleum of the venerated one, tombs of various notables, mosques, madrassas, and libraries. Imam Reza's shrine is considered the holiest. In addition to the usual shrine accoutrements, it comprises hospitals, dispensaries, a museum, and several mosques located in a series of courtyards surrounding the imam's tomb. The shrine's endowments and gifts are the largest of all religious institutions in the country. Although there are no special times for visiting this or other shrines, it is customary for pilgrimage traffic to be heaviest during Shia holy periods. Visitors represent all socioeconomic levels. Whereas piety is a motivation for many, others come to seek the spiritual grace or general good fortune that a visit to the shrine is believed to ensure. Since the nineteenth century, it has been customary among the bazaar class and members of the lower classes to recognize those who have made a pilgrimage to Mashhad by prefixing their names with the title *mashti*. Shrine authorities have estimated that at least 4 million pilgrims visit the shrine annually in the early 2000s.

There are also important secondary shrines for other relatives of the Eighth Imam in Tehran and Shiraz. In virtually all towns and in many villages, there are numerous lesser shrines, known as *imamzadehs*, that commemorate descendants of the imams who are reputed to have led saintly lives. In Iraq the shrines at Karbala and An Najaf also are revered by Iranian Shias. Pilgrimages to these shrines and the hundreds of local *imamzadehs* are undertaken to petition the saints to grant special favors or to help one through a period of troubles. The constant movement of pilgrims from all over Iran has helped bind together a linguistically heterogeneous population. Pilgrims serve as major sources of information about conditions in different parts of the country and thus help to mitigate the parochialism of the regions.

The *vaqf* is a traditional source of financial support for all religious institutions. It is a religious endowment by which land and other income-producing property is given in perpetuity for the maintenance of a shrine, mosque, madrassa, or charitable institution such as a hospital, library, or orphanage. A *mutavalli* administers a *vaqf* in accordance with the stipulations in the donor's bequest. In many *vaqfs*, the position of *mutavalli* is hereditary. Under the Pahlavis, the government attempted to exercise control over administration of the *vaqfs*, especially those of the larger shrines. This practice caused conflict with the clergy, who perceived the government's efforts as inimical to their influence and authority in traditional religious matters.

The government's interference with the administration of *vaqfs* during the Pahlavi era led to a sharp decline in the number of *vaqf* bequests. Instead, wealthy and pious Shias chose to give financial contributions directly to the leading ayatollahs in the form of *zakat,* or obligatory alms. The clergy, in turn, used the funds to administer their madrassas and to institute various educational and charitable programs, which indirectly provided them with more influence in society. The access of the clergy to a steady and independent source of funding was an important factor in their ability to resist state controls, and ultimately helped them direct the opposition to the shah.

Religious Hierarchy

From the time that Twelver Shia Islam emerged as a distinct religious denomination in the early ninth century, its clergy, or ulama, have played a prominent role in the development of its scholarly and legal tradition. However, the development of the present hierarchy among the Shia clergy dates only to the early nineteenth century. Since that time, the highest religious authority has been vested in the *mujtahids*, scholars who, by virtue of their erudition in the science of religion (the Quran, the traditions of Muhammad and the imams, jurisprudence, and theology) and their attested ability to decide points of religious conduct, act as leaders of their community in matters concerning the particulars of religious duties. Lay Shias and lesser members of the clergy who lack such proficiency are expected to follow a *mujtahid* in all matters pertaining to religion, but each believer is free to follow any *mujtahid* he or she chooses. Since the mid-nineteenth century, it has been common for several *mujtahids* concurrently to attain prominence and to attract large followings. During the twentieth century, such *mujtahids* were accorded the title of ayatollah. Occasionally, an ayatollah achieves almost universal authority among Shias and is given the title of *ayatollah ol ozma,* or grand ayatollah. Such authority was attained by as many as seven *mujtahids* simultaneously, including Ayatollah Khomeini, in the late 1970s.

To become a *mujtahid,* it is necessary to complete a rigorous and lengthy course of religious studies in a prestigious madrassa of Qom or Mashhad in Iran or An Najaf in Iraq and to receive an authorization from a qualified ayatollah. Of equal importance is either the explicit or tacit recognition of a cleric as a *mujtahid* by laymen and scholars in the Shia community. Most seminary students actually leave the madrassa after completing the primary level. They then can serve as prayer leaders, village mullahs, local shrine administrators, and other religious functionaries. Those who leave after completing the second level become preachers in town and city mosques. Students at the third level of study are those preparing to become *mujtahids.*

Unorthodox Shia Religious Movements

Sufism, or Islamic mysticism, has a long tradition in Iran. It developed there and in other areas of the Islamic empire during the ninth century among Muslims who believed that worldly pleasures distracted from true concern with the salvation of the soul. Sufis generally renounced materialism, which they believed supported and perpetuated political tyranny. Their name is derived from the Arabic word for wool, *suf,* and was applied to the early Sufis because of their habit of wearing rough wool next to their skin as a symbol of their asceticism. Over time various Sufi brotherhoods were formed, among them several militaristic orders such as the Safavis.

Although Sufis were associated with the early spread of Shia ideas in Iran, once the Shia clergy had consolidated authority over religion, by the early seventeenth century they tended to regard Sufis as deviant. Despite occasional persecution by the Shia clergy, Sufi orders continue to exist in Iran. During the

Pahlavi period, Sufi brotherhoods were revitalized as some members of the secular middle class were attracted to them. However, the orders appear to have had little lower-class following. The largest Sufi order is the Nimatollahi, which has teaching centers in several cities and has even established new centers in foreign countries. Sufi brotherhoods such as the Naqshbandi and the Qadiri also exist among Sunni Muslims in Kurdistan. There is no evidence of persecution of Sufis since the Revolution, but because individual political leaders and clergy in the governments of the Islamic Republic have regarded Sufi brotherhoods suspiciously, these groups have tended to keep a low profile.

Some Shia sects present in Iran are regarded as heretical by Twelver Shia clergy. The Ismailis have several thousand adherents in northeastern Iran and several million outside the country. The Ismailis trace their origins to the son of Ismail, who predeceased his father, the Sixth Imam. Very numerous and active in Iran from the eleventh to the thirteenth centuries, the Ismailis were forced into hiding by the Mongols. In the nineteenth century, their leader, the Agha Khan, fled to British-controlled India, where he supervised the revitalization of the sect.

Members of another Shia sect, the Ahl-e Haqq, are concentrated in Kurdish areas, especially the Kermanshah region. Smaller communities live in the provinces of East and West Azerbaijan, Luristan, Mazandaran, and in Tehran. The Ahl-e Haqq are believed to have originated in one of the medieval politicized Sufi orders. Although the Ahl-e Haqq generally revere the Twelve Imams, they do not observe many fundamental Islamic practices. Some orthodox Shias and Sunnis consider this sect heretical, and its members have been persecuted sporadically in the past. Immediately after the Revolution, some of the sect's leaders were imprisoned on the grounds of religious deviance, but since the late 1980s the government has not interfered with Ahl-e Haqq activities.

Sunni Muslims

Sunni Muslims constitute approximately 8 percent of the Iranian population. An estimated 40 percent of Iranian Kurds, virtually all Baluchis and Turkmens in Iran, and a minority of Iranian Arabs are Sunnis. There also are small communities of Persian-speaking Sunnis in the Lar region of southern Iran and in the provinces of North, Razavi, and South Khorasan. Generally speaking, Iranian Shias are inclined to recognize Sunnis as fellow Muslims whose religion is incomplete because they do not accept the doctrine of the Imamate. Shia clergy tend to ascribe value to missionary work to convert Sunnis to what Shias regard as true Islam. Because the Sunnis generally live in the border regions of the country, there has been limited Shia–Sunni tension or conflict in most of Iran. In towns with mixed populations in West Azerbaijan, the Persian Gulf region, and Sistan va Baluchistan, however, tensions between Shias and Sunnis have existed both before and after the Revolution. Religious tensions tend to be highest during major Shia observances, especially Moharram. Because most Sunnis are members of ethnic minorities, religious and ethnic identities sometimes become fused. This combination has fueled complaints of discrimination, especially among some Sunni Kurds and Sunni Baluchis.

Non-Muslim Minorities

Christians

Beginning in the twentieth century, Christians generally have been permitted to participate in the economic and social life of the country. Iran's indigenous Christians include an estimated 300,000 Armenians, some 32,000 Assyrians, and a small number of Iranians who have converted to Roman Catholicism and Protestant sects or who are the descendants of Iranians who converted to those religions in the nineteenth and twentieth centuries (see table 5, Appendix). The Armenians are predominantly urban and are concentrated in Tehran and Esfahan; smaller communities reside in Tabriz, Arak, and other cities. A majority of the Assyrians are also urban, although there are still several Assyrian villages in the Lake Urmia region. Although the Armenians and the Assyrians have encountered individual prejudice, they have not been subjected to persecution. The Armenians, especially, have achieved a relatively high standard of living and maintain several parochial primary and secondary schools.

The constitution of 1979 recognized the Armenians and Assyrians as official religious minorities. Armenians are entitled to elect two representatives to the Majlis and Assyrians, one. Both groups are permitted to follow their own religious laws in matters of marriage, divorce, and inheritance. Other Christians have not received any special recognition, and some Iranian Anglicans and Evangelicals have been persecuted. All Chris-

The Armenian Vank Church in the Jolfa quarter of Esfahan
Courtesy Nader Davoodi

tians are required to observe the laws relating to attire and gender segregation in public gatherings. However, Christians are permitted to make wine for use in religious services. Tensions have existed between the government and Armenians over the administration of the Armenian schools. The Ministry of Education insisted for a decade after the Revolution that the principals of these schools be Muslims, that courses on Islam be required in the curricula, that other religion courses be taught in Persian, and that all female students observe *hejab* inside the schools. Government supervision gradually lessened during the 1990s, although in the early 2000s Armenian schools still taught an approved course on Islam.

Baha'is

Although the Baha'is are Iran's second-largest non-Muslim minority, they do not enjoy constitutional protection as an official religious minority. There were an estimated 250,000 Baha'is in Iran in 2005 according to Iranian figures, but other estimates are as high as 350,000. The Baha'is are scattered in small communities throughout Iran, with heavy concentrations in larger cities. Most Baha'is are urban, but there are some

Baha'i villages. The majority of Baha'is are Persians, but there is a significant minority of Azerbaijani Baha'is, and Baha'is also are represented in other ethnic groups in Iran.

The Baha'i faith originated in Iran in the mid-1800s, based on the teachings of Mirza Ali Muhammad and his disciple, Mirza Hussein Ali Nur, or Baha'u'llah, the faith's prophet-founder. It initially attracted a wide following among dissident Shia clergy and others dissatisfied with society, but since its inception it has met with intense hostility from mainstream Shia clergy. Upholding many teachings of Islam and other world religions, the faith stresses the brotherhood of all peoples, the eradication of all forms of prejudice, and the establishment of world peace. By the early twentieth century, the faith had spread to North America, Europe, and Africa.

Because the Shia clergy, like many other Iranians, continued to regard their faith as heretical, Baha'is in Iran have encountered much prejudice and sometimes even persecution. Their situation generally improved under the Pahlavi shahs, as the government sought to secularize public life. Baha'is were permitted to hold government posts and allowed to open their own schools, and many were successful in business and the professions. The faith expanded significantly in the 1960s. However, major instances of discrimination occurred in 1955 and 1978, and the faith's status changed drastically in 1979. The Islamic Republic did not recognize the Baha'is as a religious minority, and adherents to the faith were officially persecuted. More than 1,000 Baha'is were imprisoned and several hundred killed. Most privileges of citizenship were revoked. Several thousand Baha'is fled the country during the 1980s. Their situation improved marginally during the 1990s. However, in the early 2000s the United Nations Commission on Human Rights reported that Baha'is faced restrictions in employment, education, and the practice of their religion. Media condemnation of the faith became more frequent in 2005, and Baha'is continue to be subject to arbitrary arrest and imprisonment.

Zoroastrians

In the early 2000s, there were an estimated 32,000 Zoroastrians in Iran. The Zoroastrians speak Persian and are concentrated in Tehran, Kerman, and Yazd provinces. Zoroastrianism initially developed in Iran during the seventh century B.C. Later, it became the official religion of the Sassanian dynasty, which ruled Iran for approximately four centuries before being destroyed by the Arabs in the seventh century A.D. (see The Sassanians, A.D. 224–642, ch. 1). With Iran's incorporation into the Islamic empire, the majority of the Iranian population had converted from Zoroastrianism to Islam by the mid-tenth century.

During the Qajar dynasty, there was considerable prejudice against Zoroastrians. In the mid-nineteenth century, several thousand Zoroastrians emigrated from Iran to British-ruled India to improve their economic and social status. Many eventually acquired wealth in India and subsequently expended part of their fortunes on upgrading conditions in the Zoroastrian communities of Iran. The emphasis placed on Iran's pre-Islamic heritage by the Pahlavis also helped Zoroastrians achieve a more respected position in society. Many of them migrated from Kerman and Yazd to Tehran, where they accumulated significant wealth as merchants and in real estate. By the 1970s, younger Zoroastrians were entering the professions.

The Zoroastrians, like the Christians and Jews, are recognized as an official religious minority under the 1979 constitution. The constitution permits the Zoroastrians to elect one representative to the Majlis, and, like the other "legal" minorities, they may seek employment in the government. They maintain houses of worship, known as fire temples, and their own cemeteries. They generally enjoy the same civil liberties as Muslims. As a group, Zoroastrians have not been singled out for discrimination or persecution because of their religious beliefs.

Jews

In the early 2000s, there were an estimated 25,000 to 30,000 Jews in Iran, a decline from about 85,000 in 1978. The Iranian Jewish community is one of the oldest in the world, being descended from Jews who remained in the region following the Babylonian captivity, when the Achaemenian rulers of the first Iranian empire permitted Jews to return to Jerusalem (see The Achaemenian Empire, 550–330 B.C., ch. 1). Over the centuries, the Jews of Iran became physically, culturally, and linguistically indistinguishable from the non-Jewish population. The overwhelming majority of Jews speak Persian as their primary language. Iran's Jews are predominantly urban; by the 1970s, they were concentrated in Tehran, with smaller communities in other cities such as Shiraz, Esfahan, Hamadan, and Kashan.

Until the twentieth century, Jews were confined to their own quarters in the towns. In general, they were an impoverished, occupationally restricted minority. Since the 1920s, Jews have had greater opportunities for economic and social mobility. They gradually gained increased prominence in the bazaars, and after World War II some educated Jews entered the professions. The Jews' legal position did not change as a result of the Revolution, and the constitution of 1979 recognized Jews as an official religious minority with the right to elect a representative to the Majlis. Like the Christians, the Jews generally have not been persecuted. They have maintained numerous synagogues, cemeteries, and private schools. In practice, however, the situation of the Jewish community has been affected by the intense hostility between Iran and Israel. The Islamic Republic does not recognize Israel and officially condemns Zionism, the ideology of Israel, as a racist creed justifying the occupation of a Muslim holy land, Palestine. Since the creation of Israel in 1948, about 45,000 Iranian Jews have emigrated there, and many Jews in Iran keep in regular contact with relatives in Israel. Although the leaders of Iran's Jewish community insist that no Iranian Jews subscribe to Zionism, the ties between Iranian Jews and their relatives in Israel have been used against them. These individual cases have not affected the status of the community as a whole, but they have contributed to a pervasive feeling of insecurity among Jews and have helped precipitate large-scale emigration.

Education

Prior to the mid-nineteenth century, education was associated with religious institutions. The clergy, both Muslim and non-Muslim, assumed responsibility for instructing youth in basic literacy and the fundamentals of religion. Knowledge of reading and writing was not considered necessary for all the population, and thus education generally was restricted to the sons of the economic and political elite. Typically, this involved a few years of study in a local school, or *maktab*. Those who desired to acquire more advanced knowledge could continue in a religious college, or madrassa, where all fields of religious science were taught. A perceived need to provide instruction in subjects that were not part of the traditional religious curriculum, such as accounting, European languages, military science, and technology, led to the establishment of the first government school in 1851. By the early twentieth century, several schools, including a few for girls, taught foreign languages and

Boys posing in a grocery store
Courtesy Nader Davoodi

sciences. These schools were run by foreign missionaries, private Iranians, and the government. Their function was to educate the children of the elite. During the Constitutional Revolution (1905–7), a number of reform-minded individuals proposed the establishment of a nationwide, public, primary school system (see The Constitutional Revolution, ch. 1). Progress in opening new schools was steady but slow, and by the end of the Qajar dynasty (1925) approximately 3,300 government schools were operating, with a total enrollment of about 110,000 students.

During the Pahlavi era (1925–79), the imperial government expanded the education system. Given responsibility for regulating all public and private schools, the Ministry of Education drafted a uniform curriculum for primary and secondary education. This entire public system was secular and was based on the French model. Its objective was to train Iranians for modern occupations in administration, management, science, and teaching. Although this education system was the single most important factor in the creation of the secular middle class, the goal of creating a nationwide education system was never achieved during the Pahlavi era. In 1940 only 10 percent of all elementary-age children were enrolled in school, and less than

1 percent of youths between the ages of 12 and 20 were in secondary school. These statistics did not change significantly until the early 1960s, when the government initiated programs to improve and expand the public school system. By 1978 approximately 75 percent of all elementary-age children were enrolled in primary schools, but fewer than half of teenagers were attending secondary schools.

Although by the 1920s the country had several institutes of higher education, modern college and university education developed under the Pahlavis. In 1934 the institutes associated with government ministries were combined to form the University of Tehran, which was coeducational from its inception. Following World War II, universities were founded in other major cities such as Tabriz, Esfahan, Mashhad, Shiraz, and Ahvaz. During the 1970s, these universities were expanded, and colleges and vocational institutes were set up in several cities.

One of the first measures adopted by the government after the Revolution was to "purify" the public school system of teachers deemed "counterrevolutionary" and of texts deemed antireligious. However, excepting the introduction of religion as a required class in the public school curriculum, the basic organization of the education system was not altered. Thus, students continued to attend primary school for five years, beginning in the first grade at age six. Then they spent three years in middle school. In high school, students aspiring to go on to college enrolled in humanities or science and mathematics programs; others enrolled in vocational programs. Students who completed the three-year cycle of the first two programs attended a fourth year of college preparatory classes.

The Ministry of Education announced that nearly 15 million students registered for elementary and secondary schools in September 2004. At the primary level, 97.8 percent of children ages six to 11 were enrolled. Attendance at secondary school is not compulsory, and consequently students begin to drop out as they reach their teen years. Nevertheless, in 2004 some 90 percent of children ages 12 to 14 were enrolled in middle school, and 70 percent of adolescents ages 15 to 18 years were enrolled in high schools. Girls and boys were enrolled in approximately equal numbers at the primary level; in 2004 girls made up 49 percent of middle-school students and 48 percent of high-school students.

In April 1980, the government closed the universities, most of which had become centers for political demonstrations by both opponents and supporters of the revolutionary regime. Over the following two and one-half years, the universities were purged of "counterrevolutionary" faculty, and courses in some disciplines of the humanities were redesigned to better reflect the worldview of the Islamic Republic. Once the universities were reopened, they expanded rapidly in response to the rising demand for college education. By 2004, more than 200 public and 30 private institutions of higher education were dispersed throughout the country, enrolling a total of nearly 1.6 million students. The largest and most prestigious public university is the University of Tehran, which has enrolled a student body of about 32,000 graduates and undergraduates annually since 1998. Collectively, the university and 115 other major public institutions of higher education in Tehran enrolled more than 95,000 students in 2004. All of Iran's other major cities also have public universities. A popular experimental public university, Payam-e Nur, was established in 1987 to provide off-campus learning for working adults who wanted to complete undergraduate and graduate degrees by taking evening classes on flexible schedules. Payam-e Nur, which charges tuition, and the other, tuition-free, public colleges and universities collectively enrolled more than 550,000 students in 2004. The private system of higher education is dominated by the Islamic Free University, whose branches in 110 cities and towns enrolled more than 700,000 students in 2004. Some 33 other private colleges offering specialty degrees collectively enrolled more than 23,000 students in 2004. Of the country's total postsecondary student population in 2004, about 57 percent were females and 43 percent males. University male and female students are segregated by rows in classes, and in 2006 authorities sought to establish separate classes.

In 2003 Iran's overall literacy rate was 79.4 percent. The literacy rate by gender was 85.6 percent for males and 73 percent for females.

Health and Welfare

After the 1978–79 Revolution, one major faction, referred to as "radicals" in the early 1980s, then as "moderates" in the mid-1980s to early 1990s, and subsequently as "reformers," held that government ought to help the poor rise out of poverty by providing subsidies for basic foods and utilities and financial assistance to families with no regular income. This faction also felt that it was inappropriate for the government to monitor the private or public behavior of its citizens. The conservative faction, in contrast, preferred private charitable efforts over public assistance as the means of helping the needy and thus encouraged religious institutions, especially mosques, to get more involved in social welfare programs. The conservatives' policies significantly enhanced the role of the mosque in society. However, while the radical/moderate faction dominated the Majlis from 1980 until 1992, it greatly expanded governmental health and welfare services, with particular emphasis on providing services for low-income populations in both rural and urban areas. The implementation of a relatively comprehensive national health insurance program, the construction of a network of nationwide primary health care clinics, and the subsidization of the cost of many common medical drugs all have been factors in a dramatic improvement in the general health of the population. Health indicators as of 2007 showed that average life expectancy had increased to 72.1 years for women and 69.1 years for men; the crude birthrate was 16.6 per 1,000 population; the crude death rate was 5.6 per 1,000 population.

Iran has a voluntary national health insurance program that delivers primary health care to more than 65 percent of the population. Individuals and families may enroll by paying a monthly fee; several levels of coverage, correlated to the amount of the monthly fee, are available. The Imam Khomeini Relief Committee and other charitable foundations pay the basic monthly enrollment fee for poor families; most factory workers and government employees pay through payroll deductions. The program covers routine health care services, including doctors' visits, but those who require specialized medical procedures generally must cover a portion of the costs. Private health insurance plans also are available; self-employed persons and those with the financial means generally prefer to enroll in private health plans and also use private hospitals and clinics.

Medical Personnel and Facilities

According to the Iranian Medical Association (IMA), an estimated 7,000 physicians—40 percent of medical doctors in Iran—emigrated during and immediately after the Revolution. This situation contributed to a critical shortage of medical personnel that lasted through the 1980s. The Ministry of Health sought to remedy this shortage by hiring doctors from other

Asian countries, a practice that continued until the early 1990s, and by expanding medical education facilities. By the early 2000s, Iran's nine major medical colleges were awarding more than 1,500 doctor of medicine degrees annually. The IMA had about 67,000 members, of whom 62,300 were practicing physicians and about 4,700 were dentists. On average, there were 0.9 physicians per 1,000 population. The IMA estimated that 46 percent of physicians were women, as were 38 percent of dentists. Nurses of all skill levels numbered more than 100,000; about 50 percent were women. There were 650 hospitals throughout the country, with a total of 73,700 beds, or an average of 1.1 hospital beds per 1,000 population.

The medical colleges provide free education for students who agree to practice for a stipulated number of years in small-town and rural clinics after obtaining their degree. This requirement has enabled the Ministry of Health to make primary health care generally available in rural areas. However, specialized health care services, including most surgical procedures, tend to be concentrated in Tehran and other large cities. Public facilities tend to have inadequate staff and equipment to treat special cases. This situation has contributed to a widespread popular perception that private clinics provide better care, although most private physicians also practice at public facilities.

Health Hazards and Preventative Medicine

For at least 100 years prior to the 1980s, the chief causes of death, apart from infant mortality, were gastrointestinal, respiratory, and parasitic diseases. However, with the gradual improvement of health in urban areas by the 1960s, the relative rate of deaths from cancer, diabetes, and heart disease began to increase. Contagious diseases, such as grippe and influenza, conjunctivitis, scarlet fever, whooping cough, pulmonary tuberculosis, and typhoid fever also were common. The improvement in overall health care after the Revolution led to dramatic declines in infant mortality and deaths from diseases and infections that can be cured with antibiotics. The infant mortality rate in 2006 was 40.3 deaths per 1,000 live births, and the maternal mortality rate was one in 370 births. The Ministry of Health has instituted preventive programs to inoculate primary- school-age children against diphtheria, measles, pertussis, poliomyelitis, and other diseases. Following earthquakes and other natural disasters, medical response measures, including mass immunizations to prevent epidemics, have been relatively effective.

Illicit drug use has become a serious national health problem. In 2004 the Ministry of Health estimated that there were as many as 3 million drug addicts in a total adult population of 40 million. Opium is the most commonly used drug. The Shia clergy have tried to discourage opium use by declaring it religiously prohibited. Although the production, sale, and consumption of opium are illegal, an estimated 20 percent of males over age 18 are believed to use it at least occasionally. Users typically consume opium by smoking it, but since the late 1990s illegal processing laboratories have been extracting heroin from opium, and dealers have been selling it for intravenous injection. By 2002 the use of heroin may have surpassed opium use in Tehran and other large cities among males ages 18 to 25. The Ministry of Health operates a network of free drug rehabilitation centers in Tehran and other large cities. These facilities do not keep records on patients after they have been discharged, however, so it has not been possible to assess their long-term effectiveness.

Initially, the primary means of human immunodeficiency virus (HIV) infection was the transfusion of blood imported from Europe before HIV testing had become routine. Since the late 1990s, however, intravenous drug injection is the main source of HIV, accounting for 65 percent of new cases in Iran. The overall incidence of acquired immune deficiency syndrome (AIDS) has been very low. In 2005 the Ministry of Health estimated that about 9,800 Iranians were infected with the HIV virus. In the early 2000s, Iran established a national HIV treatment program, including voluntary treatment centers and a needle exchange system.

Another health hazard, especially in Tehran but increasingly in several other large cities, is air pollution, which has been linked to respiratory diseases, aggravated coronary conditions, and certain cancers, among other health problems (see Environment, this ch.).

Water Supply and Sanitation

All of Iran's urban areas and at least 95 percent of its villages had safe, piped drinking water by the end of the 1990s. Access to clean water reduced the once high incidence of waterborne gastrointestinal diseases to relatively insignificant levels. Municipal sewerage systems have been established in cities, and the use of septic tanks has become common in villages (see Environment, this ch.).

Welfare

In 2005 the absolute poverty line was estimated at US$140 of income per month. Evaluations of poverty distribution have varied widely; according to a parliamentary report, 20 percent of the urban population and 50 percent of the rural population were living in poverty in 2004. This marks a significant decrease compared with the 1996 figure of 53 percent overall.

Religious and social traditions have influenced attitudes toward welfare. Most Iranians feel obligated to help the needy in accordance with religious tenets such as the giving of alms (*zakat*), which is one of the obligations of the Islamic faith. Since the Revolution, the regime has espoused an ideological commitment to assisting the less fortunate, or *mostazafin*, the social group that had been neglected to a considerable degree under the shah. The largest charity in the country, the Bonyad-e Mostazafin (Foundation of the Disinherited), was established by the last shah as the Pahlavi Foundation to fund a variety of charitable programs. After the Revolution, the government took over its administration, renamed it, and redesigned its programs to emphasize assistance to poor families. Although this foundation and three smaller charitable ones may be considered semipublic because their directors are appointed by the Leader, no governmental body reviews their income sources or expenditures (see The Leader, or *Faqih*, ch. 4). The Bonyad-e Mostazafin undertakes a great variety of income-earning and grant-giving activities; one of its major charitable projects has been the construction of low-income housing for the poor, especially in Tehran and its suburbs. Another foundation, the Imam Khomeini Relief Committee, provides various kinds of assistance to the families of "martyrs," that is, those killed during the Revolution or the war with Iraq, and victims of natural disasters.

Aside from national health insurance, the most important form of government assistance is a pension program that is partially funded by employee contributions. The first public retirement program, set up during the Pahlavi era, initially benefited only government employees. Although it was extended gradually, by the time of the Revolution less than 10 percent of the total workforce was covered. During the 1980s, the Islamic Republic gradually extended coverage to all employed persons, and in the 1990s all self-employed farmers also were covered. Female government employees may retire after 20 years of work, their male counterparts after 25 years; in other employment sectors, women may collect pensions as early as age 45 and all workers by age 60, depending on the number of years worked. Other forms of social welfare benefits, such as disability, widows' pensions, and payments for minor children of deceased heads of households, generally are provided by the Imam Khomeini Relief Committee and other semipublic foundations.

In 2005 unemployment insurance payments to eligible workers ranged from about US$140 to US$440 per month, but only about 131,000 unemployed workers received payments. Depending on family status and the insurance payments made by the worker, the program provides between six and 50 months of coverage.

*   *   *

With respect to geography, Volume 1 of the *Cambridge History of Iran, The Land of Iran*, edited by W. B. Fisher, remains the most authoritative source for comprehensive articles about Iran's climate, environment, hydrology, mineralogy, and topography. On population, the Statistical Center of Iran is an indispensable resource for recent and historical census data; English summaries of its reports and latest statistics are available on its own and other government Web sites listed in the Bibliography. Iran's diverse languages and ethnic groups are the subjects of numerous useful books and articles, including Amir Hassanpour's *Nationalism and Language in Kurdistan, 1918–1985*, Sekandar Amanolahi's "The Lurs of Iran," Lois Beck's *The Qashqa'i of Iran* and *Nomad*, Brian Spooner's "Baluchestan," and Philip Salzman's *Black Tents of Baluchistan*.

Although many books in Persian and French analyze social change in Iran since the Revolution, there is no equivalent text in English. Fariba Adelkhah's *Being Modern in Iran*, although not comprehensive, does provide insights into selected aspects of contemporary Iranian society from a cultural-anthropological perspective. *Twenty Years of Islamic Revolution*, edited by Eric Hooglund, is a collection of articles that examine social change relating to women, youth, and rural society. A special issue of the journal *Critique*, "Sociological Research in Iran," also edited by Hooglund, provides valuable statistical data on changes affecting these and other social groups.

Insight into the social structure of urban Iran is provided by Azadeh Kian-Thiébaut in *Secularization of Iran: A Doomed Failure?* On the urban poor, see Assef Bayat's *Street Politics.* On the social structure of rural Iran, see Eric Hooglund's *Land and Revolution in Iran, 1960–1980* and Ali Shakoori's *The State and Rural Development in Post-Revolutionary Iran.* Books that are particularly valuable on women in Iran include Parvin Paydar's *Women and the Political Process in Twentieth Century Iran*, Mahnaz Kousha's *Voices from Iran*, Ziba Mir-Hosseini's *Islam and Gender*, and Faegheh Shirazi's *The Veil Unveiled*. Among the scores of articles about specific issues pertaining to women, those by Roksana Bahramitash, Homa Hoodfar, Azadeh Kian-Thiébaut, Ziba Mir-Hosseini, and Jaleh Shaditalab are especially useful.

On religion, Moojan Momen's *An Introduction to Shi'i Islam* is a comprehensive survey of the history, beliefs, and practices of Twelve Imam Shiism and contains information about all other Shia sects as well. It is an excellent reference for those with little or no prior knowledge about this denomination. For a more detailed analysis of Islam in Iran, Alessandro Bausani's *Religion in Iran* generally is considered the classic study. On non-Muslim minorities, see the *Encyclopedia Iranica* entries "Armenians of Modern Iran" (by Amurian and Kasheff) and "Assyrians in Iran" (by Rudolf Macuch), and Janet Kestenberg-Amighi's book *The Zoroastrians of Iran*. (For further information and complete citations, see Bibliography.)

Chapter 3. The Economy

A ninth-century ceramic plate from Neyshabur

SEVERAL MAJOR CHARACTERISTICS of the Iranian economy have remained remarkably untouched over the past century despite dramatic differences in the social and political structures of each of the three regimes (Qajar, Pahlavi, and Islamic) that ruled the country during this period. Each regime identified a relationship between the economic structure and the roots of the social, political, and economic problems of the country. Each regime also introduced its own socioeconomic agenda and claimed to bring about necessary structural changes, but all three failed to achieve significant change in the economy's structure. This is particularly evident in the comparison of the structure of the Iranian economy before and after the 1978–79 Revolution.

Iran's postrevolutionary economy retains several continuities with the prerevolutionary economy. Oil revenues remain the main source of government income, as they have been since the 1950s. In part because of oil's central role, the government has remained a dominant force in shaping the composition of national output, as well as its production and distribution. The public sector dominates the economic scene, and the subordination of the private sector is observed in all industries and commerce. Since 1948, with some disruptions, government development planning has implemented economic projects and budget outlays. Many government projects require multiyear budget planning. The budgetary process, the format of the annual budget, and the role of oil revenues in this process have remained the same over time.

Public-sector investments in transportation (highways and railroads), utilities, telecommunications, and other infrastructure have grown over time. Although infrastructure investments have had different impacts on rural and urban development over the period, government infrastructure investments have been one of the distinctive common features of pre- and postrevolutionary Iran. Similarly, the share of international trade in the economy has grown over time but without a significant change in structure. On the export side, Iran remains a major oil exporter, with some manufactured exports such as rugs and minimally processed items such as dried fruits. On the import side, Iran has remained an importer of raw materials and spare parts, food and medicine, manufactured goods, and military equipment.

Historical Background

The Economy under the Pahlavis, 1925–79

Reza Shah Pahlavi (r. 1925–41) improved the country's over-all infrastructure, implemented educational reform, campaigned against foreign influence, reformed the legal system, and introduced modern industries. During this time, Iran experienced a period of social change, economic development, and relative political stability.

In the interwar period, modern industries were introduced. Whereas fewer than 20 modern industrial plants existed in 1925, by 1941 more than 800 new plants had been established, with the intention of reducing the country's dependence on imports. The state encouraged industrialization by raising tariffs, financing modern industries, and imposing government monopolies. Changes in the legal system, tax structure, and trade policies attracted domestic financial resources and led to the emergence of a group of new, young entrepreneurs. The shah's court became the biggest investor in the new industries. Primarily by confiscating real estate, the shah himself became the country's richest man. Increased investment in mining, construction, and the manufacturing sector occurred, and infrastructure investment grew significantly. Iran had only 250 kilometers of railroads and 2,400 kilometers of gravel roads in 1925; by 1938 these totals had increased to 1,700 and 12,000 kilometers, respectively. Industrial growth was not balanced, however. Integration among sectors and industries was absent, and the new industries met only part of the growing domestic demand. Agriculture, from which 90 percent of the labor force made its living, did not benefit from economic reform. Furthermore, the expanding areas of the economy were not labor-intensive. Modern sectors (Caspian Sea fisheries, railroads, seaports, the oil industry, modern factories, and coal fields) absorbed a total of only about 170,000 workers, less than 4 percent of the labor force.

The government managed the expansion of international trade by techniques such as the foreign-exchange controls imposed in 1936. Many new items were among the imported goods required by industry, the military, railroads, and other areas of infrastructure investment. Traditional agricultural and industrial export products were replaced by oil exports. Germany became Iran's primary trading partner by 1940, accounting for 42 percent of its foreign trade; the United States was second, with 23 percent. The Soviet Union also was a major trading partner in this period. Despite many advances in domestic and foreign economic policy, however, Iran remained an exporter of raw materials and traditional goods and an importer of both consumer and capital goods in the years before World War II.

Reza Shah Pahlavi, who abdicated in 1941, was succeeded by his son, Mohammad Reza Shah Pahlavi (r. 1941–79). No fundamental change occurred in the Iranian economy during World War II (1939–45) and the years immediately following. However, between 1954 and 1960 a rapid increase in oil revenues and sustained foreign aid led to greater investment and fast-paced economic growth, primarily in the government sector. Subsequently, inflation increased, the value of the national currency (the rial—see Glossary) depreciated, and a foreign-trade deficit developed. Economic policies implemented to combat these problems led to declines in the rates of nominal economic growth and per capita income by 1961.

In response to these setbacks, Iran initiated its third economic development plan (1962–68; see Glossary) with an emphasis on industrialization. New economic policies significantly altered the role of the private sector. The expansion of private and public banks, as well as the establishment of two specialized banks, provided reliable credit markets for medium- and large-scale private manufacturing enterprises. Not limited to cheap credit, government programs also included a wide range of incentives to encourage investment in new industries by both Iranian and foreign businesses. Most new investment was a joint effort between either the public sector and foreign investors or private businesses and foreign corporations. Investment in roads, highways, dams, bridges, and seaports also increased. With government support, part of the agricultural sector also attracted significant investment. Many large-scale agricultural operations in meat, dairy products, and fruit production were established. Small-scale farmers, however, did not benefit from the new investment opportunities.

Under the fourth and the fifth economic development plans (1968–73; 1973–78), the Iranian economy became increasingly open to imports and foreign investment. A combination of oil revenues, public spending, and foreign and domestic investments enlarged the middle class in major cities, particularly Tehran. In the wake of the spike in crude oil prices that followed the 1973 war pitting Egypt and Syria against Israel, the process of industrialization and consumption grew rapidly. Between 1973 and 1977, the specialized banks provided more than 200 billion rials to the manufacturing sector, and the increase in investment averaged 56 percent per year. A flood of imported goods and raw materials overwhelmed the capacity of seaports and warehouses. The military was also a beneficiary of the new economic and social conditions. Military personnel, modern artillery and equipment, and military training absorbed a major part of the budget.

Between fiscal year (FY—see Glossary) 1964 and FY 1978, Iran's gross national product (GNP—see Glossary) grew at an annual rate of 13.2 percent at constant prices. The oil, gas, and construction industries expanded by almost 500 percent during this period, while the share of value-added manufacturing increased by 4 percent. Women's participation in the labor force in urban areas increased. Large numbers of urban Iranian women, from varying social strata, joined the semiskilled and skilled labor forces (see Female Participation in the Workforce, ch. 2). In addition, the number of women enrolling in higher education increased from 5,000 in FY 1967 to more than 74,000 in FY 1978.

Economic growth, however, became increasingly dependent on oil revenues in the 1970s. By 1977, oil revenues had reached US$20 billion per year (79 percent of total government revenues). Other sectors of the economy and regions of the country did not experience a uniform pattern of growth during this period. Agriculture, traditional and semi-traditional industries, and the services sector did not thrive to the same extent as the "modern" state-sponsored manufacturing industries, which accounted for only 6 percent of industrial employment. As employment opportunities in rural areas and traditional industries decreased, public employment in urban areas increased. The proportion of self-employed Iranians remained stable.

Accelerated development of the middle class was a major outcome of the 1960s and 1970s (see Social Class in Contemporary Iran, ch. 2). Among this class were the new professional intelligentsia, called *motekhassesin* (experts). Their common denominator was the professional, cultural, or administrative expertise acquired through modern education. Nevertheless, the patterns of economic growth and regional development along with the political underdevelopment of the shah's regime in areas such as civil institutions, human rights, and property rights limited opportunities for the majority of Iranians to develop fully their social and economic potential. Economic and social polarization minimized competition among businesses and limited development to the part of the economy concerned with the interests of dominant groups closely tied to the shah's court and the state. Most Iranians were excluded from political and economic decision making.

The Economy after the Islamic Revolution, 1979–Present

The Iranian Revolution marked a turning point for the economy, which suffered from several fundamental problems. First, it was heavily dependent on foreign raw materials, spare parts, and management skills. On average, 57 percent of raw materials were imported from developed countries. Second, the banking system had collapsed, and capital flight had compounded the economic problems. As a result, manufacturing industries were able to utilize only 58 percent of available capacity after the Revolution. The West's economic blockade began after the occupation of the U.S. Embassy in Iran by radical Iranian students in November 1979. Under U.S. pressure, many Western countries halted exports of raw materials and spare parts to Iran, as well as imports from Iran. They also reduced or eliminated investment in Iran. In addition, the United States froze Iranian foreign assets, which were estimated at US$10 billion to US$15 billion. Iran's crude oil exports declined from 4.5 million barrels a day in FY 1978 to 780,000 barrels a day in FY 1981. Between 1980 and 1982, a credit crunch or "debt crisis" arose when domestic and foreign-owned banks decided to reduce the amount of credit to both business and the public. The major reason for the credit crunch was the outstanding debt of many manufacturing firms to the banking system, totaling an estimated US$8.5 billion to US$10.1 billion.

Following the Revolution, the Islamic Republic of Iran's primary objective was to transform the economy by rejecting both Eastern and Western economic philosophies. The government linked economic dependency with the Westernization of Iran and the existence of big businesses. This attitude was converted into an antibusiness sentiment that targeted both small-scale manufacturing establishments and big-business entities. These businesses were portrayed as pro-Western, antilabor, and anti-

Islam. The trade sector, consisting of small entities loosely connected with religious organizations and leaders, was not significantly influenced by this negative attitude. A large share of the business profits generated since the Revolution has been in trade, real estate, and construction rather than the manufacturing sector.

The Iran–Iraq War, which started in September 1980, compounded existing economic and financial difficulties and created major social problems. Managing the war forced the Iranian government to compete with the private sector in the labor, financial, and foreign-exchange markets, as well as in the markets for goods and services. The war absorbed up to 20 percent of total public expenditures as tax revenues declined throughout the 1980s. The period after the war brought greater stability to Iran along with an increase in oil revenues. The new regime's first economic development plan (1990–95; see Glossary), which resulted in an annual real economic growth rate of 7.2 percent, recognized the role of the private sector in the reconstruction of the war-damaged economy. Oil revenues accounted for 73 percent of government revenues during this period. The second and third development plans (1995–2000; 2000–2005) were enacted under similar conditions but were implemented on a broader scale. Both plans stimulated moderate economic growth. However, they failed to increase tax revenues and the role of the private sector in the Iranian economy.

The Role of Government

The government plays a significant role in Iran's economy, either directly through participation in the production and distribution of goods and services, or indirectly through policy intervention. In the 1990s and the early 2000s, Iranian governments have seen intervention as necessary to counter both the market inefficiencies frequently associated with developing countries and imbalances in the production and distribution of basic goods. Imbalances resulting from unfavorable income distribution, a lack of linkages among industries, and regional income and employment disparities seemingly increased in the recent economic history of Iran. Under the Pahlavis, the role of government expanded as oil revenues increased. The oil revenues made it possible to establish a modern army; invest in infrastructure, health, education, and new industries; and establish a complex government bureaucracy.

The economic problems of recent decades accelerated the process of government intervention in economic life. Article 44 of the Iranian constitution states that "The economic system... consists of three sectors: state, cooperative, and private. The state sector is to include all large-scale and major industries, foreign trade, major mineral resources, banking, insurance, energy, dams and large-scale irrigation networks, radio and television, post, telegraphic and telephone services, aviation, shipping, roads, railroads, and the like owned and administered by the state. The private sector consists of those activities... that supplement the economic activities of the state and the cooperative sector." Thus, the constitution treats the private sector as the means of furnishing the government's needs rather than responding to market requirements. By the end of FY 1981, under the Law of Protection and Development of National Industries, 580 large industrial enterprises had been nationalized and were operating under the control of the Ministry of Industry and the Ministry of Mining and Metals.

Beginning in the 1990s, the government's central role in Iran's economy has been formalized in a series of five-year national economic development plans. The economy is currently operating under the fourth plan, which began in March 2005. These plans set goals for national budget income and expenditures, for the allocation of resources, and for growth rates and priorities among the branches of the economy. Central themes in development planning have been the allocation of revenues between the petroleum and nonpetroleum sectors of the economy, adjustments in the relative importance of state and private enterprises, and the role of competition in the economy. In general, planners have sought a smaller role for petroleum and an expanded share for private enterprise. However, the statistical manifestations of these goals never have been met.

Influenced by policies of the International Monetary Fund (IMF) and the World Bank, as well as the economic burden of state economic enterprises (SEEs), since the end of the Iran–Iraq War the Iranian government has changed economic and industrial policy in favor of privatization and economic liberalization. This shift was apparent in the second and third economic development plans. One objective of these two development plans was to create a favorable environment for strong economic growth through increased participation by the private sector in investment and ownership. However, results were mixed, and the government share of economic activities actually increased during this period. For example, in the 1990s the number of SEEs increased from 268 to 453, and the annual budget of SEEs ballooned from US$506 million to US$18 billion. Between FY 1995 and FY 2004, the funding of SEEs absorbed more than 60 percent of the annual government budget. The government's budget for FY 2004 included funding for 510 SEEs, budget allocations for which totaled about US$49 billion—65.5 percent of the total budget that year. The private sector's share of GNP that year was 20 to 25 percent, according to the Chamber of Commerce of Iran.

The SEEs also receive financial support from both domestic and foreign sources. They received about US$11 million in loans from domestic banks and foreign sources during FY 2003; 66 percent of this amount was financed through foreign loans. Thus, SEEs have had a substantial presence in money and labor markets. The government also paid about US$2 billion in subsidies to businesses and consumers for the production and consumption of household and business necessities in FY 2003, 246 times more than it paid in FY 1978. In part, the intent was to make products such as wheat, rice, milk, and sugar affordable for low-income families and farmers. The policy of subsidies was in conformity with Article 43 of the constitution, which emphasizes the role of the government in eradicating poverty and privation and in providing for the basic needs of the general population. The second goal of the subsidy program was to support the producers of certain goods such as paper, detergent, and pesticides. One of the primary objectives of the third development plan (2000–2005) was to reduce the size of the public sector and its presence in the economy and to increase competition. According to a report by the Management and Planning Organization (MPO), however, during that period the budget for SEEs grew by more than 231 percent, and the number of SEEs also increased from 504 to 519. Thus, the Iranian economy again moved toward bigger government during the third development plan.

Government enterprises and corporations (enterprises with more than 50 percent public ownership) have a large place in the government's total general budget. Since the Revolution, the budget for government enterprises has increased. For example, between FY 2002 and FY 2005, the nominal budget of government enterprises increased from about US$57 billion to about US$121 billion.

Following the parliamentary elections of 2004, new initiatives sought to reduce the role of government in the national economy. The privatization clauses of Article 44 of the constitution were liberalized by amendment in 2005. In mid-2006, a decree by the Leader, Sayyid Ali Khamenei (in power 1989–), called for about 80 percent of state enterprises to be privatized, with the aim of energizing private input into the economy and redistributing wealth. The oil industry, state banks, and enterprises of strategic importance were the main exceptions in the decree, which was strongly supported by President Mahmoud Ahmadinejad (in office 2005–).

Human Resources

Iran has natural resources and an educated labor force sufficient to feed and provide essential services and employment to its population, the growth of which slowed dramatically in the late 1990s and early 2000s (see Population, ch. 2). According to preliminary figures from the 2006 census, Iran's total population was estimated at about 70 million. Employment growth may become a major issue if Iran remains dependent on imports of raw materials, machinery, and other necessities (sources of employment and income) and on exports of oil, gas, and other mineral commodities (nonrenewable resources). In FY 2004 the share of labor resources in the gross domestic product (GDP—see Glossary) reportedly was 29 percent, compared with 75 percent in the United States. The contribution of labor to GDP is so small because in Iran the shares of natural resources (34 percent) and physical resources (37 percent) in national output are relatively very high. The high concentration of population in urban areas (68.4 percent in 2006) and the continued high rate of urban growth are additional concerns.

Labor Force Participation

Between 1956 and 2004, Iran's labor force (all persons aged 10 years and older, employed or unemployed during the last seven days preceding an enumeration) increased from 6.0 million to 22.4 million. During this period, the total labor force participation rate declined from 32 percent to 31 percent. Factors in the decline in labor market participation by both males and females include an increased tendency for those age 10 and older to remain in school (the share of students not in the labor force increased from 10 percent in 1956 to 45 percent in 2004), a decline in the number of active job seekers among the unemployed, and an increase in the labor market's turnover rate. In 1956 the labor force's male participation rate was 57.0 percent; it increased to 63.3 percent by 2004. The female labor force participation rate increased from 6.2 percent to 11.2 percent (13.5 percent in rural areas) between 1956 and 2004. However, all of that growth occurred before 1979 and after 1996. In 2004 employed females accounted for 13.8 percent of the total employed population—an increase of only 3.1 percent over the previous 47 years. Thus, despite women's educational achievements over the half-century, their labor force participation rate and share of employment have remained relatively constant, at very low levels.

Unemployment

Iran's population is young and urbanized, with 60 percent under 30 years of age. For these reasons, in the early 2000s unemployment was one of the most challenging issues confronting the Iranian government. In the years following the 1996 census, the unemployment rate increased to 13.2 percent as large numbers of young people flooded the job market. The official unemployment rate was 12.5 percent in 2004. The unofficial rate in 2004 and subsequently was an estimated 14 percent. In 1996 female unemployment rates were estimated at 19.0 percent for the country as a whole and 14.3 percent for rural areas; during the 1976 and 1986 censuses, the rates were 25 percent and 21 percent, respectively. Between 2000 and 2004, an average of 705,000 new job seekers entered the labor market annually. Job growth, however, did not keep up. Only 2.28 million jobs were created in that period (570,000 each year)—only 78 percent of the third development plan's goal. Unemployment was highest among 15- to 19-year-olds (the largest portion of the labor force). Among 15- to 29-year-olds, the jobless rate was 14.8 percent in 1997; by 2001, the rate had increased to 27.5 percent. In 2004 the unemployment rate for this cohort reportedly was 34.0 percent, and it was estimated that if the annual unemployment rate of 13.2 percent persisted through 2007, the jobless rate among this age-group would reach 50 percent. In 2002 the parliament (Majlis—see Glossary) passed a resolution encouraging Iranian job seekers to work overseas (in other Persian Gulf countries and Southeast Asian countries) under the supervision of the government.

Since then, however, only a negligible number of Iranian blue-collar and professional workers have gained such employment.

The Distribution of Employment

In 2004 private-sector employment was 16.8 million, and public-sector employees numbered 5.6 million. The share of public-sector employment increased between 1965 and the early 2000s as oil and gas revenues grew. The private-sector share of total employment, which was 90 percent in 1956, declined to 75 percent in 2004 as the public-sector share increased from 10 percent to 25 percent—an average annual growth rate of 5.5 percent—during this period. By comparison, in the early 2000s overall employment grew at a rate of only 2.9 percent annually. Most of the public-sector job growth occurred after 1977. Meanwhile, between 1956 and 2004 private-sector employment increased at a moderate rate of 1.5 percent.

In 2004 self-employed individuals constituted the largest group within the private sector, totaling 5.3 million. The highest proportion of self-employed individuals was in the services sector (46 percent), followed by agriculture (42 percent). Wage and salary earners were the other major group in the private sector. Between 1956 and 2004, the number of employees in this group also increased, from 2.25 million to 5.06 million.

Predominant in the structure of the agricultural workforce are small farms that employ few workers and rely heavily on unpaid family members for labor (see Agriculture, Forestry, and Fishing, this ch.). In 2004 the agricultural sector had 687,000 wage and salary earners, of which the public sector (including cooperatives) accounted for only 13 percent. Some 61 percent of unpaid family workers were in agriculture that year.

Beginning in the mid-1950s, significant shifts occurred in the employment structure among the economic sectors. Between 1956 and 2004, agriculture's share of total employment declined from 56.3 percent to 21.7 percent (see table 6, Appendix). Concurrently, the services sector's share increased from 23.6 percent to 47.7 percent, at a pace corresponding to the growth of public-sector jobs in the labor market. Industry's share (including mining, manufacturing, construction, water, and energy) increased from 20.1 percent in 1956 to 34.2 percent in 1976, then declined to 25.3 percent by 1986 (see Industry and Construction, this ch.). During the 1990s and early

2000s, it again increased, reaching 30.7 percent in 1996 and 30.6 percent in 2004. The shares of manufacturing and construction employment have fluctuated less than those of the other sectors.

Organized Labor

Although Iran belongs to the International Labor Organization (ILO, which nominally guarantees workers the right to organize and negotiate with employers) and Iran's constitution guarantees the right to form unions, labor unions in Iran have suffered severe repression, particularly under the Ahmadinejad regime. In the first half of 2007, some 600 labor leaders reportedly were imprisoned, and thousands of workers have been imprisoned for activities deemed hostile to the regime. The government controls labor through the Workers' House, which is the only legal national labor organization, representing workers in labor negotiations with management representatives in Islamic labor councils. Those councils are the only forums sanctioned by the government for such negotiations. A particularly active labor organization has been the Bus Drivers' Union of Tehran, whose 17,000 members periodically have engaged anti-union regimes and staged protests in the postrevolutionary period.

National Output Measurements

Iran has systematically measured national output (the annual value of all final goods and services produced for market transaction) since 1960, when the newly established central bank (Bank Markazi) was given responsibility for collecting and computing national accounts data. Bank Markazi has employed procedures recommended by the United Nations to estimate GDP. However, reliable estimates of GDP have been hampered by a lack of trained personnel and the existence of a large proportion of nonmonetary transactions within the economy. Domestic output typically is estimated in three sectors: agriculture, industry and mining, and services. Estimates for the oil and gas sector are made separately because of that sector's importance in the economy (see table 7, Appendix).

Gross Domestic Product

The long-term growth trend of Iran's GDP between 1960 and the late 1970s was reversed during the Revolution and the

A copper artisan plies his trade on a street in Esfahan.
Courtesy United Nations

A young vegetable vendor
Courtesy Nader Davoodi

years immediately following. Both internal and external factors were responsible for this reversal, which was sharpest in the oil and gas sector. Between 1978 and 1989, GDP decreased at an average annual rate of 1.7 percent. During the same period, the agriculture sector grew at 4.5 percent annually. With reconstruction programs and a recovery in oil output, real economic growth rebounded between 1990 and 2004. GDP increased at an average rate of about 5.3 percent annually (in constant prices) during this period. Fluctuations in the GDP growth pattern during this period included a recovery period from 1989 to 1993 and a recession during 1993–94, when the economy experienced lower oil prices and economic sanctions. Between 2000 and 2004, because of increases in crude oil prices, above-average rainfall, growth in the manufacturing sector, and economic stability, the country's real GDP increased by 5.6 percent per year, its fastest rate since the Revolution. In 2006 GDP at market prices was US$194.8 billion, and GDP per capita at market prices was US$2,978, an increase of about 6 percent over 2005.

Because the country's population increased by 25 percent between 1989 and 2004, per capita GDP in constant prices remained below its 1978 level. Overall, real GDP growth in Iran averaged about 5.0 percent a year (about 2.4 percent in per capita terms) from 1960 to 2004. Nonhydrocarbon GDP grew at a faster pace of 5.8 percent, while hydrocarbon GDP grew by 2.2 percent during this period.

Although average per capita income increased substantially between 1990 and 2004, evidence suggests that the entire population did not benefit from this economic growth, and some subsets of the population remained untouched. Although overall income distribution improved, the growth primarily benefited the wealthiest 10 percent of the population, while the next 30 percent received a relatively smaller share. Reportedly, 15 percent of the population was in absolute poverty. In 2004 average annual income of an urban household (from all sources) was about US$4,500, and that of a rural household averaged about US$2,800. The average annual expenditure was US$4,822 in urban areas and US$3,021 in rural areas that year. For the average family, expenditures on housing, food, and utilities were the fastest growing.

Industry and mining was the economic sector with the highest growth rate in the early 2000s. Within this sector, between 2000 and 2004 manufacturing grew at an annual rate of 10.6

percent. At 4.8 and 4.4 percent, respectively, the growth rates for services and agriculture lagged behind the average annual GDP growth rate during this period.

Gross Domestic Expenditure

Gross domestic expenditure (GDE) figures suggest that spending for private consumption increased as GDP grew between 1960 and 2004, except during the Revolution. During this period, Iran's investment rate (average total investment divided by GDP) exceeded 30 percent—a level comparable to that in the high-growth East Asian countries. Gross investment in equipment and construction increased at a rate of 7.4 percent of GDE. However, the share of investment in equipment did not keep pace with capital formation, most of which occurred in the construction sector.

Equipment investment has been the most volatile portion of total domestic expenditures. The share of equipment investment surpassed construction investment for the first time in 1996 and continued to increase in the early 2000s. Between 1995 and 2004, the private sector's share of equipment investment increased steadily, as the second and third five-year development plans made more investment opportunities available to the private sector.

The Informal Sector

Informal-sector activities primarily engage small-scale merchants selling a variety of items. However, the informal sector of the economy also includes carpenters, masons, tailors, and other tradespeople, as well as private tutors, cooks, and taxi drivers, offering virtually the full range of basic skills needed to provide goods and services to large sections of the population. Thus, informal employment is not confined to the peripheries of the large cities, particular occupations, or even specific economic activities. Government largely ignores, rarely supports, and sometimes actively discourages informal-sector activities. Such activities are not regulated, and they operate largely outside the system of government benefits and regulations. Thus, the informal sector is not included in GDP measurements; it also does not pay its share of taxes. In the early 2000s, most experts believed that economic activity in the informal sector accounted for about 20 percent of the Iranian GDP.

The Petroleum Industry

In 2004 Iran produced 5.1 percent of the world's total crude oil (3.9 million barrels per day—bpd; see Glossary), which generated revenues of US$25 billion to US$30 billion and was the country's primary source of foreign currency and employment. At 2006 levels of production, oil proceeds represented about 18.7 percent of GDP. However, the importance of the hydrocarbon sector to Iran's economy has been far greater. The oil and gas industry has been the engine of economic growth, directly affecting public development projects, the government's annual budget, and most foreign-exchange sources. In FY 2004, for example, the sector accounted for 25 percent of total government revenues and 85 percent of the total annual value of both exports and foreign currency earnings. However, oil and gas revenues are affected by the value of crude oil on the international market. It has been estimated that at the Organization of the Petroleum Exporting Countries (OPEC—see Glossary) quota level (December 2004), a one-dollar change in the price of crude oil on the international market would alter Iran's oil revenues by US$1 billion.

Historical Overview

The Era of International Control, 1901–79

The history of Iran's oil industry began in 1901, when British speculator William D'Arcy received a concession to explore and develop southern Iran's oil resources. The discovery of oil in 1908 led to the formation in 1909 of the London-based Anglo-Persian Oil Company (APOC). By purchasing a majority of the company's shares in 1914, the British government gained direct control of the Iranian oil industry, which it would not relinquish for 37 years. After 1935 the APOC was called the Anglo-Iranian Oil Company (AIOC). A 60-year agreement signed in 1933 established a flat payment to Iran of four British pounds for every ton of crude oil exported and denied Iran any right to control oil exports.

In 1950 ongoing popular demand prompted a vote in the Majlis to nationalize the petroleum industry. A year later, the government of Prime Minister Mohammad Mossadeq formed the National Iranian Oil Company (NIOC). A 1953 coup d'état led by British and U.S. intelligence agencies ousted the Mossadeq government and paved the way for a new oil agreement

Petroleum is the engine that drives the Iranian economy.
Courtesy United Nations (E. Adams)

(see Mossadeq and Oil Nationalization, ch. 1). In 1954 a new agreement divided profits equally between the NIOC and a multinational consortium that had replaced the AIOC. In 1973 Iran signed a new 20-year concession with the consortium.

Beginning in the late 1950s, many of Iran's international oil agreements did not produce the expected outcomes; even those oil companies that managed to extract oil in their designated areas contributed very little to the country's total oil production. By the time of the Islamic Revolution of 1978–79, the five largest international companies that had agreements with the NIOC accounted for only 10.4 percent of total oil production. During this period, Iran's oil industry remained disconnected from other industries, particularly manufacturing. This separation promoted inefficiencies in the country's overall industrial economy.

The Era of Nationalized Oil, 1979–

Following the Revolution, the NIOC took control of Iran's petroleum industry and cancelled Iran's international oil agreements. In 1980 the exploration, production, sale, and export of oil were delegated to the Ministry of Petroleum. Initially Iran's postrevolutionary oil policy was based on foreign currency requirements and the long-term preservation of the natural resource. Following the Iran–Iraq War, however, this policy was replaced by a more aggressive approach: maximizing exports and accelerating economic growth. Prior to 1998, Iran did not sign any oil agreements with foreign oil companies. Early in the first administration of President Mohammad Khatami (in office 1997–2005), the government paid special attention to developing the country's oil and gas industry. Oil was defined as intergenerational capital and an indispensable foundation of economic development. Thus, between 1997 and 2004 Iran invested more than US$40 billion in expanding the capacity of existing oil fields and discovering and exploring new fields and deposits. These projects were financed either in the form of joint investments with foreign companies or domestic contractors or through direct investment by the NIOC. In accordance with the law, foreign investment in oil discovery was possible only in the form of buyback agreements under which the NIOC was required to reimburse expenses and retain complete ownership of an oil field. Marketing of crude oil to potential buyers was managed by the NIOC and by a government enterprise called Nicoo. Nicoo marketed Iranian oil to Africa, and the NIOC marketed to Asia and Europe.

Oil Production and Reserves

Total oil production reached a peak level of 6.6 million bpd in 1976. By 1978, Iran had become the second-largest OPEC producer and exporter of crude oil and the fourth-largest producer in the world. After a lengthy decline in the 1980s, production of crude oil began to increase steadily in 1987. In 2006 Iran produced 4.0 million bpd and exported 2.5 million bpd. Accounting for 5.1 percent of world production, it returned to its previous position as OPEC's second-largest producer. According to estimates, in 2005 Iran had the capacity to produce 4.5 million bpd; it was believed that production capacity could increase to 5 million bpd by 2010, but only with a substantial increase in foreign investment. Iran's long-term sustainable oil production rate is estimated at 3.8 million bpd.

In 2006 Iran reported crude oil reserves of 132.5 billion barrels, accounting for about 15 percent of OPEC's proven reserves and 11.4 percent of world proven reserves. While the estimate of world crude oil reserves remained nearly steady between 2001 and 2006, at 1,154 billion barrels, the estimate of Iran's oil reserves was revised upward by 32 percent when a new field was discovered near Bushehr. In the early 2000s, leading international oil firms from China, France, India, Italy, the Netherlands, Norway, Russia, Spain, and the United Kingdom had agreements to develop Iran's oil and gas fields. In 2004 China signed a major agreement to buy oil and gas from Iran, as well as to develop Iran's Yavaran oil field. The value of this contract was estimated at US$150 billion to US$200 billion over 25 years. A more modest yet important agreement was signed with India to explore and produce oil and natural gas in southern Iran. In 2006 the rate of production decline was 8 percent for Iran's existing onshore oil fields (furnishing the majority of oil output) and 10 percent for existing offshore fields. Little exploration, upgrading, or establishment of new fields occurred in 2005–6.

Oil Refining and Consumption

In 2006 Iran's refineries had a combined capacity of 1.64 million bpd. The largest refineries have the following capacities: Abadan, 400,000 bpd; Esfahan, 265,000 bpd; Bandar-e Abbas, 232,000 bpd; Tehran, 225,000 bpd; Arak, 150,000 bpd; and Tabriz, 112,000 bpd (see fig. 8). In 2004 pipelines conveyed 69 percent of total refined products; trucks, 20 percent; rail, 7 percent; and tankers, 4 percent. Oil refining produces a wide range of oil products, such as liquefied petroleum gas (LPG), gasoline, kerosene, fuel oil, and lubricants.

Between 1981 and 2004, domestic consumption of oil products increased from 0.6 million bpd to 1.1 million bpd—an average annual growth rate of 2.6 percent. Most of this growth in consumption occurred between 1980 and 2001. Between 1981 and 2004, consumption of gasoline grew by 6 percent annually, but domestic production met only 75 percent of demand for this product. In 2004 the country imported US$1.6 billion worth of gasoline. By 2006 it imported 41 percent of its gasoline. Most imported gasoline is purchased at very high prices from the Middle East and Venezuela. Iran had invested between US$100 million and US$150 million to expand gasoline production to 8 million liters per day by 2007.

Trade in Oil and Oil Products

In 2006 exports of crude oil totaled 2.5 million bpd, or about 62.5 percent of the country's crude oil production. The direction of crude oil exports changed after the Revolution because of the U.S. trade embargo on Iran and the marketing

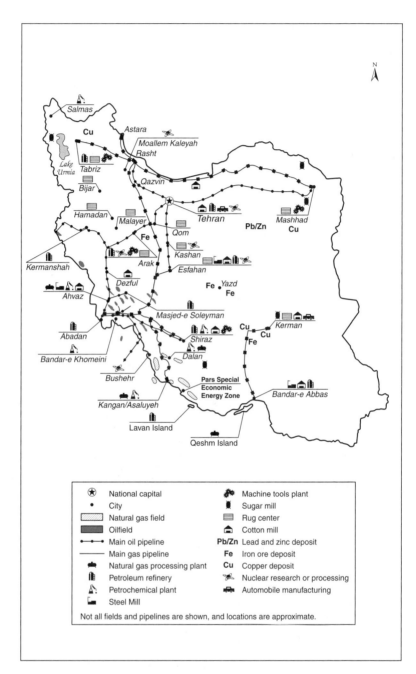

Figure 8. Industry and Mining, 2005

strategy of the NIOC. Initially, Iran's postrevolutionary crude oil export policy was based on foreign currency requirements and the need for long-term preservation of the natural resource. In addition, the government expanded oil trade with other developing countries. While the shares of Europe, Japan, and the United States declined from an average of 87 percent of oil exports before the Revolution to 52 percent in the early 2000s, the share of exports to East Asia (excluding Japan) increased significantly (see table 8, Appendix). In addition to crude oil exports, Iran exports oil products. In 2006 it exported 282,000 barrels of oil products, or about 21 percent of its total oil product output.

Natural Gas

In addition to the natural gas associated with oil exploration and extraction, an estimated 62 percent of Iran's 32.3 trillion cubic meters of proven natural gas reserves in 2006 were located in independent natural gas fields, an amount second only to those of Russia. In 2006 annual production reached 105 billion cubic meters, with fastest growth occurring over the previous 15 years. In 2006 natural gas accounted for abut 50 percent of domestic energy consumption, in part because domestic gas prices were heavily subsidized.

Since 1979, infrastructure investment by Iranian and foreign oil firms has increased pipeline capacity to support the Iranian gas industry. Between 1979 and 2003, pipelines to transport natural gas to refineries and to domestic consumers increased from 2,000 kilometers to 12,000 kilometers. In the same period, natural gas distribution pipelines increased from 2,000 kilometers to 45,000 kilometers in response to growing domestic consumption. Gas processing plants are located at Ahvaz, Dalan, Kangan, and Marun, in a corridor along the northern Persian Gulf close to the major gas fields. South Pars, Iran's largest natural gas field, has received substantial foreign investment. With its output intended for both export and domestic consumption, South Pars is expected to reach full production in 2015. The output of South Pars is the basis of the Pars Special Economic Energy Zone, a complex of petrochemical and natural gas processing plants and port facilities established in 1998 on the Persian Gulf south of Kangan.

In the 1980s, Iran began to replace oil, coal, charcoal, and other fossil-fuel energy sources with natural gas, which is environmentally safer. The share of natural gas in household energy consumption, which averaged 54 percent in 2004, was projected to increase to 69 percent by 2009. Overall, natural gas consumption in Iran was expected to grow by more than 10 percent per annum between 2005 and 2009.

With international oil prices increasing and projected to continue increasing, international demand for natural gas and investment in production and transportation of natural gas to consumer markets both increased in the early 2000s. Iran set a goal of increasing its natural gas production capacity to 300 billion cubic meters by 2015 while keeping oil production stable. To achieve this capacity, the government has planned a joint investment worth US$100 billion in the oil and gas industry through 2015. In 2004 Iran signed a contract with France and Malaysia for production and export of natural gas and another agreement with European and Asian companies for expansion and marketing of its natural gas resources. In 2005 Iran exported natural gas to Turkey and was expected to expand its market to Armenia, China, Japan, other East Asian countries, India, Pakistan, and Europe. The first section of a new line to Armenia opened in spring 2007, as a much-discussed major pipeline to India and Pakistan remained in the negotiation stage.

Petrochemicals

In the early 2000s, an ambitious state petrochemicals project called for expansion of annual output in that industry from 9 million tons in 2001 to 27 million tons in 2013. Output capacity in 2006 was estimated at 15 million tons. The goal of this expansion is to increase the percentage of Iran's processed petroleum-based exports, which are more profitable than raw materials. In 2005 Iran exported US$1.8 billion of petrochemical products (about one-third of total nonoil exports in that year). Receiving 30 percent of Iran's petrochemical exports between them, China and India were the major trading partners in this industry. Iran's domestic resource base gives it a unique comparative advantage in producing petrochemicals when international crude oil prices rise. The gain has been greatest in those plants that use liquid gas as their main input. For FY 2006, the petrochemical industry's share of GDP was projected to be about 2 percent.

Iran's petrochemical industries have absorbed a large amount of private and public investment. In the early 2000s, 43 percent of these investments was financed by Iran's National

Petrochemical Company, a subsidiary of the Ministry of Petroleum, which administers the entire petrochemical sector. Another 53 percent is owned by foreign creditors (more than 100 foreign banks and foreign companies), 3 percent by banks, and 1 percent by the capital market. Most of the petrochemical industry's physical capital is imported, and the industry does not have strong backward linkages to manufacturing industries. In 2006 new petrochemical plants came online at Marun and Asaluyeh, and construction began on three others.

Mining

In 2006 Iran produced more than 15 different nonradioactive metals and 27 nonmetal minerals. The mined products yielding the greatest value were iron ore, decorative stones, gravel and sand, coal, copper ore, and limestone. In 2003 active mines produced 99 million tons of minerals worth an estimated US$729 million. The fastest-growing nonpetroleum extraction industry is copper. An estimated 4 percent of the world's copper is in Iran, whose Sar Cheshnah deposit in the southeast is the second largest in the world. A 1997 agreement with the Svedala Company of Sweden has upgraded the copper mines and established new processing plants. Between 2001 and 2005, the industry's annual capacity increased from 173,000 tons to 300,000 tons. In 2006 copper accounted for 4 percent of total exports.

Since the Revolution, the government has retained monopoly rights to the extraction, processing, and sales of minerals from large and strategic mines. The private sector has been allowed limited access to a particular class of small mines with the approval of relevant government agencies. Since 1998, however, the private sector's role has increased. A more flexible interpretation of the constitutional definitions of state and private ownership by the Expediency Council in 2004 and a 2005 amendment to Article 44 of the constitution, which specifies conditions for privatization, were expected to increase the role of the private sector in mining.

In 2003 a total of 2,955 mines were operating. Of these, 332 were managed by the public sector (ministries, government organizations, Islamic Revolution foundations, banks, and municipalities), and 2,623 were run by the private sector (individuals or private institutions). From 2003 to 2004, the mining industry had the second-highest growth rate (12.7 percent) in value added, after oil and gas, among all industries. In 2004 total employment in the sector was estimated at more than 88,000.

Adjusted for inflation, capital formation in the mining industries increased more than eightfold between 1986 and 2003. During the fourth economic development plan, initiated in March 2005, the government planned to invest US$17 billion in mining and related industries, US$8.5 billion of which would be allocated to importing tools and intermediate goods.

Because of inefficient linkages with the manufacturing sector, most of the necessary physical capital for mining (tools, machinery, and parts) is imported at relatively high prices. Given the country's extensive metal and nonmetal mineral reserves, vertical integration of mining with other industries would provide important employment opportunities for the country's rapidly growing labor force. The rise in transportation costs is a major obstacle to further development of the mining industry. Transportation costs quadrupled from 2001 to 2005 and were expected to escalate further because of a lack of infrastructure (highways, railroads, warehouses, and seaport facilities) and oil price increases. Also, mining operations have not been able to extract sufficient metals such as copper, zinc, coke, and gold to satisfy the needs of domestic industries.

Agriculture, Forestry, and Fishing

Agriculture traditionally was Iran's primary source of food, raw materials, foreign exchange, employment, and income. In 1960 it accounted for 23.5 percent of GDP and employed 54 percent of the labor force. By 2006, however, the share of GDP had declined to 11.2 percent, and agriculture employed less than 20 percent of the labor force.

Of Iran's total area of 1.65 million square kilometers, about 11 percent is arable; the remainder is covered with mountains, rivers, lakes, roads, and residential and industrial areas or is otherwise not suitable for agriculture. The most productive agricultural land, bordering the Caspian Sea, makes up only 5.5 percent of the country's total land. The rugged mountains in the north and west are used as pastureland for meat and dairy livestock. Because of uneven rainfall distribution, only 10 percent of the country receives sufficient moisture to support agriculture without irrigation. Iran has the requisite conditions (land, water, tools, and labor) to produce sufficient agricultural products to satisfy domestic demand. It has adequate arable land and water, farm tools, and experienced and knowledgeable farmers. Obstacles to the application of these resources include inefficient water distribution, land erosion, low levels of productivity, underutilization or misuse of fertilizers, inadequate investment and technology, insufficient use of improved seed, land deterioration, domination by middlemen, and a shortage of management expertise.

Since the early twentieth century, most of the sector's public and private investments have encouraged farmers to favor cash crops for export. As a result, in some years the country has experienced shortages of staple crops, particularly wheat. Nevertheless, Iran has remained an exporter of agricultural products throughout history. In the early 1980s, the revolutionary government focused on establishing agricultural self-sufficiency and building farm communities. Since the introduction of the Islamic Republic's first five-year economic development plan, preference has been given to large-scale farming, modern production methods, a more centralized administrative approach, and relatively scaled-down government investment. Although agricultural production's share of GDP declined from 16.4 percent to 11.2 percent between 1992 and 2006, per capita food production almost doubled. Iran's state-run Agricultural Products Insurance Fund, which provides producers security against risks of low production and price fluctuation, is the only such plan in the region.

Crops and Livestock

Iran's primary crops are wheat, barley, rice, pistachios, sugar beets, sugarcane, seed cotton, potatoes, legumes, tea, tomatoes, saffron, and onions (see table 9, Appendix). Some 85.5 percent of Iran's cultivated agricultural land is allocated to crops—particularly wheat, barley, and rice. These crops are grown in several areas of the country; rice is the only crop grown exclusively under irrigation. In 2004 about 62.7 million tons of crops were produced in an area of 122,000 square kilometers. Significant gains in yield and productivity occurred in the early 2000s. During that period, the total area under cultivation remained relatively constant, but the distribution of crops changed. Between 1998 and 2003, for example, the area of wheat cultivation declined by 12 percent, and the area of barley cultivation by 56 percent, while the area of pistachio cultivation increased by 148 percent, and the area of legumes cultivation by 239 percent.

Except for declines in cotton, the production of other major crops grew significantly between 1988 and 2003. Despite its relatively small tonnage, the pistachio crop returns very high value to Iran; production reached a high of 310,000 tons in 2003.

Iran's main livestock products are mutton, lamb, beef, veal, eggs, chicken, and milk from cows, goats, and sheep. According to the Ministry of Agriculture, the output of poultry and livestock (red meat, chicken, milk, and eggs) increased from 7.2 million tons in 1987 to 8.8 million tons in 2004. During the same period, the relative contribution of livestock products (red meat and milk) increased significantly, from 4.0 million tons to 7.1 million tons. In 2004 the total number of livestock was 63.6 million head (58 percent sheep, 32 percent goats, 9 percent cattle, and 1 percent buffaloes and camels). Total milk production was 6 million tons. Although livestock and poultry raising techniques have become more sophisticated in recent years, traditional free grazing still predominates.

Government Agricultural Policy

In theory, Iranian agricultural policy is intended to support farmers and encourage the production of strategically important crops. The policy is twofold: first, to purchase certain crops at guaranteed prices and second, to encourage the production of specific crops through farm subsidies. The policy of purchasing agricultural crops from farmers at guaranteed prices was put in place in the 1989 crop year. On average, the guaranteed prices increased at the rate of inflation over the past 15 years. Individual subsidy levels for major crops, however, vary annually.

In the 1990s and early 2000s, government agricultural planning was only marginally successful. According to government figures, during the 1990s—coincident with the first two Islamic Republic economic plans—only 40.5 percent of the agricultural modernization projected by those plans was accomplished, and only 40.2 percent of government and private-sector financial commitments materialized.

Because wheat is considered Iran's most strategically important crop, it received the largest subsidies, and its production grew at the fastest rate between 1990 and 2005. From FY 2003 to FY 2004, wheat subsidies increased by 17.2 percent, reaching a record of US$1.5 billion. Between 1981 and 2004, the area cultivated with wheat remained stable at 5 million hectares, but

Siphon irrigation being used in a sugar-beet field near Qazvin
Courtesy United Nations

Women planting rice in the Caspian Sea region
Courtesy Nader Davoodi

171

wheat production increased from 5.7 million to more than 11 million tons.

Beginning in 1990, the government expanded its agricultural support programs to include a guaranteed purchase price for major agricultural crops, subsidies, favorable interest rates, government investment, and favorable foreign-trade policies. Primarily because of government support for domestic agriculture, between 1989 and 2003 the import volumes of wheat, sugar, and red meat declined by 77.7 percent, 39.6 percent, and 88.2 percent, respectively. Concurrently, the value of agricultural exports increased from US$461.5 million in 1989 to US$1.7 billion in 2004. However, over the same period total food and live animal imports increased from US$1.37 billion to US$2.65 billion.

Forestry

In 2005 Iran's forest area totaled about 11 million hectares, approximately 7 percent of the country's surface area. Adequate rainfall and a favorable climate have created 1.5 million hectares of dense forest in the Caspian region. The remainder is distributed among western forests (3.6 million hectares), southern forests (434,000 hectares), desert forests (620,000 hectares), and forests scattered in other locations. Supervised by the Department of Natural Resources, the Caspian forests produced 820,000 cubic meters of timber products in 2004, more than 90 percent of which was for industrial use. Although forests and pastures are nationalized and 12 percent of forested land is nominally protected, forest destruction by the private sector is routine. Limited forest areas, mismanagement, and destruction have compelled Iran to import lumber and wood products. In addition, forest fires destroy 20,000 hectares of forest area each year. Between 1954 and 2004, an estimated 41 percent of Iran's forest land was lost.

Fishing

Access to the Caspian Sea, the Persian Gulf, the Gulf of Oman, and many river basins provides Iran the potential to develop excellent fisheries. The government assumed control of commercial fishing in 1952. One government-owned enterprise, the Northern Sheelat Company, was established in 1952, and a second, the Southern Sheelat Company, was established in 1961. In recent years, illegal and off-season fishing, discharge of industrial and agricultural pollutants, overfishing by other Caspian littoral states, and other unfavorable conditions have endangered Caspian fish resources. Between 1990 and 2004, Iran's total annual Caspian Sea catch declined from 98,000 tons to 32,533 tons, including 463 tons of sturgeon, which yields high-quality caviar.

Iran has 1,786 kilometers of coastline on the Persian Gulf and the Gulf of Oman. These southern waters are rich in fish and other marine resources. In 2004 the catch off the southern coast totaled 299,000 tons. This represented an average annual increase of 12.6 percent since 1976. The southern catch either is used directly by households and restaurants or processed and preserved by industry. Expansion of the fishery infrastructure would enable the country to harvest an estimated 700,000 tons of fish annually from the southern waters. However, increased pollution from the oil industry and other enterprises poses a serious threat to this area's fishing industry.

Since the Revolution, increased attention has been focused on producing fish from inland waters. Between 1976 and 2004, the combined take from inland waters by the state and private sectors increased from 1,100 tons to 110,175 tons.

Industry and Construction

Iran's industries include indigenous small businesses (producers of handicrafts, carpets, and other light goods) and large-scale manufacturers of consumer or intermediate goods. While smaller industries rely on domestic sources of labor, raw materials, and tools, larger ones depend primarily on imported raw materials and investment. Introduced into the Iranian economy during the reign of Reza Shah Pahlavi (1925–41), large-scale and "modern" industries have not grown in response to the needs of the economy, but rather in response to political goals, economic concessions, regional pressures, and, most importantly, the ebb and flow of oil revenues.

Handicrafts

Throughout history, Iranians have been involved in handicraft activities that evolved in response to available resources and markets in various parts of the country. These industries include the manufacture of glassware, pottery, tile and other construction materials; architecture; jade; the working of metal and wood; and the production of leather products, textiles, apparel, paintings and sculpture, and, most notably, carpets.

Handicraft activities serve the needs of agriculture, construction, transportation, defense, households, businesses, and other sectors of the economy. These industries are complementary to the farm sector and obtain 90 percent of their resources domestically. In addition, handicrafts are a major source of employment, export revenue, and foreign exchange. Through the middle of the Qajar era (1795–1925), handicraft industries were dynamic, diversified, and competitive. These industries lost their economic standing, however, as competing manufactured goods, particularly textiles and apparel, were imported more freely, and Iran began to export more raw materials such as silk and cotton to Europe and India. Growth occurred only in handicrafts that had large domestic or international markets, such as carpets and rugs, and those that were more competitive, such as leather products.

Iranians were the earliest carpet weavers among the ancient civilizations; through centuries of creativity and ingenuity, their carpets achieved a unique degree of excellence. Persian carpets and rugs always have been an intrinsic part of Iranian culture and daily life. The craft holds a unique position in industrial production, sales, and exports. It is complementary to both agriculture and rural industries. During the Pahlavi dynasty (1925–79), the craft of carpet making was encouraged both directly, through orders for the court and government, and indirectly, through facilitated export and trade. Carpet making has played a pivotal role in rural development. In FY 1997, 1.81 million Iranians (85 percent of them female), working in a total of about 901,000 households, were engaged in cottage industries that manufactured about US$400 million of carpets and rugs. In addition, cooperatives employing a total of 114,931 workers were producing handwoven carpets. Although official statistics are not available, it has been reported that between 4 and 7 million individuals in rural and urban areas were directly and indirectly engaged in this industry in FY 2004.

After a sharp reduction in the early 1980s, carpet exports surged to a record high of US$600 million in the 1990s. Despite stagnation and intense international competition, Iran held a 20 percent market share in FY 2004, exporting carpets valued at a total of US$600 million. That year the industry directly employed 1.8 million laborers, 90 percent of whom were in rural areas.

The manufacturing of carpets and rugs is an important element in Iran's economy.
Courtesy United Nations (John Isaac)

Artisan preparing ceramic bowls
Courtesy Nader Davoodi

Manufacturing

Modern manufacturing industries (plants and companies that produce or assemble durable and nondurable goods) were introduced under Reza Shah Pahlavi. Since then, manufacturing industries have generally grown faster than GDP. Their growth, however, has been correlated strongly with the growth of oil revenues. The oil revenue booms of the 1970s and 1990s were accompanied by high rates of manufacturing growth.

Small Industries

Small, light industrial establishments (i.e., those having fewer than 10 employees) are located in both rural and urban areas. In FY 2003 about 426,000 small manufacturing establishments were in operation. They produced US$6 billion of durable goods, such as metal products, medical devices, and transportation equipment, and nondurable goods, such as food and beverages, textiles, leather, and paper products. In FY 2003 the total capital investment in small industry was US$187 million, the sector's value added was about US$3.2 billion, and small industry employed more than 1 million workers that year. Wage and salary earners made up 51 percent of the sector's total workforces, as compared to just 33 percent in 1977. Almost 100 percent of small manufacturing establishments were privately owned.

Large Industry

Since their introduction into the Iranian economy during the 1930s, large manufacturing establishments have been mostly state-run enterprises, generally funded with oil revenues and indirect taxes. The growth rates of both small and large manufacturing concerns have increased significantly since the mid-1960s because of government investment in the manufacturing sector. Since the early 1990s, the government has used privatization and other incentives to increase the private sector's role in manufacturing. Major manufacturing establishment indexes (output, employment, and total compensation) showed significant gains during this period.

The 1996 census showed 13,371 establishments in the category of large industries (those having more than 10 employees). Some 1,329 in that category had more than 100 employees. By FY 2003, the number of establishments with more than 100 employees had increased to 1,797, of which

Laborers weigh and process jute in a small mill.
Courtesy U.S. Information Agency

1,397 were privately owned. The fastest growth rates occurred among manufacturers of durable goods, with the production of transportation vehicles and equipment showing the largest gain: Its index rose from 100 to 650 from 1996 to 2003. For example, from FY 2003 to FY 2004 the number of motor vehicles produced in Iran went from 531,461 to 753,378, an increase of more than 40 percent. In FY 2003 the total number of workers in large manufacturing establishments was about 1,026,000, about half of the total manufacturing employment that year.

Among Iran's most important large industries are the manufacture of petrochemicals and automobiles and food processing. The petrochemicals industry, dominated by the state-owned National Petrochemicals Company, has grown rapidly, with output in FY 2002 worth US$1.4 billion. The industry has received substantial foreign investment. Automobile manufacture has benefited from licensing agreements with European and Asian manufacturers. In 2002 the largest plant, Iran Khodro, built about 260,000 units, and several smaller facilities produced a total of about 240,000 vehicles. In 2005 Iran ceased production of the Paykan, which had been the chief domestic automobile model since the 1970s. In 2006 Khodro introduced the Samand model to replace the Paykan. The processing of agricultural products also is an important industry, dominated by domestic private firms. Among the major subsectors are grain processing and fruit and vegetable canning.

Heavy Industry

Iran's heavy industrial factories produce metal products such as steel, aluminum, and copper; nonmetal intermediate goods; and finished industrial products such as tractors and construction equipment for both domestic and foreign markets. In the early 2000s, Iran's heavy manufacturing industry faced several serious challenges. First, it was largely dependent on imports for raw materials, spare parts, and equipment. Second, production standards were below international requirements, and therefore little excess production could be exported. Third, the concentration of heavy manufacturing industries in Tehran Province entailed high transportation costs for raw materials and finished products. Other problems associated with these industries were a lack of domestic competition (they were mostly monopolies or oligopolies), low productivity rates, low profits, insufficient internal investment, relatively small size (hence, few economies of scale), and high demand for foreign currencies.

The country's first modern steel mill, with a capacity of 550 million tons per year, opened in Esfahan in 1972. This complex, which remains a key part of the industry in the early 2000s, included factories for sheet metal and shape metal and had a total capacity of 1 million tons. An aluminum plant with a capacity of 90,000 tons and a copper mill with a capacity of 120,000 tons were established in the early 1970s. In the 1970s, joint investments with East European countries and the Soviet Union led to the establishment of several plants to produce and assemble industrial machinery. Following the Revolution, most expansion of heavy industry occurred through joint investment with the United Kingdom, France, Germany, and Italy. The role of the private sector also increased; in 2004, for example, private-sector steel production reportedly was about 2 million tons, five times more than the previous year.

The steel industry, which is centered at Ahvaz, Esfahan, and Mobarakeh, has grown rapidly since 1990. In 2004 Iran produced 19 million tons of steel and steel products (8.5 tons of raw steel and 10.5 tons of treated steel and steel products). For the period covered by the fourth economic development plan (March 2005–March 2010), Iran planned to increase the production of steel and steel products to 36 million tons. Meeting this goal would require substantial increases in joint investment and private investment and the import of appropriate raw materials and machinery. However, between 1995 and 2002 the level of investment declined. This downturn indicated that in the early 2000s the sector's growth was lagging far behind other manufacturing industries, and that its potential for future growth was uncertain. In FY 2004 investment in the large and small basic metal industries was US$11 billion.

In addition to steel products, Iran produces aluminum and copper products. Between 1997 and 2004, the production of aluminum bars increased from 77,000 tons to 181,000 tons, 60 percent of which was exported. In the early 2000s, the availability of cheap energy sources was an incentive for Iran to be more aggressive in attracting private and foreign joint investment in aluminum production. In FY 2004 Italy's investment in aluminum production was US$345 million. For the fourth economic development plan, Iran set a production capacity goal of 240,000 tons of aluminum bars. In early 2005, the production capacity of aluminum increased to 230,000 tons, when the second phase of the Al-Mahdi Aluminum Complex was opened. The fourth economic development plan calls for the production capacity of copper metal to increase to 350,000 tons. The total level of investment in this project was estimated at US$4.5 billion.

Construction and Housing

Stimulated by growing oil revenues, the economic prosperity that began in the mid-1960s encouraged construction, mostly of urban housing units. Throughout this period, advances in construction trends closely followed those in the oil industry. Similarly driven mostly by increasing oil profits, the economic prosperity of the 1990s led to another boom in the construction industry. The construction industry is labor-intensive, with strong linkages to the extraction of materials such as sand and gravel.

Between 1995 and 2004, the construction sector contributed an average of 29 percent of GDP. The nominal value of government development expenditures for construction, housing, and urban development programs also grew during this period by an annual average of 31 percent, reaching a record US$467 million in FY 2004. Most government development expenditures were allocated to urban development programs, government buildings, and housing development projects. In FY 2004 the total investment in urban housing development by the private and public sectors was about US$7 billion, 95 percent of which was private investment. Despite banks' limited financial resources, their contribution to the financing of private-sector construction and housing activities grew noticeably in the early 2000s. Major cities, particularly Tehran, received a large portion of the banks' construction investments. Between 1995 and 2004, new housing development projects in rural areas received only US$8.6 million of public development funds, however. The fourth development plan calls for work on 200,000 of the 2.5 million rural housing units estimated to need major repair. In FY 2004, new housing construction fell 18,000 units short of projections.

Services

In 2006 the value-added share of services, in constant prices, was 47.1 percent of GDP. Services include trade, lodging, and food services (30 percent), transportation and telecommunications (17 percent), finance and real estate (3 percent), professional services (27 percent), and public and household services (23 percent).

Domestic Trade and Distribution

The government's role in trade and distribution was limited prior to the Revolution; it had monopoly rights to importation and distribution of only a few socially important commodities, such as sugar, tobacco, and concrete. (The specific commodities were not fixed over time.) The private sector controlled most trade, with a few major merchants and traders managing domestic distribution of 80 to 90 percent of certain products. After the Revolution, many transportation companies, banks, and insurance companies were nationalized, and because of other internal and external factors, the production and distribution system could not continue to operate as before. Government intervention in the production and distribution of many consumer goods increased, and a new trade and distribution system emerged. Under this new system, foreign trade was solely in the hands of local and national governments, and city and local councils and cooperatives controlled the distribution channels for many goods and services. After the Iran–Iraq War, the government relaxed its control over the distribution of goods and services, and the cooperatives' role was formalized and institutionalized. Price controls and subsidies have remained as public-policy tools to combat inflation and manage the prices of those key consumer goods that are perceived to be politically important.

In 2004 a total of 11,937 rural and urban cooperatives were in operation; they had 7.4 million members and 170,000 employees. In the early 2000s, rural cooperatives supplied their members with a variety of durable and nondurable consumer goods, such as food, chemicals, apparel, and leather products.

In 2002 some 1,470,070 trade establishments (4,821 of them public enterprises) engaged in auto repair, home appliance repair, and wholesale and retail trade, 17 percent of them in rural areas and 83 percent in urban areas. Less than 1 percent of these establishments had more than five employees; their total number of employees was 2,187,658 in 2002.

Insurance

Before the Revolution, all insurance companies, with the exception of the state-owned Iran Insurance Company, were privately owned. After the Revolution, private insurance companies with joint investments were nationalized and merged into one company. The nationalization of banking, insurance, manufacturing, and some other activities in the 1980s reduced the role of the insurance industry. During the 1990s, the private sector and joint ventures with foreign interests gained an increased role in the insurance industry. In the early 2000s, insurance companies in Iran offered a range of services such as health, freight, fire, and life insurance. Between 1997 and 2004, premiums received in the insurance market increased twelvefold; in the same period, the value of claims paid in the insurance market increased ninefold. In 2004 the insurance companies issued 14.9 million contracts, a 29.6 percent increase over 2003. The insurance market has been very concentrated; the top four firms control 97 percent of the market.

Tourism

Iran's diverse cultures, climates, and historical sites have great potential to attract international tourists, and Iran is one of the safest destinations among developing countries. Although it is highly regarded for the diversity of its destinations and the quality of its historical-cultural sites, in FY 2004 only 700,000 foreign visitors (of whom reportedly only 200,000 were tourists) came to Iran, while 9.2 million Iranians visited other countries. In the early 2000s, Iran's share of the international tourism industry, 0.09 percent, ranked it seventy-sixth in the world. Religious sites have been among the most popular attractions. In the early 2000s, about 10 million people a year visited the shrine of Hazrat-e Masumeh, in Qom. This shrine, like others in Iran, has adequate regional infrastructure and facilities for large numbers of visitors. The island of Kish, located in the Persian Gulf west of the Strait of Hormuz, features what has become known as the Kish Free Zone. With most laws substantially more relaxed than those on the mainland, Kish has attracted growing numbers of foreign tourists and played a significant role in Iran's international commerce.

The Organization of Iranian Handicrafts was established in 2005 with the goal of increasing awareness of the significance of tourism in the Iranian economy through the sale of tourism-related products. In addition, the Cultural Heritage and Tourism Organization received government support to help it achieve its objective of increasing the economic contribution of the tourism industry. The fourth economic development plan calls for the number of tourists to increase to 2.5 million, by means of visits of organized foreign groups. Foreign investment in tourism is increasing; entrepreneurs in countries such as Germany, Spain, Italy, and France have shown interest in investing in hotels and historical and entertainment sites.

In FY 2003 Iran had about 69,000 restaurants and 6,000 hotels and other lodging places; about 80 percent of these establishments were in urban areas. Some 875 restaurants and hotels were publicly managed by cooperatives and government organizations. More than 95 percent of restaurants and hotels had fewer than five employees, and only 38 had more than 100 employees. In FY 2002 this sector employed more than 166,000 people, 42,000 of whom worked in places of lodging. Of the 56,618 beds in all hotels, about half were located in three- to five-star hotels.

Transportation and Telecommunications

Iran's topography, size, and inadequate internal waterways make the provision of transportation facilities expensive and challenging. Although the transportation system is capable of meeting general commercial needs, specific shortfalls exist (see fig. 9). Expansion of transportation facilities has occurred mainly in response to the needs of the oil and gas, military, and international trade sectors. In FY 2004 the transportation sector's value added was about US$8 billion, of which ground transportation accounted for 89 percent, water transportation 6 percent, and air transportation 5 percent. The total gross fixed investment in the transportation sector was about US$6 billion, 84 percent of which was for equipment.

Roads

Between 1960 and 1979, Iran's roads and highways increased from 42,000 kilometers to 63,000 kilometers. During the Iran–Iraq War, roadways were expanded to 100,000 kilometers, and by 2003 the system had expanded to 179,990 kilometers, 100,000 of which were paved. Some 36 percent of Iran's roads are classified as main roads (highways and freeways). In 2004 public roads carried approximately 348 million tons of freight and the equivalent of 404 million people. Some 281,000 transport vehicles (76 percent trucks, 6 percent buses) moved cargo and passengers. There were 2,647 transportation enterprises,

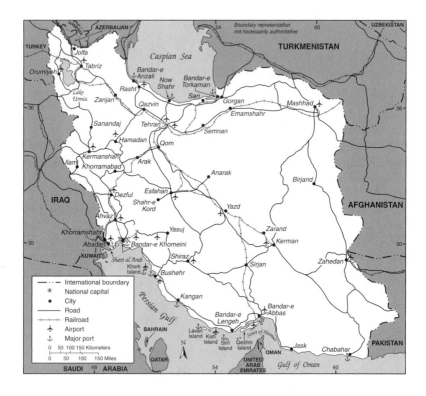

Figure 9. Transportation System, 2005

139 of which were international companies and 1,093, coopera-tives.

Since 1989, road construction has stressed ring roads around large cities and multilane highways between major met-ropolitan areas. The three national autoroutes are the A–1 across northern Iran, from the Turkish border on the west to the Afghan border on the east, and connecting Tabriz, Tehran, and Mashhad; the A–2 across southern Iran, from the Iraqi border in the west to the Pakistani border in the east; and the Tehran–Qom–Esfahan–Shiraz highway, which traverses central Iran from north to south.

Road expansion after the Revolution had spillover benefits to rural development, industry, and commerce, but it also facil-itated rural-urban migration, particularly to Tehran and other major cities. Expanded use of motor vehicles and the lack of public transportation systems have contributed to increased air

184

and noise pollution since the mid-1960s. Stimulated by government subsidization of gasoline prices, the number of registered motor vehicles increased nineteenfold between 1986 and 2004. In 2004 the number of registered motor vehicles was 1,926,449, including 634,482 passenger cars. In 2006 about three-quarters of domestic freight moved by truck.

Railroads

Foreign currency shortages, the financial burdens of war, and trade sanctions made it impossible for Iran to expand its railroads adequately in the 1980s, but railroad investment began to increase in the 1990s. In 2006 Iran had 8,367 kilometers of rail lines in good condition, compared with 5,800 kilometers in 1979. The five main lines of the system, most of which is single-track, radiate from Tehran: one runs south to Khorramshahr and Abadan at the head of the Persian Gulf; a second runs south to the Strait of Hormuz at Bandar-e Abbas; a third runs southeast to Kerman (with a route under construction in 2005 farther east to Zahedan, which was already connected to Pakistan's rail system); a fourth runs east to Mashhad and connects with the Central Asian rail system on the Turkmenistan border, and includes a spur to the east side of the Caspian Sea; and the fifth runs northwest to Tabriz and the border with Turkey, where it connects to the Turkish State Railroad and includes a spur to Azerbaijan's Nakhichevan enclave. Major rail lines connect the eastern city of Mashhad to the northwestern city of Tabriz and connect the Caspian Sea port of Bandar-e Torkaman to the Persian Gulf port of Bandar-e Khomeini.

Between 1991 and 2003, the number of rail passengers increased from 8 million to 16 million annually. The fourth economic development plan calls for further expansion to 34 million passengers, including extensive purchase of new rail cars. The annual volume of freight transported by rail increased significantly from 1991 to 2006, accounting for nearly 25 percent of the country's domestic freight shipments. Oil and mineral products accounted for about 61 percent of the total net freight transported; industrial materials and products were next with an 18 percent share. The volume of industrial materials and products transported by rail increased by 81 percent from 1991 to 2003. The cost of railroad transportation to passengers and businesses was less than that of bus and truck transportation. As a result, railroads were overused for some purposes, placing a financial burden on the government. To accommodate increased demand, in the early 2000s experts estimated that Iran needed 30,000 to 50,000 kilometers of railroads.

In 2005 the new Friendship Line reportedly was opened, providing access for Turkey and the Central Asian countries to Iran's southern coast. This 1,000-kilometer railroad links northeastern Iran to the south, bypassing Tehran and saving 800 kilometers. The Friendship Line complements an existing line that had linked Turkmenistan to Iran's main rail system. These two lines, linking Iran's northeast to its southeast, can be used by passengers and the manufacturing, mining, and steel industries. In 2006 a new rail line was under construction between Khaf in northeastern Iran and Herat in Afghanistan. Lines connecting Zahedan and Esfahan with Shiraz were scheduled for completion in 2007. A new rail connection with Armenia was in the planning stage. Construction of an ambitious North–South Corridor, linking Russia to India via Iran, was delayed by Iran's nuclear controversy.

Water Transport

Iran has 14 ports, six of which are major commercial seaports—four in the south, on the Persian Gulf and the Gulf of Oman (Bandar-e Khomeini, Bushehr, Bandar-e Abbas, and Chabahar), and two on the Caspian Sea (Bandar-e Anzali and Now Shahr). In 2004 some 6,450 vessels entered Iranian ports, about 60 percent of them on the Persian Gulf. More than one-third of the total traffic (2,204 vessels) came through Bandar-e Abbas. The concentration of sea transportation through this port illustrates its strategic importance and the overuse of its infrastructure. In 2004 some 53 million tons of cargo were unloaded and 30 million tons loaded at Iran's main commercial seaports; 49 percent of the cargo loaded consisted of oil products. In 2004 Iran's largest shipping company, state-owned Islamic Republic of Iran Shipping (IRI Shipping), had 82 ships with a total of 2,944 tons of capacity. With its three affiliates (the Iran–India Shipping Company, the Caspian Sea Shipping Company, and the Valfajr–8 Shipping Company), IRI Shipping owned a total of 107 ships, with a cargo capacity of 3,257 tons and a passenger capacity of 3,058. Some 18 shipping cooperatives and 290 private sea transport companies also were in operation in 2004.

A highway in Tehran
Courtesy Nader Davoodi

Bandar-e Anzali on the Caspian Sea
Courtesy Nader Davoodi

Air Transport

In 2006 Iran had 129 airports with paved runways, 41 of which were 3,000 meters or longer. Iran's international airports, which numbered nine in 2006, served about 4.3 million passengers on international flights in 2004. Some 67 percent of those passengers traveled on domestic airlines. Passengers carried from Iran by domestic airlines passed through more than 40 foreign international airports. About 9 million passengers passed through the country's airports on domestic flights. In 2006 the national airline, Iran Air, had a fleet of 35 aircraft and employed more than 7,500 personnel. Iran Air flew to 25 domestic destinations and 35 major cities abroad, carrying about 5.6 million passengers and 41 million tons of cargo. In the early 2000s, Iran Air suffered financial losses because of its inflated staff and inadequate technological investments. For example, in 2004 its labor cost was 48 times higher than that of Lufthansa, the German national airline, which reportedly offered eight times as many flights with a much smaller staff.

In May 2005, the new Imam Khomeini International Airport, the largest airport in Iran, was opened after long delays and about US$350 million of investment. The airport had an initial annual passenger capacity of 6.5 million; its final design capacity was 40 million passengers and 700,000 tons of cargo. However, the airport service and ground transportation were inadequate to allow operation at these levels. In the first phase of operations, the airport was able to land between 200 and 250 planes a day. During this phase, international flights were scheduled to be added gradually. At the end of the second phase of the project, the airport was to be competitive with other major international airports in the region.

Electronic Media and Telecommunications

Radio and Television

In 2005 the state-owned National Radio and Television Organization (Sazeman-e Seda va Seema) had sufficient radio and television transmission capability to reach about 95 percent of the population of Iran. In 2004 Iran had 92 radio stations with 123 main radio transmitters and nine substations for reaching overseas listeners. In addition, four short-wave radio stations with 28 transmitters were in operation. In 2002 some 28 television stations were in operation, sending signals from six main channels to about 7 million television sets. Access to international satellite channels, introduced in the early 2000s, has provided Iranians in both rural and urban areas with greatly increased opportunities to obtain information. Although domestic data were not available, unofficial statistics suggested that at least 50 percent of households had access to international channels in 2005.

Telephone

Since the introduction of telephone service to Iran, the demand for telephone lines consistently has exceeded supply. In 2004 Iran had 1.1 million intercity automatic telecommunications channels and 9,760 outgoing and 7,078 incoming international channels. Between 1987 and 2004, telephones installed in housing units, commercial units, and public buildings increased from 1.8 million to 17.7 million. During that period, the number of villages with telephone communication facilities increased from 2,329 to 41,109. Households and businesses subscribing to mobile telephone lines increased from 60,000 in 1997 to about 3.5 million in 2004. In 2006 an estimated 13.7 million subscribers had mobile telephone service. In 2005 Iran's telephone system remained inadequate to meet demand, but an ongoing modernization program was expanding services, especially in rural areas. Also, the widespread installation of digital switches increased the system's technical capabilities.

Internet

In 1998 only nine businesses provided Internet services in Iran; all nine were in Tehran. In 2004 official records indicated that 800 Internet access services were operating in major cities. Internet businesses are divided into two categories: Internet cafés and Internet service providers (ISPs). In 2005 some 319 Internet cafés, 191 ISPs, and 94 unidentified Internet businesses were in operation; Internet businesses employed 1,831 full-time and part-time personnel and had 2,309 computer units. In 2002 Internet businesses served 7,100 customers a day and had about US$13 million in sales. Capital formation was US$3.5 million that year. Between 1997 and 2006, the number of Internet subscribers increased from 2,000 to 7.5 million. However, Internet censorship increased sharply after the election of Mahmoud Ahmedinejad in 2005.

Energy Supply

Electric power plants were introduced to Iran during the late Qajar dynasty; by the turn of the twentieth century, several small power plants were operating in major cities. In 1964 the Ministry of Power and Electricity (renamed the Ministry of Energy after the Revolution) began managing the production, distribution, and consumption of electric power. Since the mid-1960s, rapid urbanization and growing economic activity have prompted increased production and consumption of electricity. Overall production reached 152 million megawatt-hours in 2004. That year, the nominal capacity of installed generators was 39,613 megawatts. Several new generating units came on line in 2005 and 2006.

In 2004 some 23 hydroelectric power plants generated 11 million megawatt-hours of electricity. Although the output of hydroelectric plants increased by 47 percent between 1987 and 2004, their share of total electricity output dropped from 33 percent to 6 percent during that period. The fourth economic development plan calls for an additional 6.4 million megawatt-hours of hydroelectric capacity by 2010. The electricity production of thermal power plants affiliated with the Ministry of Energy was 136 million megawatt-hours in 2004, an increase of 431 percent since 1987. During that period, natural gas has been the fastest growing source of electricity generation. Its share of the total rose from 8 percent in 1987 to 32 percent in 2004. In 2006 natural gas reportedly accounted for about 50 percent of domestic energy consumption (see Natural Gas, this ch.).

Iran has no capacity for nuclear power generation. Plans call for a series of nuclear reactors to be built. However, completion of the Bushehr plant, built with Russian technical assistance, has been jeopardized by disputes with Russia and international objections to the facility's potential for providing Iran with military-grade nuclear fuel (see Nuclear Issues, ch. 5).

Electricity is distributed to customers nationwide by nine regional organizations and the national Water and Electricity Company. The same state-owned company, Tavenir, oversees generation and distribution of power throughout Iran. Registered users of electricity numbered 18 million in 2004, an increase of 10 million users since 1987. This included 4.1 million registered rural users. In 1977 only 2,360 villages had access to electricity; by 2004 the number had increased to

47,359. Between 1989 and 2004, the consumption of electricity increased from 40 million to 114 million megawatt-hours. The largest consumers were households (33 percent), industry (32 percent), and agriculture (13 percent).

Subsidization of the production and consumption of electricity in Iran has caused over-consumption. In 2004, with the per capita energy consumption subsidy about US$230, per capita consumption of energy was 64 percent above the world average. Between 1967 and 2004, per capita consumption of energy increased by 5 percent per annum. The government projected that per capita consumption would grow at 7 percent per annum during the fourth development plan, the same rate as in the early 2000s. According to estimates, to satisfy demand Iran would have to invest US$20 billion in the energy sector, increasing its electricity production and distribution capacity to 55,000 megawatts. Aside from subsidized energy prices and the waste that they encourage, Iran faces the serious challenges of low energy storage capacity and obsolescence in distribution channels. In 2005 Iran's electric power industry continued to depend on foreign equipment, parts, and expertise, although to a lesser extent than in prior years. Iran is both an importer and an exporter of electricity. It has reciprocal relationships with Armenia, Azerbaijan, Pakistan, Turkey, and Turkmenistan. Both import and export levels have averaged about 2 million megawatt-hours annually.

Fiscal and Monetary Policy

In the twentieth century, oil profits became Iran's primary source of both government and foreign-exchange revenue, as the country became integrated into the world economy through its oil industry. The industry became Iran's foremost income-generating economic activity as measured by national output. Thus, national fiscal and monetary policies and resource allocation became tightly linked to oil revenue. Government fiscal policies have been carried out through the development planning process.

Fiscal Policy

Since 1964 budget preparation has been delegated to the Management and Planning Organization (MPO). In addition to the general budget, the MPO prepares fiscal positions of public enterprises and corporations. Since 1987 the MPO has prepared the foreign-exchange budget and submitted it to the parliament with the annual budget. The general budget laws are designed with consideration for international crude oil prices and in conformity with the policies and strategies set out in the existing development plan.

General Government Revenues

The structure of government revenues and expenditures has shifted as the fabric of the Iranian economy has changed. Between 1963 and 1979, oil revenue generated approximately 60 percent of total general revenues. Oil revenue continued to be an important component of general revenues after the Revolution.

In FY 2004 total government revenue was about US$30 billion, 49 percent from oil revenue and 25 percent from tax revenue. Between FY 1988 and FY 2004, the share of tax revenue in government general revenue increased from 4.5 percent to 24.7 percent. Of that amount, 49 percent came from direct taxes and 51 percent from indirect taxes. An objective of the third development plan (March 2000–March 2005) was to increase tax revenue to 10.6 percent of GDP, thus reducing the government's general revenue dependency on oil exports. After the first four years of that plan, however, Iran remained as dependent on oil exports as before; tax revenue reached only 5.9 percent of GDP in FY 2004 and remained approximately the same in FY 2005. Among the causes cited for the failure to reach the tax revenue goal were a culture of self-reporting (1.8 million businesses and individuals self-reported their taxes in FY 2004), inadequate tax laws and technical capabilities, and corruption. Because the private sector plays a small role in economic activities compared with the state and because some government enterprises are exempt from tax reporting, the tax base has remained very thin. For example, government-linked charitable foundations, or *bonyads*, were expected to pay taxes of only about US$46 million in FY 2004, although those consortiums are believed to control about 40 percent of Iran's GDP. Overall, an estimated 50 percent of Iran's GDP was exempt from taxes in FY 2004. However, for the first time since the Revolution, in FY 2004 the government was able to collect 100 percent of tax revenue projected to come from direct and indirect sources (about US$7.3 billion).

According to the budget law approved by the parliament, the total government budget for FY 2006 was expected to be about US$180 billion. The general revenues approved by the parliament were about US$60 billion (a 7.5 percent increase over the previous year), and the revenues from government enterprises and corporations were estimated at US$106 billion, a 0.2 percent increase over the previous year. One of the sources of tax revenue estimated in the FY 2006 budget law was the tax on oil revenue (projected at US$2 billion to US$3 billion), which was introduced for the first time that year. The total tax revenue estimated in the FY 2005 budget law was about US$14 billion.

In October 2000, the parliament approved establishment of the Oil Stabilization Fund (OSF). The fund was to be financed from surplus foreign-exchange revenues received from oil exports in excess of the figures projected in the annual budget. Between 2000 and 2004, about US$20 billion was deposited in the OSF account. During the same period, US$11.4 billion was withdrawn from this account, with approval of the parliament, for extrabudgetary expenditures such as compensation for the Central Bank of Iran's claims on the government, repayment of matured government debts, and compensation to farmers for drought years.

Government Expenditures

A general trend toward increased government expenditures began in FY 1972. By FY 2004, total government expenditures had increased more than sevenfold, from US$4.5 billion to US$34 billion. Government expenditures may be divided into two groups: current, or operating, expenditures and capital, or development, expenditures. These two types of expenditure are distributed among four payment categories: general affairs, national defense, social affairs, and economic affairs. Within the development plans, government priorities reflected in budget law influence fluctuations in the relative share of each payment category. Because of changes in the classification of budgetary figures, comparison of categories among different years is not possible. However, since the Revolution the government's general budget payments have averaged 59 percent for social affairs, 17 percent for economic affairs, 15 percent for national defense, and 13 percent for general affairs. (For a breakdown of expenditures for social and economic purposes, see fig. 10.) The balance of the FY 2004 operating budget showed a deficit of about US$10 billion, 15.3 percent more than the FY 2003 operating budget. The main reasons for defi-

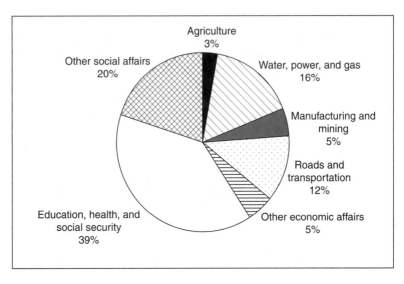

Source: Based on information from Iran, Statistical Center of Iran, *Iran Statistical Year-book 1383* [2004–5], Tehran, 2006.

Figure 10. National Budget Expenditures for Social and Economic Purposes, Fiscal Year 2004

cit growth were an increase in the projected operating budget and a concurrent reduction of tax revenue from public enterprises and corporations. During FY 2004, total government development expenditures were about US$6.8 billion.

In FY 2004 central government expenditures were divided as follows: current expenditures, 59 percent, and capital expenditures, 32 percent. Other items (earmarked expenditures, foreign-exchange losses, coverage of liabilities of letters of credit, and net lending) accounted for the remainder. Among current expenditures, wages and salaries accounted for 36 percent; subsidies and transfers to households accounted for 22 percent. Earmarked expenditures totaled 13 percent of the central government total. Between FY 2000 and FY 2004, total expenditures and net lending accounted for about 26 percent of GDP.

Banking and Monetary Policy

Structure of the Banking System

In 1960 the Central Bank of Iran (CBI, also known as Bank Markazi) was established as a banker for the government, with responsibility for issuing currency. In 1972 legislation further defined the CBI's functions as a central bank responsible for national monetary policy. In the 1960s and 1970s, the expansion of economic activity fueled by oil revenues increased Iran's financial resources, and subsequently the demand for banking services increased exponentially. By 1977, some 36 banks (24 commercial and 12 specialized) with 8,275 branches were in operation.

After the Revolution, the government nationalized domestic private banks and insurance companies. Bank law was changed under new interest-free Islamic banking regulations. The post-Revolution reduction in economic activity and financial resources required banks to consolidate. By 1982, this consolidation, in conformity with the Banking Nationalization Act, had reduced the number of banks to nine (six commercial and three specialized) and the number of branches to 6,581. Subsequently, the system expanded gradually.

The banking system in Iran plays a crucial role in transmitting monetary policy to the economic system. Each year, after approval of the government's annual budget, the CBI presents a detailed monetary and credit policy to the Money and Credit Council (MCC) for approval. Thereafter, major elements of these policies are incorporated in the five-year economic development plan.

In 2005 the Iranian banking system consisted of a central bank, 10 government-owned commercial and specialized banks, and four private commercial banks. In 2004 there were 13,952 commercial bank branches, 53 of which were foreign branches. Specialized banks had 2,663 branches. The CBI is responsible for developing monetary policy, issuing currency, and regulating national clearing and payment settlement systems. Commercial banks are authorized to accept checking and savings deposits and term investment deposits, and they are allowed to use promotional methods to attract deposits. Term investment deposits may be used by banks in a variety of activities such as joint ventures, direct investments, and limited trade partnerships (except to underwrite imports). However, commercial banks are prohibited from investing in the production of luxury and nonessential consumer goods. Commercial banks also may engage in authorized banking operations with state-owned institutions, government-affiliated organizations, and public corporations. The funds received as commissions, fees, and returns constitute bank income and cannot be divided among depositors.

In FY 2004 the balance sheet of the banking system showed that total assets and liabilities were US$165 billion, an increase of 226 percent since 1976. In that year, bank assets were divided as follows: private debt, 34 percent; government debt, 16 percent; and foreign assets (90 percent foreign exchange), 22 percent. Liquidity funds (money and quasi-money) accounted for more than 39 percent of total liabilities.

The Stock Exchange

The Tehran Stock Exchange is the main stock exchange of Iran. It began operation in 1968, dealing in shares from a small range of private banks and industries as well as government bonds and securities. The volume of transactions increased sharply during the 1970s as oil revenues grew, then shrank drastically after the Revolution's nationalization of banks and enterprises in 1979, followed by the Iran–Iraq war of 1980–88. In the 1990s, limited economic reform and privatization spurred substantial growth, interspersed with temporary reversals. The early 2000s saw another rapid expansion. Between 1996 and 2007, the number of companies listed on the exchange increased from 164 to 364.

Nevertheless, ongoing tight state control, large-scale inefficiency in the economy, and the high risk associated with foreign investment in Iran continued to limit the growth potential of the Tehran Stock Exchange. In 2007 that exchange remained smaller (total valuation US$42 billion) and less broad than all the major world stock exchanges. More than half of the capitalization is from heavy industry enterprises (automotive, chemicals, and metals), and foreign participation is minor. The Tehran Stock Exchange is directly under the control of the Iranian government, by virtue of the fact that the chairman of its High Council is the governor of the state-owned Central Bank of Iran. The bank's deputy governor also heads the exchange's board of directors. In 2005 fewer than 0.1 percent of Iran's registered companies were listed on the Tehran Stock Exchange, and fewer than 5 percent of Iranians owned stock. An ongoing modernization project aims at expanding the exchange's listings and improving transparency, in order to increase foreign investment. A set of exchange laws, heretofore lacking in Iran, have been proposed.

Efforts to Control Prices and Inflation

In the late 1990s and early 2000s, inflation rates were high in Iran for several reasons: an increase in the volume of liquidity with respect to GDP growth, an increase in the level of imports and a decrease in the terms of trade, an increase in public and private spending, and fluctuations in oil export revenues. Since its establishment in 1960, the CBI has regularly published price indices on GDP deflators, consumer goods, and wholesale products. The price development indices published by the bank do not always reflect the true picture of price changes, because markets are regulated and controlled by other countries' governments. The highest inflation, averaging 23 percent per year, occurred between FY 1977 and FY 1998. The inflation rate in FY 2006 was 15.8 percent.

International Trade and the Balance of Payments

Iran's international trade began a trend of consistent growth in the early 1920s, with imports competing freely in the domestic market. Trade expansion had several consequences. First, the growth of transportation infrastructure outpaced domestic production. This development reflects the need for infrastructure improvements required for oil and gas exports, and the subsequent import of goods and services. Second, the need for distribution channels for consumer goods led to the emergence of a small group of wealthy traders with both economic and political power. Third, with the growth of imports and domestic trade, financial services rapidly expanded to facilitate trade-related activities. Banks and insurance companies with foreign-exchange branches first grew in response to public and private foreign trade; their services later became available to manufacturers to facilitate the import of parts and machinery. Fourth, the significant volume of trade made import duties a major source of government revenue. This resulted in the emergence of sophisticated trade laws, import duty standards, and government offices specializing in imports and foreign trade. After numerous rejections for membership in the World Trade Organization, beginning in 1996, in mid-2005 Iran was approved for observer status, which could last for several years. In 2006 the United States set modification of Iran's nuclear program as a condition for full membership (see International Reactions to Iran's Nuclear Program, ch. 5).

Imports

In FY 2006 Iran's international trade volume, including oil and gas, was estimated at US$109 billion. Imports totaled US$45 billion (about 23 percent of GDP) and total exports about US$63 billion (about 32 percent of GDP). Thus, the overall trade surplus was about US$18 billion. The surplus was diminished by a hydrocarbon deficit of US$32.7 billion. Between 2000 and 2005, Iran's imports increased by 189 percent. According to an Iranian government report, nonhydrocarbon exports increased by 43 percent in 2006 after reaching a record high of US$12 billion in 2005.

The value and composition of imports have shifted with time, reflecting a change in both policy and oil revenues. The end of the Iran–Iraq War in 1988 coincided with a change in Iranian trade and foreign-exchange policies and the introduction of a new economic development plan. Thus, some imported goods received preferential foreign-exchange rates, as did public and private business enterprises. A change in valuation methods and bureaucratic processes also made it easier to import parts and finished products. Between 1989 and 2004, import volume increased from 19.2 million tons (worth US$13 billion) to 30 million tons (worth US$27 billion). This rise, representing more than a twofold increase at constant prices, mirrored the increase in oil earnings over the same period. During that period, the value of imported goods per ton grew considerably.

Prior to 1979, Iran relied on industrialized countries for imported commodities. Countries of the European Community (EC; now the European Union—EU) accounted for 43 percent of the total, with West Germany, the United Kingdom, and Italy responsible for 74 percent of the EC portion. Since that time, import composition has shifted in response to changes in economic structure and trade policy, linkages between industries, consumption patterns in the public and private sectors, and the political climate. From 1997 to 2005, the average volume of imports of raw materials and intermediate goods declined to their lowest level since 1963. The share of imported consumer goods also had declined significantly since 1990. A factor in this trend is a significant increase in smuggling into Iran that began in the 1990s. Although no official statistics on illegal imports are available, official estimates of their value during FY 2003 varied between US$2 billion and US$9 billion. Since 1995, illegal low-priced imported consumer goods have become a major problem for legitimate traders, domestic producers, and government officials.

As the proportion of consumer goods imports decreased, capital goods imports increased, reaching their highest-ever share level of 38 percent between 1997 and 2004. The increased share of imported capital goods may suggest that domestic manufacturing industries were unable to produce the tools and machinery needed for growth by the public and the private sectors. It also may suggest that the domestic currency was losing purchasing power while the values of major currencies were artificially held below true market value.

In 2005 a wide variety of goods were imported; chiefly food and tobacco, industrial raw materials and intermediate commodities, chemicals, other raw materials and intermediate commodities, and transport equipment and machinery. Since 1989 there has been a pronounced change in the origin of imports. The share of the EU remained high, at 40 percent; however, by 2004 Japan's share declined to 4 percent. Meanwhile, China and the Republic of Korea (South Korea) aggressively pursued the Iranian market, each exceeding Japan's share of total imports in 2005. Among the EU states, Italy and Germany in particular emerged as strong exporters to Iran, surpassing both Japan and the United Kingdom (see table 10, Appendix).

Nonoil Exports

Any interruption of imports would significantly affect the daily lives of Iranians, for whom foreign goods have become essential. Trade disruption would not, however, cause foreign consumers to miss many of Iran's nonoil exports. Industrial goods exports from Iran have been limited to only a few items that are exchanged primarily through barter agreements. Historically, agricultural products and carpets have made up a major portion of nonoil exports in international markets at competitive prices (see table 11, Appendix). However, since the 1990s, the Iranian government and the private sector have marketed Iranian nonoil exports aggressively, significantly increasing the sale of those goods. Between 1998 and 2004, nonoil exports averaged about US$5.1 billion per year, with industrial goods holding a 52 percent share. In FY 2005 the value of nonoil exports totaled US$10.7 billion. Of that amount, 42 percent was contributed by the sale of industrial exports, including chemical, petrochemical, and metal products. The export share of agriculture was 18.4 percent, tourism 16.0 percent, and mining and metals 11.8 percent).

Despite an increase in nonoil exports, foreign market penetration has proven difficult for Iran's goods and services. In the early 2000s, nonoil exports averaged only 20 percent of total exports. In this period, the export of durable manufacturing goods remained especially problematic. For example, in FY 2005 the export of home appliances was less than 1 percent of domestic production. In the early 2000s, obstacles to increased nonpetroleum exports included income and price inelasticity of exportable industrial goods and the lack of infrastructure (such as permanent trade offices overseas and special financial facilities) on which to base expanded activities. Because of these factors, economic growth among Iran's trading partners did not necessarily increase their demand for Iranian goods, and domestic currency depreciation has not increased export revenues. Beginning in 2006, Iran's Khodro automotive company pursued an aggressive export strategy for its new passenger car model, the Samand.

Although Iran has relied on industrial countries for imports, export sales have been concentrated in a different group of countries and have shifted with time. Prior to 1979, the EU's share of Iran's nonoil exports was 30 percent, that of China and the Soviet Union (in the form of barter trade) was 29 percent, and that of the Organization of the Petroleum Exporting Countries (OPEC—see Glossary) countries was 9.7 percent. During 1980–88, the EU's average share increased to 41 percent, while political instability in Eastern Europe reduced barter trade with Iran by the countries of that region to 9 percent. In this period, Germany and Italy remained major importers of the country's nonoil exports. Beginning in 1995, the EU's share declined to 15 percent, while the share of OPEC nations increased to 18 percent. Between 2002 and 2005, Japan was Iran's largest customer, importing an average of 19 percent of the country's total nonoil exports; the next-largest customers were China (10 percent) and Italy (6.4 percent) (see table 10, Appendix).

Balance of Payments and Debt

Although Iran's foreign-exchange balance has fluctuated primarily in response to oil revenues, the demand for foreign exchange (for imports and services) typically has exceeded the funds available. Beginning in 1990, foreign-exchange payment statistics showed continuous increases with relatively few fluctuations in payments; foreign-exchange receipts varied primarily in relation to export volume and the prices of crude oil. For example, in 1998, following a reduction in the global demand for crude oil, Iranian oil revenue declined by 36 percent while imports increased slightly, resulting in a current account deficit of US$2.1 billion. In the other years between 1995 and 2004, increased oil revenue yielded a trade surplus, and both foreign-exchange receipts and foreign reserves increased continuously. The current account also was affected by nonoil exports and services, although to a lesser degree. In 2006 the current account surplus was US$13.3 billion. Between 1991 and 2004, the value of nonoil exports increased from US$1 billion to US$7 billion, 2.9 times faster than the value of oil exports during that period. Within the services account, travel receipts increased from US$61 million to US$1.4 billion, and travel payments from US$340 million to US$2.6 billion. Payments on investment income increased from US$157 million to US$1.2 billion.

Iran's capital account has shown more fluctuations than the current account balance because of short-term and long-term foreign borrowing, debt service payments (principal and interest) on international loans, and the current account status. After continuous growth during the previous five years, in mid-2006 the total amount of foreign debt was about US$18.6 billion. Of that amount, US$8.2 billion was short-term debt. Because financial market transactions are limited in Iran, liabilities are limited, and data on private-sector investment in foreign securities are also not available. In 2006 high oil prices raised Iran's foreign currency holdings to US$58.5 billion.

The Foreign-Exchange System

After the Revolution, Iran adopted a complex multiple exchange-rate system, under which the Exchange Allocation Commission allocates foreign-exchange receipts (including nonoil exports and services) for government, commercial, and noncommercial purposes. The official basic rate of the rial (see Glossary) is pegged to the International Monetary Fund (IMF) special drawing right (see Glossary) without a link to the U.S. dollar. Since 1991 Iran's multiple exchange-rate system has been simplified and modified several times, reflecting international trade policy reforms and stable foreign-exchange receipts. For example, in 2000 external-sector policies aimed at creating transparency in the foreign-exchange market, reducing trade barriers, and easing conditions for nonoil exports. In the early 2000s, foreign-exchange policy continued to focus on moving toward a unified managed exchange-rate system and elimination of the multiple rates system. By 2006 gross international reserves had increased from US$12.1 billion to an estimated US$58.5 billion.

Foreign Direct Investment

Foreign direct investment (FDI) in Iran may be divided into the oil and gas industry and investment in other economic activities, including nonoil mining. Since the discovery of oil in Iran in the early twentieth century, exploration, extraction, and refining have been the major sources of FDI. Prior to 1979, such investments were arranged according to particular oil concession agreements or treaties. After the Revolution, the terms of such agreements between Iran and international companies changed, causing a temporary reduction in oil and gas investment. Although growth resumed in 1988, FDI in other sectors failed to reach pre-Revolution levels.

Low FDI has resulted from ambiguity in business laws, limited availability of credit, weak private-sector presence, political issues with FDI, and an unfavorable international political climate. In 2003 the approval of foreign investment in the Tehran Stock Exchange increased capital mobility and improved Iran's potential to attract foreign investment. Since that time, increased capital mobility within the Middle East has enabled Iran to attract more regional financial resources.

*　　　　　*　　　　　*

Although there have been many books in Persian and other languages analyzing the social, political, and cultural changes since the 1978–79 Revolution, no equivalent texts in any language deal with Iran's economic issues. In the case of economic statistics, the situation is the opposite. The international economic institutions, particularly the IMF, provide systematic statistics as well as some analysis on different aspects of the Iranian economy. The IMF's *International Financial Statistics Yearbook*, available in hard copy and on line, provides financial market statistics regularly. The Web sites of the *Tehran Times* and *Payvand Iran News* provide statistics and short articles on current economic issues. *Gooya.com* provides access to Iranian daily newspapers and periodicals in English and Persian. Other sources are the Economist Intelligence Unit's annual country profile on Iran, the *Middle East Economic Digest,* and the Middle East Research and Information Project (MERIP).

In Iran several official sources of statistics and analysis in Persian and English are available in print and on the Internet. The Economic Research and Policy Department of the Central Bank of Iran (Bank Markazi) provides annual and quarterly reports (*Economic Trends*) and other publications in English that deal with economic issues and economic policies via its Web site. Its annual *Economic Report and Balance Sheet* is an indispensable resource for recent and historical data. This report also discusses recent economic trends and policies and provides comprehensive statistical data in its appendix. In addition, its annual publication *National Accounts* provides current and historical statistics on national and income accounts, and its annual *Household Budget Survey* provides unique information on urban-area household budgets in Iran by year. The Central Bank of Iran's *The Law of Usury (Interest) Free Banking* provides information on the banking system and its role and objectives in Iran and will complement *The Monetary and Bank Law of Iran,* also published by the bank. The Management and Planning Organization, part of the Statistical Center of Iran (SCI), is another excellent source of economic and social statistics. The SCI provides historical census data and the most recent data provided by government agencies and departments in its annual report, *Iran Statistical Yearbook.* The SCI also provides special census and survey data such as the *Census of Agriculture* and *Household Survey.* The entire data set is available in Persian and English on its own Web site. Since 2001 the state Management and Planning Organization's annual *Economic Report* has provided helpful annual publications on the performance of development plans.

Ervand Abrahamian's *Iran Between Two Revolutions* is a very valuable book on Iran's political economy in the twentieth century. Jahangir Amuzegar's *Iran's Economy under the Islamic Republic* is a comprehensive analysis of post-Revolution economic trends and policy initiatives, particularly during the period 1980–92; it includes detailed projected outcomes. Eric Hooglund's *Land and Revolution in Iran, 1960–1980* is a classic work on the social structure of rural areas and land reform issues.

Philip Parker's *The Economic Competitiveness of Iran* provides business indicators on productivity, costs, and revenues of Iranian industries in comparison with those of the Middle East and elsewhere in the world. (For further information and complete citations, see Bibliography.)

Chapter 4. Government and Politics

Two men who came to pay tribute to Darius, ca. 500 B.C., from a bas-relief at Persepolis

THE ISLAMIC REVOLUTION OF 1978–79 brought dramatic change to the political atmosphere of Iran. Prior to the Revolution, the nation's government was a secular, pro-Western monarchy allowing substantial social liberties but using a strong security agency to maintain increasingly tight control over opposition forces. In the wake of the Revolution, Iran was transformed into a theocratic state whose fundamental law was that of the national religion and whose most influential government leaders were senior religious figures. In the decades following, the fundamental form of governance remained the same, but substantial struggles persisted over the day-to-day distribution of power and the roles of government agencies.

Beginning with its inception in early 1979, Iran's Islamic regime passed through five distinct phases before a surprising presidential election in 1997 altered the tone of governance more decisively (see Bazargan and the Provisional Government; The Bani Sadr Presidency; Terror and Repression; Consolidation of the Revolution; and The Rafsanjani Presidency, ch. 1). During that period, the regime's evolution was driven by the changing attitudes of the Iranian people and the strategies pursued by key leaders. Behind these factors stood more fundamental elements: changing social and economic conditions, the character of Iran's political institutions, and the international environment as seen from the Iranian perspective.

The unexpected election of Mohammad Khatami as president in May 1997 inaugurated a new phase of political liberalization, an eight-year period in which major political changes occurred. The changes advocated by the pro-Khatami politicians, who positioned themselves as reformists, threatened the power and status of many conservative political leaders. Following a period of disarray after the 1997 election, the conservatives gradually regrouped and began to use the courts to challenge and stymie reform initiatives. The conservatives took control of the parliament in the 2004 elections; a year later, a conservative candidate, Mahmoud Ahmadinejad, won a landslide victory in the presidential election. With his inauguration in August 2005, the political liberalization phase officially came to an end, and a new one, perhaps a phase of pragmatic authoritarianism, began.

Political Dynamics

A Reformist Comes to Power

In the presidential election of 1997, trends such as the formation of a centrist association of lawmakers called the Executives of Construction and the coalescing of progressive and democratic politicians around a reform agenda converged to catalyze the landslide victory of prominent reformist Mohammad Khatami. Khatami's unexpected election energized his supporters and led to the formation of two main political blocs, the reformists and the conservatives. Initially, there was a period of optimism and rapid change that some observers likened to the "Prague Spring" of 1968 in Czechoslovakia. Khatami named a reformist-dominated cabinet that soon was approved by the conservative-controlled parliament, demonstrating the powerful impact of his electoral victory. During his first few months in office, Khatami indicated that he intended to seek far-reaching political liberalization. The most important manifestation of this liberalization was a loosening of restrictions on the news media, which resulted in the emergence of a series of newspapers that strongly criticized the conservatives and even challenged the concept of *velayat-e faqih* (guardianship of the religious jurisprudence expert; see Glossary), the governing principle of the Islamic Republic of Iran (see Khatami and the Reform Movement, ch. 1). Khatami also broke an important taboo by calling for improved relations with the United States (see The United States and Iran, this ch.). Some Iranians responded to this looser atmosphere by challenging political and even cultural restrictions that had existed since 1979—speaking more openly about politics, interpreting Islamic dress codes less strictly, and stretching or ignoring gender roles.

Conservatives Strike Back

The conservatives responded to liberalization with vigilante attacks against reformist leaders, lawsuits, forced resignations, and the closing of reformist newspapers. Despite these setbacks, the reformist position was strong enough to achieve the relaxation of regulations for the establishment of political parties. Eighteen parties joined to form the reformist Second of Khordad coalition, named after the Iranian calendar date of Khatami's election (May 23, 1997). A large number of reformist clerics registered to contest the October 1998 elections for the Assembly of Experts, a body charged with selection and oversight responsibilities regarding the Leader (see The Leader or *Faqih*; The Assembly of Experts, this ch.). The credentials of most, however, were rejected by the Guardians Council, a body empowered to oversee the electoral process (see The Guardians Council, this ch.), ensuring a victory for the conservatives. The reformists' call for the creation of local legislative councils, which had been mandated in the constitution but never established, gained strong public support and, in 1998, parliamentary approval. Consequently, in February 1999 all cities and villages held local council elections. Reformists swept these elections amid a very high turnout, delivering another strong electoral mandate for the reformist movement.

Nevertheless, in early 1999 vigilantes continued to assault leading reformists at public functions; the judiciary arrested several reformists on dubious libel charges; parliament tried unsuccessfully to impeach Ataollah Mohajerani, the minister of culture and Islamic guidance who had virtually ended government press censorship; prosecutors arrested 13 Iranian Jews on charges of espionage; parliament gave preliminary approval to a bill imposing sharp limits on the press; and the judiciary closed down two popular newspapers.

The Power Struggle Intensifies

In July 1999, police and vigilante attacks on student demonstrators at Tehran University led to riots in several districts of Tehran. Khatami banned demonstrations, but the protests continued. In reaction, a group of commanders of the Islamic Revolutionary Guard Corps threatened a coup d'état against Khatami (see The Islamic Revolutionary Guard Corps (IRGC), ch. 5). Hundreds of protesters were injured, and some 1,400 were arrested before order was restored.

Khatami stated that he would address the protesters' concerns and crack down on vigilantes, but he also reaffirmed his support for Iran's Leader, Sayyid Ali Khamenei, who charged that foreign enemies of Iran had instigated the demonstrations. Many protesters received long prison terms. However, Khamenei replaced the conservative judiciary chief Ayatollah Mohammad Yazdi with Ayatollah Mahmoud Hashemi Shahrudi, who promised to reform the judiciary.

In preparation for the February 2000 parliamentary elections, the Second of Khordad coalition registered slates of multiple candidates to thwart potential Guardians Council vetoes. The conservatives in the judiciary and parliament closed reformist newspapers, raised the voting age from 15 to 16 to reduce the youth vote, and arrested Abdullah Nuri, the most popular reformist candidate, on spurious charges. When former president Ali Akbar Hashemi Rafsanjani announced his candidacy for one of the 30 at-large seats in Tehran, the major conservative political organizations backed him, hoping that he would be named speaker and thus prevent the reformists from taking control of that office. Despite the backing of the centrist Executives of Construction, Rafsanjani failed to gain reformist support (see The Centrist Faction, this ch.).

Because the Guardians Council unexpectedly vetoed only a small number of candidates, the Second of Khordad coalition achieved a decisive victory in the elections, winning 71 percent of the seats filled in the first round, while conservatives won only 21 percent. More women and fewer clerics won seats than in the 1996 parliamentary elections, and voter turnout was 80 percent. These results mirrored those of the 1997 presidential election and the 1999 local council elections, confirming that the reformist movement enjoyed overwhelming popular support.

The Reformists Retreat

When the new parliament convened in May 2000, it elected as its speaker the moderate reformist cleric Mehdi Karrubi. Karrubi quickly unveiled a broad agenda of reforms, starting with revision of the press law passed by the previous parliament. Khamenei then publicly opposed revision of the press law, and the judiciary closed several more newspapers and arrested several journalists on libel charges. Parliament nevertheless began work on a revised press law, leading Khamenei to demand that it cease its efforts. Karrubi reluctantly complied, provoking strong protests from some reformists. In the following months, the judiciary closed more newspapers and arrested more journalists. It pressed libel charges against numerous reformist leaders, including several members of parliament, despite their constitutional immunity from prosecution. These actions demonstrated that the conservatives were determined to stop the reformists and that the judiciary remained a potent weapon in their arsenal.

In blocking liberalization, the conservatives also drew upon the powers of the Guardians Council, which, in addition to vetting political candidates, was empowered to vet laws passed by

Sayyid Ali Khamenei
(Leader, 1989–)
Courtesy Iran Interests Section,
Embassy of Pakistan,
Washington, DC

the parliament. The conservatives' success in blocking reform and the reformists' inability to challenge them left the Iranian public—especially young people—increasingly disappointed with Khatami and his allies. In addition, new laws embodying neoliberal economic reforms often had cost jobs in newly privatized industries. They also had reduced the incomes of farmers, who had come to depend on subsidies that the reformists had reduced or rescinded. As a result, the reformist coalition began to fray after the 2000 parliamentary elections. Many student leaders and some older reformists called for a more confrontational approach or even a break with Khatami, while low-income groups abandoned the reformists en masse (see Government Institutions; Political Parties and Civil Society, this ch.).

The reformist leadership pursued a strategy of "active calm" during this period, pressing firmly for reform but avoiding confrontational actions that might give the conservatives a pretext for cracking down even further. The main political arena now was parliament, which passed legislation on matters such as the status of political crimes, defendants' rights, prison conditions, press protection, and reform of the intelligence division of the Ministry of Information and Security. However, in this period the Guardians Council vetoed or sharply diluted all major reform legislation, and the Expediency Council (in full, the Council for the Discernment of Expediency; the organization empowered to mediate disagreements between parliament and the Guardians Council) generally backed these decisions. With the reformist leadership seemingly powerless to advance its program, fissures began to emerge in the Second of Khordad coalition and the main reformist student organization, the Office for Consolidating Unity. Some reformists became increasingly critical of Khatami, Karrubi, and other moderates and openly questioned whether the Islamic regime could be reformed.

Frustrated by his lack of power, Khatami entered the June 2001 presidential election only at the last minute. The Guardians Council disqualified all but 10 of the 814 registered candidates. Khatami's nine opponents spanned the range of conservative opinion. Khatami again scored a decisive victory, winning 77 percent of the vote, although voter turnout fell to 67 percent from the 83 percent level of the 1997 presidential election.

Khatami's Second Term

Khatami's re-election had little impact on the power struggle between reformists and conservatives. The Second of Khordad coalition continued to pursue its "active calm" strategy, working mainly through parliament to promote reform and avoiding confrontation. The conservatives continued their attacks on the press and the reformist politicians, blocking political reform initiatives but supporting many economic reform policies. In the fall of 2001, the judiciary brought charges against reformist members of parliament, issuing summonses for 60 members to appear in court. In response, Khatami issued a statement warning the judiciary that this move violated the constitution, and some reformist leaders called for a referendum on the matter. A constitutional crisis was averted when Khamenei intervened, compelling the judiciary to back down and respect parliamentary immunity.

Throughout 2002, the judiciary continued to bring charges against reformist leaders and closed more reformist newspapers. In July it convicted 30 members of the Iran Freedom Movement, a reformist group that predated the Revolution, on charges of plotting to overthrow the Islamic regime and banned the organization. The reformists' ongoing failure to achieve their political goals despite their electoral success increased frustration among reformist leaders and their supporters; President Khatami even talked openly about resigning. Reformists favoring a more proactive approach called for confrontation with the conservatives and threatened to break with Khatami and the moderates. Common Iranians, many of whom were beginning to experience the negative consequences of the economic reforms, increasingly expressed disappointment with the reformists' agenda and declared that they no longer would vote for them.

In the February 2003 local council elections, reformist candidates in Tehran and other major cities were defeated decisively, although most were reelected in small towns and rural areas. A new conservative party, the Islamic Iran Builders Council, portrayed itself as pragmatic and apolitical during the campaign and swept the Tehran council elections, although voter turnout was only 12 percent of the electorate in the city. Elsewhere, voter turnout fell from a national average of 57 percent in 1999 to 29 percent. In general, voter turnout was higher in rural districts than in large cities, reflecting stronger public interest in races that were less politicized and where local councils made decisions on issues that voters deemed important.

Especially in Tehran, the results of local council elections emboldened the conservatives and left the reformists frustrated and divided. In the following months, the Guardians Council vetoed two bills Khatami had proposed, aimed at weakening the Guardians Council powers and strengthening those of the presidency. The Expediency Council sharply increased the Guardians Council's budget, enabling it to set up a nationwide network of election-monitoring offices. The judiciary arrested more reformist leaders, closed more newspapers, and began to block reformist Internet sites. Security personnel and vigilantes again attacked student protesters. In a rare triumph for the reformists, human rights lawyer Shirin Ebadi won the Nobel Peace Prize in October and quickly began to use her high-profile position to promote political and civil rights reforms.

The growing popular disenchantment reflected in the February 2003 local council elections prompted Khatami and the reformists to focus on economic development programs, but the efforts were too late to bear fruit before the 2004 parliamentary elections. A total of 8,144 candidates, most of them affiliated with a reformist party, registered to compete. In early January 2004, the Guardians Council disqualified 44 percent of the registered candidates, including almost every prominent reformist and 80 incumbent members of parliament. Under pressure from Khamenei, the Guardians Council reinstated 1,075 (30 percent) of the candidates it originally had disqualified, although no prominent reformists were among them. Of 210 incumbent deputies in parliament, a total of 75 remained disqualified, including President Khatami's brother.

The End of the Khatami Era

The first round of the parliamentary elections occurred on February 20, 2004, with more than 5,600 candidates competing for 290 seats. Karrubi, one of the few nationally known reformists who had not been disqualified, organized a nationwide list of 220 reform candidates, the Coalition for All Iran, but no one on the list won a seat. In all, only 39 reform candidates won in the first round and nine more in the second round, giving the reform bloc 17 percent of the total seats. The conservative Islamic Iran Builders Council was the big winner, picking up 154 seats in the first round and adding 43 in the second round to obtain a 68 percent majority in the parliament. The remaining 15 percent of seats were distributed among independents, a majority of whom were more conservative in their political views than the Islamic Iran Builders Council. Overall voter turnout was 51 percent, with higher participation rates in small towns and villages than in large cities.

The 2004 elections marked the end of Khatami's efforts to promote political reform and the beginning of a new era of conservative domination, inaugurated when the new parliament convened in late May and elected as its speaker the head of the Islamic Iran Builders Council, Gholam Ali Haddad Adel, who had led a small conservative bloc in the 2000–4 parliament. Adel's declared intention was to concentrate on improving the economy, and under his tutelage the parliament enacted several economic programs that restricted or reversed the neoliberal economic reforms enacted by the previous parliament. But conservatives both in the parliament and the judiciary also continued to focus on their reformist opponents. The judiciary began another crackdown on Internet sites and banned several more newspapers. A number of prominent reformist politicians and student leaders were arrested. The parliament approved three conservative nominees for the Guardians Council, including one who had been rejected twice by the previous parliament. In August Khamenei reappointed judiciary head Shahrudi and three members of the Guardians Council, signaling his approval of their records. The parliament challenged the authority of two cabinet ministers and approved a no-confidence measure against another. It also placed heavy restrictions on foreign investment, revised the five-year development plan passed by the previous parliament, and began efforts to put the Ministry of Information and Security under control of the judiciary.

In the run-up to the June 2005 presidential election, two main reformist candidates emerged: Mostafa Moin, a former cabinet minister, and Mehdi Karrubi. Many centrists backed former president Rafsanjani. Several conservative candidates emerged, including Ali Larijani, who resigned as head of Iran's state radio and television service; Mohammad Qalibaf, chief of the national police; and Mahmoud Ahmadinejad, who had served in the Islamic Revolutionary Guard Corps during the Iran–Iraq War, was elected to the Tehran city council in 2003, and later was chosen the capital's mayor.

Of the six candidates, Rafsanjani won a plurality in the June 17 balloting, but he got only 21 percent of the total. Ahmadinejad, who had conducted a populist campaign, narrowly gained second place by outpolling Karrubi, 19 percent to 17 percent. Because no candidate obtained a majority, a second round of balloting was held between the two highest vote-getters. In the June 24 second-round vote, most reformists unenthusiastically backed Rafsanjani because they feared that Ahmadinejad might win. Ahmadinejad stepped up his populist message, downplaying his conservative political views, promising to help the poor and to fight corruption, and repeating the theme that it was time for a new generation with fresh ideas to come to power. Iranian voters responded to these themes by strongly backing Ahmadinejad, who won 62 percent of the second-round vote. Ahmadinejad's victory was not only a decisive defeat for Rafsanjani but also for the "establishment" of conservative and reformist politicians who had been contesting power among themselves since 1979. Ahmadinejad was inaugurated in August 2005 and formed a cabinet consisting mostly of men with reputations as pragmatic technocrats.

Government Institutions

Iran was one of the first countries outside Europe and the Americas to adopt a constitution. Adopted in 1906 after a peaceful revolution against absolutist rule, Iran's first constitution established a constitutional monarchy, a popularly elected parliament, and a government headed by a prime minister. However, this constitution was ignored after 1925 by Iran's monarchs, who exercised almost unlimited authority (see The Constitutional Revolution, ch. 1).

The Islamists who led Iran's 1978–79 Revolution sought to abolish the monarchy and establish an Islamic republic, based on Ayatollah Khomeini's concept of *velayat-e faqih*. In the summer of 1979, a constitutional assembly drafted a new constitution that would establish the institutional apparatus for an Islamic republic, although one with strong democratic features. The draft constitution called for a mixed presidential-parliamentary system, universal adult suffrage, strong guarantees for civil and political freedoms, elected local councils, and a Guardians Council chosen by parliament, whose purpose would be to ensure that elections and legislation were compatible with Islamic law.

Seeking to strengthen the Islamic aspects of the constitution vis-à-vis its popular-sovereignty provisions, Islamist delegates made two crucial changes to the draft. First, they created the office of *faqih* (religious jurisprudence expert; see Glossary), also referred to in the constitution as the Leader of the Revolution. This office was to be vested in Khomeini during his lifetime. Then it would be occupied by a *marja-e taqlid* (a "source of imitation" in all religious matters), who would be chosen by an elected council of high-ranking Shia clerics, the Assembly of Experts. The Leader's responsibility would be to exercise general supervision (*velayat*) over the government of the Islamic Republic to ensure that its policies and actions adhere to Islamic principles. Based on his superior knowledge of Islam and Islamic law, the Leader's authority would be superior to that of any other official. Since the death of Khomeini in 1989, the degree of that authority has been the central political debate in Iran. Conservatives generally maintain that the authority of the office is absolute, while reformists assert that the constitution and any amendments approved in popular referenda limit the Leader's powers.

The Islamists also expanded the powers of the Guardians Council to veto parliamentary bills and made it an independent body, half of whose members must be clerics appointed by the Leader. These two changes gave ultimate authority over the state to the Leader and, more broadly, to Shia clerics. Although in theory the Leader would be responsible to an elected body,

President Mahmoud Ahmadinejad
Courtesy Iran Interests Section,
Embassy of Pakistan,
Washington, DC

the Assembly of Experts, this stipulation did not establish effective popular sovereignty because the Guardians Council vets candidates for elections to the assembly, and its members must be clerics. The revised constitution allowed for an elected president and parliament, political parties, women's suffrage, and many other democratic features of the draft constitution. However, it also included a number of changes sharply limiting civil and political rights. The constitution was approved in a December 1979 referendum.

During the 1980s, two important shortcomings of the 1979 constitution became increasingly clear. First, the document called for an elaborate system of checks and balances that, given the bitter factionalism that emerged during this period, produced institutional paralysis (see Consolidation of the Revolution, ch. 1). In February 1988, Khomeini tried to eliminate the primary source of paralysis by creating the Expediency Council, which he empowered to mediate disputes between the parliament and the Guardians Council. However, the structure and prerogatives of the Expediency Council remained very much in dispute, and other potential sources of paralysis still existed. Second, as Khomeini's health deteriorated, it became increasingly clear that no other *marja-e taqlid* had sufficient charisma or loyalty to the Islamic regime to succeed him as Leader. The constitutional guidelines governing succession therefore urgently needed revision.

To address these issues, Khomeini created a constitutional review panel in April 1989 to revise the constitution. The panel made several important changes. It eliminated the potential for conflict between the prime minister and the president by abolishing the office of prime minister, transferring its duties to the presidency, and strengthening the presidency in other ways. It clarified the structure and prerogatives of the Expediency Council. It dropped the requirement that the Leader be a *marja-e taqlid* and eliminated the possibility that a council of clerics could permanently assume the powers of the Leader. It expanded the Leader's powers in certain ways but removed his unilateral ability to dismiss the president and dissolve parliament. The panel made other changes as well, notably restructuring the judiciary and creating a Supreme National Security Council (SNSC), headed by the president and empowered to oversee foreign, defense, and intelligence policy. These changes were approved overwhelmingly in an August 1989 referendum. In 2006 the members of the SNSC were heads of the three branches of government; the chief of the Joint Staff of the Armed Forces; the head of the Planning and Budget Organization; two representatives nominated by the Leader; the ministers of foreign affairs, interior, and information and security; representatives from the army and the Islamic Revolutionary Guard Corps (IRGC); and any additional minister particularly concerned with a given issue. Among other policy functions, the SNSC is the lead agency on development of nuclear technology. The secretary of the SNSC is ex officio Iran's chief spokesman in international negotiations on the nuclear issue.

The Leader, or *Faqih*

The Leader of the Revolution is Iran's chief spiritual guide, exercising ultimate authority over the state apparatus and all political matters (see fig. 11). As enumerated in Article 110 of the constitution, the Leader's powers and responsibilities include: setting general state policy guidelines and supervising their implementation; declaring war and peace; commanding the armed forces; appointing and dismissing the six clerical members of the Guardians Council, the head of the judiciary, the head of state radio and television, and the commanders of the armed forces; overseeing the activities of the Expediency Council; and confirming the suitability of presidential candidates, certifying the presidential candidate elected in a popular vote, and dismissing a president found incompetent by parliament or convicted of violating the constitution by the Supreme Court.

In addition, Article 177 empowers the Leader to initiate and supervise the process of revising the constitution. The revisions are to be drawn up by a council whose members represent each branch of government, together with additional appointees of the Leader. The revised constitution then is submitted for approval by majority vote in a national referendum.

The Leader is assisted by an office with some 600 employees. In addition to a large administrative staff, this office includes 10 prominent special advisers who assist in areas such as foreign policy, military affairs, economic policy, and cultural matters. Closely connected to this office is a network of some 2,000 representatives of the Leader, who are attached to all government ministries, provincial governorates, branches of the armed forces, embassies, parastatal foundations and organizations, religious organizations, and major newspapers. The representatives monitor the activities of these bodies on behalf of the Leader to ensure that his policy guidelines are followed. Most of these representatives are Shia clerics. The Leader's office also includes the Central Council of Friday Prayer Leaders, which oversees the Friday prayer sermons given throughout the country each week. These sermons, especially the Tehran Friday prayer sermon, are the primary mechanism through which Iran's leaders explain their policies and try to mobilize and influence the Iranian public.

Finally, the Leader's office supervises a variety of parastatal foundations and organizations. The most important are: the Bonyad-e Mostazafin (Foundation of the Disinherited), a huge conglomerate that controls an estimated US$12 billion in assets and employs some 400,000 workers, and whose proceeds are intended to help the poor and the families of men killed in the Iran–Iraq War; the Imam Khomeini Relief Committee, a large social welfare organization that provides assistance to disadvantaged Iranians; the Supreme Council for Cultural Revolution, a body charged with ensuring that cultural materials used in the schools and on state television conform to Islamic values; and the Islamic Propagation Office, which seeks to promote Islam and the principles of the Islamic Republic by publishing

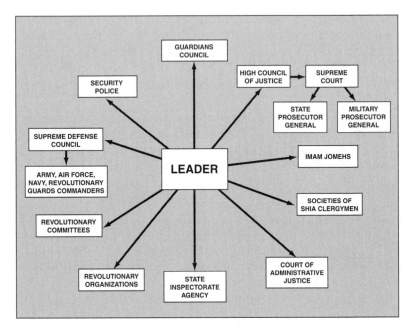

Source: Based on information from Shahrough Akhavi in Nikki R. Keddie and Eric
 Hooglund, eds., *The Iranian Revolution and the Islamic Republic*, Rev. ed.,
 Syracuse, 1986.

Figure 11. Appointive Powers of the Leader

books and other materials and sponsoring speaking engage-
ments by clerics.

The Assembly of Experts

The Assembly of Experts consists of 86 Shia clerics who have
a strong record of scholarship and loyalty to the Islamic regime
and are elected for eight-year terms in popular elections overseen by the Guardians Council. Articles 107 and 109 of the constitution empower the assembly to select the Leader, applying
three criteria: The candidate must possess a distinguished
record of Islamic scholarship, a sense of justice and piety, and
"right political and social perspicacity, prudence, courage,
administrative facilities, and adequate capability for leadership." Article 111 authorizes the Assembly of Experts to dismiss
the Leader if it determines that he no longer meets these qualifications or is unable to fulfill his duties. The assembly meets at
least once annually and in considerable secrecy, mainly to
review the performance of the Leader.

The President and Cabinet

Articles 113–142 of the constitution cover the selection and powers of the president and cabinet ministers. The president is the country's second-highest official, after the Leader, with responsibility for implementing the constitution and heading the executive branch of government. Presidents are selected for four-year terms in popular elections and can serve no more than two consecutive terms. The president must be a practicing Shia Muslim of Iranian citizenship and origin who supports the Islamic Republic and has appropriate personal qualifications. Although the constitution does not explicitly state whether a woman may serve as president, the Guardians Council disqualified women who registered as candidates in the presidential elections of 2001 and 2005.

The president appoints a cabinet consisting of the heads of the government's 21 ministries, who must be approved by parliament, as well as an unspecified number of vice presidents, who are not subject to parliamentary approval. Cabinet ministers can be dismissed either by the president or in a no-confidence vote by a majority in parliament. Article 110 stipulates that the Leader can dismiss the president after either a vote by two-thirds of the deputies or a finding by the Supreme Court that the president has violated the constitution. If the president is dismissed, resigns, or dies in office, the first vice president takes over until a new president is selected.

The Parliament

Articles 59 and 62–90 of the constitution cover the selection process and responsibilities of the parliament (Majlis—see Glossary; also known as the Supreme Consultative Assembly). Popular elections for parliament are held every four years. Seats are distributed among the country's 290 constituencies, each of which elects one deputy. In theory, each constituency has a population of just over 200,000. The actual distribution of seats favors cities, with Tehran being divided into 30 at-large constituencies. Five of the 290 seats are reserved for deputies who represent Iran's religious minorities: Christians (three seats), Jews (one seat), and Zoroastrians (one seat).

The parliament is empowered to enact laws within the framework specified in the constitution, based on bills forwarded by its members, the cabinet, or the judiciary (on judicial matters only). The parliament can vote only if two-thirds of its members are present. All legislation is subject to approval by the Guardians Council. The parliament is authorized to question cabinet ministers and approve or dismiss them. It also can authorize popular referenda with a two-thirds vote. The parliament cannot be dissolved, and members are immune from arrest or prosecution for expressing their views in parliament or otherwise carrying out their duties. The presiding officer of parliament is the speaker, who is assisted by two deputies and a system of 22 permanent committees. Select committees can be established when necessary.

The Guardians Council

The composition and responsibilities of the Guardians Council are enumerated in Articles 90–99 of the constitution. The council consists of six Shia clerical experts in Islamic law and six Shia laypeople with expertise in various areas of law, each serving a six-year term. The Leader appoints the six clerical members. The six lay members are chosen by the parliament from a list of candidates nominated by the head of the judiciary, who in turn is a cleric appointed by the Leader.

The Guardians Council has three main responsibilities. First, it is empowered to determine whether parliamentary legislation is compatible with Islamic law and with the constitution. Only the six clerical members make the determination with respect to Islamic law; all 12 members judge a law's compatibility with the constitution. Second, the council is empowered to interpret the constitution, with decisions requiring approval by at least nine of the 12 members. Third, according to Article 99, the council is responsible for supervising elections to choose the Assembly of Experts, the president, and the parliament, as well as referenda. Based on the guidelines of Article 108, the council drew up a law on the first Assembly of Experts elections, which were held in 1982. Subsequently, the assembly itself was solely responsible for amending this law. Article 110 gives the council responsibility for confirming the qualifications of candidates for the presidency. The Guardians Council has no constitutional mandate to supervise local council elections (see The Electoral System, this ch.).

The Expediency Council

Articles 110–112 of the constitution specify the three main duties of the Expediency Council. First, it mediates between parliament and the Guardians Council when these two bodies cannot reach agreement on legislation. Second, it serves as an advisory body to the Leader, who is required to consult with it in setting general policy guidelines and resolving problems that cannot be remedied by conventional means. Third, it temporarily assumes the duties of the Leader if he is incapacitated, and it plays a similar role during the transition from one Leader to another. The president, the speaker of the parliament, and several other high-ranking officials are automatically members of the Expediency Council. The Leader appoints additional members for five-year terms.

The Judiciary

From early 1979 until the end of 1982, revolutionary courts played a key role in suppressing political activity deemed counterrevolutionary. Following the failed uprising by the Mojahedin-e Khalq (People's Fighters) and some secular leftist groups in June 1981, the revolutionary courts arrested thousands of suspected opponents; many were sentenced to prison or even death in trials that lacked due process protections for the defendants. The overall situation created an atmosphere of intimidation that silenced critics of the proceedings. Subsequently, as regular civil, criminal, and special courts developed and adopted routine procedures, the role of the revolutionary courts diminished.

Articles 156–174 of the constitution cover the composition and powers of the judicial branch of government. The head of the judiciary is appointed by the Leader for a five-year term and must be a *mojtahed*—an authority on Islamic jurisprudence (see Glossary). The judiciary head has extensive powers, including responsibility for overseeing all activities of the judiciary, appointing the prosecutor general and all judges and Supreme Court justices, drafting legislation pertaining to judicial affairs, and nominating candidates for minister of justice. The minister of justice, who is chosen by the president from among the nominees, is responsible only for overseeing the administration of the ministry and coordinating relations between the judiciary and other branches of government. The chief justice of the Supreme Court and the prosecutor general also serve five-year terms and must have the status of *mojtahed*. The Supreme Court oversees the operations of 33 branch courts, to which the chief of the Supreme Court assigns cases. Branch courts are not regional in jurisdiction; all but two are located in Tehran.

Public courts, the most active judicial entities, try conventional civil and criminal cases at province and local levels. Iran also has numerous courts authorized to try and discipline persons perceived as threats to the political status quo. The revolutionary courts were established in early 1979 to cover general political offenses and matters involving national security. Special courts were established under Articles 172 and 173 of the constitution for members of the security forces and government officials. Overseen directly by the Leader, the Clerical Court was established in 1987 for cases involving members of the clergy, including those charged with "ideological offenses." Such offenses include interpretations of religious dogma that are not acceptable to the establishment clergy and activities, such as journalism, outside the realm of religion. The Press Court was established in the late 1990s for cases involving the mass media. It closed several reformist newspapers in the early 2000s (see Human Rights, this ch.).

Although the constitution provides for an independent judiciary, in practice the judicial branch is influenced strongly by political and religious institutions. Defendants have the right to public trial, choice of a lawyer, and appeal. Judicial authority is concentrated in the judge, who also acts as prosecutor and investigator to the exclusion of legal counsel. Judges must be experts in Islamic law. The prosecutor's office initiates suits against persons charged with attempting to undermine the system of government, a broad category of crimes that includes slandering or insulting leading government or clerical figures. In the early 2000s, reformers tried unsuccessfully to gain Majlis approval for the introduction of jury trials. Juries function only in specific cases related to the media. The revolutionary courts have authority to hold suspects for long pretrial periods and without benefit of counsel. Charges often are vague, such as "antistate activity" or "warring against God," and lawyers have complained of being harassed and even imprisoned.

The Problem of Dual Sovereignty

The structure of government institutions in Iran places authority over the state partly in the hands of the Iranian people and partly in the hands of Shia clerics. This configuration may be described as "dual sovereignty." All major political institutions—the Leader, the Assembly of Experts, the president, the cabinet and ministries (including the security forces), the parliament, the Guardians Council, the Expediency Council, and the judiciary—are held accountable, directly or indirectly, to the Iranian people through elections. Similarly, all of these institutions are held accountable to members of the Shia clergy through the appointment and oversight functions of the Leader, the Assembly of Experts, and the Guardians Council. Indeed, the constitution is quite ambiguous about sovereignty, as reflected in the wording of the key section on this matter, Article 56: "Absolute sovereignty over the world and man belongs to God, and it is He who has made man master of his own social destiny. No one can deprive man of this divine right, nor subordinate it to the vested interests of a particular individual or group. The people are to exercise this divine right in the manner specified in the following articles [of the constitution]."

Because of this ambiguity, the extent to which state policy reflects the will of the Iranian people or that of clerics has been determined by political practice. Since the advent of the Islamic regime, the Shia clerics associated with Ayatollah Khomeini's vision of an Islamic regime, together with their lay allies, have used government institutions to advance their views and interests, thereby sharply limiting popular input into state policy making. They have done so mainly through their control over the office of Leader, the Guardians Council, and the judiciary.

The constitution gives the Leader far-reaching power. Ayatollah Khomeini and Khamenei have wielded this power in ways that have favored their clerical allies. During his tenure, Khomeini almost invariably sided with them in their disputes with secular figures. This tendency was particularly noticeable in the process of writing the constitution. Subsequently, Khamenei strongly supported the conservatives in their disputes with President Khatami and his reformist allies. Both Leaders failed to restrain the security forces and the judiciary, which routinely work outside the law to suppress popular protest movements. Although the Assembly of Experts theoretically has oversight power over the Leader, it has yet to use this power to hold Khamenei accountable to the Iranian public. In fact, the requirement that members of the assembly be Shia clerics, together with the Guardians Council's efforts to screen candidates in elections to this body, has ensured that the assembly's actions reflect the views of the clergy.

The Guardians Council has acted to block initiatives that it has perceived as threatening to clerical prerogatives, contrary to Islam, or harmful to private property rights. It has made extensive use of its power to review legislation, blocking parliamentary initiatives in the 1980s to redistribute income and land and, more recently, bills to expand and protect civil rights. Although the Expediency Council is empowered to override the Guardians Council's vetoes, its heterogeneous membership of elected and appointed officials has greatly hindered its ability to reach consensus. This was especially true during the Khatami administrations, when conservative and reformist membership was nearly equal. The Expediency Council rarely overruled Guardians Council vetoes of key political reform legislation while Khatami was president.

Since its inception, the Guardians Council also has had responsibility for vetting candidates for political office. It has used this authority to disqualify all candidates it deemed insufficiently committed to the Islamic regime. Since the early 1990s, the members of the Guardians Council have been clerics and lawyers committed to the conservative interpretation of the institution of *velayat-e faqih* as vesting paramount or even absolute authority in the Leader. They have disqualified candidates who did not share this view, most notably prior to the 1992 parliamentary elections, the 1998 Assembly of Experts elections, the 2004 parliamentary elections, and the 2005 presidential election. Occasionally, the Guardians Council's actions have provoked such controversy that the Leader has felt compelled to intervene, as Khomeini did several times in the 1980s. The most tangible example was in 1988, when Khomeini created the Expediency Council as a mediating agency between the parliament and the Guardians Council. Since becoming Leader in 1989, Khamenei also has intervened to restrain the Guardians Council. For example, he ordered the council to accept the results of the 2000 parliamentary elections when the council seemed determined to nullify the victories of many reformists. In 2004 Khamenei demanded that the council review its disqualification of candidates for the parliamentary elections.

Local Government

Iran is divided into 30 provinces (*ostans*), which in 2007 were subdivided into a total of 321 counties (*shahrestans*). Each county encompasses one or more incorporated cities (*shahrs*) and several rural districts (*bakhshs*). There were 705 incorporated cities in 2003; the total number fluctuates, however, as large villages obtain municipal status and new towns are annexed by nearby large cities. A total of 842 rural districts encompassed 68,000 villages and 2,000 farms, the latter defined as localities in which only a single family resides. As was also the case before the Revolution, Iran's provinces are administered by a governor general appointed by the central government. The governor general, in consultation with the Ministry of Interior, appoints the governor of each county in the province, and, in consultation with the latter, the chief of each rural district. Prior to 1999, mayors and other urban officials also were appointed, but in most villages the village head (*kad-khoda*—see Glossary) was chosen by either election or consensus. In addition to the formal structure of local government, which was under the indirect supervision of the Ministry of Interior, in many areas the Leader's representatives, the Friday prayer leaders, and the commanders of the security forces also exercised considerable influence independently of the government officials.

In the 1990s, the emergence of a strong movement for political decentralization increased pressure for the implementation of Article 100 of the constitution, which provides for popularly elected local councils. Accordingly, the parliament passed a law in 1998 detailing selection procedures and the duties of local councils. This law provided for local councils to be elected for four-year terms in all cities and large villages, with small villages in proximity to each other sharing councils. Provincial, county, and district councils then would be made up of representatives from the city and village councils in their areas of jurisdiction. The city and village councils would appoint their own mayors and village heads. The powers of the councils would supersede those of the central government in the affairs of each administrative unit. Local council elections were held throughout Iran in 1999, 2003, and 2007.

The Electoral System

The constitution does not further clarify the role of the Guardians Council in presidential and parliamentary elections, stating only that the procedures for these elections will be specified in laws. The parliament has drawn up election laws that give the council considerable authority over national elections. As a result, the council exerts far more influence over presidential and parliamentary elections than is implied by the "supervisory" role stipulated in the constitution. For example, the parliamentary election law of 1984 divides responsibility for administering parliamentary elections between the Guardians

Council and the Ministry of Interior in ways that give the council a preeminent role. The law states that the council's supervisory role is "general and extends to all stages and regards all affairs related to [parliamentary] elections." Under the 1984 law, the council established the Central Oversight Committee, which reviews the credentials of all candidates according to vaguely worded criteria and verifies the authenticity of ballots. The Ministry of Interior and provincial officials are empowered to appoint executive committees in each election district to review candidates' credentials, staff and maintain voting facilities, and report election-related crimes to the Central Oversight Committee. Although the council and the ministry therefore can review and reject candidates, the Guardians Council has used this power much more assertively than the Ministry of Interior. Indeed, exercise of its vetting power is the main way in which the council has exerted control over parliamentary elections. Other provisions of the election law limit candidates to one week of campaigning, stipulate that voting is by secret ballot, provide for a second round of voting for each seat where no candidate receives 25 percent of the first-round vote, and set the minimum age for voters at 16.

The presidential election law, enacted in 1985, is broadly similar to the parliamentary law, except that the constitution gives the Guardians Council explicit authority to vet presidential candidates. As in parliamentary elections, the Guardians Council has general supervisory authority, and its Central Oversight Committee reviews candidates' credentials and verifies the validity of ballots. The Ministry of Interior's executive committees operate voting facilities and report election-related crimes to the Central Oversight Committee. Like the law on parliamentary elections, the presidential election law limits campaigning to one week, calls for a secret ballot and a second round of voting if no candidate wins a majority, and sets the minimum voting age at 16.

When parliament was developing procedures in 1998 for the first local council elections, the Guardians Council did not have the administrative capacity to supervise races for some 200,000 positions throughout the country, so it did not demand a supervisory role. Instead, the parliament created the Local Elections Supervision Board to oversee these elections. This body, which was headed by a conservative cleric, made some effort to block reformist candidates in 1999 and 2003, although to little effect. As in presidential and parliamentary elections, the Ministry of Interior operates the voting facilities and reports crimes in connection with local council elections.

The only referendum since establishment of the Guardians Council was held to approve the constitutional revisions of 1989. The procedures for that vote were decreed by Ayatollah Khomeini and not by statute. No laws governing referenda exist.

Political Parties and Civil Society

Article 26 of the constitution authorizes the existence of political parties and other civil society organizations, so long as they do not violate "the principles of independence, freedom, national unity, the criteria of Islam, or the basis of the Islamic republic." These general guidelines can be interpreted very broadly. Legislation permitting the establishment of parties was not adopted until 1998, following President Khatami's election. Nevertheless, a variety of partylike organizations and other civil society institutions have existed since the beginning of the Islamic regime, and many more have emerged since 1998.

Although in the early 2000s Iran had many parties and civil society organizations, none developed a broad base of popular support. Rather than parties, Iranians generally have preferred to identify with political factions, whose positions have evolved over time as the views of their supporters have changed. A changing constellation of parties and other civil society organizations embody these factions, representing narrow constituencies in formal or informal coalitions with like-minded organizations. Besides three main political factions, several minor factions exist that are largely or entirely outside politics. Various factions also exist among the many Iranians living abroad.

The Reformist Coalition

The 18 reformist parties of the Khatami era evolved from the Islamic leftist faction of the early 1980s to the mid-1990s. After Khatami was elected in 1997, these reformist parties established the Second of Khordad coalition, which became the reformists' main political vehicle. The coalition had two main parties. The Islamic Iran Participation Party (IIPP; Hezb-e Mosharakat-e Iran-e Islami) was established in 1998 by a group of reformist intellectuals and activists to promote Khatami's reforms, with Mohammad Reza Khatami, the president's brother, as its leader. The IIPP has tried to appeal to a broad range of Iranians. The Mojahedin of the Islamic Revolution Organization (MIRO; Sazman-e Mojahedin-e Enqelab-e Islami) was established in April 1979, when several small Islamic leftist groups united to create an organization to defend the newly established Islamic regime. The organization disbanded several years later but was reestablished in the early 1990s with a new agenda that stressed democratic practices over popular sovereignty guided by an elite vanguard. The MIRO has had a narrow following, consisting mainly of progressive-minded Islamists. The reformist faction also encompassed a number of smaller parties, including the Islamic Iran Solidarity Party (Hezb-e Hambastegi-ye Iran-e Islami) and the Islamic Labor Party (Hezb-e Islami-ye Kar).

Although it was not a party, the Militant Clerics Association (Majma-e Ruhaniyun-e Mobarez; short form Ruhaniyun) worked closely with the Second of Khordad coalition. The Ruhaniyun was a Shia clerical organization that broke off from the Combatant Clerics Association in the 1980s to pursue a reformist political agenda that stressed civil liberties and accountability of government personnel and institutions. During the 1990s, members of the Ruhaniyun began advocating democracy. In 1997 they supported the candidacy of Khatami, a member who was elected as the group's secretary general after he completed his eight-year tenure as president in August 2005.

The Office for Consolidating Unity (OCU; Daftar-e Takhim-e Vahdat), Iran's largest student organization, was created by Islamist students in 1979. It strongly supported Khatami from 1997 until after the parliamentary elections of 2000, when the OCU split into two wings. The larger wing, Allameh, broke with Khatami and advocated a more confrontational approach toward the conservatives. The smaller wing, Shirazi, favored Khatami's course of compromise with the conservatives.

Several civil society organizations also backed the reformist coalition. These included cooperatives, labor unions, professional associations, and women's organizations. Among the better-known groups were the Association of Iranian Writers and the Society for the Defense of Human Rights.

The Centrist Faction

In the early 1990s, a group of pragmatic protégés of President Rafsanjani emerged as a third faction, occupying a position between the Islamic reformers and the Islamic conservatives. They established the Executives of Construction (Kargozaran-e Sazendegi) before the 1996 parliamentary elections but won few seats. The Executives of Construction supported Khatami in 1997, and some of its members joined his cabinet. Several members became prominent reformist leaders, but the organization remained ambivalent about the reformist movement and gradually split into reformist and centrist wings. The Executives of Construction did not try to organize as a mass party and never cultivated popular support. Nevertheless, some individual members have enjoyed a national following. The party actively supported Rafsanjani in the 2005 presidential election, organizing rallies and other public events for him in Tehran and the provinces.

The Conservative Coalition

The conservative bloc is a heterogeneous grouping united on two issues: a strict interpretation of the constitution, especially the clauses empowering the Leader, and protection of private economic activities. Many older conservatives belonged to prerevolutionary Islamic organizations such as the Islamic Warriors (Fedayan-e Islami) and the Islamic Nations Party (Hezb-e Mellal-e Islami); younger ones were active in Islamic student groups in the late 1970s. The conservatives' main focus is on protecting the Islamic cultural restrictions implemented under the Islamic regime and the prerogatives and lifestyle of Iran's traditional classes, which they believe are threatened by the reformist movement and its efforts to promote political and economic reforms. The conservatives have a small but devoted base of support among the bazaar (see Glossary) merchants, urban religious families, and small farmers. Four political organizations have drawn significant conservative support.

The Combatant Clerics Association (Jameh-ye Ruhaniyat-e Mobarez; short form Jameh) was established in 1979 by Khomeini's clerical followers. A group of reform clerics broke off in the 1980s to form the Militant Clerics Association, leaving the Jameh dominated by conservatives. Its members are clergy who prefer strict, rather than liberal, interpretations of Islamic legal codes. The Islamic Coalition Organization (Jamiat-e Motalefeh-ye Islami; short form Motalefeh) was originally a coalition of traditionalist guilds and other organizations based in Iran's bazaar community before the Revolution. It advocates cultural restrictions and bazaar-oriented economic policies, and it is closely tied to the conservative Shia clergy. The Supporters of the Party of God (Ansar-e Hezbollah; short form Ansar) is an extremely conservative vigilante group notorious for assaulting and intimidating reformist leaders. Most of its members are war veterans who believe passionately that the authority of the Leader is absolute and must be obeyed without question, a position that puts them into direct conflict with the reformists. Ansar also opposes foreign cultural influences. The Islamic Iran Builders Council (Etelaf-e Abadgaran-e Iran-e Islami; short form Abadgaran) was created to contest the 2003 local council elections. Most of its members are technocrats who espouse economic development and pragmatic leadership. Abadgaran led the conservatives to victory in the 2004 parliamentary elections and the 2005 presidential election. The organization tends to take a flexible, moderate position on cultural issues.

The conservative faction also includes many smaller parties and civil society organizations, such as the Followers of the Line of the Imam and the Leader (Peyrovan-e Khatt-e Imam va Rahbari) and the Moderation and Development Party (Hezb-e Etedal va Towse'eh). Various guilds and professional and religious organizations, mainly associated with the bazaar community, also belong to the conservative faction.

Other Political Groups

Several relatively minor political groups exist in Iran but are largely or entirely excluded from politics. The "religious nationalists" (*melli mazhabi*) are Islamic modernists who support the Islamic regime but advocate transforming it into an Islamic democracy. Iran's leaders generally have tolerated this faction, although some of its members have been arrested. The most important religious nationalist organization has been the Iran Freedom Movement (Nezhat-e Azadi-ye Iran), which led the provisional government in 1979 but was marginalized as the Revolution became more radical. Most of its leaders were arrested in 2002, and the organization was banned. Several members were allowed to run as individuals in the 2003 local council elections but did poorly.

Politicians who favored either a secular democracy or reestablishment of the monarchy were repressed or went into exile in late 1978 and early 1979. Several political organizations advocating these views exist outside Iran, ranging from secular democratic organizations descended from the venerable National Front (Jebhe-ye Melli) to monarchist organizations supporting

Reza Pahlavi, son of the last shah. These organizations appeal mainly to Iranians in expatriate communities in North America and Europe. They generally have few contacts inside Iran and no organized support there. Various Marxist, Islamic socialist, and ethnic organizations also exist outside Iran. Most of these organizations are remnants of guerrilla groups that participated in the Revolution or formed shortly afterward but soon turned against the Islamic regime and were repressed severely in the early 1980s. The most important is the Mojahedin-e Khalq (People's Fighters), whose leader, Masoud Rajavi, fled to France in 1981 and subsequently relocated to Iraq, where he established a base and began cooperating with the government of Saddam Hussein during the final years of the Iran–Iraq War. This relationship with the Iraqi government made the Mojahedin deeply unpopular inside Iran, where the organization was believed to have few underground followers. The Mojahedin remained in Iraq after the U.S.-led invasion of 2003. The U.S. forces first took custody of the organization's base and seized all weapons, then allowed the dwindling force to remain, against the wishes of the Iraqi provisional government.

Civil Society Organizations

Iran has developed a strong tradition of civil society activism since 1979. Numerous nongovernmental organizations (NGOs) work with international groups on such issues as consumer protection, cultural heritage, economic development, education, the environment, media, publishing, science, trade, and women's rights. NGOs that work on legal and political issues are watched closely by judicial authorities and have experienced official harassment, but other NGOs generally operate freely. Civic organizations in cities and towns include community development groups, parent-teacher associations in schools, social services groups, and sports associations. More informal, voluntary organizations include thousands of cultural, religious, and social groups that meet weekly, monthly, or seasonally.

Human Rights

Article 4 of Iran's constitution stipulates that all laws must be based on fundamental Islamic principles. The six clerical members of the Guardians Council are empowered to ensure that this provision is observed. Articles 12 and 13 state that the official religion of Iran is Twelver Shiism, but members of the other major branches of Islam and the Christian, Jewish, and Zoroastrian religions are free to practice their own faiths (see Shia Islam in Iran, ch. 2). In matters of personal status (e.g., marriage, divorce, and probate), such individuals are to be judged by principles based on their own faiths. Article 24 guarantees freedom of the press, except "when it is detrimental to the fundamental principles of Islam or the rights of the public." Article 27 guarantees freedom of assembly, except in circumstances that are "detrimental to the fundamental principles of Islam." Article 38 bans all forms of torture. Article 165 states that all trials should be open to the public, except in cases in which this would undermine public morality or discipline or both parties request a closed trial.

Despite these constitutional guarantees, in many instances civil liberties were not protected during the early years of the Islamic Republic. More than 500 high officials, military officers, and secret police agents from the shah's regime were executed after summary trials in 1979. In the summer of 1980, the discovery of alleged plots within the military to overthrow the government led to wide-scale arrests and the execution of more than 100 officers condemned by hastily convened tribunals at which no defense was allowed. According to Amnesty International, in the year following the abortive uprising of the Mojahedin in June 1981, nearly 3,000 persons were executed following their summary trials as Mojahedin members. During the 1980s, almost all opposition organizations were suppressed; civil and political freedoms were sharply curtailed, the independent press was shut down, intellectual and artistic expression was heavily restricted, and members of the Baha'i faith were persecuted. Harsh punishments such as flogging, justified as "Islamic," were applied for violations of social mores and relatively minor crimes such as nonobservance of public dress codes, consumption of alcoholic beverages, petty theft, and premarital sex. Robbers could have their fingers amputated, and adulterers could be executed by stoning.

Beginning in the late 1980s, the judiciary began to monitor prisons and courts with the aim of ensuring respect for the constitutional rights of the accused in practice. Consequently, the human rights climate improved, and by the mid-1990s political executions had ceased. Nevertheless, Iran remained among the leading countries in executions, averaging 100 per year in the 1990s. Crimes for which offenders received capital punishment included murder, rape, treason, and adultery. Human rights lawyers such as Shirin Ebadi maintained that torture—usually in the form of prolonged solitary detention—and other arbitrary legal practices continued to occur, even though they were contrary to law.

The improvement in human rights conditions initially continued under President Khatami. However, during the Khatami administration the judiciary charged many reformist political leaders and newspaper publishers with slander, and their trials provoked considerable controversy about arbitrary trial procedures, mistreatment in prison, and restrictions on the right of expression. As the reformists became increasingly bold, the conservatives responded by enacting new laws on slander under which reformist leaders subsequently were arrested and reformist newspapers closed down.

The reformists' victory in the February 2000 parliamentary elections, which posed a serious threat to the conservatives' political control, led to an intensification of arrests and media closures. Two cases of extrajudicial killing in 2003 focused international attention on Iran's legal practices. One case involved the execution of two Iranian Kurds accused of membership in Kurdish armed opposition groups. The other involved an Iranian photojournalist, Zahra Kazemi, who died after being severely beaten in prison. Because Kazemi was a Canadian citizen, her death galvanized the international human rights community. Nevertheless, in the early 2000s political executions and other politically motivated killings did not play a major role in preserving the Islamic regime or influencing relations among the various political factions.

In the early 2000s, irregularities in Iran's legal system were widespread and had an extensive impact on the country's politics. Reformist and dissident political activists frequently were arrested and prosecuted on vague charges of insulting prominent individuals or threatening national security. Amnesty International reported "scores" of arrests of this sort annually. Defendants often were held for long periods without trial. Dozens of instances of torture were documented each year. Trials in political cases usually failed to meet minimum due process standards. Defendants often were denied access to lawyers and family members; lawyers were prevented from seeing crucial evidence and sometimes prosecuted for their work; outside observers were barred from the courtroom; sentences sometimes were inappropriately harsh; and juries were not used in legal proceedings. Although reformists and dissidents almost always were convicted, the few vigilantes or security personnel who came to trial usually were acquitted or given light sentences.

From 2000 to 2004, reformists tried to use their control of the parliament to eliminate some irregularities, introducing legislation to specify what kinds of political activity were illegal and to outlaw torture. They also proposed that Iran join the United Nations Convention on Torture. However, the Guardians Council vetoed each of these bills. The Iranian government also often prevented international human rights organizations from entering the country to examine human rights conditions.

Irregular methods used to silence political activists and bar them from engaging in politics encouraged self-censorship by other activists. By 2005, many prominent reformist leaders and dissidents had been arrested, imprisoned, harassed, or prevented from holding public office; all politically active Iranians understood that they might face such harsh treatment if the positions they advocated irritated politically powerful conservatives.

Restrictions on freedom of association also have had a powerful impact on politics in Iran. Although many political parties and other civil society organizations exist, any group that in the opinion of conservative officials does not support the Islamic regime is banned from political activity (see Political Parties and Civil Society, this ch.). Independent trade unions also have been banned. In addition, the judiciary, the security forces, and conservative vigilante groups have sharply limited the ability of Iranians to hold demonstrations and strikes, and permits for such activity are denied regularly. Security and vigilante groups often attack and arrest protesters and strikers. Hundreds of student protesters have been arrested; some have been severely beaten, imprisoned for long periods, and tortured. These restrictions on freedom of association apply almost exclusively to reformist politicians and opponents of the Islamic regime. Because reformists and regime opponents have little institutional power and rely mainly on mobilizing popular support to exercise influence, these restrictions strongly benefit the conservatives.

Many aspects of Iran's criminal justice system violate internationally accepted human rights standards and are opposed by Iranian human rights activists. In the early 2000s, some punishments, widely regarded as inhumane or inappropriate, were suspended but not legally rescinded. In addition, numerous legal practices are widely regarded as discriminatory toward women. These include stipulations that a woman's testimony is worth only half that of a man; that the monetary compensation for a woman who is killed, accidentally or otherwise, is one-half the compensation for a man who is killed; and that a woman must receive permission from an adult male relative to marry or to obtain a passport. Women also have fewer rights than men in divorce and child custody cases.

Publicity about human rights intensified after lawyer Shirin Ebadi was awarded a Nobel Peace Prize in 2003 for her work inside Iran on behalf of women's, children's, and prisoners' rights. Mahmud Hashem Shahrudi, head of the judiciary, appointed a special judicial investigator to examine conditions in the courts and prisons. The report, made public in 2005, confirmed that "un-Islamic" practices such as torture and violations of defendants' rights were a continuing problem that needed to be addressed through an educational program directed to Iranians involved in law enforcement, criminal investigations, and prosecutions.

Mass Media and the Arts

After a brief flourishing of the press following the Revolution, beginning in 1981 Iran's leaders gradually closed down or took over all newspapers and magazines that expressed opposition to the Islamic regime. Consequently, during the early and mid-1980s, the Iranian news media reflected only a narrow range of views. Iran's new leaders also inherited the monarchy's state-controlled radio and television media and continued to exercise tight control over its content.

Restrictions on the press began to ease somewhat in the late 1980s, when Mohammad Khatami was minister of Islamic culture and guidance and permitted a limited degree of relaxation to occur. This trend accelerated considerably in the early 1990s, especially with the publication of the newspapers *Salaam* (Peace) and *Asr-e Ma* (Our Era) and the magazine *Kiyan* (Foundation), which played crucial roles in the emergence of the reformist faction. The press flourished again after Khatami was elected president in 1997, and many pro-reformist newspapers appeared. However, in 1999 the conservative-controlled judiciary began to close down these newspapers and arrest some journalists and editors. Thanks to new laws on slander and the overt support of Khamenei, these closures and arrests increased sharply in April 2000 (see Political Dynamics, this ch.). By early 2005, more than a hundred newspapers had been closed and scores of journalists and editors arrested. In its annual report for 2004, the press watchdog organization Reporters Without Borders summarized the mixed status of Iran's news media, describing Iran as "the biggest prison for journalists in the Middle East, with harsh censorship but also a prolific and vigorous written press that is clearly helping the growth of civil society."

Of the major newspapers published in Iran, *Kayhan* (World), *Ettela'at* (Information), *Resalat* (Prophetic Mission), and *Jomhuri-ye Islami* (Islamic Republic) reflect the views of the conservative faction, while *Hambastegi* (Together) *Mardom Salari* (Free People), and *Shargh* (The East) have a reformist tone. The judiciary closed *Salaam, Asr-e Ma, Kiyan*, and many other major reformist newspapers and magazines. However, it generally allows some reformist publications to remain open at any given time, typically closing one after a few months but allowing new ones to open. In addition, four English-language newspapers are published in Iran: the conservative *Kayhan International* and *Tehran Times* and the reformist *Iran News* and *Iran Daily*. Newspapers opposing the Islamic regime or even reflecting the "loyal opposition" perspective of the religious-nationalist faction have not been granted publishing licenses.

All radio and television media inside Iran are under the control of a state agency, Islamic Republic of Iran Broadcasting. The head of this agency is appointed by the Leader, and the content of political programming reflects generally conservative views. In 2005 Iran had six national television channels and seven national radio stations, which offered programming on a wide range of topics. Iran also broadcast radio and television programs in Arabic, Kurdish, Turkish, English, Hebrew, and other languages to nearby countries and, by satellite and the Internet, to a global audience.

Iranians who own shortwave radios seek access to foreign broadcast media. Persian-language radio broadcasts are beamed into Iran by many governments, including those of the United States, Britain, France, Germany, Russia, Israel, China, and Japan. These broadcasts, especially those of the British Broadcasting Company and Voice of America, are popular among some Iranians. Exile opposition organizations also make radio broadcasts into Iran, usually with the help of foreign governments. However, in the early 2000s these broadcasts decreased considerably as the organizations grew weaker and the United States reduced or ended funding. In 2003 the overthrow of the government of Saddam Hussein in Iraq, which had hosted some opposition broadcasts, further reduced the range of available broadcasting. Several evangelical Christian stations and a Baha'i station also broadcast into Iran. The Iranian government jams some but not all of these foreign transmissions.

Foreign satellite television broadcasts also are watched by Iranians who have the means to purchase satellite dishes. The estimated 1.5 million satellite television receivers in Iran can pick up a wide range of foreign programming, including many commercial and government-owned news channels and a broad variety of entertainment programs in various languages. In the early 2000s, many Persian-language stations were established outside Iran to broadcast into Iran and to the Iranian diaspora. Mainly located in Los Angeles, many of these stations have a strong monarchist orientation. The U.S. government's Voice of America also broadcasts Persian-language television programs into Iran. The Iranian government tried to curb access by outlawing satellite dishes and antennas in 1995, but enforcement stopped in 1997. Thus, in 2005 satellite receivers remain ubiquitous in wealthy urban neighborhoods. At that time, surveys indicated that as many as 12 percent of Iranian adults had access to satellite television.

The Internet has become another important means of access to foreign media for many Iranians. A 2005 study estimated that as many as 7.5 million Iranians had access to the Internet at that time. Most heavy Internet users are below age 35. Most of these users patronize Internet cafés, which became common in Tehran and other large cities in the early 2000s. Iranians use the Internet to gain access to the many Persian-language news and cultural sites and chat rooms that emerged in the early 2000s and to exchange e-mail and make inexpensive telephone calls to friends and relatives abroad. Many Iranian political organizations and activists have established Web sites or blogs, which often contain highly informative and sharply critical material. The Iranian government has arrested some Internet commentators and blocked some of their Web sites. It also has attempted to block some foreign-based Persian-language Web sites and pornographic sites, with limited success.

Iran's writers, filmmakers, and other artists also face limits on freedom of expression. Publishers are not required to submit book manuscripts to the Ministry of Islamic Culture and

Guidance for prepublication approval, but they risk prosecution and heavy fines if the ministry revokes distribution of a book after its publication. A considerable amount of critical material was published in Iran in the early 2000s, including some incisive works by investigative journalists. About 35,000 new titles were published annually in that period. In contrast to book publishers, filmmakers, most of whom depend heavily on government subsidies for their work, are obliged to submit scripts and film proposals to the Ministry of Islamic Culture and Guidance for review. Nevertheless, Iran has an internationally acclaimed film industry. Iranian filmmakers produce subtle films that are often implicitly critical of the regime. Some of these films have been banned in Iran but granted licenses for distribution abroad. Iran also has a vibrant community of painters and other visual artists, with many galleries and an excellent contemporary art museum in Tehran. Some of their work also has a critical tone, although most of Iran's visual artists avoid politically sensitive topics.

Foreign Policy

After the election of President Khatami in May 1997, Iran's foreign policy continued to follow the general approach that had emerged during the last year of Rafsanjani's presidency (see The Rafsanjani Presidency, ch. 1.). Khatami and his foreign minister, Kamal Kharrazi, continued to seek better relations with Europe and with most pro-Western countries in the region. They tried to improve Iran's relations with the United States, which had been characterized by mutual suspicion and an absence of diplomatic ties since 1980. Beginning in the Khatami era, Iran's efforts to normalize relations with the United States have been impeded by ongoing U.S. suspicions that Iran supports groups such as Hizballah in Lebanon, is opposed to the Middle East peace process, and is pursuing a secret nuclear weapons program. In Iran, too, the worldview of many key officials has been shaped by nationalism and even xenophobia, and such leaders continue to distrust the United States.

Relations with Europe

Although Iran's relations with the countries of the European Union (EU) had been harmed in 1989 by Khomeini's fatwa (religious opinion) against British author Salman Rushdie

Modern Art Museum, Tehran
Courtesy Nader Davoodi

(based on Rushdie's characterization of the Prophet and his family in the novel *Satanic Verses*) and by assassinations of prominent Iranian political dissidents living in Europe, President Rafsanjani tried to improve ties during the 1990s. These efforts suffered a serious setback in April 1997, when a German court implicated top Iranian officials in the 1992 assassination of four Iranian Kurdish dissidents in Berlin. Germany and many other countries of the EU responded to the judicial finding by withdrawing their ambassadors from Tehran and suspending the EU's "critical dialogue" with Iran.

After his inauguration, President Khatami moved quickly to repair relations with the EU countries. In November 1997, Iran and the EU reached an agreement under which all EU ambassadors would return to Iran. The EU also soon authorized a resumption of ministry-level contacts with Iran, although the critical dialog remained suspended. Iran conducted intense negotiations with Britain in this period over the Rushdie affair, and in September 1998 British officials announced an agreement under which the Iranian government would not enforce the death threat against Rushdie. Although the fatwa was not revoked, British officials expressed satisfaction with the agreement. Further, the assassinations of Iranian exiles that had

241

begun in Europe in the early 1990s now had ceased. Despite potentially harmful U.S. economic sanctions, European businesses continued to increase their involvement in Iran after Khatami was elected, and many European NGOs became more involved in Iran as well.

Iran's relations with the EU countries did not improve during Khatami's second term. The arrest and trial of Iranian reformists who had participated in an April 2000 German Green Party–sponsored conference in Berlin on democracy in Iran raised concerns in Europe pertaining to human rights in the Islamic Republic. Furthermore, the August 2002 revelations that Iran had secretly built plants to enrich uranium and extract plutonium led the EU to reassess relations with Iran. A subsequent International Atomic Energy Agency (IAEA) inspection found that Iran's nuclear program was very advanced. Even though the IAEA said that Iran had the right, as a signatory to the Nuclear Non-Proliferation Treaty (NPT), to enrich uranium to use as fuel in a civilian nuclear power program, it criticized Tehran for failing to report its enrichment activities and requested that Iran provide the IAEA with information on how it had obtained the centrifuges used in enrichment experiments. Following this report, Britain, France, and Germany, acting on behalf of the EU as the "EU3," began negotiations with Iran aimed at persuading it to suspend its uranium enrichment activities voluntarily.

In 2003 the EU3 and Iran reached an agreement whereby Iran consented to suspend uranium enrichment activities voluntarily in return for verbal assurances that it would be offered a long-term trade agreement. In June 2004, citing a lack of progress in talks on a permanent agreement, Iran announced its intention of resuming uranium enrichment. This decision set in motion a new round of Iran–EU3 negotiations that yielded a new voluntary suspension agreement in November 2004. In return, the EU3 promised that talks on a permanent agreement would be held in tandem with talks on an overall trade agreement and support for Iran's application for membership in the World Trade Organization. When talks made no progress on nonnuclear issues, in 2005 Iran again announced resumption of certain uranium fuel processing activities. Iran rejected a comprehensive proposal for trade in August, on the grounds that the proposal did not deal with the issue of U.S. economic sanctions, which were harming Iran's economy. A stalemate then developed, with the EU3 contending that Iran's rejection of the proposal had ended the negotiations while Iran asserted that it was willing to continue talking. In mid-2006, the United Nations (UN) Security Council reacted to the IAEA's appeal of the stalemate by demanding that Iran suspend uranium enrichment. When Iran failed to meet the UN deadlines and renewed European diplomatic efforts failed, the Security Council imposed limited sanctions in December 2006. No substantial progress was made to resolve the issue as of late 2007.

Relations with Neighboring Arab Countries

After Khatami was elected, Iran also made concerted efforts to improve its relations with neighboring Arab countries. These relations had begun to thaw under Rafsanjani, and considerable progress had been achieved in bilateral relations with Kuwait, Oman, Qatar, and Saudi Arabia. According to scholars of Saudi foreign policy, the Saudi attitude toward Iran began to change in 1995, after the Saudi government decided to improve relations with its own Shia minority. As Saudi leaders ceased to view their Shia minority as a potential security threat, they gradually perceived Iran less as a source of subversion among this minority. This new attitude then eased the way for improved relations. The symbolic manifestation of the new cordiality was an exchange of official visits by the two heads of state in late 1997 and early 1998. This unusual exchange was followed in May 1998 by a comprehensive cooperation agreement and in April 2001 by a security agreement between the two countries.

Iran's relations with most other Arab countries also improved in the 1990s. Unrest among the majority Shia population of Bahrain, which the Sunni (see Glossary) monarchy there viewed as a security threat, had persisted throughout the 1980s and early 1990s, and the government suspected Iran of providing clandestine support to Bahrain's Shia dissidents. Saudi Arabia's rapprochement with its Shia minority put pressure on the government of Bahrain to accommodate some demands of its Shia majority. As sectarian tensions abated in the mid-1990s, the concerns of Bahrain's rulers about potential Iranian subversive activities eased considerably, and this led to relatively amicable relations by the late 1990s. Iran even established a better relationship with its archfoe Iraq, as the two countries exchanged most or all of the remaining prisoners from the war they had fought in the 1980s. They also held several high-level diplomatic meetings between 1997 and 2002. In the early stages of the 2003 conflict in Iraq, Iran adopted a neutral stance (see Contemporary Security Policy, ch. 5).

The only Persian Gulf Arab country whose relations with Iran did not improve substantially was the United Arab Emirates (UAE), which continued to dispute the sovereignty of three islands in the Persian Gulf, Abu Musa and the two Tunbs. The dispute over the islands had been dormant until 1992, when the UAE accused Iran of violating the 1971 accord on shared sovereignty of Abu Musa and also demanded that Iran end its occupation of the Tunbs. Although the dispute has persisted as an irritant in Iran–UAE relations, it has not affected trade between the two countries. The UAE, principally the emirate of Dubai, annually exports consumer goods valued at several billion U.S. dollars to Iran.

Relations with other Middle Eastern Countries

In the late 1990s, Iran began a dialogue with Egypt, which had been a bitter foe since the early days of the Islamic regime. The normalization of relations between Iran and Egypt was stalled for several years by Iran's refusal to rename a Tehran street honoring the assassin of Egyptian President Anwar Sadat. Although Iran's parliament finally voted to change the street's name in January 2004, other issues stalled the resumption of full diplomatic ties. Nevertheless, Iran's relations with Egypt improved substantially between 1997 and 2005. Meanwhile, relations with Egypt's southern neighbor, Sudan, which were not close during most of the 1980s, became cordial after a 1989 coup brought to power a military government allied with a Sudanese Islamist political party led by Hasan al-Turabi. However, relations deteriorated gradually throughout the 1990s because of Turabi's persistent criticism of Shias for not being "complete Muslims." Relations with Sudan improved after that country's rulers broke with Turabi and his followers in late 1999.

Iran continued to have a good working relationship with Syria under Khatami, despite Syria's secularist orientation. Trade (primarily Iran's concessionary sales of oil to Syria), tourism (particularly the visits of several thousand Iranian pilgrims per year to Syria), and a shared view of Middle Eastern security issues were important aspects of this relationship. Prior to 2005, Syria was a main conduit for Iran's relations with Lebanon. The largest religious community in multiconfessional

Lebanon is composed of Shia Muslims, and Iran's interest in this group's welfare long predates the Islamic Revolution of 1978–79. Beginning in the early 1980s, Iran maintained direct relations with both Lebanese Shia armed political factions, Amal and Hizballah, sometimes mediating conflicts between the rivals. Following the end of Lebanon's 15-year civil war in 1990, that country's central government tried to persuade Iran not to provide direct assistance, especially arms, to Amal and Hizballah. But Lebanon's de facto political dependence on Syria meant that Iran could ignore the government's entreaties. The withdrawal of all Syrian military forces and intelligence agents from Lebanon in 2005 and the presence of Hizballah as a political party in the coalition government that came to power in Lebanon in July 2005 reinforced Iran's position in Lebanon. Iran reportedly lent support to Hizballah's conflict with Israel in mid-2006.

In the early 2000s, Iran's relations with Lebanon and Syria were intertwined with its policy toward Israel. Iran has supported the position of both countries that the Israeli occupation of parts of their territories (part of southern Lebanon from 1978 until 2000 and Syria's Golan Heights since 1967) is illegal under international law, as is the Israeli occupation of the Palestinian territories known as the West Bank, along the Jordan River, and the Gaza Strip. Like Lebanon and Syria, Iran held that the creation of Israel in 1948 on land that a UN partition resolution had allotted to a Palestinian state was a violation of that resolution and therefore illegal. For that reason, Iran refused to extend diplomatic recognition to Israel. In fact, one of the very first foreign policy initiatives of the provisional government in February 1979 was to rescind the de facto recognition that the shah had granted to Israel in the early 1960s and to turn the Israeli trade mission in Tehran over to the Palestine Liberation Organization (PLO). Iran's relations with the PLO ended a year later, when the PLO expressed support for Iraq's invasion of and subsequent eight-year war with Iran. After Israel and the PLO signed the Oslo Accord on mutual recognition in 1993, President Rafsanjani announced a position that remained Iran's official policy on Israel and the Palestinians for the remainder of his term and throughout the Khatami administration: The peace process did not provide a just procedure for dealing with the issue of Palestinian refuges from 1948, but Iran would not oppose any agreement with Israel that the Palestinian people accepted. The regime of Mahmoud Ahmadinejad, however, took a harder overall line toward Israel, expressed by several virulent attacks in presidential speeches.

The peace process between Israel and the PLO had collapsed by winter 2001; PLO officials then established clandestine contacts with officials in Iran about obtaining weapons for the police forces of the governing Palestinian Authority. In January 2002, Israeli commandos intercepted the freighter *Karine A* in the Mediterranean Sea, carrying 50 tons of Iranian weapons. The Khatami government denied any involvement in the shipment, whose origin remained unclear. Whatever its origin, the *Karine A* affair, occurring only a few months after the September 11, 2001, terrorist attacks in the United States, had a fateful impact on the U.S. perception of Iran's role in the fight against terrorism.

With a few notable exceptions, Iran's relations with the other non-Arab countries in the region have been pragmatic, if not cordial, both during and after the Khatami presidency. In the 1980s and early 1990s, Iran and Turkey maintained diplomatic relations and engaged in considerable trade, despite the fact that armed Kurdish groups, particularly the Kurdistan Workers' Party (known by its Kurdish initials, PKK), staged attacks in both directions across their mutual border, and despite the Turkish government's avowed secularism and close relations with the United States and Israel. During the Khatami era, Iran's relations with Turkey remained good, with increased trade and Turkish investment in Iran. In the wake of the U.S. occupation of Iraq, Iran and Turkey have increasingly shared anxiety about increased activity by their respective Kurdish minorities. However, in the winter of 2006 Iran abruptly cut deliveries of natural gas to Turkey, and Turkey's public position against Iran's nuclear program also caused friction. Turkey's growing security cooperation with Israel is another matter of concern for Iran, as is competition with Turkey over pipeline routes from the Caucasus Mountains.

Relations with Neighbors to the North and East

Iran has enjoyed generally good relations with Russia and most of the other former Soviet republics since the breakup of the Soviet Union in 1991. In 1995 Russia agreed to finish construction of a large nuclear power reactor in the southern Iranian city of Bushehr, despite intense opposition from the United States. Russia's extensive trade with Iran has included the sale of military equipment. In addition, the two countries cooperated closely between 1996 and 2001 to support former Afghan government forces fighting against the Taliban government in Afghanistan. Iran meanwhile continued to maintain a cordial relationship with the former Soviet republics of Central Asia, building important pipeline and rail connections with Turkmenistan, for example.

The one country among its northern neighbors with which Iran has not had cordial relations is Azerbaijan. Iran provided de facto assistance to Armenia during the 1992–94 war between Armenia and Azerbaijan over the Armenian-populated province of Nagorno–Karabakh in Azerbaijan. That war was a disaster for Azerbaijan, ending with Armenia in control not only of Nagorno–Karabakh but also of the Azerbaijani territory between Armenia and Nagorno–Karabakh. Possibly in retaliation, Azerbaijan has not cooperated with Iran on issues of concern to Tehran, such as the decline of caviar-producing sturgeon and increased pollution of the Caspian Sea. Furthermore, newspapers and politicians in Azerbaijan continue to assert territorial claims on Iran's Azeri-speaking provinces of East and West Azarbaijan. Although such claims are not official, they have provoked angry responses from Tehran. Iran has cultivated closer relations with Armenia in economic and transportation policy, building a new pipeline and a new railroad across the mutual border.

Iran's relations with its eastern neighbors have been complex. In Afghanistan, the Taliban seized Kabul in 1996 after defeating the various Tajik, Uzbek, and Hazara militias that subsequently formed the Northern Alliance in a small area of northeastern Afghanistan outside Taliban control. Iran supported the Northern Alliance because it disliked the Taliban's puritanical, anti-Shia Islamist ideology and believed that the Taliban was a tool of Pakistan. In August 1998, Taliban forces executed several captured Iranian diplomats. In response, Iran massed some 250,000 troops along its Afghan border and seriously contemplated invading the country. In subsequent years, Iran continued to work against the Taliban, even cooperating with the United States in the overthrow of the Taliban government in late 2001 (see The United States and Iran, this ch.). In 2006 Iran was supporting anti-Taliban and anti-U.S. conservative forces in Afghanistan in an effort to solidify its influence in that country.

Iran and Pakistan maintained correct relations in the 1980s and early 1990s, but tensions existed between them as they supported different Afghan resistance forces against the Soviet-backed government in Afghanistan. After 1992, Iran also believed that Pakistan was largely responsible for creating and supporting the Taliban. Suspicions about Pakistan led Iran to develop closer ties with India, which also helped support the Northern Alliance. Trade between India and Iran became important by the 1990s, and the two countries began to discuss plans to build a pipeline to transport natural gas from Iran to both Pakistan and India. In 2003 the two countries signed a comprehensive partnership agreement, and India has not been critical of Iran's nuclear program. Plans for a pipeline route and the financing of construction costs were finalized in 2005.

Despite Iran's reservations about Pakistan's policies in Afghanistan, sometime in 1992 or later A.Q. Khan, the head of Pakistan's nuclear program, began to sell Iran plans and technology for producing nuclear fuel enriched to levels suitable for use in weapons. This activity only was revealed in 2002 by the government of Pakistan, which claimed no prior knowledge of the secret sales. The revelations caused Iran to admit that it had constructed an elaborate network of facilities for conducting research and experiments on nuclear fuel cycle activities.

The United States and Iran

The United States broke diplomatic relations with Iran in April 1980, during the hostage crisis, and relations had not been restored as of late 2007. Secret talks occurred between the United States and Iran in the mid-1980s, but their premature revelation was an embarrassment for both countries. Consequently, even though the talks had been approved at the highest levels in Tehran and Washington, some Americans and some Iranians involved in them were punished by their respective governments. New, tentative overtures toward normalizing relations were undertaken during the presidential administrations of George H.W. Bush and Ali Akbar Hashemi Rafsanjani, but these did not bear fruit by the end of Bush's term in 1993. The administration of William J. Clinton, which followed, had a more suspicious view of Iran. In early 1993, it announced a policy of dual containment to isolate both Iran and Iraq. Two years later, an executive order forbade U.S. firms and individuals from trading or having any financial transactions with Iran, and in 1996 the Iran–Libya Sanctions Act (ILSA) expanded economic sanctions against Iran. Consequently, when Khatami took office as president of Iran in 1997, the United States was not positioned to respond quickly to the opportunities his administration presented.

In a series of statements during his first few months in office, Khatami called for better relations with the West and, specifically, closer ties with the United States. In an extraordinary interview broadcast in January 1998, he expressed "great respect" for the American people, condemned the use of terrorism, and again called for closer U.S. ties. American officials reacted cautiously to these overtures, making a few minor gestures such as listing the Mojahedin-e Khalq as a terrorist organization. However, the United States continued to insist that any bilateral discussions with Iran focus on its nuclear program, its alleged support for terrorist groups, and its opposition to the Israeli-Palestinian peace process—preconditions that Iran had rejected repeatedly in the past. A few weeks after Khatami's interview, Khamenei further undermined the prospects for rapprochement in a major speech, stating that the United States was Iran's "enemy" and making it clear that he opposed better relations as long as Washington continued to act "arrogantly" toward Iran. Other conservatives quickly joined Khamenei in denouncing the United States, thereby politicizing the issue of U.S relations and making it difficult for Khatami to move forward. However, while relations between the two governments remained problematic during this period, many U.S. NGOs became much more active in Iran.

In June 1998—more than a year after Khatami was elected—U.S. Secretary of State Madeleine Albright laid out a "road map" to achieve better bilateral relations. U.S. officials made several minor gestures toward Iran during 1998 as well, declining to apply sanctions to third-country firms investing in Iran (as provided for in the ILSA), working with Iranian officials in a UN committee on Afghanistan, and removing Iran from the U.S. list of countries involved in illicit drug transit or production. In April 1999, the United States authorized sales of food and medicine to Iran. Iranian officials generally found these gestures positive but considered them small steps that did not address the crippling economic sanctions that remained in force. Moreover, faced with increasing criticism from the conservatives beginning in 1998, Khatami and his allies concluded that whatever benefits might result from responding positively to these limited U.S. actions were outweighed by the high domestic political costs of doing so.

Despite Iran's tepid response, U.S. officials continued efforts to promote rapprochement until the Clinton administration left office in January 2001. The high point of this initiative came in March 2000, when Albright officially acknowledged the U.S. role in overthrowing Iranian prime minister Mohammad Mossadeq in 1953, lifted restrictions on U.S. imports of Iranian food products and carpets, and identified areas where the United States and Iran could cooperate. However, Albright also pointedly criticized Iran's "unelected officials"—an obvious reference to Khamenei and other key conservatives. Predictably, Khamenei's negative reaction to Albright's speech nullified the important concessions she had made.

When George W. Bush was elected U.S. president in November 2000, the prospects of continued rapprochement with Iran seemed good. However, the Bush administration did not continue its predecessor's efforts. The administration's review of Iran policy was interrupted by the terrorist attacks of September 11, 2001; Iranian officials expressed deep sympathy over the loss of life and then gave assistance to the United States as it attacked the forces of the Taliban and the terrorist group al Qaeda in Afghanistan. Iran facilitated U.S. contacts with the Northern Alliance, allowed U.S. forces to use Iranian territory and airspace for various purposes, and worked closely with U.S. officials to set up a post-Taliban government. Although Iran clearly had an interest in helping to overthrow the Taliban, the Iranian assistance seemed to be a deliberate, positive gesture toward the United States.

Before the Bush administration decided on whether to reciprocate Iran's gesture in Afghanistan, the *Karine A* incident of January 2002 had the effect of putting Iran into the camp of supporters of terrorism, as seen from the U.S. perspective. Several weeks later, in his State of the Union address, Bush linked Iran with Iraq and North Korea in an "axis of evil." Iranian officials were angered that the United States had ignored the assistance they had provided in Afghanistan and had put Iran in the same category as Iraq, whose government, in their view, had committed acts of incomparable brutality.

The "axis of evil" characterization initiated a new period of mutual recriminations between Iran and the United States. Although Iran did not end its cooperation with the United States in Afghanistan, contacts were scaled back considerably, and misunderstandings were more common than consensus during 2002 and 2003. Iranian forces arrested some al Qaeda members who fled into Iran.

Iraq became another arena for cooperation and conflict with the United States. On the one hand, Iran did not welcome the prospect of a large American military force occupying Iraq. On the other hand, it did welcome Saddam Hussein's removal from power and the opportunity for Iraq's Shias finally to gain representation in national government. Iran's main ally in Iraq was the Supreme Council for the Islamic Revolution in Iraq (SCIRI), which had been based in exile in Iran since 1980, and whose militia returned to Iraq soon after the U.S. invasion of March 2003. Iran's relations with the SCIRI have provided it with influence in Iraq, but Iraq's large Shia community (estimated at 55 percent of the country's population) did not unite around a single political party.

The initial U.S. victory in Iraq prompted some official talk in Washington of the need for "regime change" in Iran. This language put Khatami and the reformists on the defensive, forcing them to demonstrate their loyalty to Iran by denouncing the United States as strongly as did the conservatives. By 2004, however, the rhetoric had abated, and both Iran and the United States seemed to have reverted to ambivalent attitudes toward each other. Washington continued to cite the need for "freedom" in Iran while simultaneously stressing the value of negotiations with Tehran on its nuclear program. In March 2005, Bush agreed with his EU allies that they should offer Iran a carrot if it would abandon efforts to enrich uranium for fuel: The United States would drop its opposition to Iran's application for membership in the World Trade Organization. In 2006 and 2007, there was persistent media speculation about a possible U.S. attack on or invasion of Iran, as tensions continued and negotiations failed to resolve issues.

Tensions around the nuclear issue diminished in the fall of 2007 when an official U.S. government intelligence report declared that Iran likely ceased work on its nuclear weapons program in 2003. However, the Bush administration maintained that the nuclear program represented an ongoing danger because of Iran's continued enrichment of uranium and that Iran's support of terrorist organizations in the Middle East remained unacceptable.

*   *   *

The most comprehensive analysis of Iran's political dynamics, especially the development of the political struggles between the reformists and conservatives during the 1990s, is Mehdi Moslem, *Factional Politics in Post-Khomeini Iran*. An updated account, which covers Khatami's second administration and the initial months of Ahmadinejad's presidency, is Ali Gheissari and Vali Nasr, *Democracy in Iran: History and the Quest for Liberty*. Several journalists who were stationed in Iran for a year or more also have written informative accounts of post-1999 politics; these books include Geneive Abdo and Jonathan Lyons, *Answering Only to God: Faith and Freedom in Twenty-First-Century Iran*; Christopher de Bellaique, *In the Garden of the Martyrs*; Azadeh Moaveni, *Lipstick Jihad;* and Afshin Molavi, *The Soul of Iran*. For a thorough description of Iran's governmental institutions, see Wilfried Buchta, *Who Rules Iran?* This book may be supplemented by Bahman Baktiari's *Parliamentary Politics in Revolutionary Iran: The Institutionalization of Factional Politics*, a detailed analysis of the first and second postrevolutionary parliaments, and Kian Tajbakhsh's article on local government councils, "Political Decentralization and the Creation of Local Government in Iran."

On the development of political parties and civil society organizations, articles by the following scholars provide useful insights: Hossein Akhavi-Pour and Heidar Azodanloo, Mark Gasiorowski, Arang Keshavarzian, Farhad Khosrokhavar, and Azadeh Kian-Thiébaut. An interesting account of the legal campaign to institutionalize basic human rights protections is the memoir by Iran's Noble Peace Prize laureate, Shirin Ebadi, *Iran Awakening*. Specific human rights issues are covered by Ervand Abrahamian in *Tortured Confessions* and Reza Afshari in *Human Rights in Iran*. On this topic, also see the annual reports of Amnesty International, Middle East Watch, and Reporters Without Borders. Mass media and the arts, especially cinema, are covered in Hamid Dabashi, *Close-Up*, as well as in the collection of articles, *The New Iranian Cinema*, edited by Richard Tapper.

The article by Arshin Adib-Moghaddam, "Islamic Utopian Romanticism and the Foreign Policy Culture of Iran," provides a succinct overview of the ideological premises that underlie the foreign policy of the Islamic Republic of Iran. Other aspects of general Iranian foreign policy are analyzed in articles contained in the edited volume by Eric Hooglund, *Twenty Years of Islamic Revolution*. U.S.-Iranian relations since the 1978–79 Revolution are examined in William O. Beeman, *The "Great*

Satan" vs. the "Mad Mullahs": How the United States and Iran Demonize Each Other, James A. Bill, *The Eagle and the Lion;* and in articles by Eric Hooglund, R.K. Ramazani, and Gary Sick. The issue of Iran's nuclear development program is discussed in Ali Ansari's *Confronting Iran: The Failure of American Foreign Policy and the Next Great Crisis in the Middle East.* (For further information and complete citations, see Bibliography.)

Chapter 5. National Security

A sword and scabbard from a bas-relief at Persepolis, ca. 500 B.C.

UNTIL THE MID-1960s, IRAN'S NATIONAL security strategy had an internal focus. The primary objective was to develop and deploy a strong national military that would put a conclusive end to resistance by tribal groups, which, as late as the 1920s, had maintained autonomy over portions of the Iranian countryside. After suppressing the last major tribal rebellions, the military began to focus on potential external threats. In 1968 two developments combined to elevate the Persian Gulf region as a primary security concern: the announcement by Britain that it would withdraw its military forces from the Persian Gulf sheikhdoms and grant its protectorates there full independence, and a coup d'état by the Sunni Baathist Party in Iraq. By the early 1970s, Iran was providing military support to a Kurdish uprising in northern Iraq against the Baathist regime and had dispatched a contingent of troops to Oman to oppose an anti-monarchical movement that had occupied the southern half of that country. Although a 1975 treaty temporarily resolved the problems with Iraq, the Islamic Revolution of 1978–79 weakened Iran's internal and external security. Within a few months after the Revolution, counterrevolutionary groups, tribes, and various ethnic minorities were engaging in armed conflict with government security forces. Then, in September 1980 Iraqi ground troops moved across the entire Iran–Iraq border, beginning a costly eight-year war of attrition that has had a lasting effect on Iran's security policy.

After 1979, a combination of internal instability and external pressures resulted in a state structure that relied on a strong military to deter foreign threats and assert domestic authority. Factional politics and increasingly problematic relations with the international community further complicated Iran's security policy. The Iran–Iraq War taught Iran that military independence was vital and that command of the air was the most important factor in military success. In the decades following the war with Iraq, Iran coped with an international arms embargo by piecing together military technology and incomplete inventories of weapons, vehicles, and aircraft. Meanwhile, it slowly assembled a missile force capable of ensuring regional domination. Concerned that Iran had clandestinely developed facilities to process nuclear fuel potentially applicable to nuclear weapons manufacture, the international community applied various diplomatic and economic strategies to persuade Iran to discontinue its uranium enrichment program. The controversy over the nuclear energy program has strongly influenced Iran's overall national security policy.

The Armed Forces

Historical Background

The Military under the Pahlavi Shahs

Iran's twentieth-century army was formed by Reza Khan, who became minister of war in 1921, prime minister in 1923, and shah in 1925, taking the name Reza Shah Pahlavi (see The Era of Reza Shah, 1921–41, ch. 1). Supposedly created to defend the country from foreign aggression, the army became the enforcer of Reza Shah's internal security policies against rebellious tribes and political opposition groups. Between 1924 and 1940, Reza Shah allocated between 30 and 50 percent of national expenditures to the army. He not only purchased modern weapons in large quantities but also created an air force and a navy as branches of the army in the 1920s. With the introduction of the new services, the army established two military academies to meet the ever-rising demand for officers. The majority of the officers continued training in Europe, however. By 1941 the army stood at 125,000 troops, five times its original size. Considered well trained and well equipped, it had gained a privileged role in society. Disloyalty to the shah, evidenced by several coup attempts, was punished harshly. The public perceived the military mainly as a tool to uphold the shah's dictatorial regime.

Disproving the high reputation of Iran's armed forces, in August 1941 British and Russian forces invaded Iran when Reza Shah, who had declared Iran neutral in World War II, refused to expel German nationals from the country. In three days, the invading forces decimated the Iranian army and completely destroyed the fledgling air force and navy. With his institutional power base ruined, the shah abdicated in favor of his 22-year old son, Mohammad Reza Shah (r. 1941–79 as Mohammad Reza Shah Pahlavi) (see World War II and the Azarbaijan Crisis, ch. 1).

Reza Shah's abdication in favor of his son did not slow the modernization of the army. In 1942 the United States sent military advisers to Iran to aid the new shah in reorganizing his

Members of the shah's Imperial Iranian Armed Forces

forces, thus establishing a relationship between the armed forces of the two nations that would last until the Revolution of 1978–79. Beginning in 1946, the parliament (Majlis—see Glossary) put limits on the military budget to keep the army from resuming its role as a base of political power. Although determined to build an effective military establishment, the shah was forced to accept the managerial control of the parliament. Mohammad Mossadeq, who with the support of the parliament gained the posts of prime minister (1951) and minister of war (1952), dismissed officers loyal to the shah. With the assistance of British and U.S. intelligence, however, officers who had been dismissed overthrew Mossadeq in August 1953 and re-installed the shah, who had fled the country (see Mossadeq and Oil Nationalization, ch. 1). Within two years, the shah consolidated his control of the armed forces. In this period, separate commands were established for the army, air force, and navy; all three branches of the military embarked on large-scale modernization programs that continued to the end of the shah's reign in 1979.

After the 1953 coup, the shah instituted an unparalleled system of control over all his officers. The monarch not only made all decisions pertaining to purchasing, promotions, and routine military affairs but also restricted interaction among his officers, who were forced to deal individually with their ruler. However, the absence of leadership at the general staff level and below that resulted from this practice literally paralyzed the military as the Revolution gathered momentum in the fall and winter of 1978–79 (see The Coming of the Revolution, ch. 1). In response to numerous mass demonstrations, the army lashed out heedlessly, killing and injuring numerous civilians. The most infamous such encounter occurred at Jaleh Square in Tehran in September 1978, shortly after martial law had been declared in Iran's major cities. In response to these incidents, demonstrators "attacked" army units, deployed to maintain order, with flowers. This tactic demoralized troops and caused conscripts to desert en masse.

In early February 1979, continued mass demonstrations brought about a declaration of neutrality by the military, leading to the collapse of the government left in power when the shah fled Iran in January. Installed in its place was a provisional government named by revolutionary leader Ayatollah Sayyid Ruhollah Musavi Khomeini. Within days, Khomeini and several other religious leaders announced that the armed forces had "returned to the nation" and cautioned against indiscriminate vengeance against service members. Nevertheless, large numbers of the shah's former officers were dismissed or fled the country.

The Postrevolutionary Period

The new government took prompt steps to reconstitute the armed forces. Intent on remolding the shah's army into a loyal national Islamic force, Khomeini made radical changes in the senior officer corps and at the command-and-control level. Troops who had heeded Khomeini's appeal to disband were called back in March 1979, and a new command group of officers with impeccable revolutionary credentials was established. General staff personnel were called back to coordinate the reorganization; division and brigade command positions were promptly filled by reliable officers. Only the personal guard units of the shah were permanently disbanded.

To protect the new regime from counterrevolutionary threats during the period when the military was being reformed, a parallel military institution, the Islamic Revolutionary Guard Corps (IRGC) or Revolutionary Guards (Pasdaran; in full, Pasdaran-e Enghelab-e Islami), was formed. The IRGC has been the most loyal and dominant armed force in Iran since the Revolution. Originally created as a protector of the regime, the IRGC became a full military force during the Iran–Iraq War (see Special and Irregular Armed Forces, this ch.). As a separate and parallel organization that eventually developed its own air and naval divisions, the IRGC became a rival of the regular armed forces. In 1989 this anomaly was resolved with the merger of all the military forces under a single command. A new position was created for the officer who would lead the combined forces: chief of staff of the armed forces and commander of the Gendarmerie (rural police). The influence of the IRGC on this joint structure is reflected in the fact that through the end of 2007 every person holding the position of armed forces chief of staff has been a senior IRGC officer.

When war with Iraq broke out in September 1980, the Islamic Republic of Iran was both internally and externally vulnerable and had no real defense strategy. Because Iran had neither expected nor prepared for the war, Iraqi troops easily occupied parts of oil-rich Khuzestan Province. Having discarded its alliance with the United States in 1979 and joined the Non-Aligned Movement, Iran fought the entire war without significant military support from a friendly state, except for tactical support from Syria. In its search for weapons, the regime was even forced to deal, clandestinely, with putative enemies such as Israel and the United States. Politically, too, Iran had very few friends and soon entered into a phase of international isolation, even among Islamic countries.

The Iran–Iraq War helped to lay the foundations for the geopolitical and military conditions that influenced many of the security decisions of the 1990s. The war highlighted the international isolation of Iran's new government and the regional pressures exerted by surrounding regimes. Furthermore, the war with Iraq forced Iran to address the problem of having two separate armed forces, one professional (the army) and the other voluntary and politically motivated (the IRGC). Coupled with a history of foreign intervention, manipulation, and exploitation, the events of the 1980s reinforced the desire for military self-reliance.

The presidency of Ali Akbar Hashemi Rafsanjani, which began in 1989, saw substantial reorganization of Iran's national security establishment in response to the shortcomings revealed by the Iran–Iraq War. A central aim of this process was to professionalize Iran's irregular forces and reform them into a conventional military organization (see Command and Control, this ch.). In the 1990s, the military reassessment process also emphasized acquisition of missiles and weapons of mass destruction (WMD), with the aim of making Iran capable of waging war independently of outside suppliers (see Arms Acquisition; Military Doctrine, this ch.).

Beginning in 1991, international events presented new considerations for Iran's national security policy makers. The Persian Gulf War of 1991 brought large numbers of U.S. troops close to Iran's borders. The terrorist attacks of September 11, 2001, again brought U.S. forces to the region, this time in both Afghanistan and Iraq. After lending some assistance to troops of the United States and the North Atlantic Treaty Organization (NATO) in Afghanistan, Iran remained neutral toward the U.S. invasion of Iraq in 2003 (see Contemporary Security Policy, this ch.).

Command and Control

Early in his presidency, Rafsanjani took steps to streamline the army while encouraging the professionalization and institutionalization of the IRGC. In effect, the IRGC's ground forces were reorganized into 21 infantry divisions, 15 independent infantry brigades, 21 air defense brigades, 3 engineering divisions, and 42 armored, artillery, and chemical defense brigades. Some 21 new military ranks (from private to general, divided among the categories of soldiers, fighters, officers, and commandants) also were created.

In 1989 the IRGC and the professional armed forces were amalgamated under the Ministry of Defense and Armed Forces Logistics (MODAFL). This measure dissolved the separate ministry that had run the IRGC, placing its command structures within the new MODAFL. The creation of the MODAFL allowed the regime to minimize potential threats from the revolutionary IRGC. Also, the assignment of ranks was a first step in professionalizing the IRGC, with the ultimate goal of further unifying the armed forces under a comprehensive defense umbrella. In further reforms, the Rafsanjani regime expanded the Joint Chiefs of Staff and created the General Command of the Armed Forces Joint Staffs. These changes strengthened the institution of the Joint Staff Office. Although resentment between the IRGC and the regular army still existed in the early 2000s, the Rafsanjani reforms resulted in more cooperation between the two forces.

Under Article 110 of the constitution of 1979, the Iranian head of state (the Leader of the Revolution) has full authority to appoint and dismiss the chief of the Joint Staff, the commander in chief of the IRGC, and as many as two advisers to the Supreme Defense Council (SDC), the body responsible for strategic planning and development of military and defense policy. On the recommendation of the SDC, the Leader also can appoint or dismiss the commanders in chief of the ground, naval, and air forces. The Leader also has authority to supervise the activities of the SDC, and, on its recommendation, to declare war and mobilize the armed forces. As Leader, Khomeini maintained the role of final arbiter, but he delegated the post of commander in chief to the president (see The President and Cabinet, ch. 4).

Article 110 stipulates that the SDC consist of the president, minister of defense, chief of the Joint Staff of the Armed Forces, commander in chief of the IRGC, and two advisers appointed by the Leader. Other senior officials may attend SDC meetings to deliberate on national defense issues. In the past, the minister of foreign affairs, minister of interior, commanders in chief of the air force and navy, and others have attended meetings. The council has representatives at operational area and field headquarters to provide political and strategic guidance to field commanders. SDC representatives may veto military decisions.

There are two chains of command below the SDC: one administrative, the other operational. To some extent, this dual chain of command is a holdover from the organizational structure of the Imperial Iranian Armed Forces, which was modeled on the U.S. division of powers between the administrative functions of the service secretaries and the operational functions of the secretary of defense and the chiefs of staff. In addition, government leaders saw this structure as a way to limit friction between the regular military and the IRGC.

In this dual structure, the MODAFL handles administrative matters for the entire armed forces. The administrative chain of command flows upward from senior unit commanders (division, wing, and fleet) to intermediate-echelon service commanders and to service commanders in chief and their staffs. Similarly, during its existence the Ministry of the Islamic Revolutionary Guard Corps handled the administrative affairs of the IRGC. The operational chain of command flows upward from senior unit commanders (operational brigades in the case of combat units) to the ministry staff officers. Even though the Ministry of Defense oversees the entire armed forces, the IRGC continues to benefit from a unique and distinguished status compared to the regular army. After the election of Mahmoud Ahmadinejad as president in June 2005, there was some indication that the operational chain of command would be weakened in order to mitigate the decision-making authority possessed by operational officials.

Decision Making

Iran's decision-making system is a complex of competing influences whose conflicts are resolved through a culturally prescribed consensus procedure. Power distribution within the system rests on the personal relationships of the primary actors rather than on a formal set of rules and regulations. The complex relationships within the hierarchy of the regular military and the parallel IRGC military organization, and the relationships of those organizations with informal power centers, are based on clan and family. Nevertheless, the decisions of military leaders generally are heavily influenced by decisions conveyed to them before their "deliberation" process begins. Because the Leader's judgment rarely is questioned, no system of checks and balances exists in most cases. Senior religious figures often involve themselves in military decision making, which has resulted in unsuccessful outcomes when expert analysis was contravened. The hierarchical system, maintained by the emphasis on consensus, discourages "rogue actions."

Organization, Size, and Equipment

Army

The estimated force level of the regular army increased from 325,000 in 2001 to 350,000 in 2007 (see table 12, Appendix). Of that number, an estimated 220,000 were conscripts. Most of the personnel who gained combat experience in the Iran–Iraq War had left military service by the mid-1990s. Experts do not rate Iran's military training highly, so the potential combat performance of the ground forces is unknown.

After the Revolution, the army underwent a structural reorganization. The ground forces of the Imperial Iranian Armed Forces had been deployed in six divisions and four specialized combat regiments that were supported by more than 500 helicopters and hovercraft. Following the Revolution, the army was renamed the Islamic Iranian Ground Forces (IIGF). In 2006 the IIGF comprised four armored divisions, each with three armored brigades, one mechanized brigade, and four or five artillery battalions; six infantry divisions; two commando divisions; one airborne brigade; one special forces brigade; six artillery groups; and aviation support units.

Prior to the Revolution, Iran had purchased matériel for its ground forces from many countries, including the United States, the United Kingdom (UK), France, the Federal Republic of Germany (West Germany), Italy, and the Soviet Union. With access to many of its traditional suppliers restricted during the Iran–Iraq War, Iran made selective purchases from a wide variety of suppliers, including the Democratic People's Republic of Korea (North Korea), China, Brazil, Israel, and the Soviet Union. The diversity of the weapons purchased from these countries greatly complicated training and supply procedures. Nevertheless, by 2000 Iran had done much to restock its arsenal, most notably by the addition of 72 combat aircraft and 108 heavy artillery weapons.

Iran's army relies primarily on main battle tanks of Soviet manufacture, together with some from China and the UK and 100 domestically produced Zulfiqar tanks (see table 13, Appendix). Armored units suffer from a lack of spare parts for their foreign tanks and from the obsolescence of most models, although the size of the armored force increased significantly in the late 1990s. The Zulfiqars and the Soviet T–72s on which they are based are the most advanced main battle tanks in the arsenal. Most of Iran's armored personnel carriers (APCs) and armored vehicles, together totaling 1,250 units in 2006, are Soviet models, supplemented by the 1960s-vintage U.S. M–113 and the domestically produced Boragh APC, which is based on a Soviet armored vehicle, the BMP.

Iran's artillery units depend heavily on towed rather than self-propelled guns. The predominant type of towed artillery is the M–46 field gun (985 of which were in service in 2006), first produced in the 1950s by the Soviet Union and China. More than two-thirds of self-propelled artillery pieces are U.S.-made M–107 and M–109 howitzers. Nearly all of Iran's multiple-rocket launchers are 107-mm and 130-mm pieces from the Type 63 series, developed by China in the 1960s. Some launchers of Iranian origin also are in service. Most of the 1,700 operable antiaircraft guns are of Soviet manufacture. The surface-to-surface rocket arsenal includes modified Soviet Scud–Bs and several models of domestic origin.

Most of the aircraft flown by the army's aviation units are U.S.-made holdovers from the Pahlavi era. Some helicopters of Italian manufacture and 25 Russian-made Mi–8 and Mi–17 helicopters have been added.

Navy

Because of the need to defend the Persian Gulf waterway, the navy is an essential combat arm. However, in 2007 that branch, always the smallest of the three services, had only about 18,000 personnel (including 2,600 in naval aviation and 2,600 marines), most of whom had limited experience. The navy operates bases at Bandar-e Abbas, Bushehr, Khark Island, Bandar-e Anzali, Bandar-e Khomeini, Bandar-e Mah Shahr, and Chabahar. The capabilities of the navy have been limited by insufficient resources. Spare-parts shortages have plagued the navy more than the other services because Western naval matériel is less widely available on world arms markets than matériel for the other branches. In particular, arms import limitations in the late 1990s and early 2000s hampered development of amphibious warfare capabilities.

With some of the navy's ships and weapons more than 50 years old, modernization is essential to achieving force readiness. In 2001 naval authorities announced that to achieve naval self-sufficiency Iran would begin building naval craft equipped with rocket launchers, as well as advanced gunboats and destroyers and missile launcher frigates. However, that plan had not materialized by mid-decade. In 2005 some 10 French-built Kaman missile patrol boats, carrying Chinese C–802 surface-to-surface missiles (first acquired in the 1990s, now being manufactured in Iran), were in service. Three 30-year-old Alvand guided missile frigates, four 35-year-old minesweepers, and two 35-year-old Bayandor corvettes also were in service. The operational capabilities of all those vessels were regarded as poor. The navy had no fixed-wing combat aircraft, and its reconnaissance aircraft were all at least 30 years old. All naval air equipment suffers from parts shortages and poor maintenance. Iran is believed to have manufactured sophisticated mines, using Chinese and Russian technology, which could be used to block the strategically vital Strait of Hormuz (see fig. 12). In 2005 the navy had three Soviet-era Kilo-class attack submarines. A new type of minisubmarine called the Qadir went into limited production in 2005.

Air Force

In the early 2000s, Iran's air force was relatively small, with an estimated 52,000 active personnel (including 15,000 assigned to air defense units) and an aging fleet of combat aircraft. After suffering severe losses in the Iran–Iraq War and losing access to U.S. equipment, Iran made some improvements in its combat aircraft fleet in the early 1990s by purchasing fighter jets from Russia, its main supplier of such items since the Revolution. The arms import reductions of the late 1990s and early 2000s resulted in a failure to modernize the air force and ground-based air defenses.

After a steady buildup by the shah in the 1970s, the air force had about 450 modern aircraft and nearly 100,000 personnel, making it the most advanced of Iran's three services. Because most of the new equipment had come from the United States, a significant portion of Iran's aircraft probably were cannibalized for spare parts during the first decade after the Revolution. The air force also was reorganized and substantially reduced in size during this period.

Iran acquired some Chinese and North Korean aircraft in the late 1980s, and in 1991 it made its last large-scale purchase of combat aircraft, consisting mainly of Soviet-made fighter and attack jets in the MiG–27, MiG–29, MiG–31, Su–24, and Su–25 series. A few Su–25 fighter jets reportedly were delivered to the IRGC in 2003. In the early 2000s, the most important combat element of the Iranian air force consisted of 30 Su–24 Fencer and 25 MiG–29A Fulcrum fighter jets. An estimated 80 percent of these Soviet-era aircraft were serviceable during that period. The air force also had seven Su–25 Frogfoot ground attack fighters of Russian manufacture. In 2005 Iran had only about 150 aging U.S.-built aircraft left. These included 65 F–4D/E interceptors and 60 F–5E/F fighters, about 60 percent of which were rated as serviceable in 2002. Iran has long tried to maintain its U.S.-made fighters, despite the U.S. arms embargo, by purchasing spare parts through third parties. Reportedly, in 2004 Iran ordered a number of Super–7 fighters, an upgrade of the J–7 design developed by China's Chengdu Aircraft Corporation. A 2005 arms agreement with Russia provided for modernization of MiG–29 fighter jets and Mi–8 helicopters. Some of the MiG–29s had been flown by the Iraqi air force to

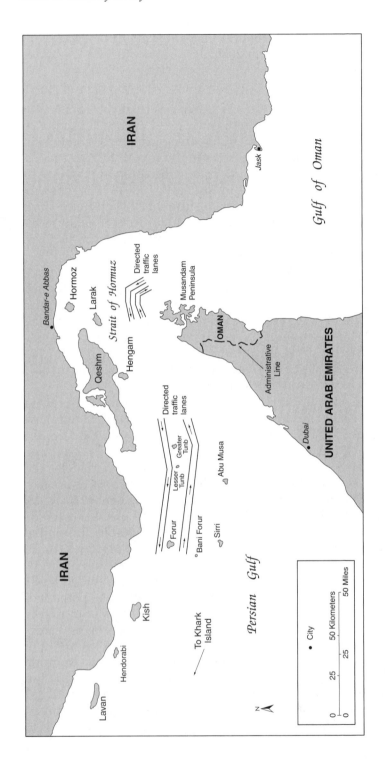

Figure 12. Strait of Hormuz and Vicinity

Iran for sanctuary during the Persian Gulf War. Iran purchased the remaining fighters and the helicopters in the early 1990s. The air force has limited air refueling capability.

In 2007 some 14 military air bases were in operation. Air force combat forces were organized in nine ground-attack fighter squadrons, five fighter squadrons, and one reconnaissance squadron. The air force's primary maintenance facility is located at Mehrabad Air Base near Tehran. The nearby Iran Aircraft Industries has supported the air force maintenance unit and provided spare parts. Several less important facilities are located at air bases in the south and near Tehran (see Arms Acquisition, this ch.).

Special and Irregular Armed Forces

The stresses that the Iran–Iraq War placed on Iran's military establishment were an important factor in the growth of the Islamic Revolutionary Guard Corps (IRGC) and another unofficial military group, the Basij, or Popular Mobilization Army, a subordinate to the IRGC. After existing in parallel during the 1980s, these two organizations were merged as part of the comprehensive force unification in the 1990s. However, the IRGC retained substantial independence as an auxiliary military force.

The Islamic Revolutionary Guard Corps (IRGC)

With the downfall of the monarchy in 1979, many of the shah's generals left Iran or were executed or purged. As a result, during the war with Iraq the officer corps was depleted, and Iran struggled to reorganize its field forces. The IRGC emerged in early 1979 as a force of about 10,000 men dedicated to preventing a counterrevolutionary coup by elements loyal to the deposed shah, especially within the military. After receiving official status in May 1979, the force was used to suppress the growing influence of largely leftist and ethnic armed groups within Iran, such as the Fedayan-e Khalq (People's Warriors), the Mojahedin-e Khalq (People's Fighters), Peykar, Komela, and a Kurdish group, the Peshmerga. The IRGC subsequently assumed an important military role in the Iran–Iraq War.

As a parallel military and defense force, the IRGC required an independent general staff and related military administrative personnel. Years of trial and error transformed the IRGC into a force rivaling the Iranian army, although both forces the-oretically were under one defense ministry. Unlike the members of the regular army, the rank and file of the IRGC initially were recruited among Khomeini supporters. Those individuals then received special compensation to extend their service after the Revolution.

Gradually, the IRGC evolved into a versatile military force entrusted with preserving the accomplishments of the Revolution through an expanding range of activities. (The regular army, by contrast, retained the primary function of safeguarding Iran's territorial integrity and political independence, as prescribed by the constitution.) Under the Ministry of the Islamic Revolutionary Guard Corps, which existed from 1982 to 1989, the IRGC became the leading institution for weapon system procurement in Iran. In the early 2000s, most weapon system purchases continue to fall under IRGC jurisdiction, rather than that of the regular military. Since the 1980s, the IRGC has played a role in military training and exercises and in nonmilitary activities such as the installation of gas pipelines in regions where no private-sector contractor is willing to work. An intelligence branch of the IRGC cooperates with the government's official security agency, the Ministry of Information and Security (MOIS; see Internal Security, this ch.). The IRGC's training in land and naval asymmetrical warfare made it a valuable asset as Iran incorporated that type of combat more fully into its military doctrine in the early 2000s.

The IRGC had an estimated 125,000 active personnel in 2007. The Qods Corps is a shadowy intelligence and military organization of the IRGC. Directly responsible to the Leader, Qods is suspected of being active in Iraq, together with IRGC and MOIS forces, since the U.S. occupation of that country in 2003, and it is suspected of having a role in several major terrorist attacks against Western targets in the 1990s. Qods agents have been reported in the Middle East, South and Central Asia, North Africa, and Europe.

The Basij

During the war with Iraq, the Basij emerged as a volunteer force organized and staffed by civilians to provide support to the IRGC and the regular military. Originally formed in late 1979 in response to Khomeini's call for a volunteer militia to confront an expected U.S. invasion, the Basij fielded an estimated 550,000 troops in the Iran–Iraq War and suffered 36,000

Troops of the Revolutionary Guard Corps in Qasr-e Shirin
Copyright Lehtikuva/PHOTRI

fatalities. The force has recruited mainly among young people, including many who drop out of high school to join. Young volunteers receive significant incentives to join the Basij. Senior political leaders often have praised the Basij for its contributions to various civilian projects such as earthquake relief work. The force is available for any situation deemed an emergency or a threat to national security. In case of war, the regular armed forces would engage the enemy first, followed by the IRGC and then the Basij. Among the Basij's domestic missions have been encouraging and enforcing the Islamization of society, nighttime patrolling of urban streets and intersections, and policing of areas where young people gather, such as universities and the sites of weekend and summer youth activities.

At the conclusion of the Iran–Iraq War, the government faced the need to reintegrate hundreds of thousands of young Basij volunteers into Iranian society. One solution was to use the Basij for reconstruction work, particularly under Iran's first postrevolutionary five-year economic development plan (see Glossary) implemented by the Rafsanjani administration. This provided Basij members, who were mostly from the lower class, with an income and a role serving the Revolution. The second solution was to assign the Basij the duty of upholding Islamic norms. In 1992 a law was enacted giving Basij members authority to arrest alleged perpetrators of felonies and deliver them to the police. This function, carried out mainly in major urban areas, integrated the Basij into Iran's law enforcement structure. However, since the law's inception the authority of the Basij has expanded to include monitoring of a wide variety of "suspicious" everyday activities of citizens. This monitoring function has included arrests of women who fail to observe the Islamic dress code and men who consume alcoholic beverages.

The IRGC, the Basij's original sponsor, no longer relies on the Basij as a military force because of its low training level. However, the IRGC has continued to encourage the Basij to participate in military groups and maneuvers. In 2007 the Basij had about 300,000 personnel, including 40,000 active personnel; they were authorized to carry small arms only. According to estimates, this force, mainly composed of youths, could expand to as many as 1 million members in the event of a national emergency.

Arms Acquisition

In the early 2000s, most of Iran's conventional military equipment was outmoded or in poor condition. The regular upgrades that occurred during the reign of the shah no longer were possible after the Revolution, and the Iran–Iraq War destroyed an estimated 50 to 60 percent of land force equipment. Beginning in the 1980s, access to foreign arms supplies has been haphazard. As a result, some types of equipment have been upgraded while others have been neglected.

Arms Imports

Historically, the role of imported matériel in supplying the regular armed forces has been broad, vital, and controversial. After World War II, the preponderance of U.S.-made weapons led to a dependence on the United States for support systems and spare parts. Because foreign technical advisers were indispensable for weapons operations and maintenance, the cessation of U.S military cooperation in 1980 was difficult for Iran. After the war with Iraq, Iran felt the need to strengthen and diversify its military hardware, but it lacked funds for a comprehensive buildup. Because of the cost of the Iran–Iraq War, U.S. economic sanctions, fluctuating oil revenues, and unwise economic policies, Iran's military procurement budget at the end of the 1980s was about half its prewar size. Iran was forced to depend heavily on low-grade weapons imports. During the 1980s, Iran was able to circumvent the U.S. embargo somewhat through third-party purchases of spare parts for U.S. military equipment, as well as additional U.S. missiles. Unverified reports alleged that Israel agreed to sell Sidewinder air-to-air missiles to Iran, as well as radar equipment, mortar and machine gun ammunition, field telephones, M–60 tank engines and artillery shells, and spare parts for C–130 transport planes.

In the 1980s and 1990s, other countries directly or indirectly supplying weapons to Iran included Syria (which transferred some Soviet-made weapons), France, Italy, Libya (which provided Scud missiles), Brazil, Algeria, Switzerland, Argentina, and the Soviet Union (later, Russia). Most purchases were arranged in international arms markets. Despite embargoes, some matériel from West European countries reached Iran. West European states often wished to keep communication channels open with Iran, even during periods of difficult political relations.

Although Iran's procurement budget increased significantly beginning in 2000 as oil prices increased and economic conditions improved, in 2003 Iran reached an all-time low in expenditures on imported combat technology (see Gross Domestic Product; The Petroleum Industry, ch. 3). Between 1996 and 1999, Iran signed new arms agreements valued at US$1.7 billion, but for the period 2000–3 the total was only US$500 million. Since the early 1990s, the main foreign supplier has been Russia, which between 1992 and 2004 signed arms contracts with Iran valued at US$7 billion despite pressure from the United States to limit such transactions. In November 2005, Iran signed a US$1 billion arms purchase agreement with the Russian government.

After 2000 Iran continued to focus its arms imports on advanced weapons and missile technology. In the early 2000s, China reportedly developed several new types of tactical guided missiles, mainly for use on missile patrol boats, specifically for sale to Iran. In 2004 Iran began negotiations with North Korea for the purchase of the Taepo–Dong 2, whose estimated range of 4,000 to 6,500 kilometers would make it Iran's first intercontinental ballistic missile. A major part of a 2005 arms agreement with Russia called for the delivery and installation of 29 TOR–M1 missile defense installations, costing

US$700 million. The TOR–M1 detects low-flying missiles that evade detection by conventional radar systems. It also operates against fixed-wing and rotary-wing aircraft and aerial drones.

Domestic Arms Production

The Iran–Iraq War and the subsequent Western arms embargo stimulated the full reorganization and expansion of Iran's defense industries. As imports remained at low levels in the early 2000s, domestic arms production played an expanding role in military procurement.

In late 1981, the revolutionary government placed all of the country's military industrial enterprises under the authority of the Defense Industries Organization (DIO), which replaced the Military Defense Organization as the oversight agency for military factories. In 1983, however, the IRGC received authority to establish its own military plants, ending the DIO's monopoly. The following year, IRGC plants began producing a variety of arms and military supplies, a function that continued in the 2000s.

Beginning in the 1990s, Iran has manufactured a variety of rockets, missiles, and multiple-rocket launchers, some based on imported technology such as the Soviet Scud–B rocket, and others fully developed by the Iranian arms industry. A mutual defense treaty concluded with India in 2003 promised technical assistance for Iran's domestic manufacture of aircraft, tanks, and artillery. The missile development and manufacturing arm of the DIO is the Aerospace Industries Organization (AIO), based at Arak, whose 13 large manufacturing plants also produce a wide variety of weapons, ordnance, and equipment for Iran's military and for export. The AIO is responsible for development of the long-range Shihab–3 missile. Domestically produced surface-to-surface missiles reportedly in the arsenal in 2005 were the Oghab, Shahin, and Nazeat, the last of which was developed with Chinese technical assistance. Since 2002 the Iran Helicopter Support and Manufacturing Industry has built small numbers of the Shabaviz 2075 transport helicopter, the Shabaviz 2061 reconnaissance helicopter, and the Shabaviz 2091 attack helicopter, all based on designs of the U.S. firm Bell Helicopter. The Iran Helicopter Support and Manufacturing Industry also has rebuilt U.S.-made Chinook transport helicopters acquired in the 1970s and 1980s. In 2001 Iran began production of the Azarakhsh fighter plane, an upgraded version of the U.S. F–5. Plans called for production of 30 such aircraft in the early 2000s. Iran is believed to have developed a substantial submarine manufacturing infrastructure, the first product of which was the Qadir minisubmarine in 2005. In 2006 two such vessels were known to exist.

Missiles

Beginning in the 1990s, Iran's leaders have cited the expansion of missile capability, based on a combination of domestic and foreign technology, as a high priority of national security. Iran's desire to acquire missile capability does not derive from a perceived threat from Iraq, but rather from Israel, a regional power that has cited Iran as a threat since 1991. In 2004 Minister of Defense and Armed Forces Logistics Ali Shamkhani explicitly stated that Israel was the potential target of the Shihab–3 missile, which Iran could mass-produce, he said, very efficiently. Shamkhani also emphasized that his task was not to devise offensive military strategies but to develop "defensive capabilities." In 2004 and 2005, statements on the purpose of the Shihab–3 by other political and military leaders were similarly ambiguous.

The domestically manufactured Shihab–3, which became fully operational in 2000, can reach Israel. In 2004 Iranian officials claimed that the range of the Shihab–3 missile had been extended to 2,000 kilometers, a substantial improvement over the previous version. The missile's capability to carry chemical, biological, or nuclear warheads extends its threat value. In the early 2000s, Iran reportedly obtained 20 North Korean liquid-fuel engines to power the Shihab–3, although that number of engines is inadequate for serial production of the rocket. The number of Shihab–3s in Iran's possession is unknown.

In recent years, with North Korean and Russian assistance Iran has started building and developing its own Scud–B and Scud–C surface-to-surface missiles, whose respective ranges of 300 and 500 kilometers enable them to reach any capital city in the Persian Gulf. In 2006 an estimated 300 such missiles were in Iran's arsenal. Reportedly, in the 1990s China sold Iran large quantities of missile guidance devices. Shihab–3 missiles test-fired in 2004 are a variation of the North Korean Nodong, whose range is about 1,300 kilometers. Reportedly, a Shihab–4 variant, whose range is estimated at about 2,500 kilometers, was at an early production stage in 2006. A Shihab–5 variant would have a range of about 3,400 kilometers.

Internal Security

During the tumultuous period between the Islamic Revolution of 1978–79 and 1989, the statements and actions of Ayatollah Khomeini were reliable indicators of political developments in Iran. In a time of political upheaval and war with Iraq, his charismatic guidance set the framework for an Islamic republic. The death of Khomeini in 1989 exposed factional politics that had been contained by the cryptic and authoritative nature of his recommendations. This crisis occurred at the same time that economic and social difficulties threatened the internal stability of the country. In this context, the role of internal security agencies increased. Nominally, the Ministry of Information and Security (MOIS) was designated the chief intelligence agency of the state. However, in the 1990s and early 2000s other, more covert agencies are believed to have performed vital intelligence functions to protect the regime.

Intelligence Services

Especially after the upheavals of the early 1950s, the shah was intensely concerned with matters of internal security (see Mossadeq and Oil Nationalization, ch. 1). He thus authorized the creation of one of the most extensive systems of law enforcement in the developing world. The forces of the Gendarmerie (the rural police) and the National Police grew in size and responsibility. In addition, the secret police organization, SAVAK (in full, Sazman-e Ettelaat va Amniyat-e Keshvar; Organization for Intelligence and National Security), gained notoriety for its excessive zeal in maintaining internal security. But, as in the case of the regular armed forces, the shah's management style virtually eliminated coordination among these agencies. A favorite approach was to shuffle army personnel back and forth between their ordinary duties and temporary positions in internal security agencies, in order to minimize the possibility of an organized coup against the throne. Cultivating an image of mystery and fear, the Iranian law enforcement agencies were perceived as powerful tools of the shah's absolute power—a perception that fostered deep resentment among Iranians.

Formed under the guidance of U.S. and Israeli intelligence officers in 1957, SAVAK developed into an effective secret agency whose goal was to sustain the government of Iran as a monarchy. At its height, SAVAK was a full-scale intelligence agency with more than 15,000 full-time personnel and thousands of part-time informants. SAVAK was attached to the Office of the Prime Minister, and its director assumed the title of deputy to the prime minister for national security affairs. Although SAVAK was officially a civilian agency, many of its officers served simultaneously in the armed forces.

After years of underground operation against opposition groups, SAVAK was a primary target for reprisals when those groups came to power in 1979. Khomeini officially dissolved the organization that year. Some 61 SAVAK officials were among 248 military personnel executed between February and September 1979.

To make intelligence gathering more publicly responsible, the new regime replaced SAVAK with the Ministry of Information and Security (MOIS). The ministry's primary role in foreign policy has been to support like-minded religious groups abroad and to suppress Iranian dissidents. Constitutionally, the MOIS has the authority to gather information and to act against perceived conspiracies against the Islamic Republic. Although open information on the MOIS is limited, the defense of the regime from internal threats is a primary function. After the election of Mohammad Khatami as president in 1997 increased the power of reformist factions, the MOIS was steadily purged of hard-liners. Against this trend, conservatives applied constant pressure to strengthen the security organization. Although the publicly acknowledged security establishment always has been the MOIS, since 1997 an undefined security force, often referred to as "officers in civilian clothes" or "unofficial civilian forces," has existed parallel to the official agency. Members of this force intervene to suppress domestic disturbances such as demonstrations and strikes and to serve generally as an instrument for preventing political dissent and civil unrest.

Law Enforcement

In the years following the Revolution, the two national police forces, called the Gendarmerie and the National Police, were under operational control of the Joint Staff of the armed forces. Joint Staff members also were empowered to integrate regular and paramilitary forces into operational planning. Beginning in 1987, the two police forces gradually lost the national defense role that they had played in the early 1980s. In

1991 the Gendarmerie and the National Police were combined to form the Law Enforcement Forces (Niruha-ye Entezami-ye Jomhuri-ye Islami), which since 1991 have fallen under the authority of the Ministry of Interior and now also are known as the Islamic Republic of Iran Police (IRIP). Smaller rural units of the IRIP correspond in function to the former Gendarmerie, whose duties were mainly outside urban areas. The officials comprising the IRIP are appointed by the Leader, and during the administrations of President Khatami the IRIP acted autonomously on some occasions. Following the deaths of demonstrating students in 1999, Sayyid Ali Khamenei (Leader, 1989–) appointed former air force commander Mohammad Qalibaf chief of the IRIP. Qalibaf remained in that position until he resigned in 2005 to be a candidate in the presidential election. Although consolidation of law enforcement and internal security agencies in the IRIP reduced bureaucratic red tape and fostered interagency cooperation, the final decision-making power of the Leader sometimes has hindered effective law enforcement because Khamenei lacks expertise in domestic security policy. Including border patrol units and marine police, the IRIP had about 40,000 personnel in 2005. In 2006 Iran announced plans to restructure and decentralize the IRIP in order to improve operational efficiency.

The Police–110 rapid-response unit, established under the IRIP in 2000, is responsible for maintaining social order and responding to emergencies in urban areas. The unit frequently has raided social gatherings deemed threatening to domestic security or in violation of Islamic law.

The Military's Relations with Society

The 1953 military coup against Mohammad Mossadeq, and the close relationship of the military with the shah, instilled in Iranians an abhorrence of military control of political policy. Consequently, the defense establishment adopted a policy of silence on political issues. This stance remained unchanged after the Revolution, with popular support. Like previous regimes, the administration of President Mahmoud Ahmadinejad, who was elected in 2005, has made a practice of excluding the military from day-to-day politics.

Despite the tradition of noninvolvement, beginning in the 1990s the IRGC, the Basij, and the regular military began efforts to redefine their respective relationships with Iranian society. The regular military has continuously presented itself as above factional politics as it provided manpower and technical assistance in civilian projects, capitalizing particularly on the remediation of damage incurred during the Iran–Iraq War. In contrast, as the proclaimed defenders of Islamic ideology, the IRGC and the Basij have felt compelled and entitled to engage in the political arena. For example, the latter organization took the position that President Khatami's reform proposals were challenges to the loyal supporters of the Islamic Republic and Khamenei.

By the early 2000s, the ideology that motivated the establishment of the IRGC had faded, decreasing the authority of the organization and the concept that the ideals of the Revolution should be protected by such an activist organization. However, beginning with the parliamentary elections of 2004, and especially since the election of former IRGC officer Ahmadinejad as president in 2005, there has been an attempt to increase the IRGC's role in internal and external policy making. Many former IRGC commanders gained seats in parliament in 2004, and under Ahmadinejad the IRGC has substantially increased its influence in the Supreme National Security Council (SNSC), the agency that coordinates defense and national security policies.

Defense Economics

Under the Islamic Republic, the armed forces budget has been prepared by the Ministry of Defense and Armed Forces Logistics in consultation with the Supreme Defense Council (SDC). The president, who also is a member of the SDC, submits the completed package to the Majlis for debate, approval, and appropriation. The ability of the Islamic Republic to commit resources to military modernization and enhancement is contingent on the success of the overall Iranian economy. The intrinsic problems of Iran's economy, however, are extremely difficult to rectify and were not ameliorated in the early 2000s by increased income from Iran's most valuable export, oil (see The Economy after the Islamic Revolution, 1979–, ch. 3). Iran's defense budget for 2006 was estimated at US$6.6 billion, up significantly from the 2004 level of US$5.6 billion.

During the reign of the last shah, high military expenditures caused severe popular discontent. Income from the oil boom of 1973–74 was disproportionately invested in military procurement at the expense of industry, agriculture, and education. Particularly in the rural areas, the civilian population disapproved of the privileged status granted to the military establishment. Despite constructive civilian activities by the armed forces (especially in education), Iranian society in general never shared the shah's commitment to a buildup that drained the treasury.

The Revolution failed to change this pattern, except for cancellation of arms procurement commitments in the first year of the new regime. At that time, the government abandoned many military projects because they involved contracts with U.S. corporations and because the Khomeini regime identified the government's first priority as satisfying the needs of the masses.

This trend was rapidly reversed, however, with the revolutionary government's first war budget in 1981. By 1987 all defense expenditures for the year, including those of the IRGC and Basij and payments to the families of war casualties, totaled as much as US$100 billion. Expenditures dropped sharply to US$6.8 billion the year after the cease-fire. However, beginning in 1989 Iran again increased procurement of arms, largely from the former Soviet Union, as well as domestic production of strategic missiles. Within the context of new external pressures in the Persian Gulf region, this policy reflects a realignment of priorities from addressing fundamental economic ills to responding to security pressures related to the Persian Gulf region. Beginning in 2003, the presence of U.S. forces both to the west in Iraq and to the east in Afghanistan has magnified the importance of military funding decisions. Because of changes in how military spending is categorized, statistics for the early 2000s are speculative. For instance, it is likely that any significant expenditures on Iran's nuclear arms program would have been concealed under energy production expenses.

Military Doctrine

The fundamental principles of Iran's military doctrine were laid out in the regulations codified for the armed forces in 1992, under the title "Iran: Complete Regulations of the Islamic Republic of Iran Armed Forces." Because Iran's armed forces and equipment were exhausted by the war with Iraq and subsequent arms resupply was severely limited by an international embargo and by Iran's poor economic position, the 1992 doctrine depended heavily on a deep supply of manpower, the strategic advantages provided by the nation's geography, and the patriotic ideology inherited from Ayatollah Khomeini. The primary goals of the doctrine were defensive: to protect the territory of Iran and the practice of Islam on that territory. Increasingly in the 1990s and early 2000s, Iran's long-term historical effort to preserve influence in its region was focused on ending what it considered the most urgent threat to that influence: the U.S. presence in the Persian Gulf region. In the early 2000s, the doctrine still relied on manpower, territory, and ideological fervor, and the fundamental goals remained the same. However, by 2000 the offensive and defensive phases of the doctrine had been refined by external events and by Iran's improved financial and technological resources.

The Legacy of the Iran–Iraq War

In the aftermath of the war with Iraq, changes in Iran's regional, political, and geo-strategic situation required adjustments of military strategy and defense doctrine for which the revolutionary government was unprepared. However, the Iran–Iraq War had the positive result of highlighting grave military shortcomings. The war proved to the government that without a system of alliances Iran needed more aggressive "defensive" weapons, or some type of WMD, that could deter a ruthless enemy such as Iraq's president Saddam Hussein. During the war, Iraq had used its missile capability to hit Tehran and other targets, while Iran could hardly respond. In the last stages of the war, Iraq also used chemical weapons to inflict severe casualties on Iranian troops and civilians.

The war experience enabled Iran to identify two military prerequisites: access to high technology to enhance military capacity and military self-reliance. During the war, the lack of replacements for U.S.-supplied aircraft, coupled with Iraq's missile attacks, further motivated a shift of emphasis from aircraft to missiles.

After the Iran–Iraq War, Iran's security policy generally shifted from revolutionary adventurism to a more conservative, less confrontational approach. However, this policy faced a new strategic environment after the U.S. military presence in the Persian Gulf began to expand in the early 1990s. The conflict with the United Arab Emirates over the Persian Gulf islands of Abu Musa and the Tunbs, the steady buildup of Iran's capacity to threaten tanker traffic, Iran's development of long-range ballistic missiles, and allegations of an active WMD program in Iran alienated the Persian Gulf states and the West. Furthermore, after the Persian Gulf War of 1991, Iran confronted a strong coalition dominated by the United States and continued exclusion from the Gulf Cooperation Council, the regional security organization that included all the other Persian Gulf states except Iraq when it was founded in 1981.

Contemporary Security Policy

The military doctrine that Iran has chosen in the postwar years includes a narrow range of options that focus mainly on deterrence. The emphasis on self-reliance has placed a higher priority on domestic arms production and on a small number of foreign military supply relationships. The quest for international military prestige through conventional and (potential) nuclear missile capability has led to regional and international isolation that contradicts the doctrinal goal of improving relations and security within the Persian Gulf region.

Until the Persian Gulf War, most threats to Iran involved regional territorial disputes or conflicts with neighboring states. The arrival of U.S. troops in the region in 1991 created a new strategic situation in which Iran felt insecure. Although U.S. troops withdrew from Iraq later that year, during the 1990s the direct and indirect influence of the United States in the region combined with Israel's maturing missile programs to exacerbate Iran's insecurity. To the west was the still-hostile Iraqi regime of Saddam Hussein, and, in the second half of the decade, to the east was the hostile, fundamentalist regime of the Taliban in Afghanistan. Although Iran moderated its public revolutionary stance during this period, the doctrine of protecting Islam came to involve supporting such Islamic organizations as the Palestinian Hamas and the Lebanese Hizballah. However, links with these groups had the result of further isolating Iran. At the end of the 1990s, the Iranian government shifted its doctrine to emphasize joint military operations with neighboring countries, with the goal of reducing U.S. influence in the region. This approach met with considerable skepticism among adjacent states, and international events soon overtook Iran's efforts in that direction.

The terrorist attack on the United States of September 11, 2001, had a strong impact on Iran's military thinking. After September 11, the United States, which Iran continued to perceive as its principal enemy, received an outpouring of international sympathy, during which it established a military presence in Afghanistan. Against a background of deep internal political divisions, Iran's sense of encirclement intensified. The U.S.

Severe damage inflicted on the port of Khorramshahr
by Iraqi forces in October 1980
Copyright Lehtikuva/PHOTRI

invasion of Iraq in 2003 exacerbated Iranian insecurities. Iran responded with increased claims about a U.S. psychological war against the revolutionary government and warnings that it would retaliate for hostile military acts.

In 2001 Iran had taken a conciliatory approach toward the war in Afghanistan led by the United States, offering limited assistance to U.S. and North Atlantic Treaty Organization (NATO) troops. On the issue of the threatened U.S. invasion of Iraq, however, Iranian policy makers believed that national security was at stake and a clear position was needed. To ensure international control of Iraq's ostensible WMD arsenal, Iran advocated a solution involving the United Nations rather than military action. It also opposed a unilateral attack by the United States because such an action might create a precedent for attacking Iran itself. The Iranian government took the position that Iraqi political boundaries should remain intact and that the people should choose their own government. Factors in this position were Iran's fears that a potential Kurdish state in northern Iraq would arouse internal instability among Iran's Kurds and that a pro-U.S. government in Iraq would encourage antiregime sentiment in Iran (see Other Indo-Iranian–Speaking Groups, ch. 2).

Realizing that a U.S. invasion of Iraq might be unavoidable, Iran adopted a stance of active neutrality. Under this policy, which temporarily strengthened Iran's role regionally and internationally, the Iranian government first used diplomatic means to attempt to circumvent the invasion, then rejected the use of force against the invasion once it materialized. Because of the unexpected difficulties experienced by the U.S. occupation, Iran continued to benefit from that complicated situation in subsequent years.

Because of ongoing concerns about a potential preemptive military strike by Israel on its nuclear facilities, Iran accelerated development of its defensive capabilities, despite uncertainties about the range, targeting, and effectiveness of missiles such as the Shihab–3. The Iranian government made unsubstantiated claims about the potential of the Shihab–3 to discourage attack and to otherwise improve Iran's regional bargaining position. Both the exaggerated claims about its ballistic missiles and the renewal of uranium enrichment had the goal of bolstering Iran's geopolitical stature by calling attention to its military potential. The advancement of the nuclear program appeared to transcend party ideology within Iran, even as other aspects of military doctrine became subject to heated debate.

In the wake of the 2003 U.S. invasion of Iraq, Iran's military doctrine included three basic objectives: to foster long-term recovery from the Iran–Iraq War by enhancing the stability of the region; to defend Iranian territory and interests against any form of external intrusion or attack; and to safeguard Islamic values and the nation's right to live in freedom (as defined by Islamic laws) "without resorting to military operation." Beginning in 2003, increasing alarm about a possible U.S. invasion led to expansion of Iran's capacity to fight an "asymmetrical war," in which an invading force would be absorbed into Iran and then subjected to guerrilla warfare, supplemented by attacks against the enemy's interests overseas. The basic elements of such irregular warfare would be surprise, speed, and security. Presumably to advance its irregular-warfare capability, Iran started to increase recruiting of new Basij personnel in 2004 and incorporated irregular operations into the training of regular military units. In any case, the ground forces' outmoded armor and artillery support, and their heavy dependence on mobilization of IRGC forces, severely limited Iran's potential to fight a conventional land war.

The naval phase of Iran's military doctrine emphasizes utilization of the geographical configuration of the Persian Gulf in asymmetrical warfare. Iran's limited naval resources are to be used for small-scale attacks on military and oil-related targets and blockades of oil shipping in the gulf. Small attack boats, minisubmarines, and mines are key elements in this strategy. The air phase of the doctrine has two main elements: ballistic missiles and air defense. The missile force is the main element of the air doctrine. Its value is to be enhanced by the intimidation effect of rhetoric hinting at weapons of mass destruction, increased range, and possible targeting of Israel or the capitals of Persian Gulf states. Air defenses have been strengthened only minimally since they were found wanting in the Iran–Iraq War. Iran has sought to maximize its limited air-defense forces by strategic location, hardening, and concealment.

Nuclear Issues

Iran's official position is that it has no program for the development of nuclear weapons and never would use such weapons. However, certain aspects of its civilian nuclear power program, especially its development of facilities for the conversion of uranium to nuclear fuel, were not disclosed to the International Atomic Energy Agency (IAEA) until 2002, long after they had been constructed and become operational. This lack of disclosure aroused suspicion in the United States and member countries of the European Union, as well as elsewhere, that Iran was using the development of nuclear reactors to generate electric power as a cover for the clandestine development of nuclear weapons. Iran denied that this was the case, however (see Relations with Europe; The United States and Iran, ch. 4). As of late 2007, no documentary evidence had confirmed that Iran's military doctrine includes a scenario for the use of nuclear weapons. However, if Iran had a nuclear weapons program, only a very limited number of political and military leaders would know of its existence.

Before the Revolution, the shah's government contracted with the German corporation Siemens to build a nuclear power plant at Bushehr on the Persian Gulf (see fig. 8). When the Revolution halted the project, 85 percent of the first reactor was complete, but it sustained serious damage in the Iran–Iraq War. When the Islamic Republic attempted to resume work in the late 1980s, Siemens declined to participate, and Iran turned to Russia to complete the plant. The agreement reached between the Iranian and Russian governments in 1995, worth an estimated US$800 million, was attractive to Russia because it established a nuclear market in the Middle East. The station was to include a 1,000-megawatt light water reactor, and Russia was to provide 2,000 tons of uranium fuel. Completion of the first reactor, originally scheduled for 1999, was delayed several times, causing friction between Iran and Russia. A 2005 addendum to the agreement provided for Russia to train several hundred Iranians to run the plant. The delay of scheduled fuel deliveries from Russia and late payments by Iran further set back the opening of Bushehr, until at least 2008. Meanwhile, Iran announced plans to build a large number of additional nuclear power plants.

International Reactions to Iran's Nuclear Program

As early as the 1990s, a lack of transparency regarding nuclear activity was a major factor in Iran's international isolation. In October 2003, Iran acknowledged that it had enriched small quantities of uranium using imported centrifuge components and had conducted plutonium separation experiments without declaring these activities to the IAEA. Iran never has agreed that it seriously violated its obligations under the Nuclear Non-Proliferation Treaty (NPT), to which it is a signatory, and it has continuously asserted that its nuclear program is permissible under the treaty because it is intended for producing energy. Despite ongoing inspections, the IAEA was not able to resolve all questions about Iran's compliance. Meanwhile, Iranian conservatives were advocating withdrawal from the NPT; former president Mohammad Khatami resisted such pressure, but conservative President Mahmoud Ahmadinejad, who succeeded Khatami in 2005, displayed a more ambivalent attitude. In 2005 and 2006, Iran threatened to withdraw if its right to nuclear technology were not recognized.

In 2005 the failure of Iranian officials and those of the United Kingdom, France, and Germany to reach a mutual agreement on the nuclear issue created an international impression of an ongoing cover-up. Soon after Ahmadinejad assumed office in August 2005, he ended Iran's unilateral commitment to cease uranium enrichment activities at the Esfahan nuclear conversion plant; a renewal of that activity was announced in February 2006. Iran justified construction of nuclear facilities by citing a need to process domestically extracted uranium for use in the 30 nuclear power plants that nominally were in the planning stage. The decision to build those plants enjoyed national support and was approved by both reformist and conservative factions within the regime.

The secret nature of the project to give Iran nuclear technology, the limitations on available technology, fear of a U.S. or Israeli military response, and the U.S. military presence in the region combined to make rapid completion of the Bushehr nuclear project a key goal. Project completion also was important because the Bushehr reactor had become a symbol of national pride. However, the project was slowed by Russia's concerns about jeopardizing its relations with the West.

Nuclear Facilities

International concerns have focused not on the Bushehr site but on several other nuclear facilities, whose existence Iran confirmed only in 2002, after it was revealed that Pakistan's leading nuclear scientist, A. Q. Khan, had provided Iran with crucial information on making nuclear weapons. Iran disclosed its previously undocumented facilities in a report to the IAEA in 2002, then agreed to open the sites for IAEA inspection in 2003 and 2004. According to the IAEA, several of these facilities were involved, or could be involved, in the nuclear fuel cycle, thus requiring IAEA monitoring to ensure that their products are not diverted for use in the manufacture of weapons-grade fuel. Concerns about such diversion were not allayed when the IAEA discovered in 2005 that Iran had partial documentation for preparation of the explosive core of an atomic bomb.

It is known that Esfahan, at the center of the Iran nuclear controversy, has reactors designated for university research and the burning of highly enriched uranium, as well as a Chinese-made uranium hexafluoride conversion facility. (Uranium hexafluoride is a key compound in uranium enrichment both for energy and weapons production.) The Esfahan reactors serve the Nuclear Technology Research Center, Iran's largest nuclear research facility. Besides the threat posed by the conversion facility, Esfahan attracted attention because its scientists may have requested military-grade plutonium from China in the 1990s and because a portion of the nuclear facility is believed to be concealed underground, beyond observation by the IAEA.

Moallem Kaleyah, the primary fissile material production center in Iran, has been under intense international scrutiny and heavily guarded by the IAEA in 2006–7. Previously, the center, strategically located in a mountainous region northwest of Tehran, had been suspected as a probable facility for the development of nuclear weapons.

In 2005 a heavy water manufacturing facility was in the last stages of construction near Arak, southwest of Tehran. The heavy water could supply a reactor manufacturing bomb-grade plutonium. Although existence of the Arak facility per se was not a violation of international rules on nonproliferation, its potential role prompted an international call for construction stoppage after the site was discovered in 2002.

*   *   *

The *Military Balance*, published annually by the International Institute for Strategic Studies, and similar publications such as the yearbook of the Stockholm International Peace Research Institute (SIPRI), remain the best sources for recent data on the size, budget, and equipment of the armed forces of Iran. Other sources provide information on aspects of complex national security issues. *Iran's Security Policy in the Post-Revolutionary Era*, by Daniel Byman, Shahram Chubin, Anoushiravan Ehteshami, and Jerrold Green, is of great value, as are Anthony Cordesman's *Iran's Military Forces in Transition* and *Iran's Evolving Military Forces*. Three recent works of particular value are *Iran: Time for a New Approach*, a task force report of the Council on Foreign Relations by Zbigniew Brzezinski, Robert Gates, and Suzanne Maloney; a journal article by Steven R. Ward, "The Continuing Evolution of Iran's Military Doctrine," which provides an extensive discussion of the motivations and conditions that shaped military doctrine in the early 2000s; and Mehdi Moslem's *Factional Politics in Post-Khomeini Iran*. Although somewhat outdated, Wilfried Buchta's *Who Rules Iran? The Structure of Power in the Islamic Republic* remains a unique work on the anatomy of political power in Iran. Kenneth M. Pollack's study of U.S.-Iranian relations, *The Persian Puzzle: The Conflict Between Iran and America*, also is of interest.

In regard to Iran's military industry and weapons technology and other security-related matters, the analysis and data provided by the Global Security Web site and its online library on Iran are most helpful for current conditions and updates. Similar information is provided by the on-line database of the Institute for Science and International Security.

In the absence of daily access to Iranian newspapers and journals, one should consider sources in Persian (Farsi), including the Islamic Republic News Agency and other Iranian journals and newspapers available on the Internet. Most, if not all, Persian sources available on the Internet are free and do not require a subscription, although in many cases archive availability is limited. (For further information and complete citations, see Bibliography.)

Appendix

Table 1. Metric Conversion Coefficients and Factors

When you know	Multiply by	To find
Millimeters	0.04	inches
Centimeters.........................	0.39	inches
Meters	3.3	feet
Kilometers...........................	0.62	miles
Hectares.............................	2.47	acres
Square kilometers....................	0.39	square miles
Cubic meters........................	35.3	cubic feet
Liters	0.26	gallons
Kilograms	2.2	pounds
Metric tons	0.98	long tons
....	1.1	short tons
....	2,204	pounds
Degrees Celsius (Centigrade)	1.8 and add 32	degrees Fahrenheit

Table 2. Population of the Eight Largest Cities, Preliminary Census Data, 2006

City	Population
Tehran............................	7,160,094
Mashhad	2,837,734
Esfahan	1,573,378
Tabriz.............................	1,523,085
Karaj..............................	1,460,961
Shiraz.............................	1,279,140
Qom...............................	1,046,961
Ahvaz	841,145

Source: Based on information from Iran, Statistical Center of Iran, *Preliminary Report on Census of Population and Housing for 1385* [2006–7] [in Persian], Tehran, December 2006.

Table 3. Population of Principal Cities, 1996 Census

City	Population
Tehran............................	6,758,845
Mashhad	1,887,405
Esfahan	1,266,072
Tabriz.............................	1,191,000
Shiraz.............................	1,053,025
Karaj..............................	940,968
Ahvaz	804,980
Qom...............................	777,677
Kermanshah	673,000
Orumiyah	435,200
Zahedan...........................	419,517

Table 3. Population of Principal Cities, 1996 Census (Continued)

City	Population
Rasht	417,000
Hamadan	401,000
Kerman	384,991
Arak	380,755
Ardabil	340,386
Yazd	326,776
Qazvin	291,117
Zanjan	286,295
Sanandaj	277,808
Bandar-e Abbas	273,578
Khorramabad	272,815
Eslamshahr	265,450
Borujerd	217,804
Abadan	206,073
Dezful	202,639
Kashan	201,372
Sari1	195,882
Gorgan	188,710
Najafabad	178,498
Sabzevar	170,738
Khomeynishahr	165,888
Amol	159,000
Neyshabur	158,847
Babol	158,300
Khoi	148,944
Malayer	144,000
Bushehr	143,641
Qaemshahr	143,286
Sirjan	135,024
Bojnurd	134,835
Maragheh	132,217
Birjand	127,604
Ilam	124,346
Saqqez	115,394
Gonbad-e Kavus	111,253
Saveh	111,245
Mahabad	107,500
Varamin	107,233
Andimeshk	106,925
Khorramshahr	105,936
Shahrud	104,765
Marv Dasht	103,579
Zabol	100,887
Shahr-e Kord	100,488

Source: Based on information from Iran, Statistical Center of Iran, *Report on Census of Population and Housing for 1375* [1996–97] [in Persian], Tehran, 1998.

Table 4. Ethnic and Linguistic Groups, 1996

Ethnic Group	Language	Population[1]	Percentage of Total Population
Persians	Persian	38,900,000	64.8
Azerbaijani Turks	Azeri Turkish	9,500,000	15.8
Kurds	Kurdish	4,100,000	6.8
Lurs[2]	Luri	3,410,000	5.7
Afghans[3]	Persian, Pushtu, and Turkic dialects	1,408,000	2.3
Baluchis	Baluchi	1,000,000	1.6
Arabs	Arabic	1,000,000	1.6
Fars Turks[4]	Turkic dialects	600,000	1.0
Turkmens	Turkic dialects	500,000	0.8
Armenians	Armenian	300,000	0.5
Assyrians	Assyrian	32,000	0.05
Other	Various	50,000	0.08
TOTAL		60,000,000[5]	100.0[5]

[1] Estimated.
[2] Lurs include Bakhtiaris and other Luri-speaking tribal groups as well as non-tribal Lurs.
[3] Afghans include refugees who entered Iran between 1979 and 1989 and their Iran-born children.
[4] Group includes, in order of size, Qashqais, Afshars, Baharlus, Inanlus, Abivardis, and others.
[5] Column does not add to total because of rounding.

Source: Derived from statistics on primary language reported as being spoken at home in Iran, Statistical Center of Iran, *Report on Census of Population and Housing for 1375* [1996–97] [in Persian], Tehran, 1998, passim.

Table 5. Non-Muslim Religious Minorities, 2005

Religious Minority	Language	Estimated Population
Armenian Christians	Armenian	300,000
Baha'is	Persian, Azeri	250,000
Assyrian Christians	Assyrian	32,000
Zoroastrians	Persian	32,000
Jews	Persian, Kurdish	30,000
Protestant Christians (Anglicans, Evangelicals, Presbyterians)	Persian, Azeri	10,000

Source: Adapted from tables and data in Iran, Statistical Center of Iran, *Iran Statistical Yearbook 1383* [2004–5], Tehran, 2006.

Table 6. Employment by Economic Sector, Selected Years, 1956–2004 (percentage of total workforce)

Sector/Year	1956	1976	1986	1996	2004
Agriculture	56.3	34.0	29.0	22.8	21.7
Total Industry	20.1	34.2	25.3	30.7	30.6
Manufacturing	13.8	19.0	13.2	17.5	16.5
Construction	5.7	13.5	11.0	11.3	12.3
Services	23.6	31.8	45.7	46.5	47.7
Total Employment, in thousands	5,908	8,799	11,002	14,572	22,400

Source: Based on information from Iran, Statistical Center of Iran, *Iran Statistical Yearbook*, Tehran, various years and sections.

Table 7. Gross Domestic Product by Sector, Selected Years, 1960–2006 (in percentages)

Category/Year	1960	1978	1990	2004	2006
Hydrocarbons*..............	38.3	35.6	16.4	11.8	18.7
Agriculture	23.5	8.6	19.5	14.1	11.2
Industry and Mining	7.8	15.5	17.0	24.0	23.0
Services	30.4	40.3	47.1	50.1	47.1

*Includes oil and gas extraction, refining, and distribution.

Sources: Based on information from Iran, Central Bank of Iran, Tehran, various publications, http://www.cbi.ir.

Table 8. Destinations of Crude Oil Exports Before and After the Revolution (in percentages)

Destination/Period	1971–76	1998–2003
Western Europe	42	30
Japan.......................................	33	22
Asia and Far East except Japan	5	34
United States	12	0
Africa......................................	6	4
Other countries	2	10

Sources: Based on information from Ebrahim Razzaghi, *The Iranian Economy*, Tehran, 1988, and Iran, Central Bank of Iran, *Summary of Economic Activities*, various years, http://www.cbi.ir.

Table 9. Production of Major Crops, 2001–4 (in thousands of tons)

Crop/Year	2001	2002	2003	2004
Wheat	9,459	12,450	12,900	11,031
Sugar beets	4,649	6,098	5,300	5,140
Barley	2,423	3,085	3,100	3,186
Rice	1,990	2,888	3,300	3,552
Sugarcane	3,195	3,712	3,650	5,415
Seed cotton..............	412	345	330	114
Pistachios	112	249	310	51

Source: Based on information from Economist Intelligence Unit, *Iran Country Profile 2006*, London, 60.

Table 10. Main Commercial Partners, 2002–5

	Export Partners, Percentage of Total			
Country/Year	2002	2003	2004	2005
Japan	19.5	21.3	18.4	16.9
China	9.7	9.5	9.7	11.2
Italy	7.3	6.1	6.0	6.2
South Africa	4.2	3.9	5.8	5.5
	Import Partners, Percentage of Total			
Country/Year	2002	2003	2004	2005
Germany	16.9	10.8	12.8	13.9
China	4.7	8.3	7.2	8.3
Italy	6.2	8.0	7.7	7.1
United Arab Emirates	9.6	7.8	7.2	6.7

Sources: Based on information from *Europa World Year Book 2005*, London, 2220, and Economist Intelligence Unit, *Iran Country Profile 2006*, London, 2006.

Table 11. Composition of Nonoil Exports, Selected Years, 1963–2003 (in millions of U.S. dollars)

Category/Year	1963	1977	1989	2003
Agriculture	373	264	522	1,414
Carpets	108	114	345	573
Industrial Goods	106	153	122	3,268
TOTAL	634	540	1,044	6,755

Source: Based on information from Iran, Central Bank of Iran, *Summary of Economic Activities*, various years, http://www.cbi.ir.

Table 12. Armed Forces Personnel by Service, Selected Years, 1979–2007

Service	1979*	1984	1986	1999	2001	2003	2007
Active Armed Forces	415,000	555,000	704,000	545,000	513,000	520,000	545,000
Army	285,000	250,000	305,000	350,000	325,000	325,000	350,000
Navy	30,000	20,600	14,500	20,600	18,000	18,000	18,000
Air Force	100,000	35,000	35,500	50,000	45,000	52,000	52,000
IRGC	n.a.	250,000	350,000	125,000	125,000	125,000	125,000
Total Basij	n.a.	2,500,000	3,000,000	200,000	200,000	300,000	300,000
Active Basij	n.a.	n.a.	n.a.	40,000	40,000	40,000	40,000

*Prerevolutionary figures.
n.a.—not available.

Source: Based on information from International Institute for Strategic Studies, *The Military Balance*, London, various years.

Table 13. Selected Weapons of the Armed Forces, 2005

Service	Weapon	Number
Army	T–54 and T–55 Main Battle Tank	540
	T–72 Main Battle Tank	480
	Chieftan Mk–3 and Mk–5 Main Battle Tanks	100
	M–47 and M–48 Main Battle Tanks	168
	Zulqifar Main Battle Tank	100
	Scorpion and Towsan Light Tanks	80
	BMP–1 Armored Infantry Fighting Vehicle	210
	BMP–2 Armored Infantry Fighting Vehicle	400
	BTR–50 and –60 Armored Personnel Carriers	300
	M–113 Armored Personnel Carrier	200
	Boragh Armored Personnel Carrier	140
	M–101A1 Towed 105-mm Gun	130
	D–30 Towed 122-mm Gun	540
	Type 54 Towed 122-mm Gun (Chinese)	100
	M–46 and Type 59 Towed 130-mm Gun	985
	D–20 Towed 152-mm Gun	30
	M–114 Towed 155-mm Gun	70
	GHN–45 Towed 155-mm Gun	120
	2S1 Self-Propelled 122-mm Gun	60
	M–109 Self-Propelled 155-mm Gun	180
Navy	Kilo Submarine	3
	Alvand (Vosper) Frigate	3
	Bayandor (PF-103) Corvette	2
	Kaman (Combattante) Missile Craft	10
	Hejaz Mine Layer	2
Air Force	F–4D and F–4E Fighter Aircraft	65
	F–5E and F–5F Fighter Aircraft	60
	Su–24 MK Fighter Aircraft	30
	Su–25K Fighter Aircraft	7
	Mirage F–1E Fighter Aircraft	24
	F–14 Fighter Aircraft	25
	F–7M Fighter Aircraft	24
	MiG–29A and MiG–29UB Fighter Aircraft	25

Source: Based on information from International Institute for Strategic Studies, *The Military Balance 2004–2005*, London, 2005, 124–25.

Bibliography

Chapter 1

Abrahamian, Ervand. *Iran Between Two Revolutions.* Princeton: Princeton University Press, 1982.

Abrahamian, Ervand. *Khomeinism: Essays on the Islamic Republic.* Berkeley: University of California Press, 1993.

Abrahamian, Ervand. *Tortured Confessions: Prisons and Public Recantations in Modern Iran.* Berkeley: University of California Press, 1999.

Afary, Janet. *The Iranian Constitutional Revolution of 1906–1911: Grassroots Democracy, Social Democracy and the Origins of Feminism.* New York: Columbia University Press, 1996.

Akhavi, Shahrough. *Religion and Politics in Contemporary Iran: Clergy-State Relations in the Pahlavi Period.* Albany: State University of New York Press, 1980.

Alam, Asadollah. *The Shah and I: The Confidential Diary of Iran's Royal Court, 1969–1977.* Ed., Alinaghi Alikhani. New York: St. Martin's Press, 1992.

Algar, Hamid. *Islam and Revolution: Writings and Declarations of Imam Khomeini.* Berkeley: Mizan Press, 1981.

Algar, Hamid. *Religion and State in Iran, 1785–1906.* Berkeley: University of California Press, 1969.

Amanat, Abbas. *Pivot of the Universe: Nasir Al-Din Shah Qajar and the Iranian Monarchy, 1831–1896.* Berkeley: University of California Press, 1997.

Amuzegar, Jahangir. *The Dynamics of the Iranian Revolution: The Pahlavis' Triumph and Tragedy.* Albany: State University of New York Press, 1991.

Amuzegar, Jahangir. *Iran's Economy under the Islamic Republic.* London: Tauris, 1993.

Arjomand, Said Amir. *The Shadow of God and the Hidden Imam.* Chicago: University of Chicago Press, 1984.

Arjomand, Said Amir. *The Turban for the Crown: The Islamic Revolution in Iran.* New York: Oxford University Press, 1988.

Arjomand, Said Amir, ed. *From Nationalism to Revolutionary Islam.* Albany: State University of New York Press, 1984.

Avery, Peter. *Modern Iran.* London: Benn, 1965.

Bacharach, Jere L. *A Middle East Studies Handbook.* Seattle: University of Washington Press, 1984.

Bakhash, Shaul. *Monarchy, Bureaucracy and Reform under the Qajars.* London: Ithaca Press, 1978.

Bakhash, Shaul. *The Reign of the Ayatollahs: Iran and the Islamic Revolution.* Rev. ed. New York: Basic Books, 1990.

Bakhtiari, Bahman. *Parliamentary Politics in Revolutionary Iran: The Institutionalization of Factional Politics.* Gainesville: University Press of Florida, 1996.

Banani, Amin. *The Modernization of Iran, 1921–1941.* Stanford: Stanford University Press, 1961.

Bartol'd, Vasilii Vladimorovich. *Turkestan down to the Mongol Invasion.* London: Luzac, 1968.

Bashiriyeh, Hossein. *The State and Revolution in Iran, 1962–1982.* New York: St. Martin's Press, 1984.

Bayat, Mangol. *Iran's First Revolution: Shi'ism and the Constitutional Revolution of 1905–1909.* London: Oxford University Press, 1991.

de Bellaigue, Christopher. *In the Rose Garden of Martyrs: A Memoir of Iran.* New York: HarperCollins, 2005.

Bharier, Julian. *Economic Development in Iran, 1900–1970.* New York: Oxford University Press, 1971.

Bill, James A. *The Eagle and the Lion: The Tragedy of American-Iranian Relations.* New Haven: Yale University Press, 1988.

Bill, James A. *Iran: The Politics of Groups: Classes and Modernization.* Columbus, Ohio: Meril, 1972.

Bill, James A., and William Roger Louis, eds. *Musaddiq, Iranian Nationalism, and Oil.* Austin: University of Texas Press, 1988.

Boroujerdi, Mehrzad. *Iranian Intellectuals and the West: The Tormented Triumph of Nativism.* Syracuse: Syracuse University Press, 1996.

Bosworth, E. C. *The Ghaznavids: Their Empire in Afghanistan and Eastern Iran, 994–1040.* Edinburgh: Edinburgh University Press, 1963.

Browne, E. G. *A Literary History of Persia.* 4 vols. Cambridge: Cambridge University Press, 1925–28.

Browne, E. G. *The Persian Constitutional Revolution of 1905–1909.* London: Cambridge University Press, 1910. Reprint. Washington, DC: Mage Publishers, 1995.

Brumberg, Daniel. *Reinventing Khomeini: The Struggle for Reform in Iran.* Chicago: University of Chicago Press, 2001.

Buchta, Wilfried. *Who Rules Iran? The Structure of Power in the Islamic Republic.* Washington, DC: The Washington Institute for Near East Policy and the Konrad Adenauer Stiftung, 2000.

The Cambridge History of Iran. 7 vols. Cambridge: Cambridge University Press, 1968–91.

Chubin, Shahram, and Charles Tripp. *Iran and Iraq at War.* London: Tauris, 1988.

Chubin, Shahram, and Sepehr Zabih. *The Foreign Relations of Iran.* Berkeley: University of California Press, 1974.

Cottam, Richard. *Iran and the United States. A Cold War Case Study.* Pittsburgh: University of Pittsburgh Press, 1988.

Cottam, Richard. *Nationalism in Iran.* Pittsburgh: University of Pittsburgh Press, 1964.

Cronin, Stephanie. *The Army and the Creation of the Pahlavi State in Iran, 1910–1926.* London: Tauris, 1997.

Curzon, George. *Persia and the Persian Question.* 2 vols. London: Frank Cass, 1966.

Dabashi, Hamid. *Theology of Discontent: The Ideological Foundation of the Islamic Revolution in Iran.* New York: New York University Press, 1993.

Ehteshami, Anoushirvan. *After Khomeini: The Iranian Second Republic.* New York: Routledge, 1995.

Elwell-Sutton, L. P. *Modern Iran.* New York: Gordon Press, 1976.

Elwell-Sutton, L. P. *Persian Oil: A Study in Power Politics.* London: Lawrence and Wishart, 1955.

Frye, Richard. *The Golden Age of Persia.* London: Weidenfeld and Nicolson, 1975.

Frye, Richard. *The Heritage of Persia.* London: Weidenfeld and Nicolson, 1962.

Garthwaite, Gene. *The Persians.* Malden, Massachusetts: Blackwell Publishing, 2005.

Gasiorowski, Mark J., and Malcolm Byrne, eds. *Mohammad Mossadegh and the 1953 Coup in Iran.* Syracuse: Syracuse University Press, 2004.

Gasiorowski, Mark J., and Malcolm Byrne, eds. *U.S. Foreign Policy and the Shah: Building a Client State in Iran.* Ithaca: Cornell University Press, 1991.

Ghani, Cyrus. *Iran and the Rise of Reza Shah: From Qajar Collapse to Pahlavi Power.* London: Tauris, 1998.

Gheissari, Ali. *Iranian Intellectuals in the 20th Century.* Austin: University of Texas Press, 1998.

Ghirshman, Roman. *Iran: From the Earliest Times to the Islamic Conquest.* London: Pelican, 1954.

Graham, Robert. *Iran: The Illusion of Power.* London: Croom Helm, 1978.

Halliday, Fred. *Iran: Dictatorship and Development.* Harmondsworth, New York: Penguin Books, 1979.

Hammond World Atlas. Maplewood, New Jersey: Hammond, 1971.

Hiro, Dilip. *Iran under the Ayatollahs.* London: Routledge and Kegan Paul, 1985.

Hiro, Dilip. *The Longest War: The Iran–Iraq Military Conflict.* London: Grafton, 1989.

Historical Atlas of the Muslim Peoples. Amsterdam: Djambatan, 1957.

Hodgson, Marshall G. S. *The Venture of Islam.* 3 vols. Chicago: University of Chicago Press, 1974.

Hooglund, Eric. *Land and Revolution in Iran, 1960–1980.* Austin: University of Texas Press, 1982.

Hunter, Shireen T. *Iran and the World: Continuity in a Revolutionary Decade.* Bloomington: Indiana University Press, 1990.

Issawi, Charles. *The Economic History of Iran, 1800–1914.* Chicago: University of Chicago Press, 1971.

Keddie, Nikki R. *An Islamic Response to Imperialism: Political and Religious Writings of Sayyid Jama'l ad-Di'n "al-Afgha'ni."* Berkeley: University of California Press, 1983.

Keddie, Nikki R. *Modern Iran: The Roots and Results of Revolution.* New Haven: Yale University Press, 2003.

Keddie, Nikki R. *Religion and Rebellion in Iran: The Tobacco Protest of 1891–1892.* London: Frank Cass, 1966.

Kinzer, David. *All the Shah's Men: An American Coup and the Roots of Middle East Terror.* Hoboken, New Jersey: John Wiley and Sons, 2003.

Kurzman, Charles, *The Unthinkable Revolution in Iran.* Cambridge, Massachusetts: Harvard University Press, 2004.

Ladjevardi, Habib. *Labor Unions and Autocracy in Iran.* Syracuse: Syracuse University Press, 1985.

Lambton, Ann K. S. *Landlord and Peasant in Persia: A Study of Land Tenure and Land Revenue Administration.* London: Oxford University Press, 1969.

Lambton, Ann K. S. *The Persian Land Reform, 1962–1966.* Oxford: Clarendon Press, 1969.

Lambton, Ann K. S. *Qajar Persia.* London: Tauris, 1987.

Lapidus, Ira. *A History of Islamic Societies.* 2d ed. Cambridge: Cambridge University Press, 2002.

Lenczowski, George, ed. *Iran under the Pahlavis.* Stanford: Hoover Institution Press, 1978.

Lockhart, Laurence. *The Fall of the Safavid Dynasty and the Afghan Occupation of Persia.* Cambridge: Cambridge University Press, 1958.

Lockhart, Laurence. *Nadir Shah: A Critical Study Based Mainly on Contemporary Sources.* London: Luzac, 1938.

Martin, Vanessa. *Islam and Modernism: The Iranian Revolution of 1906.* London: Tauris, 1989.

Moin, Baqer. *Khomeini: Life of the Ayatollah.* New York: St. Martin's Press, 2000.

Morgan, David. *Medieval Persia 1040–1797.* London: Longman, 1988.

Moslem, Mehdi. *Factional Politics in Post-Khomeini Iran.* Syracuse: Syracuse University Press, 2002.

Mostowfi, Abdollah. *The Administrative and Social History of the Qajar Period.* 3 vols. Costa Mesa, California: Mazda, 1997.

Mottahedeh, Roy P. *Loyalty and Leadership in an Early Islamic Society.* Princeton: Princeton University Press, 1980.

Mottahedeh, Roy P. *The Mantle of the Prophet.* New York: Simon and Schuster, 1985.

Mowlavi, Afshin. *Persian Pilgrimages: Journeys Across Iran.* New York: Norton, 2002.

Olmstead, A. T. *History of the Persian Empire.* Chicago: University of Chicago Press, 1948.

Parsa, Misagh. *Social Origins of the Iranian Revolution.* New Brunswick, New Jersey: Rutgers University Press, 1989.

Perry, John R. *Karim Khan Zand: A History of Iran, 1747–1779.* Chicago: University of Chicago Press, 1979.

Potter, Lawrence G., and Gary G. Sick, eds. *Iran, Iraq, and the Legacies of War.* New York: Palgrave Macmillan, 2004.

Ramazani, Ruhollah K. *The Foreign Policy of Iran, 1500–1941: A Developing Nation in World Affairs.* Charlottesville: University Press of Virginia, 1966.

Ramazani, Ruhollah K. *Iran's Foreign Policy, 1941–1973: A Study of Foreign Policy in Modernizing Nations.* Charlottesville: University Press of Virginia, 1975.

Ramazani, Ruhollah K. *Revolutionary Iran: Challenge and Response in the Middle East.* Baltimore: Johns Hopkins University Press, 1986.

Rubin, Barry. *Paved with Good Intentions: The American Experience and Iran.* Oxford: Oxford University Press, 1982.

Savory, Roger. *Iran under the Safavids.* Cambridge: Cambridge University Press, 1980.

Schirazi, Asghar. *The Constitution of Iran: Politics and State in the Islamic Republic.* London: Tauris, 1997.

Sciolino, Elaine. *Persian Mirrors: The Elusive Face of Iran.* New York: Free Press, 2000.

Sick, Gary. *All Fall Down: America's Tragic Encounter with Iran.* New York: Random House, 1985.

Simpson, John. *Inside Iran: Life under Khomeini's Regime.* New York: St. Martin's Press, 1988.

Soroush, Abdolkarim. *Reason, Freedom and Democracy in Islam: Essential Writings of Abdolkarim Soroush.* Oxford: Oxford University Press, 2000.

Spuler, Bertold. *Die Mongolen in Iran: Politik, Verwaltung und Kultur der Ilchanzeit 1220–1350.* Leiden, Netherlands: Brill, 1985.

Upton, Joseph M. *A History of Modern Iran: An Interpretation.* Cambridge: Harvard University Press, 1960.

Vreeland, Herbert H., ed. *Iran.* New Haven, Connecticut: Human Relations Area Files, 1957.

Wilber, Donald. *Riza Shah Pahlavi, 1878–1944.* Hicksville, New York: Exposition Press, 1975.

Wright, Robin. *The Last Great Revolution.* New York: Random House, 2000.

Zonis, Marvin. *The Political Elite of Iran.* Princeton: Princeton University Press, 1971.

Chapter 2

Abrahamian, Ervand. *Khomeinism: Essays on the Islamic Republic.* Berkeley: University of California Press, 1993.

Abrahamian, Ervand. *Tortured Confessions: Prisons and Public Recantations in Modern Iran.* Berkeley: University of California Press, 1999.

Adelkhah, Fariba. *Being Modern in Iran.* New York: Columbia University Press, 2000.

Afary, Janet. "Portraits of Two Islamist Women: Escape from Freedom or Escape from Tradition?" *Critique: Critical Middle Eastern Studies,* no. 19 (Fall 2001): 47–78.

Afshar, Haleh. *Islam and Feminisms: An Iranian Case Study.* New York: St. Martin's Press, 1998.

Aghajanian, Akbar. "Family Planning and Contraceptive Use in Iran, 1967–1992." *International Family Planning Perspectives* 20, no. 2 (June 1994): 66–69.

Aghajanian, Akbar. "Some Notes on Divorce in Iran." *Journal of Marriage and the Family* 48 (1986): 749–55.

Ahmadi, Hamid. "Unity Within Diversity: Foundations and Dynamics of National Identity in Iran." *Critique: Critical Middle Eastern Studies* 14, no. 1 (Spring 2005): 127–47.

Amanolahi, Sekandar. "The Lurs of Iran." *Cultural Survival* 9, no. 1 (1985): 65–69.

Amurian, A., and M. Kasheff. "Armenians of Modern Iran." Pages 478–83 in Ehsan Yarshater, ed., *Encyclopedia Iranica.* Vol. 2. New York: Columbia University Press, 1990.

Ansari, Sarah, and Vanessa Martin. *Women, Religion and Culture in Iran.* Richmond, United Kingdom: Curzon, 2002.

Ashraf, Ahmad, and Ali Banuazizi. "Iran's Tortuous Path Toward 'Islamic Liberalism.'" *International Journal of Politics, Culture, and Society* 15, no. 2 (Winter 2001): 237–56.

Azkia, Mostafa. "Modernization Theory in a Tribal-Peasant Society of Southern Iran." *Critique: Critical Middle Eastern Studies,* no. 10 (Spring 1997): 77–90.

Azkia, Mostafa. "Rural Society and Revolution in Iran." Pages 96–119 in Eric Hooglund, ed., *Twenty Years of Islamic Revolution: Political and Social Transition in Iran since 1979.* Syracuse: Syracuse University Press, 2002.

Azkia, Mostafa, and Eric Hooglund. "Research Note on Pastoral Nomadism in Post-revolution Iran." *Critique: Critical Middle Eastern Studies* 11, no. 1 (Spring 2002): 109–14.

Bahramitash, Roksana. "Market Fundamentalism versus Religious Fundamentalism: Women's Employment in Iran." *Critique: Critical Middle Eastern Studies* 13, no. 1 (Spring 2004): 33–46.

Bahramitash, Roksana, and Shahla Kazemipour "Myths and Realities of the Impact of Islam on Women: Changing Marital Status in Iran." *Critique: Critical Middle Eastern Studies* 15, no. 2 (Summer 2006): 111–28.

Bausani, Alessandro. *Religion in Iran.* New York: Bibliotheca Persica Press, 2000.

Bayat, Asef. *Street Politics: Poor People's Movements in Iran.* New York: Columbia University Press, 1997.

Beck, Lois. *Nomad: A Year in the Life of a Qashqa'i Tribesman in Iran.* Berkeley: University of California Press, 1991.

Beck, Lois. *The Qashqa'i of Iran.* New Haven: Yale University Press, 1986.

Beeman, William O. *Language, Status, and Power in Iran.* Bloomington: Indiana University Press, 1986.

Chehabi, H. E. "The Westernization of Iranian Culinary Cuisine." *Iranian Studies* 36, no. 1 (March 2003): 43–61.

Ehsani, Kaveh. "'Tilt but Don't Spill': Iran's Development and Reconstruction Dilemma." *Middle East Report*, no. 191 (November–December 1994): 16–21.

Fisher, W. B. "Physical Geography." Pages 3–110 in W. B. Fisher, ed., *The Cambridge History of Iran: Volume I, The Land of Iran.* Cambridge: Cambridge University Press, 1968.

Haeri, Shahla. *Law of Desire: Temporary Marriage in Shi'i Iran.* Syracuse: Syracuse University Press, 1989.

Hassanpour, Amir. "The Kurdish Experience." *Middle East Report*, no. 189 (August 1994): 2–7.

Hassanpour, Amir. *Nationalism and Language in Kurdistan, 1918–1985.* San Francisco: Mellen Research University Press, 1992.

Higgins, Patricia J., and Pirouz Shoar-Ghaffari. "Women's Education in the Islamic Republic of Iran." Pages 19–43 in Mahnaz Afkhami and Erika Friedl, eds., *In the Eye of the Storm:*

Women in Post-revolutionary Iran. Syracuse: Syracuse University Press, 1994.

Hoodfar, Homa. "Devices and Desires: Population Policy and Gender Roles in the Islamic Republic." *Middle East Report,* no. 190 (September–October 1994): 11–17.

Hoodfar, Homa. "The Veil in Their Minds and on Our Heads: The Persistence of Colonial Images of Muslim Women." *Resources for Feminist Research* 22, nos. 3–4 (1995): 5–18.

Hoodfar, Homa. *Volunteer Health Workers in Iran as Social Activists: Can "Governmental Non-governmental Organizations" Be Agents of Democratization?* The Women's Movement Series Occasional Paper, No. 10. Grabels Cedex, France: Women Living under Muslim Laws, December 1998.

Hoodfar, Homa. *The Women's Movement in Iran: Women at the Crossroad of Secularization and Islamization.* The Women's Movement Series Occasional Paper, No. 1. Grabels Cedex, France: Women Living under Muslim Laws, 1999.

Hooglund, Eric. "Iran." *Encarta Reference Library 2004.* Redmond, Washington: Microsoft Corporation, 2003.

Hooglund, Eric. "Khatami's Iran." *Current History* 98, no. 625 (February 1999): 59–64.

Hooglund, Eric. *Land and Revolution in Iran, 1960–1980.* Austin: University of Texas Press, 1982.

Hooglund, Eric. "Letter from an Iranian Village." *Journal of Palestine Studies* 27, no.1 (August 1997): 76–84.

Hooglund, Eric, ed. "Sociological Research in Iran." *Critique: Critical Middle Eastern Studies* 14, no.1 (Spring 2005).

Hooglund, Eric, ed. *Twenty Years of Islamic Revolution: Political and Social Transition in Iran since 1979.* Syracuse: Syracuse University Press, 2002.

Iran. Statistical Center of Iran. *Iran Statistical Yearbook* [in Persian with English summary reports]. Tehran, 1992–2006.

Iran. Statistical Center of Iran. *Preliminary Report on Census of Population and Housing for 1385* [2006–7] [in Persian]. Tehran, December 2006.

Iran. Statistical Center of Iran. *Report on Census of Population and Housing for 1375* [1996–97] [in Persian]. Tehran, 1998.

Jazayery, Mohammad Ali. "Persian." Pages 1819–20 in Philip Mattar, et al., eds., *Encyclopedia of the Modern Middle East and*

North Africa. Vol. 3. Farmington Hills, Michigan: Thomson Gale, 2004.

Kalinock, Sabine. "Between Party and Devotion: *Mowludi* of Tehran Women." *Critique: Critical Middle Eastern Studies* 12, no. 2 (Fall 2003): 173–88.

Kamalkhani, Zahra. *Women's Islam: Religious Practice among Women in Today's Iran.* London: Keegan Paul, 1998.

Kar, Mehranguiz. "Women and Personal Status Law in Iran: An Interview." *Middle East Report,* no. 198 (January–March 1996): 36–38.

Kestenberg-Amighi, Janet. *The Zoroastrians of Iran: Conversion, Assimilation or Persistence.* New York: AMS Press, 1990.

Kheirabadi, Masoud. *Iranian Cities: Formation and Development.* Syracuse: Syracuse University Press, 2000.

Khosrokhavar, Farhad. "Toward an Anthropology of Democratization in Iran." *Critique: Critical Middle Eastern Studies,* no. 16 (Spring 2000): 2–29.

Kian-Thiébaut, Azadeh. "Gendered Occupation and Women's Status in Post-Revolutionary Iran." *Middle Eastern Studies* 31 (1995): 407–21.

Kian-Thiébaut, Azadeh. *Secularization of Iran: A Doomed Failure? The New Middle Class and the Making of Modern Iran.* Paris: Institut d'études iraniennes, 1998.

Kian-Thiébaut, Azadeh. "Women and Politics in Post-Islamist Iran: The Gender Conscious Drive to Change." *British Journal of Middle Eastern Studies* (London) 24, no. 1 (1997): 75–96.

Kousha, Mahnaz. *Voices from Iran: The Changing Lives of Iranian Women.* Syracuse: Syracuse University Press, 2002.

Macuch, Rudolf. "Assyrians in Iran." Pages 817–22 in Ehsan Yarshater, ed., *Encyclopedia Iranica.* Vol. 2. New York: Columbia University Press, 1990.

Mahmoudian, Hossein. "Socio-demographic Factors Affecting Women's Labor Force Participation in Iran, 1976–96." *Critique: Critical Middle Eastern Studies* 15, no. 3 (Fall 2006): 233–48.

Mehran, Golnar. "Lifelong Learning: New Opportunities for Women in a Muslim Country (Iran)." *Comparative Education* 32, no. 2 (1999): 201–15.

Milani, Farzaneh. *Veils and Words: The Emerging Voices of Iranian Women Writers.* Syracuse: Syracuse University Press, 1992.

Mir-Hosseini, Ziba. "Fatemeh Haqiqatjoo and the Sixth Majlis: A Woman in Her own Right." *Middle East Report*, no. 233 (Winter 2004): 34–39.

Mir-Hosseini, Ziba. *Islam and Gender: The Religious Debate in Contemporary Iran.* Princeton: Princeton University Press, 1999.

Mir-Hosseini, Ziba. *Marriage on Trial: A Study of Islamic Family Law: Iran and Morocco Compared.* London: Tauris, 1993.

Mir-Hosseini, Ziba. "The Rise and Fall of Fa'ezeh Hashemi: Women in Iranian Elections." *Middle East Report*, no. 219 (Summer 2001).

Momen, Moojan. *An Introduction to Shi'i Islam: The History and Doctrines of Twelver Shi'ism.* New Haven: Yale University Press, 1985.

Moslem, Mehdi. *Factional Politics in Post-Khomeini Iran.* Syracuse: Syracuse University Press, 2002.

Najmabadi, Afsaneh. "Feminism in an Islamic Republic: Years of Hardship, Years of Growth." Pages 50–84 in Yvonne Yazbeck Haddad and John Esposito, eds., *Islam, Gender, and Political Change.* Oxford: Oxford University Press, 1998.

Paydar, Parvin. *Women and the Political Process in Twentieth Century Iran.* Cambridge: Cambridge University Press, 1995.

Poya, Maryam. *Women, Work, and Islamism: Ideology and Resistance in Iran.* London: Zed Books, 1999.

Ramezani, Nesta. "Women in Iran: The Revolutionary Ebb and Flow." *Middle East Journal* 47, no. 3 (1993): 409–28.

Rejal, Darius. "Studying a Practice: An Inquiry into Lapidation." *Critique: Critical Middle Eastern Studies*, no. 18 (Spring 2001): 67–100.

Salzman, Philip Carl. *Black Tents of Baluchistan.* Washington, DC: Smithsonian Institution Press, 2000.

Shaditalab, Jaleh. "Iranian Women: Rising Expectations." *Critique: Critical Middle Eastern Studies* 14, no. 1 (Spring 2005): 35–55.

Shakoori, Ali. *The State and Rural Development in Post-Revolutionary Iran.* Houndmills, United Kingdom: Palgrave, 2001.

Shirazi, Faegheh. "A Dramaturgical Approach to *Hijab* in Post-revolutionary Iran." *Critique: Critical Middle Eastern Studies*, no. 7 (Fall 1995): 35–52.

Shirazi, Faegheh. *The Veil Unveiled: The Hijab in Modern Culture.* Gainesville: University Press of Florida, 2001.

Spooner, Brian. "Baluchestan." Pages 598–632 in Ehsan Yarshater, ed., *Encyclopedia Iranica*. Vol. 3, fascicle 6, 1988.

Tapper, Richard. "History and Identity among the Shahsevan." *Iranian Studies* 21, nos. 3, 4 (1988): 84–108.

Tapper, Richard, ed. *The Conflict of Tribe and State in Iran and Afghanistan*. London: Croom Helm, 1983.

Tohidi, Nayereh. "The Global-local Intersection of Feminism in Muslim Societies: The Case of Iran and Azerbaijan." *Social Research*, Fall 2002.

Tohidi, Nayereh. "Modernity, Islamization, and Women in Iran." Pages 110–47 in Valentine Moghadam, ed., *Gender and National Identity: Women and Politics in Muslim Societies*. London: Zed Press, 1994.

Torab, Azam. "Piety as Gendered Agency: A Study of *Jalaseh* Ritual Discourse in an Urban Neighborhood of Iran." *Journal of the Royal Anthropological Institute* (London) 2, no. 2 (1996): 235–52.

U.S. Census Bureau. International Data Base. "IDB Population Pyramids." http://www.census. gov/ipc/www/idbpyr-html.

Vaziri, Mostafa. *Iran as an Imagined Nation: The Construction of National Identity*. New York: Paragon House, 1993.

Vosooghi, Mansour. "Treatment of Addicts in a Tehran Drug Rehabilitation Center." *Critique: Critical Middle Eastern Studies* 14, no. 1 (Spring 2005).

Yavari, Neguin. "Baluchistan." Pages 385–86 in Philip Mattar et al, eds., *Encyclopedia of the Modern Middle East and North Africa*. Vol. 1. Farmington Hills, Michigan: Thomson Gale, 2004.

Zekavat, Seid M. "The State of the Environment in Iran." *Journal of Developing Societies* 13, no. 1 (1997): 49–72.

(Various issues of the following periodicals also were used in the preparation of this chapter: *Iran Daily* (Tehran), *Iran Times* (Washington, DC), and *Tehran Times*. In addition, the following Web sites were used: Embassy of Pakistan (Washington, DC), Interests Section of the Islamic Republic of Iran, http://www.daftar.org/eng; "Iranworld: Your Portal to the Iranian Legal System," http://www.IRANworld.com; Permanent Mission of the Islamic Republic of Iran to the United Nations, http://www.un.int/iran; Statistical Center of Iran, http://www.sci.org.ir; and United Nations Development Programme,

"You and AIDS: The HIV/AIDS Portal for Asia Pacific," http://www.youandaids.org/.)

Chapter 3

Abrahamian, Ervand. *Iran Between Two Revolutions*. Princeton: Princeton University Press, 1982.

Akhavi-Pour, Hossein. "Barriers to Private Entrepreneurship in Iran." *Critique: Critical Middle Eastern Studies*, no. 1 (Fall 1992): 82–93.

Akhavi-Pour, Hossein. "Privatization in Iran: Analysis of the Process and Methods." In Hamid Zangeneh, ed., *Islam, Iran, and World Stability*. New York: St. Martins Press, 1994.

Algar, Hamid. *Constitution of the Islamic Republic of Iran*. New York: Mizan Press, 1980.

Amirahmadi, Hooshang. *Revolution and Economic Transition: The Iranian Experience*. Albany: State University of New York Press, 1990.

Amuzegar, Jahangir. *Iran's Economy under the Islamic Republic*. London: Tauris, 1993.

Amuzegar, Jahangir. *Technical Assistance in Theory and Practice: The Case of Iran*. New York: Praeger, 1966.

Azimi, Hossein. *Circuits of Underdevelopment in the Iranian Economy*. 3d ed. Tehran: Nashre Nei Press, 1993.

Azkia, Mostafa, and Gholamreza Ghaffari. *Rural Development with Emphases on Rural Community of Iran*. Tehran: Nashre Nei Press, 2004.

Bharier, Julian. *Economic Development in Iran, 1900–1970*. London: Oxford University Press, 1971.

Brend, Barbara. "Fervour, Opulence, and Decline." In *Islamic Art*. London: British Museum Press, 1991.

Chaquéri, Cosroe. *Origins of Social Democracy in Modern Iran*. Seattle: University of Washington Press, 2001.

Dunn and Bradstreet. *D and B Country Report: The Islamic Republic of Iran*. New York, 2006.

Esmaeilnia, Aliasghar. *Analysis of Budget of State Enterprises*. Tehran: Organization of Budget and Planning, 2004.

Farmanfarmaian, Manucher, and Roxane Farmanfarmaian. *Blood and Oil*. New York: Random House, 1997.

Fazel, Mohammed, and Jan-Ole Ray. *Business Culture in the Middle East: The Case of Iran.* Stockholm: Scandinavian Institutes for Administrative Research, 1979.

"Foreign Investment in the Iranian Oil Industry." *Shana Khabar* (Tehran), September 3, 2005.

Geeti, Nesha-at. "From Traditional Bazaar to Modern Bazaar: Iran in the 19th Century." *Goft-o-Gu* (Tehran) 41 (2005).

Hooglund, Eric J. *Land and Revolution in Iran, 1960–1980.* Austin: University of Texas Press, 1982.

International Monetary Fund. *IMF International Financial Statistics Yearbook 2005.* Washington, DC, 2005.

International Monetary Fund. *Islamic Republic of Iran: Selected Issues.* Washington, DC, 2004.

International Monetary Fund. *Islamic Republic of Iran: Statistical Appendix.* Washington, DC, 2006.

International Monetary Fund. *The Islamic Republic of Iran's Financial Position in the Fund as of March 2005.* Washington, DC, 2005.

Iran. Central Bank of Iran. *Iran National Accounts: 1353–56.* Tehran, 1991.

Iran. Central Bank of Iran. *The Law of Usury (Interest) Free Banking.* Tehran, 2005.

Iran. Central Bank of Iran. *The Monetary and Bank Law of Iran.* Tehran, 2005.

Iran. Central Bank of Iran. *Survey of Economic Affairs of Iran after the Revolution.* Tehran, 1983.

Iran. Management and Planning Organization. "Budget Law of 1384 (2005)." Tehran, 2005.

Iran. Management and Planning Organization. *Economic Report: 1383.* Tehran, 2005.

Iran. Management and Planning Organization. "The First Five-Year Economic, Social, and Cultural Development Plan of the IRI, 1990." Tehran, 1990.

Iran. Statistical Center of Iran. *Census of Agriculture 1382* [2003–4]. Tehran, 2004.

Iran. Statistical Center of Iran. *Iran Statistical Yearbook 1374* [1995–96]. Tehran, 1996.

Iran. Statistical Center of Iran. *Iran Statistical Yearbook 1382* [2003–4]. Tehran, 2004.

Iran. Statistical Center of Iran. *Iran Statistical Yearbook 1383* [2004–5]. Tehran, 2006.

Issawi, Charles. "The Iranian Economy 1925–1975: Fifty Years of Economic Development." In George Lenczowski, ed., *Iran under the Pahlavis*. Stanford: Hoover Institution Press, 1978.

Jazani, Bizhan. *Capitalism and Revolution in Iran: Selected Writings of Bizhan Jazani*. London: Zed Press, 1980.

Jensen, Jesper Bo, and David Tarr. *Trade, Foreign Exchange, and Energy Policies in the Islamic Republic of Iran: Reform Agenda, Economic Implications, and Impact on the Poor*. Washington, DC: World Bank Development Research Group, 2002.

"Joint Investment of 100 Foreign Companies and Banks in Petrochemical Industries." *Iran Newsletter* (Tehran), May 9, 2005.

Karshenas, M., and H. Pesaran. "Economic Reform and the Reconstruction of the Iranian Economy." *The Middle East Journal* 49, no. 1, 89–111.

Katouzian, Homa. *The Political Economy of Modern Iran: Despotism and Pseudo-Modernism*. New York: New York University Press, 1981.

Mafi, Homayoun. *Some Legal Aspects of International Trade of Iran*. Nijmegen: GNI, 1999.

Milani, Mohsen M. *The Making of Iran's Islamic Revolution: From Monarchy to Islamic Republic*. Boulder, Colorado: Westview Press, 1988.

Mofid, Kamran. *Development Planning in Iran: From Monarchy to Islamic Republic*. Cambridgeshire, United Kingdom: Middle East and North African Studies Press, 1987.

Mohseni, Maryam. "The Effects Of Economic Adjustment Plans on the Status of Iranian Workers." *Farhang-e Touse'e* (Tehran), nos. 34 and 35, 1998, 12–14.

Mousavi, Shafaee, and Seyed Masoud. "Globalization and Contradiction Between the Nation and the State in Iran: The Internet Case." *Critique: Critical Middle Eastern Studies* 12, no. 2 (October 2003): 189–96.

Parker, Philip. *The Economic Competitiveness of Iran: Financial Returns, Labor Productivity and International Gaps*. Dublin: Icon Group International, 2002.

Ra-ees Daana, Fariborz. *Political Economy of Development*. Tehran: Negah, 2000.

Razzaghi, Ebrahim. *Introduction to the Iranian Economy.* 4th ed. Tehran: Nashre Nei Press, 2003.

Razzaghi, Ebrahim. *The Iranian Economy.* Tehran: Nashre Nei Press, 1988.

Razzaghi, Ebrahim. *The Iranian Economy.* Tehran: Nashre Nei Press, 2003.

Shakiba-ei, Alireza, and Hossein Sadeghi. "Measuring the Informal Sector with Fuzzy Method." *Journal of Economic Research,* no. 61 (Fall 2004).

(Various issues of the following publications and Web sites also were used in the preparation of this chapter: *Donya-e-eghtesad* (Tehran); *Gooya.com,* http://www.gooya.com; Iranian News Agency (Tehran); *Iran Newsletter* (Tehran); *Middle East Economic Digest*; Middle East Research and Information Project (MERIP), http://www.merip.org; Payvand Iran News, http://www.payvand.com; *Shargh Newsletter* (Tehran); and *Tehran Times,* http://www.tehran times.com. Other useful sources included annual and quarterly publications of the Central Bank of Iran, http://www.cbi.ir, including *Economic Report and Balance Sheet, Economic Trends, Household Budget Survey, National Accounts,* and *Summary of Economic Activities*; annual profiles on Iran by the Economist Intelligence Unit, London; annual editions of the *Europa World Year Book,* London; and data and publications of the Statistical Center of Iran (SCI), http://www.sci.or.ir, available in English through the SCI's "National Portal of Statistics," http://www.sci.or.ir/portal/facces/public/sci_en.)

Chapter 4

Abdo, Geneive, and Jonathan Lyons. *Answering Only to God: Faith and Freedom in Twenty-First-Century Iran.* New York: Holt, 2003.

Abrahamian, Ervand. *Iran Between Two Revolutions.* Princeton: Princeton University Press, 1982.

Abrahamian, Ervand. *Khomeinism: Essays on the Islamic Republic.* London: Tauris, 1993.

Abrahamian, Ervand. *Radical Islam: The Iranian Mojahedin.* New Haven: Yale University Press, 1989.

Abrahamian, Ervand. *Tortured Confessions: Prisons and Public Recantations in Modern Iran.* Berkeley: University of California Press, 1999.

Adelkhah, Fariba. *Being Modern in Iran.* New York: Columbia University Press, 2000.

Adib-Moghaddam, Arshin. "Islamic Utopian Romanticism and the Foreign Policy Culture of Iran." *Critique: Critical Middle Eastern Studies* 14, no. 3 (Fall 2005): 265–92.

Afshari, Reza. *Human Rights in Iran: The Abuse of Cultural Relativism.* Philadelphia: University of Pennsylvania Press, 2001.

Akhavi-Pour, Hossein, and Heidar Azodanloo. "Economic Bases of Political Factions in Iran." *Critique: Critical Middle Eastern Studies,* no. 13 (Fall 1998): 69–82.

Alizadeh, Parvin, ed. *The Economy of Iran: Dilemmas of an Islamic State.* London: Tauris, 2000.

Amirahmadi, Hooshang. *Revolution and Economic Transition: The Iranian Experience.* Albany: State University of New York Press, 1990.

Amuzegar, Jahangir. *Iran's Economy under the Islamic Republic.* London: Tauris, 1993.

Amuzegar, Jahangir. "Khatami's Legacy: Dashed Hopes." *The Middle East Journal* 60, no. 1 (Winter 2006): 57–74.

Ansari, Ali M. *Confronting Iran: The Failure of American Foreign Policy and the Next Great Crisis in the Middle East.* New York: Perseus Books Group, 2006.

Ansari, Ali M. *Iran, Islam, and Democracy.* London: Royal Institute of International Affairs, 2000.

Arjomand, Said Amir. *The Turban for the Crown: The Islamic Revolution in Iran.* New York: Oxford University Press, 1988.

Bakhash, Shaul. *The Reign of the Ayatollahs: Iran and the Islamic Revolution.* Rev. ed. New York: Basic Books, 1990.

Baktiari, Bahman. *Parliamentary Politics in Revolutionary Iran: The Institutionalization of Factional Politics.* Gainesville: University Press of Florida, 1996.

Bayat, Asef. *Street Politics: Poor People's Movements in Iran.* New York: Columbia University Press, 1997.

Bayat, Asef. *Workers and Revolution in Iran: A Third World Experience of Workers Control.* London: Zed Books, 1987.

Beeman, William O. *The "Great Satan" vs. the "Mad Mullahs":
How the United States and Iran Demonize Each Other.* New York:
Greenwood, 2005.

Beeman, William O. *Language, Status, and Power in Iran.* Bloomington: Indiana University Press, 1986.

Behrooz, Maziar. *Rebels with a Cause: The Failure of the Left in
Iran.* London: Tauris, 1999.

de Bellaique, Christopher. *In the Garden of the Martyrs: A Memoir
of Iran.* New York: HarperCollins, 2005.

Benard, Cheryl, and Zalmay Khalilzad. *"The Government of God"
– Iran's Islamic Republic.* New York: Columbia University Press,
1984.

Bill, James A. *The Eagle and the Lion: The Tragedy of American-Iranian Relations.* New Haven: Yale University Press, 1988.

Boroujerdi, Mehrzad. *Iranian Intellectuals and the West: The Tormented Triumph of Nativism.* Syracuse: Syracuse University
Press, 1996.

Brumberg, Daniel. *Reinventing Khomeini: The Struggle for Reform
in Iran.* Chicago: University of Chicago Press, 2001.

Buchta, Wilfried. *Who Rules Iran? The Structure of Power in the
Islamic Republic.* Washington, DC: The Washington Institute
for Near East Policy and the Konrad Adenauer Stiftung,
2000.

Chehabi, H. E. *Iranian Politics and Religious Modernism.* Ithaca:
Cornell University Press, 1990.

Chubin, Shahram, and Charles Tripp. *Iran and Iraq at War.* London: Tauris, 1988.

Cordesman, Anthony H., and Abraham R. Wagner. *The Lessons
of Modern War.* Vol. 2, *The Iran–Iraq War.* Boulder, Colorado:
Westview Press, 1990.

Dabashi, Hamid. *Close-Up: Iranian Cinema, Past, Present, and
Future.* New York: Verso, 2001.

Draper, Theodore. *A Very Thin Line: The Iran–Contra Affairs.*
New York: Simon and Schuster, 1991.

Ebadi, Shirin. In collaboration with Azadeh Moaveni. *Iran
Awakening.* New York: Random House, 2006.

Ehteshami, Anoushiravan. *After Khomeini: The Iranian Second
Republic.* London: Routledge, 1995.

Ehteshami, Anoushiravan, and Raymond A. Hinnebusch. *Syria and Iran: Middle Powers in a Penetrated Regional System.* London: Routledge, 1997.

Entessar, Nader. *Kurdish Ethnonationalism.* Boulder, Colorado: Lynne Rienner, 1992.

Esposito, John L., ed. *The Iranian Revolution: Its Global Impact.* Miami: Florida International University Press, 1990.

Farsoun, Samih K., and Mehrdad Mashayekhi, eds. *Iran: Political Culture in the Islamic Republic.* London: Routledge, 1992.

Fuller, Graham E. *The "Center of the Universe": The Geopolitics of Iran.* Boulder, Colorado: Westview Press, 1991.

Gasiorowski, Mark J. "Iran under Khatami: Deadlock or Change?" *Global Dialogue* 3, nos. 2–3 (Spring/Summer 2001): 9–18.

Gasiorowski, Mark J. "The Power Struggle in Iran." *Middle East Policy* 7, no. 4 (October 2000): 22–40.

Gasiorowski, Mark J. *U.S. Foreign Policy and the Shah.* Ithaca: Cornell University Press, 1991.

Gheissari, Ali. *Iranian Intellectuals in the 20th Century.* Austin: University of Texas Press, 1998.

Gheissari, Ali, and Vali Nasr. *Democracy in Iran: History and the Quest for Liberty.* Oxford: Oxford University Press, 2006.

Gieling, Saskia. *Religion and War in Revolutionary Iran.* London: Tauris, 1999.

Harik, Judith. *Hezbollah: The Changing Face of Terrorism.* London: Tauris, 2004.

Hooglund, Eric. "Iran and the Persian Gulf." Pages 156–75 in Eric Hooglund, ed., *Twenty Years of Islamic Revolution: Political and Social Transition in Iran since 1979.* Syracuse: Syracuse University Press, 2002.

Hooglund, Eric. "Iran: Wary Neutral." Pages 173–85 in Rick Fawn and Raymond Hinnebusch, eds., *The Iraq War: Causes and Consequences.* Boulder, Colorado: Lynne Rienner, 2006.

Hooglund, Eric. "Mythology versus Reality: Iranian Political Economy and the Clinton Administration." *Critique: Critical Middle Eastern Studies*, no. 11 (Fall 1997): 37–52.

Hooglund, Eric, ed. *Twenty Years of Islamic Revolution: Political and Social Transition in Iran since 1979.* Syracuse: Syracuse University Press, 2002.

Houghton, David Patrick. *U.S. Foreign Policy and the Iran Hostage Crisis.* Cambridge: Cambridge University Press, 2001.

Iran. Statistical Center of Iran. *Iran Statistical Yearbook 1381* [2002–3]. Tehran, 2003.

Iran Yearbook '96. Bonn: MB Medien & Bucher Verlagsgesellschaft, 1995.

Karimi-Hakkak, Ahmad. "Introduction: Selections from the Literature of Iran, 1977–1997." *Iranian Studies* 30, nos. 3–4 (Summer–Fall 1997): 193–213.

Katzman, Kenneth. *The Warriors of Islam: Iran's Revolutionary Guard.* Boulder, Colorado: Westview Press, 1993.

Keddie, Nikki R., and Eric Hooglund, eds. *The Iranian Revolution and the Islamic Republic.* Rev. ed. Syracuse: Syracuse University Press, 1986.

Keddie, Nikki R., and Mark J. Gasiorowski, eds. *Neither East Nor West: Iran, The Soviet Union, and the United States.* New Haven: Yale University Press, 1990.

Keshavarzian, Arang. "Contestation Without Democracy: Elite Fragmentation in Iran." Pages 63–88 in Marsha Posusney and Michele Angrist, eds., *Authoritarianism in the Middle East: Regimes and Resistance.* Boulder, Colorado: Lynne Rienner, 2005.

Khadduri, Majid. *The Gulf War: The Origins and Implications of the Iran–Iraq Conflict.* New York: Oxford University Press, 1988.

Khatami, Mohammad. *Islam, Dialogue and Civil Society.* Canberra: Centre for Arab and Islamic Studies, 2000.

Khosrokhavar, Farhad. "Neo-conservative Intellectuals in Iran." *Critique: Critical Middle Easterm Studies,* no. 19 (Fall 2001): 5–30.

Khosrokhavar, Farhad. "Postrevolutionary Iran and the New Social Movements." Pages 3–18 in Eric Hooglund, ed., *Twenty Years of Islamic Revolution: Political and Social Transition in Iran since 1979.* Syracuse: Syracuse University Press, 2002.

Khosrokhavar, Farhad. "Toward an Anthropology of Democratization in Iran." *Critique: Critical Middle Eastern Studies,* no. 16 (Spring 2000): 2–29.

Kian-Thiébaut, Azadeh. "Women and the Making of Civil Society in Post-Islamist Iran." Pages 56–73 in Eric Hooglund, ed., *Twenty Years of Islamic Revolution: Political and Social Transition in Iran since 1979.* Syracuse: Syracuse University Press, 2002.

Majles Publishing House. *The Majles Election Laws.* Tehran, 1362/1982–83. (English translation published in Foreign Broadcast Information Service, no. 00N13002A.)

Martin, Vanessa. *Creating an Islamic State: Khomeini and the Making of a New Iran.* London: Tauris, 2000.

Menashri, David. *Education and the Making of Modern Iran.* Ithaca: Cornell University Press, 1992.

Menashri, David. *Iran: A Decade of War and Revolution.* New York: Holmes and Meier, 1990.

Menashri, David, ed. *The Iranian Revolution and the Muslim World.* Boulder, Colorado: Westview Press, 1990.

Middle East Watch. *Guardians of Thought: Limits on Freedom of Expression in Iran.* New York, 1993.

Milani, Mohsen. M. *The Making of Iran's Islamic Revolution: From Monarchy to Islamic Republic.* Rev. ed. Boulder, Colorado: Westview Press, 1994.

Milani, Mohsen M., "The Transformation of the *Velayat-e Faqih* Institution: From Khomeini to Khamenei." *The Muslim World* 82, nos. 3–4 (July–October 1992): 175–90.

Moaddel, Mansoor. *Class, Politics, and Ideology in the Iranian Revolution.* New York: Columbia University Press, 1993.

Moaveni, Azadeh. *Lipstick Jihad: A Memoir of Growing Up Iranian in America and American in Iran.* New York: Perseus Books Group, 2005.

Moghadam, Val. "Socialism or Anti-Imperialism? The Left and Revolution in Iran." *New Left Review* 166 (November/December 1987): 19–21.

Moin, Baqer. *Khomeini: Life of the Ayatollah.* London: Tauris, 1999.

Molavi, Afshin. *The Soul of Iran: A Nation's Journey to Freedom.* New York: Norton, 2005.

Moses, Russell Leigh. *Freeing the Hostages.* Pittsburgh: University of Pittsburgh Press, 1996.

Moslem, Mehdi. "Ayatollah Khomeini's Role in the Rationalization of the Islamic Government." *Critique: Critical Middle Eastern Studies,* no. 14 (Spring 1999): 75–92.

Moslem, Mehdi. *Factional Politics in Post-Khomeini Iran.* Syracuse: Syracuse University Press, 2002.

Moslem, Mehdi. "The State and Factional Politics in the Islamic Republic of Iran." Pages 19–35 in Eric Hooglund, ed., *Twenty*

Years of Islamic Revolution: Political and Social Transition in Iran since 1979. Syracuse: Syracuse University Press, 2002.

Mottahedeh, Roy P. *The Mantle of the Prophet: Religion and Politics in Iran.* New York: Simon and Schuster, 1985.

Mottahedeh, Roy P. "Shi'ite Political Thought and the Destiny of the Iranian Revolution." Pages 70–80 in J.S. al-Suwaidi, ed., *Iran and the Gulf: A Search for Stability.* Abu Dhabi: The Emirates Center for Strategic Studies and Research, 1996.

Pollack, Kenneth M. *The Persian Puzzle: The Conflict Between Iran and America.* New York: Random House, 2004.

Qanbari, Sakineh, and Robabeh Shahintab. *Presidential Election Collection.* Tehran: National Department of Laws and Regulations Printing and Publication Office, 1375/1996–97. (English translation published in Foreign Broadcast Information Service, no. 00N13003A.)

Rahnema, Ali. *An Islamic Utopian: A Political Biography of Ali Shari'ati.* London: Tauris, 1998.

Rahnema, Ali, and Farhad Nomani. *The Secular Miracle: Religion, Politics, and Economic Policy in Iran.* London: Zed Books, 1990.

Rahnema, Saeed, and Sohrab Behdad, eds. *Iran After the Revolution: Crisis of an Islamic State.* London: Tauris, 1996.

Ram, Haggay. *Myth and Mobilization in Revolutionary Iran: The Use of the Friday Congregational Sermon.* Washington, DC: American University Press, 1994.

Ramazani, Ruhollah K. "Ideology and Pragmatism in Iran's Foreign Policy." *The Middle East Journal* 58, no. 4 (Autumn 2004): 549–59.

Ramazani, Ruhollah K. *Revolutionary Iran: Challenge and Response in the Middle East.* Baltimore: Johns Hopkins University Press, 1986.

Roshandel, Jalil. "Evolution of the Decision-Making Process in Iranian Foreign Policy." Pages 123–42 in Eric Hooglund, ed., *Twenty Years of Islamic Revolution: Political and Social Transition in Iran since 1979.* Syracuse: Syracuse University Press, 2002.

Rouleau, Eric. "European Union and French Views of the Islamic Republic." Pages 143–55 in Eric Hooglund, ed., *Twenty Years of Islamic Revolution: Political and Social Transition in Iran since 1979.* Syracuse: Syracuse University Press, 2002.

Samii, Abbas William. "The Contemporary Iranian News Media." *Middle East Review of International Affairs* 3, no. 4 (December 1999): 1–10.

Samii, Abbas William. "Dissent in Iranian Elections: Reasons and Implications." *The Middle East Journal* 58, no. 3 (Summer 2004): 403–23.

Samii, Abbas William. "Iran's Guardians Council as an Obstacle to Democracy." *The Middle East Journal* 55, no. 4 (Autumn 2001): 643–62.

Schirazi, Asghar. *The Constitution of Iran: Politics and the State in the Islamic Republic.* London: Tauris, 1997.

Sciolino, Elaine. *Persian Mirrors: The Elusive Face of Iran.* New York: Free Press, 2000.

Sick, Gary. *All Fall Down: America's Tragic Encounter With Iran.* New York: Random House, 1985.

Sick, Gary. "Iran: Confronting Terrorism." *The Washington Quarterly,* Autumn 2003, 83–98.

Sick, Gary. *October Surprise.* New York: Random House, 1991.

Sreberny-Mohammadi, Annabelle, and Ali Mohammadi. "Post-Revolutionary Iranian Exiles: A Study in Impotence," *Third World Quarterly* 9, no. 1 (January 1987): 108–29.

Stempel, John. *Inside the Iranian Revolution.* Bloomington: Indiana University Press, 1981.

Tajbakhsh, Kian. "Political Decentralization and the Creation of Local Government in Iran: Consolidation or Transformation of the Theocratic State?" *Social Research* 67, no. 2 (Summer 2000): 377–404.

Tapper, Richard, ed. *The New Iranian Cinema: Politics, Representation, and Identity.* London: Tauris, 2002.

Workman, W. Thom. *The Social Origins of the Iran–Iraq War.* Boulder, Colorado: Lynne Rienner, 1994.

Wright, Robin. *In the Name of God: The Khomeini Decade.* New York: Simon and Schuster, 1989.

Wright, Robin. *The Last Great Revolution: Turmoil and Transformation in Iran.* New York: Vintage, 2001.

(Resources available on the following Web sites also were used in the preparation of this chapter: Amnesty International, http://web.amnesty.org/library/eng-irn/index; Human Rights Watch, http://www.hrw.org/doc?t=mideast&c=iran; Iran Internet Pages, http://www.middle-east-pages.com/Iran; Iran Virtual Library, http://www.irvl.net; Middle East Network Information Center, http://menic.utexas.edu/menic/Countries_and_Regions/Iran; Payvand Iran News, http://www.payvand.com; Radio Free

Europe/Radio Liberty, *Iran Report,* http://www.rferl.org/reports/iran-report; Reporters Without Borders, http://www.rsf.fr/country-43.php3?id_mot=92& Valider=OK; and U.S. Department of State, *Country Reports on Human Rights Practices,* http://www.state.gov/g/drl/hr/c1470.htm.)

Chapter 5

Adib-Moghaddam, Arshin. "Islamic Utopian Romanticism and the Foreign Policy Culture of Iran." *Critique: Critical Middle Eastern Studies* 14, no. 3 (Fall 2005): 265–92.

Albright, D., and C. Hinderstein. "The Iranian Gas Centrifuge Uranium Enrichment Plant at Natanz: Drawing from Commercial Satellite Images." *ISIS Issues Brief,* March 14, 2003. http://www.isis-online.org/publications/iran/natanz03_02.html.

Arnett, Eric, ed. *Military Capacity and the Risk of War: China, India, Pakistan, and Iran.* Oxford: Oxford University Press, 1997.

Brzezinski, Zbigniew, Robert M. Gates, and Suzanne Maloney. *Iran: Time for a New Approach.* Washington, DC: Council on Foreign Relations, 2004.

Buchta, Wilfried. *Who Rules Iran? The Structure of Power in the Islamic Republic.* Washington, DC: The Washington Institute for Near East Policy and the Konrad Adenauer Stiftung, 2000.

Byman, Daniel, Shahram Chubin, Anoushiravan Ehteshami, and Jerrold Green. *Iran's Security Policy in the Post-Revolutionary Era.* Santa Monica: RAND Corporation, April 1, 2001.

Cain, Anthony C. "Iran's Strategic Culture and Weapons of Mass Destruction: Implications for U.S. Policy." *Maxwell Papers,* no. 26 (April 2002).

Chubin, Shahram. *Iran's National Security Policy: Capabilities, Intentions and Impact.* Washington, DC: Carnegie Endowment for International Peace, 1994.

Chubin, Shahram. "Iran's Strategic Predicament." *The Middle East Journal* 54, no. 1 (Winter 2000).

Cordesman, Anthony H. *Iran's Evolving Military Forces.* Washington, DC: Center for Strategic and International Studies, 2004.

Cordesman, Anthony H. *Iran's Military Forces in Transition.* Westport, Connecticut: Praeger, 1999.

Cordesman, Anthony H. "Iranian Arms Transfers: The Facts." Washington, DC: Center for Strategic and International Studies, October 2000.

Ehsani, Kaveh, and Chris Toensing. "Neo-conservatives, Hardline Clerics and the Bomb." *Middle East Report* 34, no. 233 (Winter 2004).

Ehteshami, Anoushiravan. "Iran's International Posture in the Wake of the Iraq War." *The Middle East Journal* 58, no. 2 (Spring 2004).

Fitzpatrick, Mark. "Assessing Iran's Nuclear Progress." *Survival* 48, no. 3, 5–26.

Fuller, Graham E. *The Center of Universe: The Geopolitics of Iran.* Boulder, Colorado: Westview Press, 1991.

Gertz, Bill, and Rowan Scarborough. "Iran's Missile Boats." May 17, 2002. http://www.gertzfile.com/gertzfile/ring051702.html.

Harkavy, Robert, and Geoffrey Kemp. *Strategic Geography and the Changing Middle East.* Washington, DC: Brookings Institution Press, 1997.

Hooglund, Eric. "Iran: Wary Neutral." Pages 173–85 in Rick Fawn and Hinnebusch, eds., *The Iraq War: Causes and Consequences.* Boulder, Colorado: Lynne Reinner, 2006.

"Iran Asserts Right to Develop Nuclear Technology." *Foreign Policy Bulletin* 16, no. 1, 36–53.

"Iran Boasts It Can Mass-Produce Shahab–3 Missile." Iranian Student News Agency, November 9, 2004. http://www.turkishpress.com/news.asp?id=33260.

"Iran Hardliners Attack EU Deal." Deutsche Presse–Agentur, November 16, 2004. http://www.expatica.com/source/site_article.asp?subchannel_id=52&story_id=13982&name=Iran's+conservatives+attack+EU+nuclear+deal.

"Iran Making First Locally Built Submarine." Associated Press, May 11, 2005. http://www.spacedaily.com/news/submarine-05f.html.

"Iran Produces Engines for Shahab–3." *Middle East News Line,* November 11, 2004. http://www.menewsline.com/stories/2004/november/11_11_1.html.

"Iran Promises to Keep Out of US-Iraq War." Agence France Presse, October 1, 2002. http://mid-day.com/news/world/2002/october/32864.htm.

"Iranian Cleric: Iran Will Not Be Deceived by Softer U.S. Tone." Associated Press Online, April 23, 1999. http://cnn.com/WORLD/meast/9904/23/BC-Iran-US.ap/index.html.

"Iranian Conservatives Pledge Continued Cooperation with UN Nuclear Watchdog." Agence France Presse, February 24, 2004. http://www.spacewar.com/2004/040224151317.hianea 1a.html.

"Iranian FM Sees Israel as a Threat, Denies Nuke Arms Program." Islamic Republic News Agency, October 4, 2004. http://www.globalsecurity.org/wmd/library/news/iran/2004/ iran-041004-irna01.htm.

"IRGC Commander Warns Zionist Regime Against Targeting Iran." Islamic Republic News Agency, August 11, 2004. http://www.globalsecurity.org/wmd/library/news/iran/2004/iran-040811-irna04.htm.

Katzman, Kenneth. *Iran: Arms and Technology Acquisitions.* Washington, DC: Congressional Research Service, 2001.

Katzman, Kenneth. *Iran: Arms and Weapons of Mass Destruction Suppliers.* Washington, DC: Congressional Research Service, 2003.

Kemp, Geoffrey, ed. *Iran's Bomb: American and Iranian Perspectives.* Washington, DC: Nixon Center, March 2004.

Kharrazi, Kamal. "The View from Tehran." *Middle East Policy* 12, no. 1 (Spring 2005).

Kile, Shannon N., ed. *Europe and Iran: Perspectives on Non-proliferation.* Oxford: Oxford University Press, 2005.

Mokhtari, Fariborz. "No One Will Scratch My Back: Iranian Security Perceptions in Historical Context." *The Middle East Journal* 59, no. 2 (Spring 2005).

Moslem, Mehdi. *Factional Politics in Post-Khomeini Iran.* Syracuse: Syracuse University Press 2002.

Pollack, Kenneth M. *The Persion Puzzle: The Conflict Between Iran and America.* New York: Random House, 2004.

Ramazani, Ruhollah K. "Ideology and Pragmatism in Iran's Foreign Policy." *The Middle East Journal* 58, no. 4 (Autumn 2004): 549–59.

Roshandel, Jalil. "Iran's Foreign and Security Policies: How the Decision-making Process Evolved." *Security Dialogue* 31, no. 1 (March 2000).

Schake, Kori N., and Judith S. Yaphe. *The Strategic Implications of a Nuclear-Armed Iran.* Washington, DC: National Defense University, 2001.

Stockholm International Peace Research Institute. *SIPRI Yearbook 2005: Armaments, Disarmament, and International Security.* Oxford: Oxford University Press, 2005.

"Straw Completes Mid-East Mission." BBC News, October 10, 2002. http://news.bbc.co.uk/2/hi/uk_politics/2315473.stm.

Taremi, Kamran. "Beyond the Axis of Evil: Ballistic Missiles in Iran's Military Security Thinking." *Security Dialogue* 36, no. 1 (2005): 93–108.

Taremi, Kamran. "Iranian Policy Towards Occupied Iraq." *Middle East Policy* 12, no. 4 (Winter 2005).

Traynor, I., and S. Goldenberg. "Fresh Suspicion over Iran's Nuclear Aims." *Guardian Online*, November 20, 2004. http://www.guardian.co.uk/iran/story/0,12858,1355587,00.

United States Arms Control and Disarmament Agency. *World Military Expenditures and Arms Transfers, 1996.* Washington, DC, 1997.

Ward, Steven R. "The Continuing Evolution of Iran's Military Doctrine." *The Middle East Journal* 59, no. 4 (Autumn 2005).

(Various issues of *Iran Daily* (Tehran), http://www.irandaily.com; *Iran Times* (Washington, DC); and International Institute for Strategic Studies, *The Military Balance* (London) also were used in preparing this chapter. In addition, the following Web sites offer ongoing coverage of subjects discussed in this chapter: Federation of American Scientists, http://www.fas.org/; Global Security, http://www.globalsecurity.org/; Institute for Science and International Security, http://www.isis-online.org/; Iran Virtual Library, http://www.irvl.net; Islamic Republic News Agency, http://www.irna.com; Middle East Network Information Center, http://menic.utexas.edu/menic/Countries_and_Regions/Iran; Payvand Iran News, http://www.payvand.com; and Radio Free Europe/Radio Liberty *Iran Report*, http://www.rferl.org/reports/iran-report.)

Glossary

barrels per day (bpd)—Production of crude oil and petroleum products frequently is measured in this unit, which often is abbreviated bpd or bd. As a measurement of volume, a barrel is the equivalent of 42 U.S. gallons. Conversion of barrels to tons depends on the density of the specific product in question. About 7.3 barrels of average-density crude oil weigh one ton, and seven barrels of heavy crude have an equivalent weight. Lighter products such as gasoline and kerosene average about eight barrels per ton.

bazaar—Term referring to the area of an urban center where merchants and artisans traditionally sold their wares and, beginning in the nineteenth century, to the influential class of society to which merchants and artisans belong.

economic development plan(s)—Iran's economic development plans have been of varying lengths and have had various nomenclature. Under Mohammad Reza Shah, five plans were completed, and a sixth was in progress at the time of the Islamic Revolution of 1978–79. The Islamic Republic has had formal five-year economic development plans since 1990, the fourth of which began in March 2005. The plans begin and end in March in accordance with Iran's fiscal year (*q.v.*) and the Iranian calendar year (*q.v.*).

faqih—An expert in religious jurisprudence, specifically a Shia (*q.v.*) cleric whose mastery of the Quran, the traditions of the Prophet and the Twelve Imams, and the codices of Shia Islamic law permit him to render binding interpretations of religious laws and regulations. A prominent *faqih*, chosen by a body of senior *faqihs*, is empowered to rule as the Leader of the Revolution in accordance with the concept of *velayat-e faqih* (*q.v.*) enunciated by Ayatollah Khomeini.

fiscal year (FY)—Coincides with the Iranian calendar year (*q.v.*), which runs from March 21 through March 20.

gross domestic product (GDP)—The total value of goods and services produced within a country's borders during a fixed period, usually one year. Obtained by adding the value contributed by each sector of the economy in the form of compensation of employees, profits, and depreciation (consumption of capital). Subsistence production is included and consists of the imputed value of production by the farm family for its own use and the imputed rental value of owner-occupied dwellings.

gross national product (GNP)—Gross domestic product (*q.v.*) plus the income received from abroad by residents, less payments remitted abroad by nonresidents.

hejab—Modesty in attire, generally interpreted by the Shia clergy to mean that by age 10 females must cover all their hair and flesh except for hands and face when in public. In the Islamic Republic, *hejab* became a symbol of the rule of Islamic law over society and a source of irritation in some social circles.

hezbollahi(s)—Literally, a follower of the party of God. *Hezbollahis*, originally followers of a particular religious figure, eventually came to constitute an unofficial political party. Although they often acted like vigilantes in breaking up meetings of politicians whom they deemed too liberal, they were not an irregular military or paramilitary group.

imam—Among Twelver Shias, the principal meaning is a designation of one of the 12 legitimate successors of the Prophet Muhammad. Also used by both Shias (*q.v.*) and Sunnis (*q.v.*) to designate a congregational prayer leader or cleric.

Iranian calendar year—The Iranian calendar is a solar calendar that begins each year at the vernal equinox (usually March 21). The Iranian calendar begins counting years from 622 A.D., the year of Muhammad's flight from Mecca to Medina. The current Iranian calendar year, which began in March 2008, is 1387.

kadkhoda—In rural Iran, a village headman; also used as the title for leaders of some tribal clans.

madrassa—A religious college or seminary that trains students in Islamic jurisprudence.

mahriyeh—A stipulated amount of money and/or property that a groom provides his bride according to their marriage contract.

Majlis—A term used in two senses: the legislative body of imperial Iran, which included a senate and an elected lower house of representatives, or the lower house alone. After the

Revolution of 1978–79, the Islamic Republic abolished the senate, retaining an elected lower house known as the Majlis.

maktab—A primary school operated by Shia clergy.

mojtahed—In Shia religious law, a religious leader who has achieved high status by passing through a series of prescribed stages of education and experience, and thus is worthy of emulation and entitled to issue rulings and decrees.

mostazafin—Literally, the disinherited; originally, a religious term for the poor, which subsequently was popularized.

mullah—General term for a member of the Islamic clergy; usually refers to a preacher or other low-ranking cleric who has not earned the right to interpret religious laws.

Organization of the Petroleum Exporting Countries (OPEC)—An organization encompassing 12 of the world's major oil-producing countries: Algeria, Angola, Indonesia, Iran, Iraq, Kuwait, Libya, Nigeria, Qatar, Saudi Arabia, the United Arab Emirates, and Venezuela. OPEC coordinates the petroleum policies of its members, with the exception of Iraq, whose oil production has not been included in OPEC production agreements since 1998. OPEC members account for about two-thirds of world oil reserves and more than 40 percent of world oil production.

rial—Basic unit of Iranian currency. Between 1984 and 2001, Iran had multiple exchange rates, including official and unofficial rates. Since 2001 there has been a single exchange rate. In late February 2008, the exchange rate was about 9,400 rials to the U.S. dollar.

sharia—Islamic canon law. Among Shias (*q.v.*) the sharia includes the Quran and the authenticated sayings of the Prophet Muhammad and the Twelve Imams.

Shatt al Arab—"The Stream of the Arabs," Arvandrud in Persian, a river about 200 kilometers in length, formed by the confluence of the Euphrates and the Tigris at the town of Qurnah in southern Iraq. The southern end of the river constitutes the border between Iraq and Iran. Control of the waterway has been a source of friction since at least the seventeenth century; it was a major cause of the Iran–Iraq War of 1980–88.

Shia(s)—A member of the smaller of the two great divisions of Islam. The Shias supported the claims of Ali and his line to presumptive right to the caliphate and leadership of the world Muslim community, and on this issue they split from the Sunnis (*q.v.*) in the first great schism of Islam. Later schisms produced further divisions among the Shias.

special drawing right—A standardized monetary unit used by the International Monetary Fund (*q.v.*) for the transactions of several international institutions. It is standardized against all currencies using it rather than the home country's currency and is drawn from a pool of contributions by member countries.

Sunni(s)—A member of the larger of the two great divisions of Islam. The Sunnis, who rejected the claim of Ali's line to leadership of the world Muslim community, believe themselves to be the true followers of the sunna, the guide to proper behavior that includes the Quran and the words of the Prophet Muhammad.

velayat-e faqih—The guardianship of the religious jurisprudence expert. The concept was elaborated by Ayatollah Khomeini to justify political rule by the clergy.

White Revolution—Term used by Mohammad Reza Shah Pahlavi to designate the program of economic and social reforms that he initiated in 1963.

Index

331

Iran: A Country Study

Central Asia, xxxix, 247
Central Bank of Iran (*see also* Bank Markazi), 62, 156, 194–95
Central Council of Friday Prayer Leaders, 219
Central Intelligence Agency (CIA), 34
Central Oversight Committee, 228
Central Plateau, 85, 87, 91
Central Treaty Organization (CENTO), 35, 42
Chabahar, 186, 266
chain of command, military, 263, 264
chador, 115, 116, 117
Chahar Mahall va Bakhtiari, 95
Chaldeans, 101
Chaldiran, Battle of, 20
checks and balances, constitutional, 217
chemical weapons, 281
Chengdu Aircraft Corporation, 267
chief of staff of the armed forces and commander of the Gendarmerie, 261
China: and sanctions issue, xlvi; arms sales to Iran, 68, 265, 273, 274; guerrilla movements, 45; investment in Iran, xlviii; nuclear technology to Iran, 287; petroleum and gas purchases, xlviii, 163; trade with Iran, 199, 200
Chinook helicopter, 274
Chorasmia, 7
Chosroes I, 11–12
Chosroes II, 13
Christ (*see also* Jesus), 13
Christians in Iran, 128–29; representation in Majlis, 221
Churchill, Winston, 31
cities, largest (*see also* urbanization), 89
civic organizations, 233
civilian-military relations, 278–79
civil law, 224
civil liberties (*see also* human rights), 234–37
civil service code, 28
class structure, 104–8, 116, 149
Clerical Court, 224
clergy–state relations, xl, xlii
clerical powers, xxxix, xlii, 224–25
climate, 87
Clinton, William J., 72, 248
Coalition for All Iran, 214
coastal lowlands, 85
Combatant Clerics Association, 75, 76, 77, 230, 231

Conoco oil company, 72
conservatives: political coalition, xlii, 75–77, 231–32; strategy against reform, 1997–2003, xliv, 208–12; success of, xliv, 210–15; views on democracy, xliv
constitution of 1906, 25, 215–16
constitution of 1979: amendments of 1989, 70, 218; and religious minorities, 128, 130, 131, 132; established, xlii, 56, 216; human rights provisions, 233–34; shortcomings, 217
constitutional assembly of 1898, 70
constitutional assembly of 1989, 216
Constitutional Revolution, 1905–7, xl, 25–26
construction industry, 180
consumer goods, xlvii, 173, 176–80
convertibility, currency, 73
cooperatives in retail trade, 181
copper industry, 167, 179
corvettes, 266
Council for the Discernment of Expediency. *See* Expediency Council
counties, 226
criminal law, 224
Croesus, 7
Crusade for Reconstruction, 54, 110
Ctesiphon (*see also* Madain), 11
Cuba, guerrilla movements, 45
Cultural Heritage and Tourism Organization, 182
cuneiform, 92
current account deficit, 201
Curzon, Lord, 26
Cyrus II, 7, 41
Cyrus the Elder. *See* Cyrus II
Cyrus the Great. *See* Cyrus II

Dalan, 165
Dar ol Fonun, 23
Darayarahush. *See* Darius I
d'Arcy, William, 160
Darius I, 7
Darius III, 9
Darius the Great. *See* Darius I
Dasht-e Kavir (Salt Desert), 85
Dasht-e Lut (Desert of Emptiness), 85
data (legal system), 9
Davar, Ali Akbar, 28, 29
death, causes of, 137–38
death rate, 89

334

Iran: A Country Study

Republic of Korea. *See* South Korea
Resalat (newspaper), 238
resettlement: by Reza Shah Pahlavi, 27, 28;
 of Lurs, 95; of nomadic societies, 110–12;
 of Qashqais, 98; of Turkmens, 98
restaurants, 183
retail trade (*see also* bazaar; merchants),
 181
retirement programs, 139–40
revolutionary committees, 51, 52, 65
Revolutionary Council, 52–53, 57
revolutionary courts, 53, 58, 223
Revolutionary Guards. *See* Islamic Revolutionary Guard Corps
Rex Cinema fire, 48
Reza (eighth Imam), 124
Reza Khan (*see also* Pahlavi, Reza Shah), 27
Reza Shah Pahlavi. *See* Pahlavi, Reza Shah
Rezaiyeh, Lake. *See* Lake Urmia
rial, 73, 74, 147
ring roads, 184
rivers, 86
roads, 183–85
Roman Catholics in Iran, 128
Roman Empire, 10, 11, 13
Roosevelt, Franklin D., 31
Roosevelt, Kermit, 34
Roshanak. *See* Roxana
Roxana, 10
Ruhaniyun. *See* Militant Clerics Association
Rumi, 93
rural development, 109–10, 180, 184, 188,
 189, 190–91
rural districts, 226
rural society, 108–10
Rushdie, Salman, 69, 241
Russia: activities in Iran in World War I, 26;
 and Bushehr nuclear plant, 285–86, 287;
 and sanctions issue, xlvi; arms sales to
 Iran, 273, 275; loans to Iran, 25; relations
 with Qajar dynasty, 22–24; relations with
 Islamic Republic, 246–47; splits Iran with
 Britain, 26; war with Iran, xl

Sadat, Anwar, 244
Saddam Hussein. *See* Hussein, Saddam
Sadi, 93
Sadr, Abolhasan Bani. *See* Bani Sadr, Abol-
 hasan

Safavi Empire, xxxix, 15, 18–21; establish-
 ment of state religion, 119; external
 threats, 18–20; structure, 18
Saffarids, 16
Safi ad Din, 18
Saidi Sirjani, Ali Akbar, 75
Salaam (newspaper), 75, 237, 238
Salamis, Battle of, 9
Salghurid dynasty, 17
salt lakes, 86
Samand, 178
Samanids, 16
sanctions, xlv, xlvi, xlvii, 72, 158, 242, 243,
 248–50, 272–73
Sanjabi, Karim, 49, 50
Sar Cheshnah, 167
Sarkuhi, Farhad, 76
Sasan, 11
Sassanian Empire, xxxix, 11–14, 130
The Satanic Verses (novel), 69, 241
satellite television, 239
satrap, 9
satrapy(ies), 9
Saudi Arabia, 44, 71, 243
SAVAK, xlii, 35, 48, 53, 276–77
Sawad, 14
sawm (fasting), 119
scholars, Iranian, xxxix
schools. *See* education; elementary schools;
 secondary schools
SCIRI. *See* Supreme Council for the Islamic
 Revolution in Iraq
Scud–B rocket, 266, 274, 275
Scud–C rocket, 275
Scythians, 6
SDC. *See* Supreme Defense Council
secondary schools, 134
Second of Khordad coalition, 208, 209,
 210, 229–30
security forces (*see also* internal security):
 and suppression of protests, 225; independent authority, 225, 227; under
 Islamic Republic, 277; under Mohammad
 Reza Shah Pahlavi, 35, 276–77
security law of 1992, 74
segregation by sex, 115–16
SEE. *See* state economic enterprise
Seleucids, 10
Seleucus, 10
self-censorship, 236
self-employment, 155
self-propelled artillery, 265

Contributors

Hossein Akhavi-Pour is professor of economics at Hamline University, Saint Paul, MN.

Shaul Bakhash is Clarence J. Robinson professor of history at George Mason University, Fairfax, VA.

Glenn Curtis is senior research analyst for the former Soviet Union and Eastern Europe in the Federal Research Division of the Library of Congress, Washington, DC.

Mark Gasiorowski is professor of political science at Louisiana State University, Baton Rouge, LA.

Eric Hooglund is visiting professor of politics at Bates College, Lewiston, ME.

Jalil Roshandel is associate professor of political science and director of security studies at East Carolina University, Greenville, NC.

Published Country Studies

(Area Handbook Series)

Afghanistan
Albania
Algeria
Angola
Argentina

Armenia, Azerbaijan,
  and Georgia
Australia
Austria
Bangladesh

Belarus and Moldova
Belgium
Bolivia
Brazil
Bulgaria

Burma
Cambodia
Cameroon
Chad
Chile

China
Colombia
Commonwealth Caribbean,
  Islands of the
Congo
Costa Rica

Côte d'Ivoire (Ivory
  Coast)
Cuba
Cyprus
Czechoslovakia

Dominican Republic
  and Haiti
Ecuador
Egypt
El Salvador

Estonia, Latvia, and
  Lithuania
Ethiopia
Finland
Germany

Ghana
Greece
Guatemala
Guinea
Guyana and Belize

Honduras
Hungary
India
Indian Ocean
Indonesia
Iran

Iraq
Israel
Italy
Japan
Jordan

Kazakstan, Kyrgyzstan,
  Tajikistan, Turkmenistan,
  and Uzbekistan
Kenya
Korea, North

Korea, South
Laos
Lebanon
Liberia
Libya

Malawi
Malaysia
Mauritania
Mexico
Mongolia

Morocco
Mozambique
Nepal and Bhutan
Nicaragua
Nigeria

Oceania
Pakistan
Panama
Paraguay
Persian Gulf States
Peru

Philippines
Poland
Portugal
Romania
Russia

Rwanda and Burundi
Saudi Arabia
Senegal
Sierra Leone
Singapore

Somalia
South Africa
Soviet Union
Spain
Sri Lanka

Sudan
Syria
Tanzania
Thailand
Tunisia

Turkey
Uganda
Uruguay
Venezuela
Vietnam

Yemens, The
Yugoslavia
Zaire
Zambia
Zimbabwe

GPO U.S. GOVERNMENT PRINTING OFFICE: 2008—344-703